Antique GOLF Collectibles

A Price and Reference Guide

Chuck Furjanic

Edited by Maria Furjanic

Published by

 **krause publications**

700 E. State Street • Iola, WI 54990-0001
Telephone: 715/445-2214

Please call or write for our free catalog.
Our toll-free number to place an order or obtain a free catalog is 800-258-0929
or please use our regular business telephone 715-445-2214
for editorial comment and further information.

Library of Congress Catalog Number: 97-073034
ISBN: 0-87341-519-1

Printed in the United States of America

Dedication

To Julia, for her patience and love

Table of Contents

Acknowledgments

I would like to express my sincere gratitude to the many people who helped put this book together, without them this presentation would have never become a reality: Wayne Aaron, Hank Alperin, Archie Baird, Paul Biocini, Bob Burkett, Jim Cooper, Lee Crist, Mike Daniels, Art DiProspero, Mark Emerson, Jim Espinola, Pete Georgiady, David Griffiths, Roger Hill, Johnny Henry, Tom and Karen Kuhl, Bob Kuntz, George Lewis, Ralph Livingston, Dick Moore, Norm Moreau, Joseph Murdoch, Will Roberto, Tim Smartt, and Jerry Sprung. Dan Alexander provided the impetus and a multitude of photographs for this reference.

A special thank you to Teresa Ferrieri-Bisigato for her enthusiasm and research assistance.

Preface

For the past ten years, I have heard thousands of collectors, club professionals, antique dealers, and curious people with collectibles, ask the same questions: "What is this worth?" and "Is there a reference book giving current pricing for all golf collectibles?"

This book is designed to answer both these questions.

Collecting old golf memorabilia, clubs, books and balls is not a new fad. Classified advertisements for "Feather Balls," old "Gutta Percha Balls" and wooden head clubs made by "Hugh Philp" were published in the British publication, "Golf Illustrated" circa 1900. Harry B. Woods assembled a very fine collection and, in 1911, published *Golfing Curios and the Like.*

In 1987, my thirst for information concerning collectible golf equipment was at its peak. The references available were Stirk and Henderson's *Golf in the Making,* The *Encyclopedia of Golf Collectibles* by the Olman's, the Golf Collectors Society's *Bulletin,* a few dealers publishing catalogues, and auction catalogues from several British auction houses.

Determined to acquire and share up-to-date information, I began publishing a retail catalogue in 1989. In 1991, interesting articles by expert collectors and dealers were also included helping the catalogues become both informative and a retail sales vehicle. The catalogues include a wide variety of golf collectibles, such as wood shaft clubs, balls, books, tees, memorabilia and emphemera, all offered for sale. There is also a listing of events, gatherings and meetings involving golf collectors and collectibles, articles that will bring you back to the nostalgic times, and offerings of hard to find grips, tacks and whipping for care and repair of old hickories. I am presently the only dealer publishing a monthly catalogue for the golf collectibles hobby, and have published nearly 100 as of this writing.

In 1993, I began conducting Mail Auctions that provided two essential services to the collector: A way to sell duplicates from their collection and a way to add collectibles at "their price." Chuck Furjanic, Inc. now holds two public auctions: One in the spring, the other in the fall. If a collector cannot attend the auction "in person," where lots may be viewed prior to sale, a profusely illustrated catalogue allows them to bid confidently by mail.

When Dan Alexander, former president of Books Americana, suggested I write a price and reference guide on golf collectibles, the intent was clearly set in producing a truly comprehensive work encompassing the entire spectrum of golf collectibles. To accomplish this, I called for input from a number of knowledgeable, well respected dealers and collectors who are experts in their field. Throughout the years, I have been privileged of knowing the finest, and several of them assisted in presenting accurate, up-to-date information and pricing of collectibles. Their perspective and knowledge are a refreshing and valued addition to this price and reference guide.

It was also the goal of my publisher, the contributors, and mine, to provide as many photographs as possible to make these listings and prices come alive for the collector. Anyone using this guide will find the photographs incredibly helpful in bringing you back to the times and the history of the game, as well as providing visual references to the collectibles.

Thus, this guide is the result of such an effort; I am very confident it will be of great help to the numerous collectors asking that familiar question, "How much is this item worth?"

Golfingly,
Chuck Furjanic
Irving, Texas, 1997

Foreword

by Rives McBee

People often ask me, what do you collect and why do you collect? My answer to them is, "I collect almost anything that is related to the game of golf," and that includes classic clubs; hickory shafted clubs; clubs with unique shafts, fancy faces and clubheads; golf balls; logo golf balls; golf bags; golf books; golf art; golf autographs; and golf bronzes. I have done exactly what most expert collectors say *don't do*—that is, get into many areas of different collectibles. Most collectors choose one particular area such as scorecards, pencils or tees and stay with just these items. I have chosen to spread out into several areas because I have yet to find the one area that intrigues me the most. I usually can't resist buying something if it is different from what I am looking for originally. An old leather bag may contain a putter or a wood that I want and I buy the whole bag full of clubs.

Why do I collect? It all started in 1966 after my first major tournament appearance, the 1966 United States Open Championship at the Olympic Club in San Francisco. In the second round of the tournament I shot a score

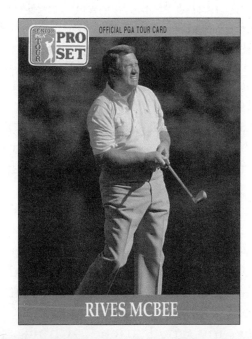

RIVES MCBEE

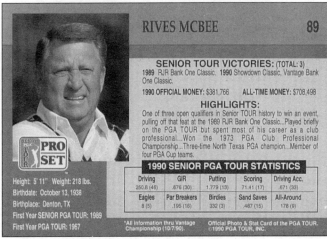

of 64, which set the course record and tied the all-time low round for an Open. I went on to finish tied for thirteenth in the championship and returned to Midland, Texas, and my job as an assistant golf professional. When I got home I put the clubs (I had used in the Open) in the closet along with a placemat autographed by all of the contestants at the Open. I still have the clubs and the placemat. This started me in the wonderful world of golf collectibles. Adding to my collection has given me many hours of pleasure and meeting fellow collectors around the country has been a fabulous experience.

Collecting can be fun and it can be expensive. Sometimes the pleasure of finding a unique club or ball far outweighs the cost of the item. When a fellow collector asks if he paid too much for a particular find I usually respond with, "You bought it because you wanted it, so you didn't pay too much." An item is worth what you are willing to pay for it. Most people who sell memorabilia are willing to negotiate and this too can be fun if you know what you are doing.

Now my good friend, Chuck Furjanic, has found a way to help the collector, old and new, by providing this reference and pricing guide. It is filled with illustrations of clubs, golf balls, pottery and ceramics, autographs, golf cards, and many more antique golf collectibles. This book should help all of the new collectors in their search for those "precious finds" at the garage sale or auction, and give them an approximate price for these items. I wish that I would have had this book to help me in my early years of collecting, but I probably would have done what so

many of my fellow collectors do. If I like it and can afford it, I buy it!

Golfingly,
Rives McBee
Irving, Texas

Foreword

by Pete Georgiady

Twenty years ago there was nothing.

By that I mean there were no ready resource materials for the collectors of old golf clubs and other golf memorabilia. It didn't much matter because there were almost no collectors. The prospect changed abruptly in 1978 when Englishmen David Stirk and Ian Henderson wrote *Golf in the Making*, an eclectic volume combining colorful bits of golf history with profiles of important club makers and short but tantalizing notes on old clubs and other golf items that were rapidly becoming collectible. It is a book that many consider to be the "Bible" for golf collectors and deserves a great deal of credit for launching the activities of many of today's collectors.

Without going into great detail, I can say that the shortcomings of one or two of the club-related sections of the Stirk and Henderson book gave me cause to begin my own explorations into the whos, whys and wherefores of old clubs and club makers. The result of my research is a small group of books devoted to clubs and club makers, the two topics which I have found most self-enlightening. Thus, the pioneering contribution of Stirk and Henderson

spawned other collector-writers like myself who will leave teachings for the next generation of golf enthusiasts. After all this time, there is a crying need for even more information about many aspects of the golf collectibles field. Frequently I am asked if a guide book has been written on this topic or another and, sadly, the answer is usually "No, not yet." Perhaps golf collectors, most of whom are also golfers, take their game so seriously that it leaves no time for scholarship. Who can blame them?

Voids still remain in the information web but sooner or later they will be filled. One addition to the collector's library is undoubtedly the volume you are now holding. It has emerged from one among us who has espoused the spirit of old golf with an evangelical fervor. Chuck Furjanic possesses a unique story within the golf collectibles field. A lifelong golfer, coach and friend of the game, he has made the world of golf collectibles his business. His ability to amass considerable familiarity with clubs, balls, art and other areas of golf collectibles, as well as a knowledge of the persons who were specialists in those areas, has made him a beacon in the field of golf collectibles. This book is a marriage of those two worlds: His daily handling of the game's antiques and his regular contact with collecting novices and experts.

There is no single person who knows everything about all the disciplines of the collectibles we seek, so the natural ideal is a book with an aggregation of information from those highly knowledgeable in the different fields. Chuck has delivered just that. In the years ahead more books to assist and instruct golf collectors will materialize. Maybe the authors of those future volumes will have been inspired by this price and reference guide just as we were inspired by another book of twenty years ago.

Pete Georgiady
Greensboro, N.C.

The seeds of Pete's interest in old golf clubs germinated while he was a graduate student at Scotland's Dundee University in the early 1970s. After many years of research and gathering information on old club makers and the clubs they produced, his knowledge has been disseminated in a series of books which include the Compendium of British Club Makers, Collecting Antique Golf Clubs, Views and Reviews: Golf Clubs in the Trade Press, Wood Shafted Golf Club Value Guide *and* North American Club Makers.

A collector of over 20 years, Pete is a regular contributor on golf topics to golf magazines, the GCS Bulletin *and Chuck Furjanic's monthly catalog.*

About the Author

Charles Michael Furjanic Jr. began playing golf at age 10 during the summer of 1953. Thanks to the parish priest, Father Charles Georgavich, Chuck was gifted his first set of clubs—two woods, four irons and a putter—all with hickory shafts. In his sophomore year at Swissvale High School in Pittsburgh, Pennsylvania, Chuck persuaded a faculty member to sponsor the school's first golf team. Chuck attended Slippery Rock University of Pennsylvania, where he played without compensation. Chuck would, in 1979, establish the "Doc-Chuck" Golf Scholarship Fund in co-sponsorship with coach Dr. Albert "Doc" Schmittlein, providing financial assistance to more than thirty golf students through 1996.

Chuck's life-long love of golf and collecting led him to turn professional in two areas. Golf came first. He taught lessons at a driving range and played in tournaments, good enough not to embarrass himself, but not well enough to win much more than gasoline money. After nearly four years, he was convinced professional golf was not going to be his lifelong vocation.

Turning to his other love, numismatics, Chuck became one of the nation's leading coin experts and enjoyed working with collectors, building meaningful collections. Chuck was a contributing editor for *A Guide Book of United States Coins* (Red Book) for nearly fifteen years, and for the *Handbook of United States Coins* (Blue Book). He authored articles for *CoinWorld*, *Numismatic News* and *CoinAge*, gave talks and presentations at local and national organizations and taught numismatic courses at Allegheny College in Pittsburgh.

In 1986, when packing to move from Pittsburgh to Irving, Texas, Chuck found some old friends in a corner of the garage. The original seven wooden shafted clubs rekindled his interest in golf collectibles and he began in earnest to develop a business around golf, centering attention on the collector.

He published his first retail golf collectibles catalogue for the hobby in February 1989 and launched a new career, not as a professional golfer, but as a golf professional, dealing with collectors and collectibles.

Conducting several successful Mail Bid Sales gave him the expertise to sell the late Linda Craft's golf estate in May 1995 (Linda was an LPGA pro and long-time golf collector). Because of that auction's success, Chuck now conducts spring and fall public sales geared to the collector from both the consignment and sales aspect.

Nearly a hundred catalogues and this book later, Chuck has found his comfort zone—golf, collectors and collectibles.

"My philosophy has always been the collector should come first. Customer satisfaction is my most important product, and if the collector is not happy, I'm not happy.

"Yes, we all would like to make mega-thousand dollar sales each time the phone rings, but the collector, who spends his grocery money to buy that $50 ball or $65 hickory shafted club, is the real foundation of the hobby. I take as much time and care filling a $50 order and helping the collector get what he wants, just as I do for the $1,000 buyer. I personally try to answer every incoming call because listening to collectors, and helping them find the collectibles or information they seek, is very important to me and essential to the hobby.

"If you are in the Dallas area, bring your hickories, not your collectibles, but your playables; there's always a 'game' available! On second thought, bring your collectibles and your stories too, and we will sit down for a friendly chat—after the 'game.'"

To Contact The Author:

Chuck Furjanic
P.O. Box 165892
Irving, TX 75016
Phone: (972) 594-7802
Fax: (972) 257-1785
furjanic@onramp.net

Chapter 1

Collecting Antique Golf

Chapter 1

Collecting Antique Golf

The Heritage of Golf

by Archie Baird, Aberlady, Scotland

Archie Baird is an avid golf collector and historian as well as a good golfer and past Captain of Gullane. He is a member and a Director of both the British and American Golf Collectors' Societies and founder and curator of the Golf Museum next to the pro-shop at Gullane Links, Gullane, Scotland. He is one of the most knowledgeable and respected authorities on clubs, balls, books, and golf memorabilia in the hobby.

Early Golf 1300-1700 AD

We begin with the Dutch derivation and by means of paintings, prints and photographs show the variety of conditions and costumes in which the game was played. It was played in church yards, on the streets and roads, on the fields and harvest, and on the ice in winter.

Who brought it to Scotland? It may have been soldiers or sailors. There were many Scottish mercenary soldiers in Holland and dozens of marriages with Dutch girls are recorded. Scotland's main export was wool and if the wind was unfavorable Scottish sailors would be forced to stay in Holland for days or weeks. The Van der Velde painting of 1668 shows two kilted players with clubs.

The flowerings of Dutch landscape paintings coincided with the popularity of the game and in most outdoor scenes, at least one figure car-

e.g. Dunbar, North Berwick, Aberlady, Mussel-burgh, Leith, Elie, St. Andrews, and so on up the coast to Dornoch. The earliest inland golf was at Bruntsfield Links, just South of Edin-burgh Castle.

In all these places there were rolling links land where rabbits and grass vied for exist-ence. Smooth areas nibbled short and marked by rabbit "scrapes" (the 1st hole?) alternated with rough grass. The "greens" were con-nected by sheep paths of varying widths. Rab-bits and sheep were therefore the first golf course architects!

The Feathery Ball Era

Up until 1850 the feather ball was used. It was a leather stitched case stuffed with a top-hat full of boiled feathers. It was a skilled and arduous job to make a feather ball and a man could only complete two or three in a day. This made them as expensive as a club and con-trolled, to some extent, the popularity of golf.

Because the "feathery" was easily damaged by iron clubs, irons were only used in sand or in a rut. The player carried nearly all wooden clubs and there was a great variation in loft and length. The first club makers were bow makers who fashioned beautiful delicate woods and carpenters who made heavier, clumsier clubs. There were no "sets" of clubs as the player chose or ordered them to his preference, and no two clubs made before 1890 were exactly the same. The heads were

ries a club. The game disappeared about 1700 and was succeeded by an indoor variation.

The spread to Scotland from Holland looks likely when the early Scottish links are marked on a map. They are all near east coast ports

Antique Dutch Kolf Balls
Made out of Boxwood (hardwood root)
two decorated with nails and screw heads.
c. 1845

long, narrow and shallow with a concave or "hooked" face. They were made of beech, apple, pear or thorn. The shafts were ash or hazel until about 1830 when hickory was found to make much better shafts.

The wood heads were attached to the shaft by a long diagonal splice or "scare." These are known as "scared head" clubs. They had lead poured into the back and a strip or horn was fitted into the leading edge of the sole. Very early clubs had no grips and the shafts were thick enough to grip. Sheepskin was used as a grip from about 1800. Leather became popular much later, about 1880. Early irons were

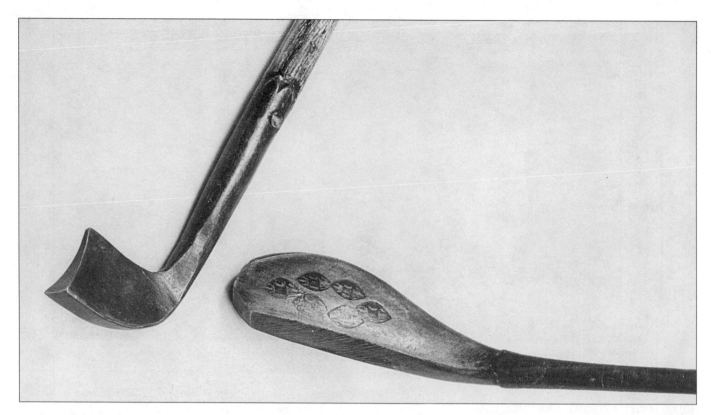

made by blacksmiths and were heavy and cumbersome. They were only used "in extremis" for fear of damaging the leather cover of the feather ball. The hosel was thick and the shaft fitted into the socket which was "knurled" to help grip the wood shaft. The cruder the "nicks" the earlier is the iron. During the "feather" era there were two main irons, the sand iron with a large concave face and the rut iron with a very small head to

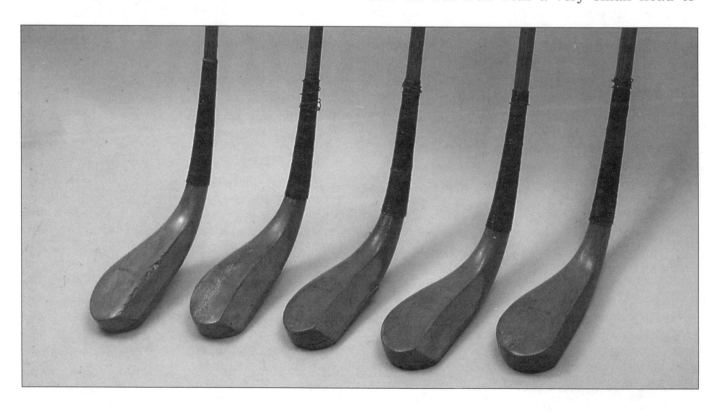

play out of the tracks formed as carts brought back sand from the beach.

The courses at this time were as nature made them. There was very little green keeping and they played the ball as it lay. Rules were simple and about 14 in number. Stroke play was very rare, match play was almost always the game. Societies were few, only 17 being formed by 1850. Dress was a personal choice except that most societies made the wearing of red jackets compulsory so that golfers could be seen easily on the busy links. Colored facings and lapels were often inscribed, and silver or brass buttons with club insignia and motto were increasingly popular.

Costume

The story of golf clothing is more varied than the clubs and the balls.

In the "feathery" era, red coats with swallow tails and even the occasional top hat were

seen. A man's everyday suit was considered correct and the ladies wore the long-skirted gowns that were fashionable at the time. An unbuttoned jacket was rare before 1920.

Waterproof clothing and spike shoes are fairly recent innovations. There is surely a wonderful book to be written on golfing costume.

Personalities

Being essentially a solo game, golf has had its share of personalities. The Parks and the Morrises; the Triumvirate; Braid, Taylor and Vardon; Harold Hilton and John Ball, Hoylake's tremendous pair; the prince of them all Bobby Jones; Joyce Weathered and Babe Zaharias; Hagen and Hogan; Player and Palmer; Nicklaus and Watson are only a few. Any golfer could add a hundred names because no two people ever played the game the same way.

What Gutta-Percha Did for Golf

Just before 1850, probably in Musselburgh, the first gutta-percha balls were produced by immersing the gum-like substance in hot water and hand rolling until round. They were cheap and tough and a man could make dozens in a day. But they would not fly properly while they were smooth. At first they were hand hammered to produce a rough surface, then they were made in molds with a wide variety of patterns. Bramble, dimple squares and circles are only a few. They were never painted successfully and survivors are all dark brown. Like the featheries, they were made in varying weights and sizes. Their moderate price and resilience allowed golf to grow quickly. The Scots had kept the game alive for 400 years but now it expanded rapidly.

Golf Clubs and Societies

Year	1850	1870	1890	1910
No. of Clubs and Societies	17	34	387	4135

This expansion was aided by the spread of the railways but the "gutta" and its composition successor, the "guttie," made it possible.

They also changed the shape and the choice of clubs. The long-nose woods that swept the "featherie" along could not stand up to the "gutta-percha." Leather faces and vulcanite insets, brass soles and broader heads all appeared. Irons became more popular and blacksmiths who made clubs became "cleekmakers," refining the sand iron and the rutiron into niblicks, mashies, and cleeks. They even made iron putters!

Greenkeeping became a necessary and canny craft. The skills became more specialized and numerous, and the local club makers or professional had seldom the time or the inclination to "keep the green."

Rubber Core

At the turn of the century from the U.S.A. came the "Haskell" ball. This was made by winding hundreds of feet of elastic onto a central core, then coating it with gutta-percha. These balls flew farther and a bad shot could still go a long way. The rubber core ball traveled so far, golf courses had to be changed to contain it.

On the negative side, the cover was easily cut on these new balls and many improvements were tried over the last 75 years. Recently, some solid one-piece balls have gained in popularity with manufacturers who are always trying to improve them further.

During the gutta and rubber core domination, club face design became important. Lines or dots on the face enabled backspin to be applied to the ball. When the grooves became too deep the R & A ruled them illegal. Hickory shafts finally gave way to steel in the 1920s partly due to steel's superiority, but mostly because the hickory forests were depleted.

The Heritage of Golf

by Johnny Henry

I've known Johnny Henry for nearly ten years. He can still shoot his age with steel or hickory clubs (70), has a fine collection of golf artifacts, and just about the finest collection of golf related memories and friends of anyone I know. A book on collecting golf would not be complete without including his impressions.

People frequently ask me when I started collecting old golf items, and I always reply, "I don't know, but I was collecting for a long time before I knew it." Golf has been a large part of my life since I started playing at age 6 (in 1933) with a set of Spalding juvenile, hickory-shafted clubs. Since then, I have been involved with golf-oriented occupations: Toro turf equipment salesman, golf course irrigation designer, PGA professional, golf architect and greenkeeper. Over the years, the opportunity had arisen to probe for clubs at the various golf courses and I had amassed some 18-20 hickory clubs. Then, in 1975, my wife gave me a golf trip to Scotland for an anniversary gift, and that was a serious mistake! While on the trip, I met Ken Smith (GCS #0076); he suggested I join the Golf Collectors Society, then, just a small group of people who had the same interests as us.

Before Phillips, Christie's and Sotheby's auction houses began to have golf sales about 1980, it was possible to ferret out collectible clubs from individuals—retired professionals, widows, caddies, "boot sales" as well as thrift shops and pros at old courses in Great Britain. This was the "fun era" of collecting.

While touring the various courses in Scotland and England, I would find pros who would

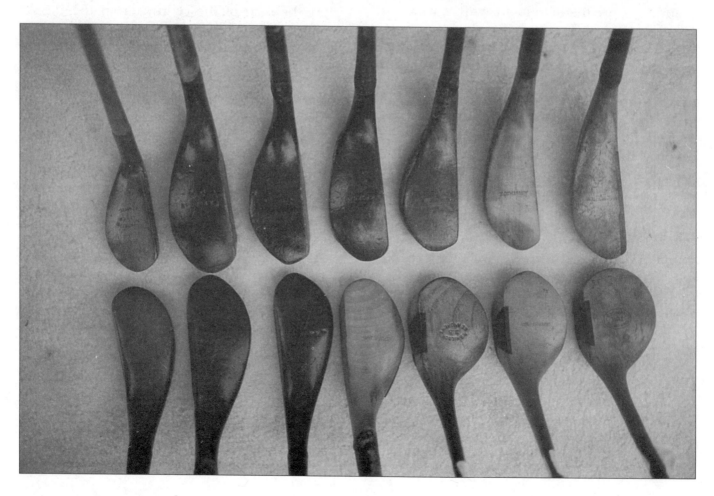

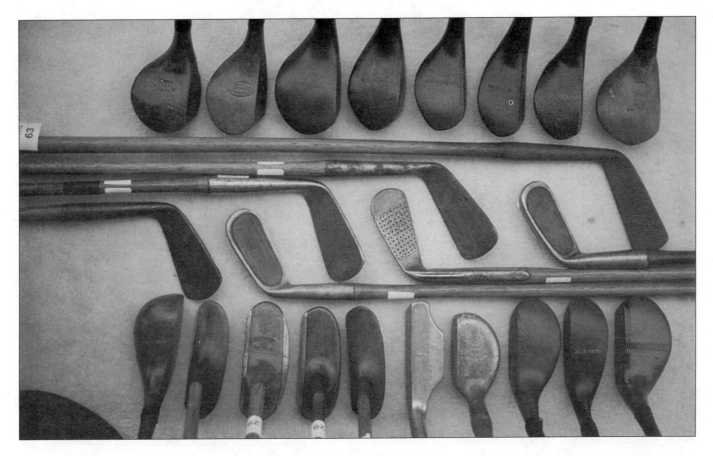

have a few hickories on the wall or back in the club storage area that were for sale. In many cases, they would also give me leads as to where I might find clubs in the area.

Sadly, those days are gone forever. With headlines in the *London Times* reading "GOLF CLUB MAKES RECORD PRICE AT SOTHEBY'S SALE" the public became reluctant to sell for fear the old clubs in their possession were worth more than this "Colonist" was offering to pay. Other than flea markets, estate sales, thrift shops and other collectors, probably the best source is purchasing items from dealers. They attend auctions here in the USA and in the UK to maintain inventories of items we all look for.

My collection, while modest in quantity (240 clubs), is adequate in quality. It consists of 25 long-nose clubs, including a Philp and an 18th century play club made by a bow and spear maker. I also have most of the patent clubs such as the Cran, Seeley, spring face, Lard whistler, anti-shank irons, Mills aluminum clubs, along with a giant niblick, transitional woods, bulger scares and deep-grooved

irons. There are about 50 putters including: a Calamity Jane, Gassiat, Schenectady, a Kismet with rollers on sole, Ivora Perfection, and various blade and Mills putters.

My collection of balls include 2 featheries, 20 gutties, and about 100 wound balls with different markings.

Scattered about in my golf room are various miscellaneous items relating to golf, including pottery by Doulton, O'Hare, Carlton, Wedgewood, Weller, and others. There are also silver and gold medals, silver hat pins, spoons and glass items by Cambridge and Steuben. My library has about 150 books, none of which are "classic" volumes, but those that I like to read.

This room is an excellent place to relax after a hard day on the links. While sipping a beverage, I can scan the walls, and each club has a story behind it. I can remember where I was, from whom it was acquired, and the circumstances and haggling that transpired. Collecting memories, friends and reminiscing is as important to me as the collection itself. It's amazing how close a bond exists among people with a common interest.

Collecting Pre-1875 Golf Artifacts

by Will Roberto

Will Roberto, Attorney at Law, is a long-time collector who specializes in pre-1875 golf collectibles and artifacts. Mr. Roberto has

kindly outlined this era.

Pre-1875 golf artifacts are very scarce and seldom offered at auction or private sale. The

few examples known are in museums, club-house displays and in several advanced collectors hands. The USGA at Far Hills, New Jersey, has an outstanding display of long-nose and early hammer-forged iron head clubs. In St. Andrews, Scotland, there is a museum, and in the Royal & Ancient Club House the Members Room is adorned by many golfing artifacts. Historical courses such as Royal Liverpool, Prestwick, and The

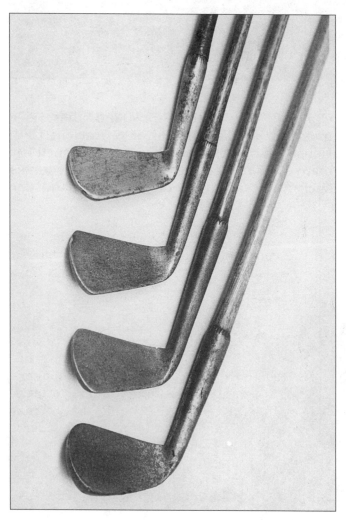

Royal Company of Edinburgh Golfers at Muirfield, have extensive displays of clubs and balls. The clubhouse at Gullane has an outstanding display of balls, one of which is the "Map of the Globe" ball. Archie Baird also has a small museum next to the pro shop at Gullane where, by appointment, Dr. Baird will conduct a personal tour.

Pre-1875 Artifacts

This period of collecting covers the era starting in 1457—a span of nearly 420 years of golf history—but is really a short blip on the collecting scene. Golf during these times was limited to royalty, clergy and the wealthy businessman, as only the affluent had the time and money to pursue the sport. Most of the highest quality artifacts are impounded in museums and clubhouse displays, and of those available to collectors, there are many below average or damaged pieces not worth having in a *serious* collection. As a result, very few quality collectibles are available and collectors diligently seek them when offered privately or at public auction.

Golf Clubs

During this era, very few iron-head clubs were marked with manufacturers identification and are difficult to date and authenticate. Wooden-head clubs were usually marked with the maker's name, but use, abuse, refinishing and repair render many unidentifiable, some not worthy of an advanced collection. With these items, accurate provenience, or opinions from experts would be the only way a collector could feel comfortable before and after acquisition. There are about fifty major collectors worldwide and a few dealers who concentrate on pre-1875 memorabilia and they could be good sources for identification, dating and authentication. Elsewhere in this book is mention of the Golf Collectors Society and other worldwide organizations who can supply names of experts.

The most difficult to obtain are pre-1800 clubs. There are very few authenticated and properly dated pre-1800 clubs in collector hands. Most of these are wooden-headed clubs as the early players only carried a few irons for use from trouble lies. There are also some pre-1800 iron putters to be found, but not many.

The period from 1800 to 1850 provides the collector more clubs than the pre-1800 period—most likely based on age and preservation rather than numbers originally manufactured.

The numbers of golfers did not vary substantially from 1750 to 1845; in fact, during the period from 1820 to 1845 golf nearly died out in Edinburgh. Robert Forgan wrote in a letter dated Feb. 3, 1899, "...there was not work for three men making golf clubs in 1856 when I first went to it...". The attrition rate of pre-1800 artifacts was far greater than clubs from the first half of the 19th century. Again, most of the clubs from the 1800-1850 period in collectors hands are woods with a few bunker, rut and putting irons.

Clubs from the period 1850 to 1875 are somewhat more plentiful but can not be considered common. Some pre-1875 clubs have a maker's name or mark on them that can help date them.

How can a collector date woods and smoothface irons with or without identifying markings? Many wood clubs were marked with the maker's name and sometimes with his mark. Reference books listing known makers can help place a "McEwan", "Philp" or "Jackson" stamped club in a probable time period by size and shape of the stamping and general overall construction of the head and neck.

Many uninformed collectors assume unmarked irons are rare. Most clubs forged in the 1880s and early 1890s were made to look

like the old style but were imprinted with the maker's name or mark. Caddies used "Emory" paper to clean rust from the iron heads and while sanding away the rust, the caddies also sanded away the markings. Rare unmarked irons were usually made by a blacksmith and have a crude hammered appearance, longer hosels, heavier hosel nickings and usually exhibit forging lines or seams. The hole at the top of the hosel where the shaft is inserted is usually wider in diameter than clubs forged by the post-1885 club maker. Many pre-1875 irons had shafts made of ash, not hickory.

Collectibility of these pre-1875 clubs is determined by quality, provenience, the maker's place relating to the history of the game as a player, maker, or both, and the scarcity of a particular club. A club from 1870 would be far more valuable if the owner could produce a provenience verifying Young Tom Morris used this particular

club while winning three British Opens, versus one without provenience probably belonging to a businessman or clergyman.

Balls

As with clubs, pre-1800 balls are scarce. Pre-1860 gutty balls are scarcer than feather-ies. Named maker balls of both types are even scarcer. Balls with markings on them from this period are among the rarest. There are also a few balls painted for winter play that are highly sought after. While most are red or orange, there have been blue, yellow and black balls noted.

Early gutty balls were smooth and were hand rolled. The early players realized they flew poorly and marked them by hand using a hammer or knife. (Some gave the smooth spheres to caddies to knock them around before play rendering them with cuts and marks, thus making their flight more consistent.) Later patterns, such as those made by Forgan, became more common and other makers developed different styles as a form of advertising. Just as club making became more sophisticated so did ball making.

As golf grew, and with it the demand for balls, heavy iron molds (rare and very collectible) were used to mold and mark the gutttapercha spheres. Various devices to cut patterns in the balls were developed in an attempt to improve the flight of the ball.

Books

Pre-1875 books are very scarce as few were written. Major titles are Robert Clark, *Golf—A*

Royal and Ancient Game, 1875; H.B. Farnie, *A Golfer's Manual,* 1857; Robert Chambers, *A Few Rambling Remarks on Golf,* 1862.

Easier to come by and equally important are some books published 1875 to 1910.

Art

Very little pre-1800 art, not already in museums, is available to private collectors and these pieces rarely appear at auctions. There are, however, many fine prints, pieces of sculpture, and paintings being offered from time to time. Also many later generation reproductions of fine quality are available to decorate a collection room.

General

Many important items associated with the game are available. Original letters between players challenging one another are very rare

and expensive. Written documents of the game such as rules, scorecards, receipts, club secretary records, and notebooks, occasionally become available.

Clothing, such as the red coats worn by the captains at St. Andrews, leather caps, top hats, tweed waistcoats and wool plus fours are prized pre-1875 collectibles.

Smoking-pipes with carved golfing scenes, pottery, mugs and beer bottles as well as jewelry, watch fobs, and whiskey flasks are also highly sought after by the historically bound collector.

Clubmaker's tools and maker's die stamps are another avenue as well as feather ball maker's tools. At an auction in 1989, a complete set of feather ball tools in a wooden case was offered for sale.

Medals

The early clubs and golf societies gave prizes of balls or clubs, a claret of wine, but most often medals. There are numerous medals won by competitors on display at old links like Muirfield, St. Andrews, Prestwick and in museums. On occasion, medals are sold through auction and their value determined by the club giving the medal, names of winners thereon, and whether the medal is gold or another metal. Most British-made medals were of 9kt. gold, sterling or bronze.

Even Presidents Enjoy Golf Collectibles

Former President George Bush visited Montgomery, Alabama, November 8, 1996, and played golf at the Montgomery Country Club. While at the club, President Bush expressed an interest in the golf collectibles on display there. Forrest McConnell, the club's historian, gave the president the grand tour of the collectibles on display in the club house. The president seemed knowledgeable about antique golf artifacts, wooden-shafted golf clubs and the makers.

On display were several clubs made by Willie Park Sr. and Willie Park Jr. and President Bush was keenly aware of the Parks, when and where they made their clubs. He was also keenly aware of their collectible popularity, value and historical significance in the development of modern-day golf equipment. He was entranced by the long nose putter and rut iron made by Willie Jr. and inspected them closely with the help of Mr. McConnell.

The president expressed that he was a student of golf history and has visited many of the old courses in Scotland and England. He is especially fond of the club room at the Royal and Ancient, and the Museum at St. Andrews.

Forrest McConnell is a long-time collector specializing in the history and club making of the Park family. As the historian at Montgomery C.C., Forrest has developed interesting and informative golf displays centering around the Parks. We thank Mr. McConnell for sharing the president's visit with our readers.

Chapter 2

Golf Collector Societies and Organizations

Chapter 2

Golf Collector Societies and Organizations

No one likes to collect alone. Collectors want to hear from others with their same interest, meet, talk and show off their prized possessions. One way to meet others is to join an organization or society. Here we will list five which provide a printed bulletin or newsletter for their members.

Welcome to the Golf Collectors Society!

by Tom Kuhl, Editor of the Bulletin, *GCS Newsletter*

Any new collector of golf memorabilia (or antiques in general) will eventually come to the point where he or she will seek broader horizons, to branch out, to meet other people who share the same enthusiasm for the game and its various artifacts. Golf collectors have been around for many years, long before the game arrived in America, but they were always scattered hither and yon and never organized. A famous early collector was Harry Wood, an Englishman from Manchester who wrote the masterpiece on collecting, *Golf Curios and the Like* in 1911, now a valuable item in any golf book collector's library. Other early prominent golf collectors of the 20th century include Alex Findlay, O.M. Leland, Jack Level, and Otto Probst. They, and others like them, shared an intense pas-

sion for the memorabilia of the game, but not until 1970 was an official body of golf collectors organized under the title of the Golf Collectors Society.

It began with a small band of 27 collectors in September 1970; on the 25th anniversary of the Golf Collectors Society (GCS) in 1995 there were more than 2,000 members from America, with nearly 200 others from all parts of the golfing globe. The largest foreign contingent is from the United Kingdom and Canada, with other members from Japan, Taiwan, Australia, South Africa, continental Europe, and a dozen or so other nations.

GCS co-founder Bob Kuntz (left) and a collector examine some clubs.

Buying and selling at a GCS annual meeting.

From the very start, and on into the present day, the purpose of the GCS is: *To serve as a means of getting golf collectors together...To establish friendships between those who share a love of the game...And to facilitate the exchange of information about collecting and the game.* Founded in 1970 by J. Robert Kuntz of Dayton, Ohio, and Joseph

The author (center) at a GCS trade show.

Murdoch of Philadelphia, the GCS remains a not-for profit fraternal organization.

GCS members collect all golf memorabilia from A to Z. Some specialize in old hickory-shafted clubs, or even earlier valuable long-nose playclubs from the mid-19th century. Others might collect balls, books, ceramics and artwork, medals, old tees and ephemera, early magazines and tournament programs, or maybe just modern era putters only, or a varied combination of all the numerous collecting categories...and a whole lot more!

While some members might specialize in collecting items as small as ball markers or scorecards, there are others who own museum quality collections of the highest caliber. And speaking of museums—the curators, many of the world's great golf museums are GCS members as well, including the USGA's Golf House; the R&A Museum at St. Andrews; the James River (Virginia) CC Museum, the oldest private golf museum in the United States; the Ralph Miller Library and Museum at City of Industry, California, named after one of the GCS founding members; and the new World Golf Hall of

Bob Kuntz gives an interesting talk at a "Club Forum" during a GCS annual meeting.

Fame, now under construction near St. Augustine, Florida. All of these people have a mutual love for the game and its artifacts, equally sharing in the express purpose of the Society to bring people together and to exchange memorabilia and information. The fact that several dozen books exist on golf collecting, authored by GCS members, indicates that information on collecting for new and veteran members alike is a highly sought after commodity.

One of the single most unifying events toward this stated purpose is the regional trade show and Hickory Hacker. Based on membership population density, the GCS has a Board of Directors covering ten geographical regions. Several times per year, within each region, a GCS

gathering of varying size occurs. Generally speaking, it comprises a one- or two-day show where golf memorabilia is bought, sold, traded or just simply exhibited for educational or entertainment purposes. Members enjoy these events if for nothing more than to meet and share their knowledge, ideas, and experiences concerning the game, its artifacts and treasures.

But the accumulation of knowledge and golf memorabilia is not always the primary focus for many GCS members at these regional meetings. To get out on the golf course and play with the old "weapons of the game" is a fun occasion that members look forward to. In these Hickory Tournaments—or Hickory Hackers, as some like to affectionately refer to them—participants often outfit themselves in the old plus fours (or knickers as they are called here in the USA) and play with the old hickory-shafted clubs from the 1920s or earlier. Like Jones, Sarazen, Vardon, Hagen, and all of the early golfers before them, the GCS Hickory Tournament participants go back in time to the days of golf when wood—not steel or graphite—was the shaft that made the ball go "far and sure."

At these regional trade shows—and especially the GCS Annual Meeting in late September or early October at various locales across the country—expect to find any golf collectible your little heart desires. The Annual Meeting is by far the largest show, with more than 200 display tables and 500-600 collectors commonly in attendance. Among a number of other locations, the following large and long-running regional golf collecting shows annually take place, and all members and collectors, from anywhere in the world, are always invited.

- Dayton, Ohio in January, "Cabin Fever"

- USGA, Far Hills, New Jersey, in the early spring

- The Texas gathering in Irving during March or April

- A South Florida event in February, and another at Dunedin, usually in March

- The Midwest event in Chicago, at Rolling Meadows, in May

- Three or four events throughout the year in the Mid Atlantic region, near Washington, D.C.

- The Carolinas gathering, at least twice per year

- Western meeting, in Southern California in November or December

- Heart of America in June, in either Kansas City, Omaha, or Iowa

- Two or three Canadian events in the Toronto area

You won't find anyone pitching golf resorts or golf course real estate, and very little of the overpriced and oversized "new stuff" at these shows. Instead, you will find tables full of the old hickory-shafted clubs, common and rare, or the more valuable and unusual implements of the game. Then there are collectible clubs of the more "modern era" of the game, for example Tommy Armour woods. Pings and highly collectible Wilson putters from the 1960s. Back to the good old days, you will discover mesh and gutty balls, and usually some pre-1850 featherie balls; early and modern books offered by a number of collectors, as well as recognized golf book dealers; fine old golf pottery, ceramics, jewelry, and the like; long out-of-print golf magazines, hard-to-find autographs, medals, and much, much more. As our GCS co-founder, Joe Murdoch, has stated time and again when talking about the regional and Annual Meeting trade shows: "If you think you have seen everything there is in golf, you'll be pleasantly surprised to see something new and different at the trade show."

Each GCS member receives our newsletter, *The Bulletin*, on a quarterly basis. Articles include golf history, featured collections and collectors, golf book reviews, patent information, unusual clubs and artifacts, current golf auction news and results, and coverage of GCS Regional Events. It also has a small classified ad section, where members are offered buy/sell/trade opportunities.

Members also receive an annual Membership Directory issued in the first quarter of the year. Among the address, telephone and e-mail numbers, vital collecting interests of each individual member are identified.

The Administrator of the Golf Collectors Society is Karen Kuhl. The mailing address is: P. O. Box 20546, Dayton, Ohio 45420 (phone 937-256-2474; Fax 256-2974). The e-mail address is KKuhl67615@aol.com. For more information you may also contact the GCS Website, http//www.golfcollectors.com.

The Golf Club Monthly

This newsletter is published monthly. Its address is 4620 Deer Creek Trail, Bessemer, AL

35020. Phone 205-428-0078. For a membership fee of $40 per year, members are entitled to a 75-line free advertisement each month. An average of 50 dealers/collectors advertise on a regular basis. Most of the ads deal with steel-shafted "classic" clubs from the 1950s to the 1980s, modern clubs and accessories for play.

This is an excellent source for finding a replacement for a lost or broken club, finding out how much your "Ping" putter is worth, or buying a used set of clubs for play. This is a very worthwhile organization.

The Golf Club Collectors Association

Dick Moore, Executive Director
640 E Liberty St.
Girard, OH 44420-2308
330-545-2832
330-545-2718 (FAX)
Internet: gccagolf@aol.com

The GCCA was founded in 1987 and was organized to include collectors of Classic Clubs as well as collectors of wooden-shafted clubs and related memorabilia. The purpose of the GCSA is to introduce golf collectors to each other, and to identify, trade, and share information.

A newsletter is published every three months and a membership directory is published annually that includes names, addresses, phone numbers and collecting interests of all active members. Annual dues are $30.

Members are informed through the newsletter by articles of interest on the increasing desire to collect golf clubs and golf related items and by the use of classified ads. They are encouraged to submit articles, classified ads, or news of trade shows and auctions.

Regional get-togethers are encouraged, and a mail and telephone auction is held annually. At a nominal charge, a catalogue is available for the identification of classic golf clubs.

The Golf Club Historical Society of Canada

555 Eastern Avenue
Toronto, Ontario, Canada, M4M 1C8
Tel. 416-465-8844

The Golf Historical Society of Canada was formed in 1988 when four founding members reasoned that there must be other souls who share a love of golf and the game's rich heritage. Today, this collective helps members indulge in their passion for golf history, its artifacts and treasures.

A quarterly bulletin is published covering a wide range of member interests. Trade shows are organized so that members can share their knowledge and build their collections of golf books, trophies, clubs and memorabilia. Special interest is placed on the preservation of Canadian golf history and traditions. A spring and fall "Hickory Hacker" golf tournament is held and many sets of restored wooden-shafted clubs are once again helping their owners enjoy the "Grand Ould Gayme."

The British Golf Collectors Society

The British Golf Collectors Society exists to promote an interest in the history of golf and the collecting of items connected with that history. The Society journal, *Through The Green*, is published quarterly and distributed to some 460 members who reside in the UK and in seventeen overseas countries, including 80 members in the USA. It contains articles of historical interest and collecting topics.

The Society has three major golfing meetings: President's Day at the Royal Liverpool G.C., Hoylake, in May; The Scottish Hickory Championship, in which wooden-shafted clubs must be used, at Gullane near Muirfield, in May; and The Open Championship meeting at a course (usually one of the Open qualifying courses) in the vicinity of the Open on the Wednesday before it starts. There are also a number of regional meetings and the Society regularly fields a team, in period dress and playing with wooden-shafted clubs, in matches associated with the Centenary celebrations of clubs.

Contact address: The Hon. Secretary, BGCS, PO Box 13704, North Berwick, East Lothian, Scotland EH39 4ZB.

Chapter 3

A Guide to Values

Chapter 3

A Guide to Values

"How much is this Calamity Jane putter worth?"

"What condition is this book, The Curious History of the Golf Ball?*"*

"How much is this sterling silver trophy worth in this condition?"

"How would you rate that Vardon Flyer ball on a 1 to 10 scale?"

Condition affects value, and experience is the collector's best ally in understanding how it affects the value of golf collectibles. Many collectors purchase only the best quality items; though their collection may be small, it is of high quality. Other collectors acquire items simply because they are available regardless of condition. The ultimate common thread is receiving value for dollar spent, no matter what golf collectible you buy. There is an old cliche worth mentioning here: "Quality remains long after the price has been forgotten." Quality and value go hand in hand.

How to Receive the Best Value For Dollar Spent

Set collecting goals. If your goal is to collect everything related to golf, or only long-nose putters made by Robert Forgan during September 1886, stick with your goal. Acquire what you like and achieve your collecting goals rather than purchasing golf collectibles touted as a good buy.

Acquire collectibles in the best condition you can afford, even if it means buying a G-2 condition scarcity or rarity that fills a void in your collection. Most of all, be happy with the items you acquire. Sort out the items that do not conform to your collecting goals and find collectors or dealers who will take them in trade towards items that will enhance your collection.

Learn as much as possible about the golf collectibles you have set goals to acquire. Building a good reference library to go with your golf collectibles will be an invaluable asset.

Once you have set your goals and have armed yourself with knowledge, you can begin locating dealers and collectors who will respect your collecting aspirations and help you fulfill them. If purchasing from a dealer, buy only from those who offer return privileges regardless of reason. If you buy at auction, inspect lots or have someone you trust inspect and bid on your behalf. You can bid confidently by mail if the auction company will allow you to return lots you are not happy with.

A Grade Scale for Golf Collectibles

Any golf collectible that has deviated from its initial manufactured mint new condition must be evaluated by how much change it exhibits. A grade scale (G-) on a basis of 1 to 10 has been formulated to evaluate the golf collectibles in this reference.

G-10

Absolutely mint new as it left the factory. Showing no signs of wear, circulation, play or any deviation from "as made."

G-9

The ultimate collectible, but not mint new. Exhibits "as made" originality with virtually no imperfections.

G-8

An outstanding example with minor imperfections and minimal wear.

G-7

A desirable collectible in an above average state of preservation. A nice example exhibiting all the characteristics of originality, but with evident imperfections and visible wear.

G-6

A slightly better than average collectible. Should look original with evident imperfections and wear. Still very desirable to the collector who cannot locate a better example because of rarity or financial reasons.

G-5

An "average" example showing moderate to heavy wear. An affordable collectible with moderate desirability.

G-4

A below average collectible, with moderate to major problems. Unless the collectible is very scarce or rare, the advanced collector will not be interested in an item of this grade.

G-3

Collectibles with obvious major problems such as broken parts, and or replacement parts that are not matching. Unless the collectible is very scarce or rare, the advanced collector will not be interested in an item of this grade.

G-2

A collectible that borders on being a non-collectible. Only the scarce or rare items will have any collectible interest.

G-1

A non-collectible item.

What Determines the Value of a Golf Collectible?

Value is based on condition, rarity, availability, competition and desirability.

Rarity is based on the availability of a golf collectible factored by its condition and desirability.

For example, a McEwan Play Club from 1880 is moderately scarce, but frequently available in the marketplace in grades ranging from G-5 to G-8. In near mint condition (G-9), it is decidedly rare and highly desirable.

Common mesh pattern golf balls—circa 1930 from Worthington, Dunlop or Spalding—in above average condition (G-7) sell for about $75. An identical ball, but with a cover cut, or teeth marks from the family pet, will bring only $10 or $15. A "Faroid" or "Park Royal" are balls so rare and seldom offered, even damaged examples are highly sought after and bring premium prices.

Availability of a golf collectible has a great affect on the price, especially at public auctions. Let's imagine a nice example of John Kerr's *The Golf Book of East Lothian*, limited edition, signed and numbered, is offered at auction. We know the book is not rare because there were 250 copies printed in 1896. But, this is the only example to be offered publicly for nearly a year and three book collectors attending the sale are interested in bidding on the book. In this case, availability and competition will determine the ultimate value.

In another example, two Royal Doulton punch bowls in similar condition were offered by two different companies at their July auctions held during British Open week. Only two serious pottery buyers were in attendance, and each is able to acquire one at a reasonable price. Availability, in this scenario, has had an adverse affect on value, even though the punch bowls are quite rare.

Let's use our imagination again. We are back in 1980 and a famous collection is being auctioned. A circa 1865 rut iron by Carrick is touted as the finest example available to collectors. At the time, only four or five collectors worldwide have enough sophistication and knowledge to believe the cataloguer; only one attends the auction and the club brings a modest $200.

Ten years from now, let's say the same club is offered when literally thousands of collectors are actively seeking clubs and several hundred have the knowledge, sophistication and resources to take the cataloguer seriously. Several hop a flight, inspect the club, and try to determine who in attendance will be competition for acquiring it. Dealers carefully inspect the club, try to "feel the mood" of those present, and contact anxious clients to determine if a high "four-figure" or low "five figure" bid is appropriate.

If you think the last paragraph is pure folly, think again! Lets look at what actually took place at an auction during 1996. A Willie Dunn "Stars & Stripes" ball in mint condition was estimated at the $6,000 level. Three bidders were actively bidding at $18,000 and the final hammer price was $26,000 plus a 10% buyer's fee for a total of $28,600! And to top that off, the collector who purchased the ball was offered a handsome profit (which he graciously refused) within a short time after the auction.

What does this mean to the antique golf collector? Since the mid-1980s, thousands of new collectors have entered the hobby. In addition, tens of thousands have expressed curiosity in golf antiques. The highly visible collectibles such as long-nose woods, feather balls, art, pottery and any other collectibles will be the center of attention, and quality will become the determining factor of value.

Chapter 4

Golf Clubs

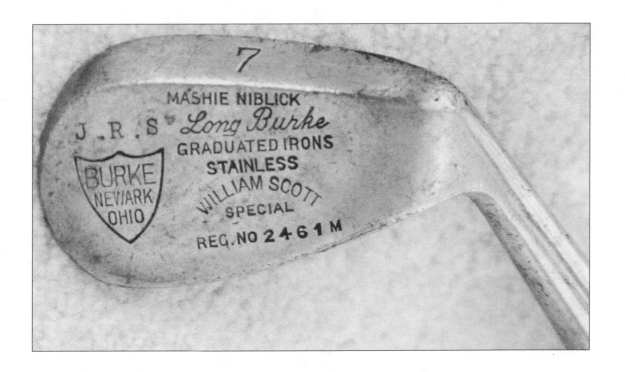

Chapter 4

Introduction to Collecting Wood-Shaft Clubs

Feather ball-era clubs were usually made by carpenters, bow makers, barrel makers, wheelwrights and other craftsmen with woodworking backgrounds. The irons were forged by the local armor maker or black-smith.

The woods were very long and narrow, almost half-pear-shaped, with a head usually measuring between 5 and 6 inches in length. The face was shallow and slightly hooked to promote control of the feather ball. The neck was delicate and curved usually producing a flat lie. The shaft was long and whippy, about 44 to 47 inches, which permitted the ball to be "swept" from the turf. The head and shaft were joined together by a "scare" or "splice" usually 5 to 7 inches in length. The shaft and neck were glued together and a heavy linen twine was wrapped over the splice to help reinforce and strengthen. The linen twine was treated with "pitch" to act as adhesive and preservative for the splice. The grip was formed by an underlisting of wool wrappings tacked to the end of the shaft and covered by goat, lamb, sheep or deer skin.

A "play club" was used from the teeing ground, a "brassie" was used to strike long, low shots from the fairway. The "long spoon" and "mid-spoons" were used to hit moderately long-lofted shots and the "short spoon" (sometimes also called a baffie) was used to hit short-lofted shots around the green or over trouble. Next time you play golf, look at the variety of woods in the bags: Ginties with runner soles, No. 5, 7, 9 and 11 woods—even some I've not heard of. The feather ball era was not much different, as many players had variations made of a long spoon or baffie to suit a particular playing style or a specific type of terrain where most of their golf was played.

The iron-head clubs generally consisted of three, although all golfers did not carry all three. The "rut" iron had a small, rounded head with the face concave or cupped. The hosel was generally 5 to 6 inches long and very thick as this club was a "trouble" club. It was used to extricate the ball from cart ruts, hoof prints or bad lies in the gorse and heather. The club was designed to propel the ball for only a few yards from impending disaster to a more playable lie. According to the player's preference, there were tiny heads (2 to 2-1/4 inches wide) and larger heads (2-1/2 to 2-3/4 inches wide) with anything in between. The concavity of the face also varies from being nearly straight to "ice cream scoop" proportions, and some were made with twisted hosels. During this era the blacksmith didn't make clubs until he had an order; the clubs were, therefore, made to the golfer's specifications. In many cases the golfer brought the club back to the blacksmith having him re-heat and re-hammer the head to produce just the right loft or concavity to suit his game.

The "bunker" or "sand" iron was a large-head, concave-faced, heavy gauge metal iron with the similar use of our modern sand wedge. Most courses were laid out over links land between the sea and arable land, and most of the terrain was sandy. The head was rounded and generally 3 to 4 inches wide with a thick hosel usually about 5 inches long. The stoutness of shaft and hosel combined with the heavy weight of the head, afforded the golfer to take a forceful slash at the ball, propelling it, with moderate distance, back into play, or onto the green.

The "cleek" was an iron with very little loft and a long face that could measure 4 to 5 inches in length. Usually the heel and toe were nearly the same depth giving the head a "rectangular" appearance. The hosel was generally very long, as much as 6 inches, and the shaft was held in place with heavy nicking hammered down into the shaft. Many old re-shafted irons had the nicking sawed off to remove the shaft. When I see an older style club without nicking, this indicates to me that the shaft is a replacement and the original heavy sawtoothed hosel nicking was sawed away when removing the original shaft. Use of the hosel pin replaced niching in head and shaft fastening. The cleek was primarily used for hitting long, low shots from bad lies instead of using a long spoon or brassie which were more susceptible to damage when not swung with a sweeping motion. The cleek was also used to hit low shots into a strong wind or to hit running approach shots to the green.

Many players carried two putters, sometimes three. The "driving" putter had a large thick head with a rather deep face and a large heavy back weight. This was used to approach the hole from a long distance over a relative flat area. The approaching cleek or putter was a slightly lofted iron with a shaft shorter than a cleek, but longer than a putter. This was used to run the ball to the hole when the terrain prohibited the use of the driving putter. The "holing out" putter was either a delicately made wood-head putter or an iron head putter with minimal loft used for more control and accuracy when in close proximity to the hole.

A very heavy white linen thread or cord was used at both ends of the grip. It was coated with pitch and many weathered whippings appear more brown than black. This same thick thread or cord was used for covering the splice joint of shaft and head on the woods and putters. A thick coating of tar or pitch was used to cover the splice whipping for added protection from moisture and handling.

During the boom period beginning with the 1890s, many innovations in club making took place. There were many patents filed on clubs with aluminum heads, adjustable heads, laminated heads, laminated shafts, one-piece woods, screw-socket woods, bifurcated hosels, steel sockets, one-piece grips, various back weightings, socket wood joint, cushioned iron face, wooden face irons, rake irons, waterfall irons, concave face irons—the list goes on and on.

Club makers went from hand forging to drop forging to conserve time and increase production. In time, factories replaced cleek makers, increasing club production by the thousands. With the advent of the rubber-cored "Haskell" ball, golf went into another gear and companies such as Spalding, MacGregor, Stewart, Anderson, Nicoll, Forgan, and Gibson produced millions of clubs yearly.

During the roaring 1920s and early 1930's new American companies such as Burke, Hillerich & Bradsby, Wilson, Kroydon, Draper-Maynard and Scottish companies Cochrane's Lt'd, Hendry & Bishop as well as the aforementioned Forgan, Nicoll, etc. produced more

Wooden-shafted clubs in this section will be valued on a scale of ten grades as outlined in Chapter 3. Current prices will be provided in conditions G-5, G-7 and G-9. The criteria for these conditions are as follows:

G-9

The ultimate collectible, but not *mint new*. Exhibits "as made" originality with virtually no imperfections. The head, shaft and grip must be original. Head, whether wood or metal, must be "as made." Shaft will be straight and have original finish. Grip must be an original or a replacement done "in-period" in order to appear as the original when inspected by the most fastidious experts. Whipping may be replacement, but must be the correct size and color for the club's period.

G-7

A desirable collectible in an above average state of preservation. A nice example exhibiting all the characteristics of originality, but with evident imperfections and visible wear. Imperfections may include an "in period" grip, signs of moderate play or a weak "maker's mark." A very desirable collectible. Clubs prior to 1890 will show more use and the woods may have slight grain separations or a leather face insert nicely done "in period." This club must be esthetically appealing. For the collector who wants the best, but finds it difficult to locate a better example.

G-5

An "average" example showing moderate to heavy wear. An affordable collectible with moderate desirability. May exhibit a slight warping of the shaft or a tattered original looking grip. If there are any markings on pre-1900 clubs, they should be readable enough to properly identify the maker. An acceptable example for the person not seeking perfection, or on a limited budget. A well done in-period cracked shaft repair can actually add "character" and desirability.

than 100 million wood-shaft clubs of various quality. Millions upon millions of low quality clubs were made by Burke, Wright & Ditson, and others to be marketed at department, hardware and sporting good stores.

With the advent of legalization of steel-shaft clubs for the 1926 season in America, and 1930 in Great Britain, Spalding, MacGregor, Walter Hagen, Hillerich & Bradsby, Forgan, Sayers, Nicoll, Gibson and other mainstream makers began to market sets of high quality hickory-shaft clubs. The Gibson "Stella" series was a great playable iron, as well as MacGregor's "Duralite," Burke's "Long Burke" and Spalding's "Kro-Flite" series just to name a few.

Golf Clubs: The Top 100 Makers and Prices

	G-5	G-7	G-9

AITKIN, ALEX

GULLANE, SCOTLAND

Aitkin was the professional at Royal Portrush from 1892-1895 and at Gullane Links from 1905-1917.

	G-5	G-7	G-9
RUSTLESS PUTTER	$50	75	125

Circa 1915. Offset blade. Stamped "Alex Aitkin, Maker, Gullane".

ACCURATE PUTTER	$55	75	110

Circa 1910. Offset blade. Stamped "Alex Aitkin, Maker, Gullane".

SOCKET WOODS	$90	120	175

Circa 1910-1915. Driver, brassie or spoon marked "A. Aitkin".

SPLICED NECK WOODS	$250	375	775

Circa 1890-1895. Transitional bulger beech head play club marked "Aitkin".

JOHN ALLAN

WESTWARD HO!

Allan was the professional at Royal North Devon (Westward Ho!) from 1867-1886 and at Prestwick, St Nicholas from 1886-1895. He made long nose and transitional putters and woods. He was a well respected clubmaker.

LONG NOSE PUTTER	$1450	2250	4000

Circa 1880-1890. Beech head driving putter stamped "J. Allan".

LONG-NOSE WOODS	$1900	3000	6000

Circa 1880-1890. Beech head play club marked "J. Allan".

TRANSITIONAL WOODS	$450	650	1350

Circa 1885-1895. Beech head play club or brassie marked "J. Allan".

AMPCO MFGR CO.

MILWAUKEE, WI

Ampco began forging clubs about 1926 and by the early 1930s went out of business. They made irons and putters from an alloy resembling bronze or brass. When cleaned or polished they have a golden appearance.

AMPCO PUTTER	$65	80	120

Circa 1926-1930. Line scored face.

AMPCO IRONS	$50	70	110

Circa 1926-1930. Line scored. All irons.

AMPCO ALUMINUM WOODS	$300	400	550

Circa 1926-1930. Driver, brassie or spoon. "Ampco, Milwaukee, Wis." on crown with a brass face insert.

ANDERSON, ANDERSON & ANDERSON

Anderson, Anderson & Anderson clubs were made by Anderson of Anstruther and bear the large "Lion and Globe" mark.

LONG BLADE PUTTER	$200	325	550

Circa 1895-1905. "Lion and Globe" maker's mark. Smooth-face blade.

PUTTING CLEEK	$175	275	450

Circa 1900. "Lion and Globe" mark.

BRASS BLADE
PUTTER   **$250**   **350**   **550**

Circa 1900. Steel face inlay. "Lion and Globe" mark.

LION & GLOBE IRONS   **$190**   **300**   **500**

Circa 1895-1905. Smooth face iron, mashie or mashie-niblick. Large "Lion and Globe" mark.

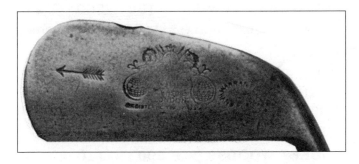

ANDERSON & BLYTHE

ST. ANDREWS, Scotland

The firm of Anderson & Blythe was began operations shortly before 1910 and was dissolved prior to 1915. They made wooden-head putters, but iron-head clubs with their stampings were forged by other makers, principally Tom Stewart.

WEYMESS
PATENT IRON   **$100**   **125**   **200**

Circa 1910. Dot-faced iron. Two level back marked "R. E. Weymess Patent No 16070".

SOCKET WOODS   **$100**   **125**   **175**

Circa 1910. Driver brassie or spoon marked "Anderson & Blythe Special".

WOODEN-HEAD
CLEEK   **$125**   **150**   **225**

Circa 1910. Small persimmon head. Lofted wooden cleek.

ANDERSON, D & SONS

ST. ANDREWS, SCOTLAND

LONG-NOSE PUTTERS   **$600**   **900**   **1650**

Circa 1890-1900. Spliced neck, beech head stamped "D. Anderson".

BRASS-HEAD
PUTTERS   **$70**   **85**   **125**

Circa 1910. Dot Ball face.

GLORY PUTTER   **$80**   **100**   **150**

Circa 1915. "Diamond" back design.

LINE SCORED
PUTTER   **$50**   **60**   **85**

Circa 1920s. "Double Circle and Ribbon" mark.

EXCELSIOR PUTTER   **$60**   **75**   **110**

Circa 1910. "Diamond-Dot" face scoring.

SPECIAL
ACCURATE PUTTER   **$45**   **55**   **80**

Circa 1920s. "Calamity Jane" style offset blade.

MONARCH PUTTER   **$45**   **60**   **80**

Circa 1920s. "D. Anderson & Sons" in a circle mark.

BENT NECK PUTTER   **$70**   **100**   **150**

Circa 1900-1910. "Criss-cross" with "diamond-dot" face scoring.

D. ANDERSON IRONS   **$60**   **80**   **135**

Circa 1900. Cleek, iron and lofting iron. Smooth face.

MAXWELL
HOSEL PUTTER $70 90 125

Circa Teens. Flanged back with Maxwell holes drilled into hosel.

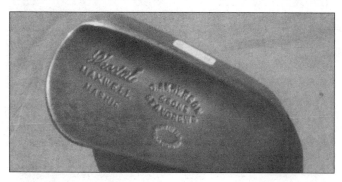

MONARCH IRONS $45 55 80

Circa 1920s. All irons.

SPLICED
NECK WOODS $175 250 375

Circa 1900. Beech head driver, brassie or spoon marked "D. Anderson, St Andrews". May have a leather face insert.

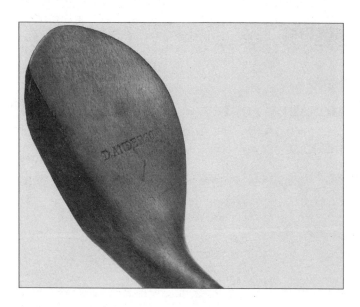

GLORY IRONS $55 75 120

Circa 1915. "Diamond" back design. Dot punched face.

MAXWELL
HOSEL IRONS $55 70 125

Circa 1910-1915. Flanged back with Maxwell drilled holes in hosel.

SAMMY IRON $70 100 150

Circa 1910-1915. Rounded sole. "Diamond" back.

GLORY
JIGGER OR CLEEK $75 95 140

Circa 1915. "Diamond" back design. Dot punched face.

ANTI-SHANK IRONS $150 200 275

Circa 1920s. Stainless steel "Smith's Mashie".

SPLICED
NECK WOODS $160 225 325

Circa 1910. Driver, brassie or spoon. "D. Anderson & Sons, St. Andrews, Special" in Gothic lettering.

SOCKET WOODS $90 110 150

Circa 1915. Driver, brassie or spoon with "D. Anderson & Sons, St Andrews" on the head.

ANDERSON OF ANSTRUTHER, SCOTLAND

by Pete Georgiady

Most collectors have seen the circular mark containing the name "Anderson-Anstruther" at one time or another but few realize the history behind the firm. That mark was used by a father and son whose club production spanned 75 years. Their business was located in the Fife coastal town of Anstruther (pronounced "anster") located about 25 miles from St. Andrews.

The firm's founder, James Anderson, was born in 1845 and became a blacksmith and ferrier. He was undoubtedly approached to make a club head or two at some point and did such a fine job that more such work was sent his way. This is conjecture but it makes for a sound hypothesis since at that time, the early 1860s, Anstruther had no golf links and Anderson himself was never known to have played golf.

There is no acknowledged year when he made his first club heads but several sources suggest either 1862 or 1865, in a decade when John Gray and the Carricks would have been his chief competition. Anderson quickly prospered and by 1880 he had moved primarily into golf club heads and was probably not shoeing horses any longer.

He eventually became a master smith and among the alumni of those once apprenticed to him was Robert Condie who started his own golf club forge in St. Andrews and achieved considerable fame in later years.

In 1892 Anderson patented his first club, a roll face putting cleek that he named the Kurtos model—Kurtos meaning curved in ancient Greek. Since he ran the premier cleek-making business of his day, many other makers and patentees sought him out to produce their iron heads. He forged Carruthers' (drilled hosel), Forrester's (concentric) and George Lowe's (anti-shank) patent club heads as well as many others for F. H. Ayers, Willie Park Jr., and Robert Anderson.

Some people credit James Anderson with the invention of the diamond-back shaped iron club head. Whether or not this is true, he produced some magnificent old irons with that design in the late 1880s and early 1890s.

James Anderson died early in life in 1895 and was succeeded in the business by his son Alexander. Alex did a fine job of transitioning the company from his father's moderately sized shop to a large volume production company making heads in the hundreds of thousands yearly.

Anderson used several cleek marks over the years. James' first mark appeared in about 1875 and was used up to his death in 1895. It is the classic Anderson-Anstruther name in a circle measuring only 1/2 inch diameter usually stamped in the center of the back of the club head. Alex then switched to a similar mark with a double circle that he used for about 15 years before reverting to the original design his father used, only in a slightly larger 5/8 inch circle.

It was Alex who began to use the "arrow" cleek mark for which the firm is now so famous. Also around this time, 1905, Anderson devised a numbering system for club heads to increase sales through catalogs. A two- or three-digit model number can be found stamped on most of their heads. Many Anderson heads were exported to North America and one of the largest seller of Anderson headed clubs was The Golf Shop, Chicago, a MacGregor retail outlet. Alex Anderson produced a registered design bent neck putting cleek (#277771) similar to that of Willie Park Jr. around 1900 and he produced a wide variety of iron heads in many styles including concave faced irons, "Hold-em" model deep groove irons as well as a healthy variety of putter types.

To today's golf collectors, the Andersons are the quintessential cleek making firm. James Anderson was known even in the 1890s as the original hand-forged cleek maker and his iron club heads were viewed as examples of the finest craftsmanship as golf entered its first modern era. Later, in Alex's generation, the company continued to produce a quality product while keeping up with modern production methods and new designs until their demise before World War II.

BRASS-HEAD
PUTTERS $125   150   250

Circa 1890. Straight blade putter with small "Circle" mark.

BRASS
MALLET PUTTER $225   300   500

Circa 1915. Brass head with a steel face plate. Double circle mark.

SMOOTH-FACE
PUTTER $125   150   250

Circa 1895-1900. Rounded back with small "Circle" mark.

DEEP-FACE PUTTER   **$60**   **80**   **150**

Circa 1905. Smooth face with small "Circle" mark.

**BRASS BLADE
PUTTER**   **$90**   **120**   **200**

Circa 1900. Smooth face blade. Small circle mark. Large "P" stamped at the toe.

**DIAMOND
BACK PUTTER**   **$50**   **70**   **125**

Circa 1910. Smooth face. Bent neck hosel. Small circle mark.

RIDGE BACK PUTTER   **$190**   **250**   **400**

Circa 1915-1920. "Ridge" runs along the center of the back. Dot punched face. "Arrow" mark at toe.

TRIUMPH PUTTER   **$225**   **300**   **500**

Circa 1920. Pyramid top line of blade. "Diamond-dot" face scoring.

**JAMES
ANDERSON IRONS**   **$300**   **375**   **550**

Circa 1880-1890. Lofted general purpose iron with small "Circle" mark.

**JAMES
ANDERSON IRONS**   **$450**   **600**   **1500**

Circa 1870-1880. Cleek. Small "Circle" mark. Five inch hosel.

**SHORT BLADE
CLEEK**   **$70**   **90**   **175**

Circa 1900. Small "Circle" mark.

LOFTING IRON   **$75**   **90**   **175**

Circa 1900. Smooth face. Small "Circle" mark.

**VARDON
SIGNATURE IRONS**   **$65**   **80**   **125**

Circa 1905-1910. All irons. Arrow mark at toe.

**FOR ARMY &
NAVY STORES**   **$100**   **125**   **225**

Circa 1900. Cleek, iron, or lofting iron marked "A N C S L" with small "Circle" mark.

**VARDON
SIGNATURE IRONS**   **$250**   **350**   **700**

Circa 1905-1910. Small smooth face niblick. "Arrow" mark at toe.

LOFTING IRON   **$275**   **475**   **875**

Circa 1900. Smooth face rut niblick. Small "Circle" mark.

**SMOOTH-FACE
CLEEK**   **$55**   **75**   **120**

Circa 1910-1915. Large double circle mark.

DEEP-FACE MASHIE   **$60**   **75**   **120**

Circa 1910. Smooth face. Large double circle mark.

OVAL-HEAD NIBLICK   **$60**   **80**   **125**

Circa 1915-1920. Arrow and large double circle marks.

**MUSSEL BACK
IRONS**   **$60**   **80**   **125**

Circa 1920s. Cleek, iron, mashie or mashie-niblick. Arrow and large double circle marks.

**CRISS-CROSS
FACE IRON**   **$60**   **75**   **125**

Circa 1905-1910. "Arrow" mark at toe.

**CONCAVE
FACE IRONS**   **$100**   **125**   **175**

Circa 1915. Mashie-niblick 30. Dot punched face. 'Arrow" at toe.

**DIAMOND
BACK IRONS**   **$50**   **65**   **95**

Circa 1920. Driving iron, mid-iron, mashie, jigger, mashie-niblick or niblick. Large double circle mark.

**PYRAMID
BACK IRONS**   **$50**   **65**   **100**

Circa 1920s. All irons. Arrow and large double circle mark.

**BALL FACE
LOFTING IRON**   **$60**   **80**   **125**

Circa 1905-1910. Deep face. Small circle mark.

"A 5" SAMMY IRON   **$150**   **200**   **300**

Circa 1920. Ridge bisects the back from heel to toe. Box-dot scoring.

MAGIC MASHIE   **$100**   **125**   **200**

Circa 1920-1925. A raised ridge bisects back from heel to toe. Lined face. Large double circle mark.

RUSTLESS NIBLICK   **$45**   **55**   **75**

Circa 1925-1930. Dot face. Large single circle mark.

**SMITH
ANTI-SHANK IRONS**   **$150**   **200**   **275**

Circa 1920-1925. All irons.

**JAMES ANDERSON
RUT IRON**   **$800**   **1000**   **2000**

Circa 1885. Tiny rounded head. Small "Circle" mark.

ANDERSON, ROBERT

EDINBURGH, SCOTLAND

Began making clubs during the early 1890s. Patented the first through-hosel shafted woods.

**BRASS-HEAD
PUTTERS**   **$90**   **125**   **200**

Circa 1890-1900. Smooth face blade marked "R. Anderson & Sons, Princess St. Edinburgh".

**CONCENTRIC-BACK
CLEEK**   **$80**   **125**   **190**

Circa 1900. Shallow smooth face cleek.

**SMOOTH-FACE
IRONS**   **$90**   **135**   **225**

Circa 1895-1905. Cleek, iron, or lofter. Marked "R. Anderson & Sons, Edinburgh".

**GENERAL
PURPOSE IRON**   **$125**   **200**   **400**

Circa 1890-1895. Long, moderately lofted smooth face. "Anderson & Sons, Princess St., Edinburgh" markings.

**THROUGH HOSEL
PATENT WOODS**   **$150**   **200**   **375**

Circa 1900. Driver, brassie or spoon marked "Anderson & Sons, Edinburgh, Patent".

ALUMINUM WOODS   **$275**   **375**   **600**

Circa 1900-1910. Various lofts. Head marked "Anderson, Edinburgh".

ARMY & NAVY COOPERATIVE STORES, LTD

Began selling clubs about 1885 and began manufacturing and assembling clubs during the early 1890s. The mark they used was "A & N C S L" and usually included "London" on the pre-1900 wood head putters and semi-long nose woods.

STEEL BLADE PUTTER $50   70   100

Circa 1905-1910. Large double circle mark.

LONG-NOSE PUTTER $550   850   1500

Circa 1890-1900. Beech head spliced neck marked "Army & Navy C S L, London".

DEEP-FACE MASHIE $100   140   250

Circa 1900-1905. Stamped "Hold Fast" and "A & N C S".

SPLICED-NECK WOODS $225   300   500

Circa 1900-1910. Driver, brassie or spoon. "Army & Navy A N C S L, London".

SMOOTH-FACE IRONS $125   160   275

Circa 1890-1900. Iron or lofting iron. "A & N C S L" on head.

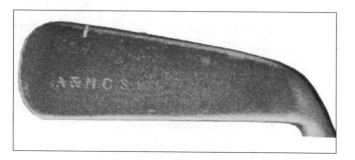

LONG-NOSE WOODS $1150   1750   3450

Circa 1890. Play club or brassie. Beech head marked "Army & Navy C S L, London".

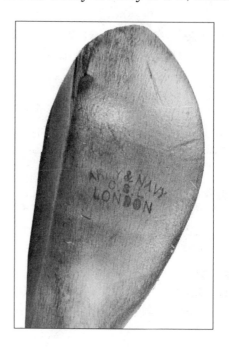

ASHFORD, W & G

BIRMINGHAM, ENGLAND

Made clubs during the mid-1890s. They used a "Fox" head as a maker's identification mark. Many clubs had the patented one-piece sewn grip.

SMOOTH-FACE IRONS $200   225   450

Circa 1893-1897. General purpose iron or lofting iron. Marked "W & G Ashford, Mild Steel" with "Cat" mark. Many have a one-piece leather grip.

SHORT-BLADE CLEEK $225   350   500

Circa 1893-1897. Stamped "W & G Ashford, Mild Steel" with "Cat" mark. Many have a one-piece leather grip.

DRIVING IRON $250   375   500

Circa 1893-1897. Driving iron marked "W & G Ashford, Mild Steel" with "Cat" mark. Many have a one-piece leather grip.

SPLICED-NECK
WOODS $450   750   1500

Circa 1893-1897. Pear-shaped heads with "Cat" and "W G Ashford" markings. Many have a one-piece leather grip.

AUCHTERLONIE, D & W

ST. ANDREWS, SCOTLAND

David and Willie Auchterlonie formed their company during the late 1890s. Their mark was simply "D & W Auchterlonie, St. Andrews".

SOCKET WOODS $90   110   150

Circa 1920s. Driver, brassie or spoon. Stamped "T. Auchterlonie, St. Andrews, Deluxe".

RIDGE-BACK PUTTER $200   250   350

Circa 1905-1910. Patent No. 405445. Fancy "Chain Link" face scoring.

D & W BRAN
PUTTER $90   120   175

Circa 1910-1915. Patent No. 726896. Two-level back. Dot face.

STAINLESS
STEEL PUTTER $50   60   85

Circa 1930-1935. Offset flanged back blade putter. Marked "D & W Auchterlonie, St. Andrews".

ALL SMOOTH-FACE
IRONS $65   85   125

Circa 1905-1910. Stamped "D & W Auchterlonie, N B, St. Andrews".

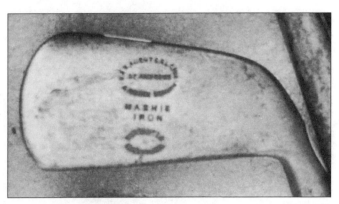

SOCKET WOODS $90   110   160

Circa 1915-20. Driver, brassie or spoon. Marked "Auchtie" in script below "D & W Auchterlonie, St. Andrews".

SPLICED
NECK PUTTERS $300   550   950

Circa 1910-1915. Long nose style persimmon head. Marked "Auchterlonie Special".

AUCHTERLONIE, TOM

ST. ANDREWS, SCOTLAND

He began his business in St. Andrews at the turn of the century and continued until the 1980s. His mark was "T Auchteronie" in block lettering.

ELLICE PUTTER $50   60   80

Circa 1925-1930. Bent-neck line-scored blade.

SOCKET WOOD
HEAD PUTTER $200   250   350

Circa 1920. "Auchterlonie" on persimmon head.

WOOD HEAD
SOCKET PUTTER $250   350   475

Circa 1910-15. Marked "T. Auchterlonie".

HOLING-OUT PUTTER $275   375   550

Circa 1920. Wide sole and beveled heel and toe.

SPLICED-NECK
PUTTERS $300   450   750

Circa 1910. Long-nose style putter. Marked "T. Auchterlonie".

"AUCHTERLONIE"
IRONS $45   55   75

Circa 1925. All irons. "Auchterlonie" in large script.

"IT-Z-IN" SERIES
IRONS $75   100   150

Circa 1920s. All irons. Marked "Patented by Tom Auchterlonie"

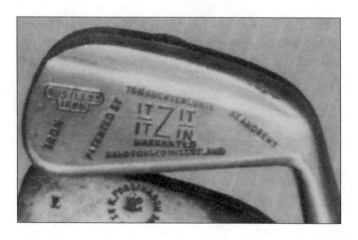

DELUXE
HAND MADE SOCKET
WOODS $90   110   150

Circa 1920s. Driver, brassie or spoon. Stamped "Auchterlonie Special, Hand Made".

GOLD MEDAL
SOCKET WOODS $90   110   150

Circa 1920s. Driver, brassie or spoon. Stamped "Auchterlonie Gold Medal".

AYRES, F. H.

LONDON, ENGLAND

F.H. Ayres began as a sporting goods house at the beginning of the 19th century. About 1885 it purchased clubs from different manufacturers, and stamped them with their "F H Ayres, London" block letters mark. It also began making its own clubs and used the same mark until about 1900 when it began to use the "Maltese Cross" mark. The business ended during the dark days of the Great Depression. Many of the original shafts were marked "F. H. Ayres & Co."

FLANGED
BACK PUTTER $60   80   135

Circa 1915-1920. Offset blade stamped with the "Maltese Cross" mark.

GEM PUTTER $60   75   125

Circa 1915. "Maltese Cross" mark and "Putter" at toe.

STRAIGHT
BLADE PUTTER $80   100   160

Circa 1890. Smooth face with "P" at toe. Steel head.

FACET PUTTER $90   120   160

Circa 1915-1920. "The Facet" in a "Triangle Sweet Spot" on a dot faced straight blade. "Maltese Cross" mark at toe.

STRAIGHT
BLADE PUTTER $100   125   190

Circa 1890. Brass head. Smooth face with "P" at toe.

WINKWORTH
SCOTT PUTTER $250   325   475

Oval hosel and oval shaft putter similar to the "Winkworth Scott" Patent. "Rainbow" face.

LONG NOSE PUTTERS   **$500   750   1450**

Circa 1890-1900. Transitional shorter rounded-head putter. Beech head.

LONG NOSE PUTTERS   **$650   1250   2250**

Circa 1885-1895. Long-nose putter. Beech head.

BOBBIE IRON   **$55   65   95**

Circa 1915. Rounded sole. "Maltese Cross" mark.

SMOOTH FACE IRONS   **$100   175   350**

Circa 1885-1895. Large block letters.

VARDON SERIES IRONS   **$60   75   110**

Circa 1920s. All irons. "Maltese Cross" mark at toe.

ROUND FACE NIBLICK   **$65   75   125**

Circa 1910-1915. "Maltese Cross" mark. Dot-punched face.

THE CERT IRONS   **$175   200   300**

Circa 1920s. "Maltese Cross". Sole extends below the heel and toe.

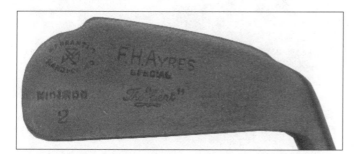

DRIVING IRON   **$100   125   225**

Circa 1890-1900. "D" marked at toe. "F. H. Ayres, London" mark.

ANTI-SHANK IRONS   **$125   175   275**

Circa 1915-1925. All Smith Patent irons.

LONG-NOSE WOODS   **$475   725   1475**

Circa 1895-1900. Transitional semi-long nose driver, brassie or spoon. "F. H. Ayers" stamping.

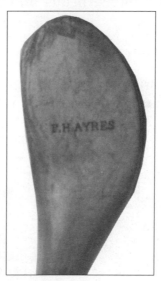

ANTI-SHANK IRONS $175   225   350

Circa 1900-1910. All Fairlie Patent irons with smooth face.

**SMALL-HEAD
NIBLICK** $190   250   475

Circa 1900-1905. "Maltese Cross" mark.

RUT IRON $375   650   1450

Circa 1885-1895. "Maltese Cross" mark.

SOCKET WOODS $90   110   160

Circa 1915-1925. Driver, brassie or spoon. "F. H. Ayres" mark.

SOCKET WOODS $110   125   190

Circa 1915-1925. Wood cleek or Bull Dog trouble wood.

**SPLICED-NECK
WOODS** $200   300   475

Circa 1895-1910. Traditional head shape. Driver, brassie or spoon. "F. H. Ayers" stamping.

LONG NOSE WOODS $1000   1650   2750

Circa 1885-1895. Play club, brassie or spoon. "F. H. Ayres" on beech head.

BLACKSMITH MADE

Clubs made by makers of armor, wheelwrights, metal workers, etc. and blacksmiths. Usually made prior to the 1870s and have crudely forged heads and heavy hosel nickings.

**SMOOTH-FACE
CLEEK** $1500   2700   5500

Circa 1840-1860. Five-inch-long hosel with crude heavy nicking.

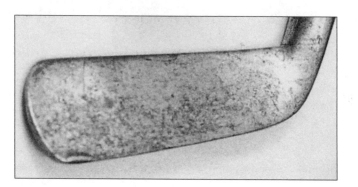

**HOLING-OUT
PUTTER** $1750   3200   6500

Circa 1840-1860. Very thick long hosel with crude heavy nicking.

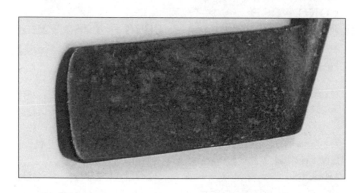

RUT IRON $2000   3500   7000

Circa 1840-1860. Small cupped face. Long thick hosel with heavy nicking.

**BUNKER OR
SAND IRON** $2000   4500   9000

Circa 1840-1860. Very thick long hosel with crude heavy nicking. Usually with a concave face.

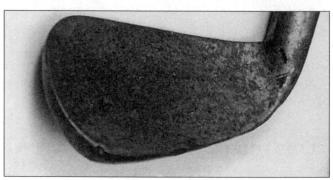

BRADDELL

BELFAST, IRELAND

**BRASS BLADE
PUTTER**   **$125   160   275**

Circa 1895-1900. Stamped "Braddell, Belfast".

**ALUMINUM-HEAD
WOODS**   **$400   600   1150**

Circa 1900-1910. Model C or G. Stamped "Braddell Patent". "Carruthers" shafting and a leather face insert.

**ALUMINUM-HEAD
WOODS**   **$450   650   1250**

Circa 1894-1900. "Braddell Patent 4624". Leather face insert.

BRAND, CHARLES

CARNOUSTIE, SCOTLAND

Charles Brand was from Carnoustie and began making clubs about 1890. He used "C. Brand, Carnoustie" in block letters, inside a double oval and also used a "Lion" mark. He produced clubs until his death in 1922.

**IRON-HEAD
BLADE PUTTER**   **$60   80   140**

Circa 1910-1915. Stamped "C. Brand, Carnoustie". Hatched face scoring.

**BRASS-HEAD
PUTTERS**   **$100   125   175**

Circa 1900-1910. Stamped "C. Brand, Carnoustie". Smooth face.

**WOOD-HEAD
SOCKET PUTTER**   **$250   350   600**

Circa 1900-1910. Stamped "C. Brand".

**SPLICED-NECK
PUTTER**   **$500   800   1500**

Circa 1895. Stamped "C. Brand" on beech head.

**LINE-SCORED
IRONS**   **$50   60   90**

Circa 1920s. All irons. Stamped "C. Brand, Carnoustie" in a double circle.

**SMOOTH-FACE
IRONS**   **$90   125   200**

Circa 1895-1905. Cleek, iron, and lofter. Stamped "C. Brand, Carnoustie".

BRIDGEPORT GUN & IMPLEMENT CO.

Bridgeport Gun Implement Co. produced clubs from 1897 to about 1905. Most pre-1899 clubs sold by BGI were imported or made by Spalding before the J. H. Williams Co., Brooklyn, New York, became its major supplier. Many aluminum-head putters and fairway woods were imported from Standard Golf Company, Sunderland, England, and were marked "B G I, CO" on the sole.

The clubs were of high quality and very popular in their day. Today many collectors focus on BGI clubs as they represent a good portion of early American golf history.

Jim Cooper has written the definitive work on Spalding, which is profusely illustrated. Every Spalding collector should have this reference in his/her library. It is available from the author, or Jim Cooper. There are also BGI Retail Catalogue reprints from 1900, 1903 and 1904 available from the author of this book.

SMOOTH-FACE
BLADE PUTTER $60   95   140

Circa 1900. "BGI Co" oval mark.

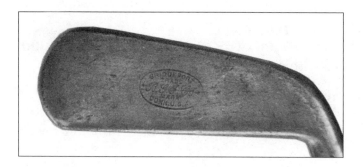

PUTTING CLEEK $65   115   175

Circa 1900. #110 on shaft. "Diamond W" mark on the hosel.

SPLICED-NECK
PUTTER $500   900   1500

Circa 1900. "Arrow-BGI-Arrow" mark. Dogwood head.

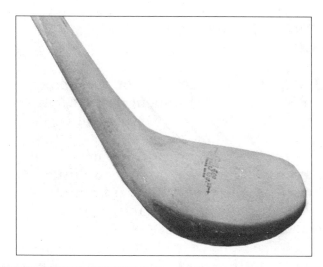

FAIRFIELD PUTTER $65   110   175

Circa 1900. "Fairfield" in script. "220" on the shaft.

DEEP FACE
BLADE PUTTER $75   125   225

Circa 1900. Smooth face. "BGI" oval mark. "Diamond W" mark on the hosel.

BRASS-HEAD
PUTTERS $75   125   225

Circa 1900. Two-way blade. "BGI" oval mark.

ONE-PIECE WOOD $1500   2000   3200

Circa 1898-1902. Driver or brassie one-piece hickory head and shaft. Has a leather face insert.

PARK-STYLE
PUTTERS $100   175   325

Circa 1900. Severely offset blade. "BGI Arrow" mark.

SCHENECTADY-TYPE
PUTTER $200   375   475

Circa 1903-1905. "BGI Co" on the sole.

SMOOTH FACE
IRONS $50   90   160

Circa 1900. All irons. "BGI" oval mark.

FAIRFIELD IRONS	$50	90	150

Circa 1900. All irons.

CARRUTHER'S MODEL CLEEK	$75	125	225

Circa 1900. #103 on shaft. Carruther's through hosel shafting.

SOCKET WOODS	$100	150	250

Circa 1900-1905. "Arrow-BGI-Arrow" mark. All woods.

FAIRFIELD WOODS	$100	150	250

Circa 1900. "Fairfield" in script. All woods. Socket heads.

SPLICED NECK WOODS	$175	325	475

Circa 1900. "Arrow-B G I-Arrow". All woods.

FORKED SPLICE WOODS	$400	700	1000

Circa 1900. All woods.

BUHRKE CO., R.H.

CHICAGO, IL

Began making clubs in the early 1920s. R.H. Buhrke made many different clubs, mostly department or sporting goods quality clubs. The most sought after series is the "Classic" with a brass "plug" in the face. They used a "Key" mark and used trade names of "Medalist", "Burr-Key-Bilt", "Classic", "Finalist" and others.

ANDY ROBERTSON IRONS	$35	45	65

Circa late 1920s. All irons. Line scored face. Chromed head.

ANDY ROBERTSON PUTTER	$40	50	70

Circa late 1920s. Line scored face. Chromed head.

CLASSIC SERIES PUTTER	$70	100	125

Circa 1920s. Brass plug face insert in sweet spot.

STYLIST SERIES

IRONS	$35	45	65

Circa 1925-1930. All irons. Line scored blade, "Flower" at the sweet spot. Chromed head.

MAJESTIC SERIES IRONS	$35	45	65

Circa 1920s. All irons. Line scored face.

PRETTY FACE WOODS	$125	175	250

Circa 1925. Half-moon aluminum face insert. Driver, brassie or spoon.

CLASSIC SERIES IRONS

Circa 1920s. All irons. Brass plug face insert in sweet spot.

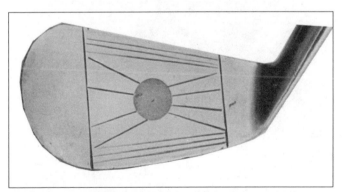

KILROY IRONS	$65	85	115

Circa 1920s. All irons. "Burr-Key-Bilt" mark with "Key".

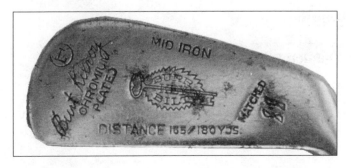

**PRETTY FACE
WOODS**   **$95   115   160**

Circa 1925. "Burr-Key-Bilt Regal". Driver, brassie or spoon.

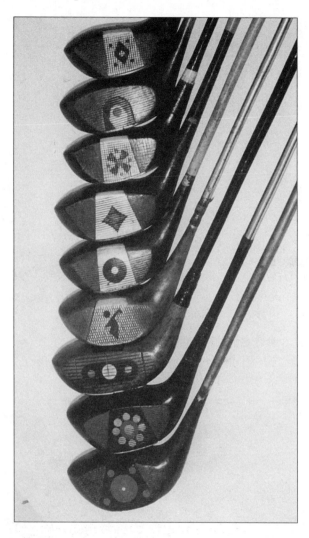

**MAJESTIC
SERIES PUTTER**   **$40   50   70**

Circa 1920s. Line scored face.

**STYLIST
SERIES PUTTER**   **$40   50   70**

Circa 1925-1930. Line scored blade. Chromed head.

BURKE MFG CO.

NEWARK, OH

Burke began forging irons about 1910. They made millions upon millions of low and medi- um quality clubs that were sold in dry good and department stores throughout the Midwest. They used many marks including a "Hand with Scales", "Bee", "Daisy", "Thistle", "Crown" and others. Their top-of-the-line clubs were the "Grand Prize" series.

MONARCH PUTTER $40   50   75

Circa 1920. Flanged back hyphen scored blade with a large "Crown" mark.

**PICCADILLY
PUTTER**   **$90   120   175**

Circa 1920s. Large flange with a "Swastika" type mark.

STERLING PUTTER $40   50   75

Circa 1920. Square punch marked face. Crown and Lion marks.

PRESTWICK PUTTER $40   50   75

Circa 1920. Line scored blade putter.

**ST. ANDREWS
SPECIAL PUTTERS $40   50   75**

Circa 1915-1920. Dot punched face. "Crown" mark.

**GRAND PRIZE
PUTTERS**   **$40   50   75**

Circa 1920s. Hyphen scored face.

**BEE AND FLOWER
MARK PUTTERS $40   50   75**

Circa 1920s. Various assemblers.

**COLUMBIA
SPECIAL PUTTERS $40   50   75**

Circa 1915-1925. "Rampant Lion" and "Crown" markings.

GLENCOE PUTTERS $80   100   150

Circa 1920s. Flanged back putter with alternating "Line and Dot Punched" face scoring.

**GRAND PRIZE
PUTTERS**   **$40   50   75**

Circa 1920s. Offset hosel blade.

X 69 PUTTER $100   140   200

Circa 1920s. Flanged back, wide sole.

Hagen's Own Clubs—for You!

WALTER HAGEN—the Incomparable Sir Walter—has granted Burke (and only Burke) the right to copy his bag of clubs.

So here are shown the leading Burke-Hagen models—*actual duplicates* of his record-breaking clubs, each autographed *Walter Hagen*.

If Walter uses them, they MUST be unrivalled in design, in material, in finish. Have you ever wondered how a set of these *proven* clubs will help your score?

Quit wondering—and find out!

In Monel metal or in steel at Pros and Sporting Goods Stores

Hagen Driver: Socket model. Deep face with metal insert. Easy to learn.

Hagen Brassie: Made exactly as the Driver but with a little more loft.

Hagen Driving Iron: A confidence-building club for the long one-shotters.

Hagen Mashie Iron: His pet club. You will use it more than any other in a round.

Hagen Mashie: Well lofted. Medium in size and weight. Practical in every way.

Hagen Mashie Niblick: Heavy head but a small blade. An excellent trouble-escape.

Hagen Putter: Slightly gooseneck. His selection from 100 models.

GRAND PRIZE

BURKE
CLUBS · BAGS · BALLS

A COPY of the new Burke Catalog, picturing and describing the full line, sent on request.

GIRAFFE-NECK PUTTER $120 150 225

Circa 1920s. Six-inch-long pencil-thin hosel.

ALUMINUM-HEAD PUTTER $100 125 175

Circa 1920s. Mills-type aluminum-head mallet.

X 78 BENT-NECK PUTTER $100 125 175

Circa 1920s. Park-style, severely bent neck, smooth-face putter.

CRESCENT-HEAD PUTTER $125 150 225

Circa late Teens. Crescent head, broad sole and pointed toe.

COLUMBIA SPECIAL IRONS $35 40 65

Circa 1915-1925. All irons. "Rampant Lion" and "Crown" markings.

END GRAIN PUTTER $325 400 650

Circa 1920. Rectangular wood head.

DIAMOND BACK IRONS $50 65 90

Circa 1910-1915. "Rampant Lion" mark at the toe.

PRESTWICK IRONS $35 40 65

Circa 1920. All irons.

ST. ANDREWS SPECIAL IRONS $35 45 70

Circa 1915-1920. Dot punched face. "Crown" mark at the toe.

GLENCOE IRONS $35 40 65

Circa 1920s. All irons.

COMMANDER IRONS $35 40 65

Circa late 1920s. All irons. Grip has aluminum end cap.

BURKE STAINLESS IRONS $35 40 65

Circa 1925-1930. All irons.

GRAND PRIZE IRONS $35 40 65

Circa 1920s. All irons.

GRAND PRIZE IRONS $100 125 175

Circa 1915. Foulis-type concave head.

HARRY VARDON SIGNATURE IRONS $35 45 75

Circa 1925-1930. All irons.

TED RAY SIGNATURE IRONS $35 45 75

Circa 1925-1930. All irons.

ROTARY ILLEGAL IRONS $300 425 675

Circa 1920. All clubs. Half waffle pattern, half slot deep groove. Monel metal.

MONEL METAL IRONS $40 50 75

Circa 1920-1930. All clubs.

DEEP GROOVE IRONS $95 120 160

Circa 1915-1922. Corrugated deep grooves. All irons.

LONGER "LIFE"—BETTER TIMING
PERFECT BALANCE

Golfers everywhere will be pleased to learn of the association of two great golf experts, now organized into a company producing new and superior model golf clubs in 3 Woods and 12 Irons.

Butchart-Nicholls clubs are a distinct advance in the art of clubmaking. They are the final achievement of two skilled clubmakers. Made of laminated bamboo and hickory by a new patented process, the shafts of B-T-N clubs maintain enduring straightness. Possessing all the advantages of first-grade hickory shafts, they retain longer "life" and in addition are uniform, durable and more dependable. Players of every class are finding the perfectly balanced B-T-N clubs an aid to greater distance on every shot.

Facilities for manufacture of B-T-N clubs at the up-to-date Glenbrook, Conn., factory include only the newest and most modern equipment. Every improved device for excellence and precision in clubmaking has been installed.

BTN

MADE IN
3 WOODS
12 IRONS

EVERY SHAFT
GUARANTEED

Now golfers, professionals and sporting goods dealers should acquaint themselves with the superior qualities of the Butchart-Nicholls clubs. Exponents of the game have long awaited golf clubs which measure up to Butchart-Nicholls quality—a superiority that is carefully built into each club shaft and each club head by expert craftsmen.

Write, wire or telephone us today for additional information. Our representative will gladly call and display these models and quote you prices.

PLAY BETTER GOLF WITH B=T=N CLUBS

BUTCHART=NICHOLLS COMPANY, INC.

Glenbrook, Connecticut · · · Telephone: Stamford 6785

DEEP GROOVE IRONS $110 135 175

Circa 1915-1922. All clubs. Monel metal heads.

DEEP GROOVE IRONS $120 150 225

Circa 1915-1922. Slot deep grooves. All irons.

LONG BURKE IRONS $35 45 75

Circa 1925-1930. All irons. "Shield" mark.

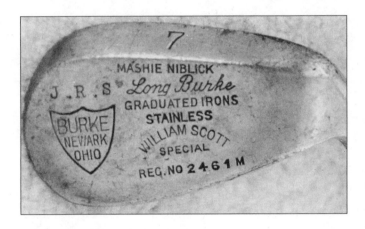

BRASS HEAD NIBLICK $150 175 250

Circa 1925. Large hyphen scored brass head.

CHAMPION WOODS $75 95 135

Circa 1920s. Driver, brassie or spoon.

GRAND PRIZE WOODS $75 95 135

Circa 1915-1925. Driver, brassie or spoon.

GLENCOE WOODS $75 95 135

Circa 1920s. Driver, brassie or spoon.

COLUMBIA SPECIAL WOODS $75 95 135

Circa 1915-1925. Driver, brassie or spoon.

VARIOUS WOODS $75 95 135

Circa 1925-1928. Driver, brassie or spoon. "Golfrite", "De Luxe", "Plus-Four", "Autograph Series", "Sportsman" and "Skippers".

PRESTWICK WOODS $75 95 135

Circa 1920s. Driver, brassie or spoon.

JUVENILE CLUBS $30 35 60

Circa 1920s. All irons and putter. Smooth faces.

JUVENILE CLUBS $60 80 125

Circa 1920s. All woods.

HAGEN SERIES IRONS $40 50 75

Circa 1925. All clubs.

BUSSEY & CO.

LONDON, ENGLAND

George Bussey began making clubs in London during the late 1880s and made a two-piece club called the "Patented Steel Socket. He also patented a one piece grip that was sewn up the back. He used the monogram "GGB" mark with an arrow through it and "Thistle". On many clubs the name of the club, (mashie, iron, etc.) was stamped on the shaft.

STEEL SOCKET PATENT PUTTER $175 250 375

Circa 1890-1900. "Bussey & Co, London" and "Thistle" marks.

STEEL SOCKET PATENT PUTTER $275 400 800

Circa 1890-1900. Brass blade, steel socket. "Bussey & Co, London" and "Thistle" marks. Many have a one-piece leather grip.

STEEL SOCKET PATENT IRONS $175 250 400

Circa 1890-1900. Smooth iron or mashie. "Thistle" below "Bussey & Co., London".

STEEL SOCKET			
PATENT IRONS	$225	275	450

Circa 1890-1900. Smooth face cleek. "Thistle" below "Bussey & Co., London".

BUTCHART-NICHOLS

GLENBROOK, CT

They were famous for shafts made of alternating strips of bamboo and hickory. They used a "Bird" mark and the letters "BTN".

BAMBOO-SHAFT			
PUTTER	$55	65	90

Circa 1920s. Dot punched face.

BAMBOO-SHAFT			
IRONS	$45	55	80

Circa 1920s. All irons. Dot punched face.

BUTCHART BILT			
WOODS	$100	125	175

Circa 1920s. Driver, brassie or spoon. Many have steel face inserts. Laminated bamboo shaft.

CANN & TAYLOR

LONDON, ENGLAND

A London-area firm. They used "Cann & Taylor, Winchester" in block letters 1894-1897, a "J. H. Taylor" signature and an odd looking "Flywheel" mark into the 1930s.

DOT FACE			
BLADE PUTTER	$50	60	90

Circa 1910-1915. "Cann & Taylor" with "J. H. Taylor" signature marks.

GEM PUTTER	$80	100	150

Circa 1910-1920. Flywheel mark. Rounded back. Dot punched face.

SMOOTH			
FACE PUTTER	$90	120	190

Circa 1900. "Cann & Taylor, Winchester and Richmond" stampings.

CYNOSURE			
SERIES IRONS	$45	55	75

Circa 1925. All irons. "Flyweel" mark.

AUTOGRAPH			
MODEL IRONS	$50	60	90

Circa 1915. All irons. Bordered hyphen face.

CONVEX FACE			
NIBLICK	$60	70	100

Circa 1920.

SMOOTH FACE			
AUTOGRAPH IRONS	$75	95	150

Circa 1900-1910. Cleek, iron, mashie and lofting iron.

RADIAL SOLE			
DRIVING MASHIE	$80	110	150

Circa 1915. "Flywheel" mark.

DRIVING MASHIE	$80	100	150

Circa 1920. "Flywheel" mark.

RUT NIBLICKS	$140	190	300

Circa 1900-1905. Stamped "Cann & Taylor Niblick".

CYNOSURE			
SERIES WOODS	$95	115	160

Circa 1920s. Driver, brassie or spoon.

SPLICED NECK			
WOODS	$150	200	300

Circa 1910-1915. Driver, brassie or spoon.

SPLICED NECK			
WOODS	$300	400	750

Circa 1891-1897. Transitional beech head. Leather face insert. Bulger driver or brassie.

CARRICK, F & A

MUSSELBURGH, Scotland

The Carrick brothers, who were initially blacksmiths, began forging iron heads about 1860 through the early 1900s. They used two marks: "F & A Carrick, Musselburgh" and simply "Carrick" in block letters. All their clubs carried a "Cross" cleek mark. They are quite scarce and highly collectible.

STEEL-BLADE			
PUTTER	$350	500	1000

Circa 1890-1895. Smooth face blade putter. "Cross" mark.

EARLY STEEL-BLADE
PUTTER $475   650   1250

Circa 1870-1885. Smooth face straight blade. "Cross" mark.

GENERAL
PURPOSE IRON $450   650   1150

Circa 1870-1880. "F & A Carrick, Musselburgh" above the "Cross" mark.

CROSS
MARKED CLEEK $500   700   1250

Circa 1870-1880. Stamped "F & A Carrick, Musselburgh".

CROSS MARKED
CLEEK $500   700   1250

Circa 1870-1880. Stamped "Carrick". "Cross" mark.

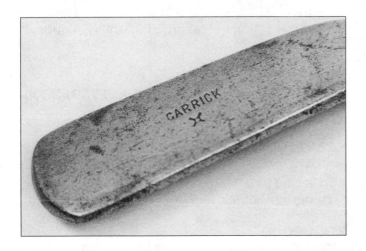

CLARK, J & D

MUSSELBURGH, SCOTLAND

The Clark brothers apprenticed under Willie Park and many of their clubs were made by Park or in his style. In the short period of time during the late 1890s and early 1900s, they used two marks: "J & D Clark, Musselburgh" in a circle similar to Park's mark, and the same in very tiny letters.

SMOOTH FACE
BLADE PUTTER $100   125   200

Circa 1895-1905. Stamped "J & D Clark Musselburgh".

BRASS BLADE
PUTTER $125   160   275

Circa 1895-1905. Stamped "J & D Clark Musselburgh".

MARKED FACE IRONS $60   80   135

Circa 1910-1920. All irons. Stamped "J & D Clark Musselburgh".

SMOOTH FACE IRONS $90   120   190

Circa 1895-1905. Cleek, iron and lofting iron. Stamped "J & D Clark Musselburgh".

COCHRANE'S LT'D

EDINBURGH, SCOTLAND

This Edinburgh-based firm used several marks including the "Knight" in armor holding a sword, and a "Bowline Knot". They also used "J. P. Cochrane's, Lt'd, Edinburgh" in script. The company made clubs well into the late 1930s.

OFFSET
BLADE PUTTER $50   60   95

Circa 1915. Knight mark. Dot punched face.

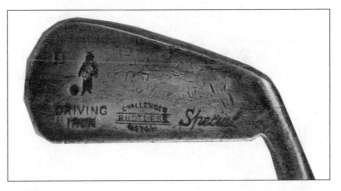

PUTTING CLEEK $50   60   90

Circa 1910-1915. "Knight" mark. Hyphen scored straight blade putter.

MUSSEL
BACK PUTTER $55   65   95

Circa 1920. "Knight" mark.

WALTER
HAGEN PUTTER $55   65   90

Circa 1925-1930. Stainless steel putter. "Bowline" mark.

PUTTING CLEEK	$55	65	90

Circa 1920. Dot faced blade. "Bowline Knot" mark.

FLANGED BACK PUTTER	$60	70	100

Circa 1920-1925. "Knight" mark.

BENT NECK PUTTER	$60	75	120

Circa 1915. Stamped "Bent Neck Putter". "Knight" mark.

HOLEM PUTTER	$80	95	140

Circa 1915. "Mussel" back. "Knight" mark.

CHALLENGER RUSTLESS PUTTER	$90	135	200

Circa 1920s. "Knight" mark. Park-style severely bent neck hosel.

"X X X" FLANGED PUTTER	$100	125	175

Circa 1920. Flat hosel and shaft.

U O T PUTTER	$450	650	950

Circa 1920. "Knight" mark. "Spur" at toe.

CRUICKSHANK SIGNATURE IRONS	$45	55	80

Circa 1925-1930. "Bowline Knot" mark.

CARDINAL SERIES IRONS	$45	55	75

Circa 1920s. 1 through 9 irons. Dot punched face.

HAGEN SERIES IRONS	$50	60	80

Circa 1930. All irons marked rustless. "Bowline Knot" mark.

STAINLESS IRONS	$55	65	90

Circa 1925-1930. All stainless irons. "Bowline" mark.

LIGHT MASHIE	$60	70	100

Circa 1920-1925. "Knight" mark. Line-scored face.

MAXWELL HOSEL IRONS	$60	75	125

Circa 1910-1920. All flanged back irons. Maxwell holes drilled in hosel.

CARDINAL SERIES IRONS	$85	100	150

Circa 1920s. Dreadnought niblick.

DEEP GROOVE IRONS	$120	150	250

Circa 1915-1922. "DEDLI" pitcher with five slot grooves.

GIANT NIBLICK	$1250	1750	2600

Circa 1925-1930. "Mammouth Niblick". "Stainless" "Fort Mason, Picadilly, London" "Bowline Knot" mark.

CARDINAL GIANT NIBLICK	$1250	1750	2600

Circa 1920s. Bowline Knot mark.

PRETTY FACE WOODS	$100	125	175

Circa 1910-1920. Driver, brassie or spoon. "Triangular" black face insert.

KIRKWOOD SERIES WOODS	$100	125	175

Circa 1925-1930. Driver, brassie or spoon. "Genuine Joe Kirkwood Model".

HAGEN SERIES WOODS	$100	125	175

Circa 1925-1930. Driver, brassie or spoon. "Genuine Walter Hagen Model".

SEMI-SOCKET PATENT	$140	175	250

Circa 1910.

SPLICED NECK WOODS	$150	225	350

Circa 1900-1910. Driver, brassie or spoon. Persimmon head.

CONDIE, ROBERT

ST. ANDREWS, SCOTLAND

Robert Condie began as a cleek maker during the early 1880s in St. Andrews. His mark was "R. Condie, St. Andrews" surrounding a "Flower" mark. More than ten different sizes and shapes of Condie's "Flower" have been catalogued. During the 1890s he briefly used single and double "Fern" marks. Clubs with the "Fern" marks are very scarce and are highly sought after by collectors.

EXCELSIOR PUTTER $60   70   120

Circa 1920. Dot faced blade. "R. Condie, St. Andrews" surrounding his "Flower" mark.

CALAMITY JANE TYPE $60 75 125

Circa 1910. Offset blade. "Flower" mark.

PUTTING CLEEK $70 95 150

Circa 1900-1910. Smooth face blade. "Flower" mark.

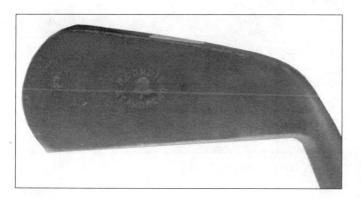

**BRASS-HEAD
PUTTERS** $80 100 160

Circa 1900-1910. Smooth face blade. "Flower" mark.

**LINE-SCORED
JIGGER** $50 60 85

Circa 1920. "Flower" mark.

**ROUND-HEAD
NIBLICK** $55 65 95

Circa 1915-1920. "Flower" mark. Dot punched face.

OVAL-HEAD NIBLICK $55 65 95

Circa 1915-1920. "Flower" mark. Dot punched face and offset hosel.

**SMOOTH-FACE
IRONS** $60 75 120

Circa 1900-1910. Iron or lofter. "Flower" mark.

**SMOOTH-FACE
CLEEK** $60 75 120

Circa 1900-1910. "Flower" mark.

**EARLY CONDIE
IRONS** $90 120 190

Circa 1890-1900. Smooth face iron or lofter. "Flower" mark. Shafted and stamped by D. McEwan, Ben Sayers, R. Simpson and others.

SWILCAN PITCHER $90 120 175

Circa 1920. "Flower" mark. Wide sole, beveled heel and toe. Dot punched face.

**SMOOTH FACE
NIBLICK** $95 125 190

Circa 1900-1910. "Flower" mark.

SINGLE FERN IRONS $275 350 550

Circa 1890-1895. Iron or lofter.

**EARLY CONDIE
CLEEKS** $100 130 200

Circa 1890-1900. "Flower" mark surrounded D. McEwan, Ben Sayers, R. Simpson and others.

**CONCAVE
FACE LOFTER** $120 150 225

Circa 1895. "Flower" mark.

ANTI-SHANK IRONS $140   200   325

Circa 1900-1910. Fairlie Patent smooth face iron, lofter or niblick. "Flower" mark.

SINGLE FERN CLEEK $300   375   600

Circa 1890-1895.

DOUBLE FERN IRONS $325   425   650

Circa 1890-1895. Iron or lofter.

DOUBLE FERN CLEEK $350   450   650

Circa 1890-1895.

CRAIGIE, J & W

MONTROSE, SCOTLAND

The Craigie brothers began forging clubs during the mid-1890s and continued through the 1920s. Their mark was "J & W Craigie, Montrose" in block letters and they used a "Rifle" cleek mark.

OFFSET BLADE PUTTER $55   65   100

Circa 1915-1920. "Rifle" mark.

SPLICED NECK PUTTER $500   850   1500

Circa 1895. Transitional shaped beech head. "Craigie" in block letters.

DOT PUNCHED FACE IRONS $55   65   90

Circa 1915-1920. All irons. "Rifle" mark.

RUT NIBLICK $200   275   450

Circa 1900-1905. Smooth face. "Rifle" mark.

DINT PATENT GOLF CO., LTD

Made wood clubs with "Dint" in script on the sole plate. The one-piece face and sole plate were made of silver.

SILVER DINT WOODS $200   275   450

Circa 1915. Driver, brassie or spoon. Patented one piece Silver face and sole plate. "Pat No. 22777/13".

SILVER DINT WOODS $225   300   475

Circa 1915. Wooden baffie. Patented one-piece silver face and sole plate. Pat. No. 22777/13".

DONALDSON, J.

GLASGOW, SCOTLAND

James Donaldson made clubs from the early 1920s through the early 1930s. He used a "Rangefinder" circular mark.

RANGEFINDER IRONS $55   65   85

Circa 1925-1930. All rustless irons. Dot-punched face.

THE SKELPIE IRONS $60   75   110

Circa 1925-1930. All rustless irons. Dot punched face.

RANGEFINDER
WOODS $100   120   160
Circa 1925-1930. Driver, brassie or spoon. Two-tone heads.

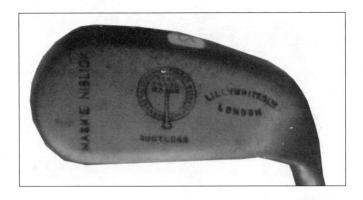

DUNN, JOHN D.

BOURNEMOUTH, ENGLAND
Began making clubs in the early 1890s. He patented the "One-Piece" wood while in Bournemouth, England, circa 1894. He later moved to New York.

BRITISH MAKE
IRONS $70   90   135
Circa 1900. All smooth face irons.

ONE-PIECE WOOD $1400   1900   3000
Circa 1895. "John D. Dunn, Bournemouth" on shaft.

PARK-STYLE PUTTER $125   150   250
Circa 1900-1910. "Dunn Selected" mark. Severely bent neck.

IONIC IRONS $60   75   100
Circa 1915-1920. All line scored irons.

CROWN MARKED
WOODS $100   135   190
Circa 1905-1910. All socket woods.

DUNN, SEYMOUR

LAKE PLACID, NY
Made clubs in America circa 1910-1920. Used a large "Crown and Ribbon" mark.

DOT FACE IRONS $60   75   110
Circa 1915. Large "Crown and Ribbon" mark.

ANTI-SHANK IRONS $175   250   450
Circa 1910. Fairlie style. Smooth face mashie-niblick or niblick. Large "Crown and Ribbon" mark.

SMOOTH FACE
IRONS $75   95   135
Circa 1905-1910. All irons. Large "Crown and Ribbon" mark.

SOCKET WOODS $100   135   175
Circa 1910. Driver, brassie or spoon. Large "Crown and Ribbon" mark.

DUNN, WILLIE

NEW YORK
Willie Dunn began forging clubs in the late 1880s at Westward Ho! In 1895 he began a clubmaking business in New York. His clubs were marked "Ardsley C. C., New York". During the period from 1897 to 1900 he worked as club designer for B.G.I., MacGregor, and Spalding. After 1900 his clubs were marked

"Dunn Selected" or "Willie Dunn, New York" in block letters.

OFFSET BLADE
PUTTER   **$70**   **85**   **125**
     Circa 1910. "Rampant Lion" mark.

BALL-FACE BLADE
PUTTER   **$70**   **85**   **135**
     Circa 1910. "Rampant Lion" mark.

SMOOTH-FACE BLADE
PUTTER   **$80**   **100**   **175**
     Circa 1900-1905. Stamped "Willie Dunn, New York".

DUNN SELECTED
IRONS   **$85**   **120**   **175**
     Circa 1900-1905. All smooth face irons.

APPROACHING
CLEEK   **$120**   **150**   **250**
     Circa 1897-1903. "Willie Dunn, New York" in block letters.

SMOOTH-FACE
IRONS   **$125**   **150**   **275**
     Circa 1897-1903. All irons stamped "Willie Dunn, New York" in large block letters.

DUNN SELECTED
WOODS   **$125**   **175**   **275**
     Circa 1900-1905. Socket-head driver, brassie or spoon.

SPLICED-NECK
WOODS   **$200**   **300**   **450**
     Circa 1900-1905. Spliced-head driver, brassie or spoon.

DUNN SELECTED
WOODS   **$225**   **300**   **500**
     Circa 1900-1905. Spliced-neck driver, brassie or spoon.

FORGAN, ANDREW

GLASGOW, SCOTLAND

Brother to Robert Forgan. He made clubs only during the mid-1890s. He used the marks "A. Forgan, Glasgow" in block letters and a "Pear" tree with "Regd" beneath.

BRASS BLADE
PUTTER   **$150**   **200**   **300**
     Circa 1900. Pear Tree mark. "Andrew Forgan, Glasgow" stamping.

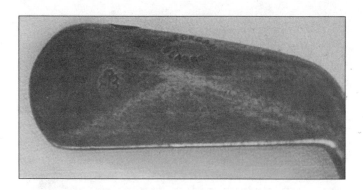

SPLICED NECK
WOODS   **$250**   **375**   **650**
     Circa 1895-1900. Driver, brassie or spoon. "Tree" mark.

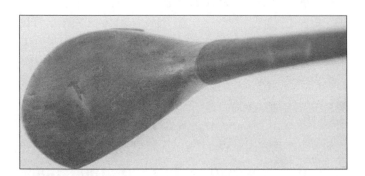

STEEL BLADE
PUTTER   **$125**   **150**   **250**
     Circa 1895-1900. Pear Tree mark. "Andrew Forgan, Glasgow" stampings.

FORGAN, ROBERT

ST. ANDREWS, SCOTLAND

Robert Forgan was one of the foremost and prolific clubmakers of his time. His shop was adjacent to the 18th green of the Old Course in St. Andrews, Scotland.

     Robert apprenticed under Hugh Philp (Philp died in 1856). During that time, his reputation had grown to capture the Prince of Wales' attention, who commissioned him to make his clubs. This explains why the firm used the Prince of Wales "Plume" mark as their trademark from the 1880s onward. The Prince became King Edward in 1901; the firm adopted the "Crown" mark using it until about 1910 and, subsequently, during the late 1920s.

When the firm of James Spence was acquired in 1926, its "Flag in the Hole" makers mark was also used. Each club had "R. Forgan & Son, St. Andrews" stamped into the head as well as the "mark" (woods sometime did not bear the "trade mark"). Pre-1910 clubs and post-1910 premium quality clubs usually had "R. Forgan & Sons, St. Andrews Selected" stamped into the shaft just below the grip.

Today the St. Andrews Woolen Mills occupies the building, which still has "R. Forgan & Son" spelled out on the sidewalk in front of the main entrance as a reminder of their glorious clubmaking past.

EARLY STEEL
PUTTERS   **$250**   **350**   **500**

Circa 1880-1890. "R. Forgan and Sons, St. Andrews" marking. Face nearly two inches vertically.

CROWN MARKED
PUTTERS   **$70**   **120**   **200**

Circa 1901-1908. Smooth face. Heavy gauge steel.

PLUME MARK
PUTTERS   **$100**   **150**   **250**

Circa 1895. Smooth face brass blade with a short, straight, thick hosel. "R. Forgan & Sons, St. Andrews" mark.

CROWN MARKED
PUTTERS   **$70**   **110**   **150**

Circa 1901-1908. #100 dot faced, centraject back weighted.

TOLLEY PUTTER   **$250**   **350**   **550**

Circa 1925-30. Heel shafted socket putter made of "Forganite", a plastic-type material.

CROWN MARKED
PUTTERS   **$75**   **100**   **175**

Circa 1901-1908. Brass blade with "R. Forgan & Sons, St. Andrews" mark.

SCOTIA
SERIES PUTTER   **$35**   **50**   **90**

Circa 1920. Line scored blade.

GEM PUTTER   **$70**   **100**   **150**

Circa 1926-1930. Wide rounded back broad sole. "Forgan" in large block letters on back.

GIRAFFE NECK
PUTTER   **$150**   **200**   **300**

Circa 1920. "Flag" mark. Slender five-inch-long hosel.

MAXMO PUTTER   **$175**   **275**   **450**

Circa 1920. Persimmon head mallet. Metal sole plates at heel and toe. Wood portion of sole marked "R. Forgan, St. Andrews".

PUTTERS EXPORTED
TO INDIA   **$125**   **175**   **275**

Circa 1901-1908. Brass blade putter. "Crown" mark. "Wager & Co., Bombay" stamping.

LONG-NOSE
PUTTERS   **$1500**   **2500**   **4500**

Circa 1860-1880. Beech head. "R. Forgan" large block letters mark. Long head. Large lead back weight.

LONG-NOSE PUTTERS $1250   1800   3000

Circa 1880-1890. "R. Forgan" and "Plume" mark. Medium-size head. Medium weight.

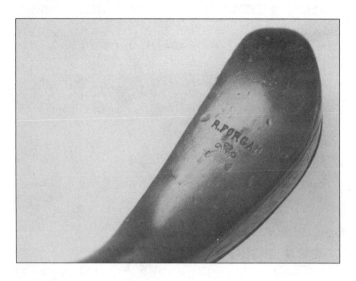

SPLICED NECK PUTTERS $225   350   700

Circa 1910-1920. "R. Forgan" in block letters on long narrow head.

GOLD MEDAL SERIES IRONS $45   55   90

Circa 1920s. All irons with line scored face.

PLUME MARKED IRONS $90   140   275

Circa 1890-1900. Lofting iron marked "R. Forgan & Sons, St. Andrews".

DIAMOND BACK IRONS $50   60   90

Circa 1920s.

PLUME MARKED IRONS $100   150   300

Circa 1890-1895. Long blade cleek marked "R. Forgan & Son, St. Andrews".

PLUME MARKED IRONS $225   350   700

Circa 1880-1890. Large head lofting iron marked "R. Forgan & Sons, St. Andrews".

CROWN MARK IRONS $60   80   150

Circa 1901-1908. Cleek or driving iron with a smooth face.

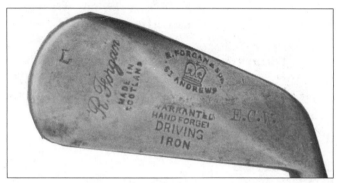

PLUME MARKED IRONS $900   1500   3000

Circa 1880-1890. Rut iron with a small cupped head. "R. Forgan & Sons, St. Andrews" marks.

CROWN MARKED IRONS $75   100   150

Circa 1901-1908. Jigger marked "R. Forgan & Sons".

CROWN MARKED IRONS $75   100   150

Circa 1901-1908. Diamond back and dot punched "BALL" face.

CROWN MARKED IRONS $100   140   225

Circa 1901-1908. Driving mashie with a smooth face marked "R. Forgan & Sons, St. Andrews".

CROWN MARKED IRONS $300   450   750

Circa 1901-1908. Niblick with a rounded head and smooth face. "R. Forgan & Sons, St. Andrews" markings.

CELTIC SERIES
IRONS $45   55   90

Circa 1920s. All irons with dot punched face.

FLAG-IN-HOLE
SERIES IRONS $45   55   90

Circa 1926-1930. All irons with dot or lined face.

SELECTED
SERIES IRONS $45   60   90

Circa 1920s. All irons with line scored face.

BIG BALL
SERIES IRONS $45   65   100

Circa 1930. All irons marked "Made especially for the big ball".

ROYAL SERIES
IRONS $45   55   90

Circa 1930. All irons line scored face.

SCOTIA SERIES
IRONS $45   55   90

Circa 1920s. All irons with dot punched face.

PLUME MARKED
WOODS $400   600   1300

Circa 1890-1900. Spliced-neck bulger face play club, brassie and spoon.

SMITH
ANTI-SHANK IRONS $120   160   250

Circa 1915-1920. Dot face. Cleek, mid-iron, mashie, mashie-niblick and niblick.

ANTI-SHANK IRONS $140   175   275

Circa 1900-1915. "Fairlie's Patent" cleek, mid-iron, mashie, mashie-niblick and niblick.

JUVENILE CLUBS $40   60   90

Circa 1926-30. Smooth face. "Flag-in-Hole" mark.

LONG NOSE WOODS $2000   3500   7000

Circa 1860-1880. Long nose without "Plume" mark.

PLUME MARKED
WOODS $500   900   1500

Circa 1885-1895. Play club, brassie, spoon. Beech transitional pear-shaped head.

CROWN MARKED
WOODS $100   125   200

Circa 1901-1908. Driver, brassie or spoon. "R. Forgan, St. Andrews" above "Crown" mark.

GOLD MEDAL
SERIES WOODS $85   110   160

Circa 1920s. Driver, brassie or spoon marked "Forgan, St. Andrews Gold Medal" on persimmon head.

SCOTIA SERIES
WOODS $85   110   160

Circa 1920. Driver, brassie or spoon. "R. Forgan & Son, St. Andrews" mark.

FORGANITE WOODS $100   150   225

Circa 1910-1915. Driver, brassie and spoon. "Forganite" in an elongated "Diamond". Forganite is a plastic-type material. No sole plate.

DREADNOUGHT
WOODS $120   150   225

Circa 1920. Large head driver, brassie or spoon. "R. Forgan" in block letters. Black triangular face insert.

**ANGLE-SHAFT
WOOD** $175 250 450

Circa 1905-1910. "Crown" mark, "Angle-Shaft Patent No. 10194" and "R. Forgan" markings. The shaft is oval shaped and "Angled" for strength.

FORRESTER, G

EARLSFERRY, ELIE, SCOTLAND

George Forrester began making clubs in the late 1880s and continued through 1930. His mark was "Geo. Forrester, Elie, Earlsferry" in block letters.

**BRASS HEAD
PUTTERS** $80 120 175

Circa 1895-1900. Long face blade putter. "George Forrester, Earlsferry, Elie" circle mark.

**CONCENTRIC
BACK IRONS** $100 135 225

Circa 1900. Smooth face. Patent "No. 125240".

**GENERAL
PURPOSE IRON** $150 200 350

Circa 1890. Smooth long face. "George Forrester, Earlsferry, Elie" circle mark.

**ROUNDED
FACE IRONS** $175 250 400

Circa 1895-1900. "Patent #53386" rounded back cleek or iron. The face is rounded from heel to toe, much like a "bulger" face wood.

**SPLICED
NECK WOODS** $175 250 375

Circa 1900-1910. Driver, brassie or spoon. Stamped "George Forrester, Elie, Earlsferry".

FOSTER BROTHERS

ASHBOURNE

The Foster Brothers produced clubs for only a short time after WWI. They used a human "Skeleton" swinging a club as their mark. They also made clubs bearing "The Bogee" stampings.

**ALUMINUM
BOGEE PUTTER** $250 300 400

Circa 1920. "Registered No. 696416". Wide soled sloped back aluminum-head putter. Square hosel.

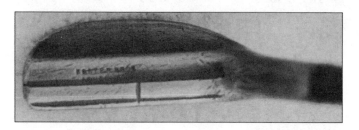

BOGEE IRONS $75 110 150

Circa 1915-1920. All irons. Dot punched face. Their mark was a "Skeleton" swinging a club.

FOULIS, JAMES,

WHEATON, IL
by Pete Georgiady

On his first day attending St. Andrews University, Charles Blair MacDonald was taken to meet the Grand Old Man of Golf, Tom Morris. The Morris shop was one of Scotland's golfing headquarters. Situated close to the 18th green, it was a place where golfers gathered and stories were told by the game's early devotees. Spending time in the company of those golfers left its mark on the student MacDonald and he knew exactly who to call when the club he formed, the Chicago Golf Club, required a pro—a real Scottish pro. Old Tom, himself, was entrusted to nominate a suitable candidate for the Chicago Golf position. Thus Tom went to his foreman James Foulis Sr., the father of five sons each of whom played a highly respectable game, and encouraged him to send his best to America where golf missionaries were required.

But James Foulis Jr. was not the first choice for the position. Brother Robert was already a professional at the Ranfurly Golf Club, Bridge o' Weir, and the most experienced, but he turned down the opportunity. Instead of moving to Chicago, he chose to honor his one year contract and suggested that Jim take the job offer instead. Jim was, after all, the better golfer and he arrived in Wheaton, Illinois, in March 1895 ready to assume his responsibilities.

Strictly speaking, young Jim Foulis was not a golf professional in 1895. Foulis' occupation was a clubmaker in the Robert Forgan works, at the time the world's largest clubmaking firm. The rules defining golf professionalism allowed him to compete as an amateur. A member of the famed St. Andrews Golf Club, he was a skilled competitor and at age 22 won the club's 1893 medal competition. Although not highly competitive, his family had been in the golfing world for many years. James' great-grandfather, a shepherd, had also mown the grass on the St. Andrews links during the time of George III. His father was employed in the Morris club works for more than thirty years.

With golf courses being created all across America, the need for more professionals and greenkeepers was quickly growing. Once in Chicago, Jim sent for younger brother David to be his assistant. Soon after that, Foulis wired home again and instructed Robert to join him immediately, "expenses paid!" Once Bob arrived, he was quickly put to work overseeing the final phases of construction at the Lake Forest Golf Club (the name would shortly be changed to Onwentsia) finishing the work Jim had begun that spring. He was appointed Lake Forest's first pro and stayed for another five years.

Jim played in the first U.S. Open at Newport in 1895, winning $50 for finishing third behind Horace Rawlins and Willie Dunn. The following year the Open was played at Shinnecock Hills and the train from Illinois carried two challengers from the American West, Jim Foulis and C.B. Mac-Donald.

The '96 Open would be remembered for two important non-events outside the tournament. The threatened boycott of professional contestants opposed to the entry of two local Shinnecock caddies, John Shippen

and Oscar Bunn fell apart two days before the championship. The other mix up occurred when Willie Park Jr., the odds-on favorite to clean the field, arrived a day after the tournament had ended, having missed his original steamship to New York.

In the early days of the U.S. Open only two 18-hole rounds were played, both on the same day. Jim Foulis shot a 78 in the morning round, leaving him in a six-way tie for the lead among the 33 contestants. In the afternoon, he deftly stroked a 74 to outdistance defending champ Horace Rawlins by three, setting an 18-hole record that was not broken until the advent of the rubber-wound ball. It is interesting to note that James Foulis Jr. stood only 5 feet 5 inches tall, but had a barrel chest, stout arms and legs, and enormous hands which gave him excellent club control.

One of the trademarks Jim Foulis applied to the game was the invention of the special Foulis patent mashie-niblick. The American game differed from Scottish golf in large part because of course design and native vegetation. Thick long grass around greens prohibited the traditional Scottish approach shot we now refer to as the "bump and run." A lofted shot, hopefully stopping dead, was required and to this end Foulis perfected a new club. It had a deeply concaved face with a blade rounded on top and very flat at the sole. It assumed the name of the "Foulis club" and every manufacturer on both sides of the Atlantic copied it after its introduction in 1904. Earlier, he had invented a club called the Octagon Niblick with its modified diamond-back design.

America was good to the Foulis family. In 1899, with three sons enjoying successes in American golf, James Sr. brought the remainder of the family—wife, daughter and two sons—to Chicago to live permanently. Robert subsequently moved to Minneapolis and, afterward, St. Louis, initially to Glen Echo then becoming the first pro at Bellerive. David worked with Jim at Chicago Golf (clubs marked "J & D Foulis") and was made the club's professional after Jim moved to Calumet C.C. on Chicago's far south side in 1905. Later Jim received the appointment to the pro's post at Olympia Fields. The fourth brother John Foulis worked at Chicago Golf as a ball maker until his untimely death in 1907. The youngest brother, Simpson, remained an amateur throughout his career.

The life and career of James Foulis are interwoven with the very heart of early American golf history. He was the second national champion and had a close relationship with C.C. MacDonald, a founding father of the USGA, Chicago Golf and National Links clubs. He served as the first professional at America's first full 18 hole course and the first golf pro west of the Alleghenies. Foulis was an expert clubmaker and inventor, and with his brothers he had a hand in laying out more than 20 courses in the Chicago and St. Louis areas.

SMOOTH-FACE IRONS   **$150   200   275**

Circa 1900. Iron or lofter. "J & D Foulis, Selected" mark.

SMOOTH FACE CLEEK   **$175   225   325**

Circa 1900. "J & D Foulis, Selected" mark.

PATENTED MASHIE-NIBLICK   **$175   250   375**

Circa 1905. Concave smooth face.

SOCKET WOODS   **$150   250   425**

Circa 1905. Driver, brassie or spoon.

SPLICED NECK WOODS   **$275   400   750**

Circa 1905. Driver, brassie or spoon.

GASSIAT, JEAN

BIARRITZ, FRANCE

He made the famous "Grand Piano"-style head putter circa 1910 that today is called simply "The Gassiat". He used his name in script as his mark.

PIANO-SHAPED WOOD PUTTER   **$500   750   1200**

Circa 1910."Jean L Gassiat" and "Regd. No. 627732" on the broad wood head.

GIBSON, CHARLES

WESTWARD HO!

Charles Gibson began making clubs about 1890 and used the mark "Charles Gibson, Westward Ho!" in block lettering on his earliest clubs. About 1910 he adopted a "Rampant Stallion" mark and later the "Phoenix" bird mark.

RUSTLESS PUTTER   **$125   175   250**

Circa 1925-1930. Long blade with "G-in-Star" mark. Corrugated sole.

RUT NIBLICK   **$190   275   450**

Circa 1895-1900. Stamped "C. Gibson, Westward Ho!"

OFFSET BLADE PUTTER   **$75   95   125**

Circa 1915-1920. Rampant Stallion mark.

SOCKET WOODS   **$90   115   150**

Circa 1910-1915. Driver, brassie or spoon. "C. Gibson, Westward Ho!" mark.

SOCKET-HEAD PUTTER   **$250   325   450**

Circa 1915-1920. Persimmon mallet. Stamped "C. Gibson Special".

PHOENIX MARKED IRONS   **$50   60   80**

Circa 1925. All irons. Line-scored face. "Phoenix" bird mark.

EXCELLAR IRONS $55   65   85

Circa 1920. All irons. "Phoenix" bird mark.

MAXWELL
HOSEL IRONS $60   75   110

Circa 1915-1920. All irons. Flanged back. "Rampant Stallion" mark.

GENERAL
PURPOSE IRON $125   175   275

Circa 1890. "C. Gibson" mark.

GIBSON, WILLIAM

KINGHORN, SCOTLAND

One of the most prolific clubmakers during the wood-shaft era, Gibson began forging iron-head clubs in the mid-1890s in Edinburgh. Before the turn of the century, he relocated in Kinghorn on the northern shore of the Firth of Fourth. His maker's mark was a "Star" which varied in size and style during the nearly 50 years it was used.

He produced the first "flanged" back irons and the "Maxwell" drilled hosel irons in large quantities for a variety of clients who assembled clubs. He forged many patent clubs including the heel and toe weighted "Smith's Patent" anti-shank irons. Collecting only Gibson forged clubs would be a formidable task.

KINGHORN
SERIES PUTTERS $50   80   135

Circa 1910. Emoried smooth face straight blade.

BRAID SERIES
PUTTERS $55   75   120

Circa 1915. Putting cleek.

STAR MAXWELL
SERIES $45   55   90

Circa 1915. Blade putter, regular hosel.

STAR MAXWELL
SERIES $60   75   125

Circa 1915. Flanged back with Maxwell holes drilled in hosel.

SAVILLE SERIES
PUTTER $45   55   80

Circa 1930. Stainless steel blade putter.

FIFE GOLF CO.
SERIES PUTTERS $60   80   125

Circa 1930. Flanged back offset blade putter with "Maxwell" holes drilled in the hosel.

ESKIT RUSTLESS
PUTTER $45   65   95

Circa 1930-1935. Offset blade, dot face. "G" inside a "Star" mark.

VARSITY PUTTER $125   200   325

Circa 1910. Crook in hosel. Bulge weight at toe.

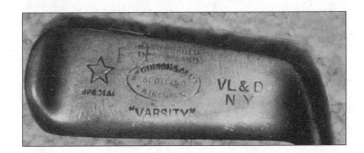

"G" IN CIRCLE
MARKED PUTTER $40   55   75

Circa 1930. Stainless blade. "Star" inside circle.

DOT FACE
GIBSON IRONS $50   60   85

Circa 1915-1920. 1 through 9 irons.

ORION PUTTER $125   175   300

Circa 1910-1920. Flanged back with flat hosel and shaft.

GEM PUTTER $90   110   135

Circa 1920-1925. Stainless steel head.

BROWN-VARDON PUTTER $125   150   250

Circa 1910-1915. Crescent shaped steel head. Oval hosel and shaft.

AKROS MODEL IRONS $55   70   100

Circa 1915. All irons. Geo. Duncan signature.

BRAID SERIES IRONS $55   75   115

Circa 1915. James Braid signature. "Full" or "light" irons.

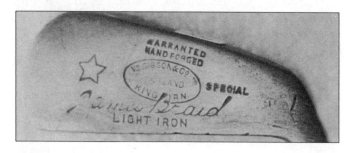

BRAID SERIES IRONS $45   55   85

Circa 1915. James Braid signature mid-iron, mashie, mashie-niblick, or niblick.

BRAID SERIES IRONS $140   175   250

Circa 1915. "James Braid Autographed Dreadnought" niblick.

GENII MODEL IRONS $50   60   100

Circa 1915-1920. Marked face irons with offset hosel.

GENII MODEL IRONS $60   75   125

Circa 1910. Smooth face irons with offset hosel.

STAR MAXWELL IRONS $40   50   80

Circa 1915. Regular hosel.

STAR MAXWELL IRONS $55   70   100

Circa 1915. Maxwell holes drilled in hosel.

FIFE GOLF CO. SERIES IRONS $40   60   80

Circa 1925. Stainless steel head. All irons.

SAVILLE SERIES IRONS $40   60   80

Circa 1930. Stainless steel 1 through 9 irons.

STELLA SERIES IRONS $45   55   75

Circa 1925-1930. 1 through 9 irons.

KINGHORN SERIES IRONS $45   55   75

Circa 1930. "Star-in-Circle". All irons.

SUPERIOR SERIES IRONS $40   50   75

Circa 1925-1930. Stainless steel heads. 1 through 9 irons.

SUPERIOR SERIES IRONS $150   200   275

Circa 1925-1930. Anti-shank irons.

PIXIE SAMMY $75   90   125

Circa 1920. Line scored face.

BAXPIN SERIES $120   150   200

Circa 1914-1922. Corrugated deep groove irons.

BAXPIN SERIES $125   160   225

Circa 1914-1922. Slot deep groove irons.

JERKO DEEP GROOVE IRONS $150   190   275

Circa 1920. Mashie, mashie-niblick or niblick.

RUT NIBLICK $450   650   1000

Circa 1895. Small rounded head. "Wm Gibson & Co, Kinghorn" in an oval with his "Star" mark inside.

ANTI-SHANK IRONS $150   190   275

Circa 1910. Fairlie style anti-shank irons. Various face scoring.

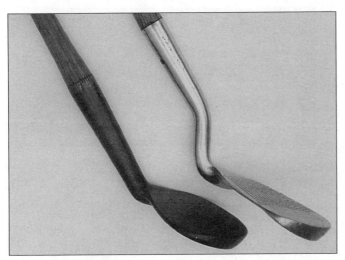

Examples of both the Fairlie's and Smith's anti-shank patent irons.

SKOOGEE SAND IRON $300   400   600

Circa late 1920s. Wide flat sole and deeply concave face.

GIANT NIBLICK $1400   1800   2500

Circa 1925. Big Ben Model.

GIBSON KINGHORN WOODS $85   100   150

Circa 1920s. Driver, brassie or spoon.

GOURLAY, JAMES

CARNOUSTIE, SCOTLAND

James Gourlay began forging clubs during the mid-1890s and continued into the Great Depression. He had a number of marks including an "Anchor", a "Crescent and Star", a "Crescent" and small circle, and a "Horseshoe"-type mark.

OFFSET BLADE PUTTER $50   60   90

Circa 1915-1920. "Crescent and Star" mark.

MUSSEL BACK PUTTER $60   75   110

Circa 1910-1915. Smooth face. "Crescent and Star" mark.

DIAMOND BACK PUTTER $65   85   125

Circa 1905-1915. Smooth face. "Crescent and Star" mark.

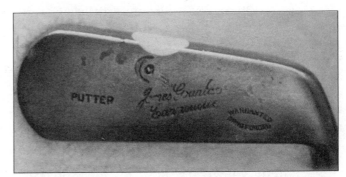

PARK STYLE PUTTER $95   125   190

Circa 1910. Severely bent neck. "Crescent and Star" mark.

BRASS HEAD MALLET PUTTERS $225   300   450

Circa 1915. Brass head, steel face insert. "Crescent and Star" mark.

SWAN NECK PUTTER $400   600   800

Circa 1905-1910. P.A. Vaile Patent of 1905.

DIAMOND BACK IRONS $55   70   100

Circa 1905-1915. All irons. "Crescent and Star" mark.

SMOOTH FACE IRONS $60   80   125

Circa 1900-1910. Iron or lofter. "Crescent and Star" mark.

MAXWELL HOSEL IRONS $60   75   110

Circa 1910-1915. All irons. Smooth face, flanged back. "Crescent and Star" mark.

SMOOTH FACE
CLEEK $65   85   135

Circa 1900-1910. "Crescent and Star" mark.

SAMMY IRON $70   90   135

Circa 1915. Dot face. Rounded sole. "Crescent and Star" mark.

JUMBO NIBLICK $100   125   175

Circa 1925. Dot punched face. Head size is 3-3/4 x 2-3/4 inches.

ANTI-SHANK IRONS $150   200   300

Circa 1905-1910. All irons. Fairlie's Patent. "Crescent and Star" mark.

RUT NIBLICK $175   275   450

Circa 1900-1910. Smooth face. "Crescent and Star" mark.

PERFECT
BALANCE IRONS $350   600   850

Circa 1910. All irons. "Lump" back weighting. "Patent No. 21307" and "R. Simpson, Carnoustie" at toe. "Crescent and Star" mark.

GRAY, JOHN

PRESTWICK, SCOTLAND

John Gray started as a blacksmith in Prestwick and began forging iron heads from about 1850 to the 1880s. He used at least two stampings to identify his clubs. "J. Gray", "Jn. Gray" and I've seen several simply marked "Gray". His clubs are very scarce and highly prized by collectors.

SMOOTH FACE
CLEEK $900   1450   3200

Circa 1860-1880. Long blade, 5 inch hosel. Stamped "Jn. Gray".

GENERAL
PURPOSE IRON $800   1200   2500

Circa 1870-1885. Hooked face iron. Stamped "Jn. Gray".

RUT IRON $1800   3500   6000

Circa 1860-1880. Small cupped head. 5 inch hosel. Stamped "Jn. Gray".

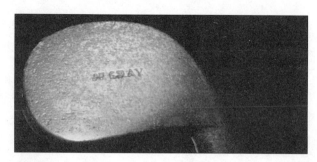

DISHED FACE
LOFTER $850   1350   2750

Circa 1860-1875. Stamped "Gray".

HACKBARTH, OTTO

CINCINNATI, OHIO

Circa 1920. Famous for manufacturing the bifurcated hosel putter commonly known as "The Hackbarth".

HACKBARTH
PUTTER $300   500   750

Patented 1901. Bifurcated hosel.

SPLICED NECK
CLEEK $175   250   500

Circa 1920. Wooden cleek marked "Otto Hackbarth".

HALLEY & CO., JAMES B

LONDON, ENGLAND

Halley & Co. began selling golf clubs about 1900, but did not make its own brands until much later. It had several marks: The "Pyramid" most often found on brass putters, a "Shell", "Circled 'H'" and a "Crossed Swords" mark.

RUSTLESS PUTTER $60   75   100

Circa 1925. Monel metal head. "Pyramid" mark.

SPECIAL PUTTER $55   65   85

Circa 1920. Offset hosel. "Crossed Swords" mark.

BRASS-HEAD PUTTERS $60   70   100

Circa 1920s. "Pyramid" mark. Line scored blade.

LINE SCORED IRONS $45   55   75

Circa 1925-1930. All irons. "Crossed Swords" mark.

CONCENTRIC BACK IRONS $50   60   85

Circa 1915. All irons. Dot punched face.

CIRCLE "H" MARKED IRONS $55   65   90

Circa 1920. All irons. "Diamond-dot" scoring.

MAXWELL HOSEL IRONS $60   75   110

Circa 1915. All irons. Circle "H" mark. Flanged back.

DREADNOUGHT NIBLICK $70   95   135

Circa 1915-1920. Hyphen scored face. "Pyramid" mark.

PRETTY FACE WOODS $100   125   175

Circa 1920s. Ivorine pegs in circular configuration.

JUVENILE CLUBS $30   40   65

Circa 1920. Putter, iron, mashie or niblick. "Crossed Swords" mark.

JUVENILE CLUBS $75   100   150

Circa 1920. Juvenile wood. "Crossed Swords" mark.

HENDRY & BISHOP, LT'D

EDINBURGH, SCOTLAND

Hendry & Bishop began producing clubs about 1910 and used the "Bishop's Hat" mark. It also made the "Cardinal" brand by which many of its clubs can be identified.

WRY-NECK PUTTER $50   60   80

Circa 1920s. Chromed head. "Bishop's Hat" mark.

THE SNIPER PUTTER $150   190   250

Circa 1920s. "Pencil" thin seven inch hosel. "Bishop's Hat" mark.

PER WHIT PUTTER $450   650   850

Circa 1920. "Patent No 247116". Hollowed out back and rounded face. The head gives the appearance of a pipe sawed lengthwise. "Bishop's Hat" mark.

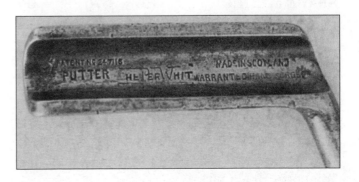

THE EAGLE PUTTER $50   60   85

Circa 1920s. "Bishop's Hat" mark.

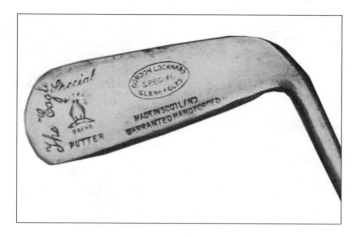

THE VIPER PUTTER $60   75   100

Circa 1920s. Long blade. "Bishop's Hat" mark.

**CARDINAL
SERIES IRONS** $45   55   75

Circa 1925. All irons. Dot punched face.

DEEP FACE MASHIE $50   60   85

Circa 1915. Dot punched face. "Bishop's Hat" mark.

**LARGE-HEAD
SPADE MASHIE** $60   70   90

Circa 1915. Dot punched face. "Bishop's Hat" mark.

**CONCENTRIC
BACK IRONS** $60   70   95

Circa 1915. All irons. "Mitre Brand" mark.

**DREADNOUGHT
NIBLICK** $75   100   150

Circa 1920. Large head, dot punched face. "Bishop's Hat" mark.

PITCH-EM IRON $75   95   125

Circa 1915. Dot punched face. "Bishop's Hat" mark.

**CARDINAL DREADNOUGHT
NIBLICK** $100   150   225

Circa 1925. Head measures 3-1/2 x 2-5/8 inches. "Bishop's Hat" mark.

**DEEP GROOVE
IRONS** $100   150   225

Circa 1915-1922. All "Stopum" corrugated face irons.

HIATT & CO.

BIRMINGHAM, ENGLAND

Made irons during the mid-1890s. They had at least two marks, one "Hiatt's Mild Steel" in an oval configuration with very tiny lettering, the other with slightly larger lettering. Their irons are very scarce and desirable.

**STEEL-HEAD
PUTTERS** $100   140   200

Circa 1895. Smooth face blade. "Hiatt" stamped on back.

**BRASS HEAD
PUTTERS** $125   160   250

Circa 1895. Smooth face blade. "Hiatt" stamped on back.

LOFTING IRON $120   150   250

Circa 1895. Smooth face lofting iron. Marked "Hiatt's Mild Steel".

**GENERAL
PURPOSE IRON** $125   175   300

Circa 1895. Stamped "Hiatt's Mild Steel".

**SMOOTH-FACE
CLEEK** $150   200   325

Circa 1895. Long face. Stamped "Hiatt's Mild Steel".

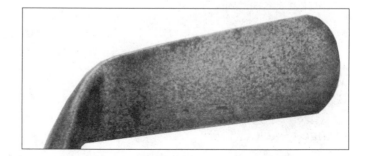

RUT NIBLICK $550   750   1250

Circa 1895. Small smooth face head. Marked "Hiatt's Mild Steel".

HILLERICH & BRADSBY

LOUISVILLE, KY

Began manufacturing clubs during the mid-teens. Its early "Invincible" series irons were smooth faced. In 1918 they patented a "Kork" grip for clubs. The "Deck of Cards", "Par-X-L" and "Lo-Skore" markings were the most common on commercial quality clubs during the 1920s.

GRAND SLAM
SERIES PUTTER $35   45   70

Circa 1920s. "Hand Holding Playing Cards" mark.

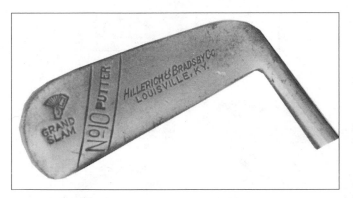

LO-SKORE
SERIES PUTTER $35   45   70

Circa 1920s. Chrome plated head.

INVINCIBLE
SERIES PUTTER $40   50   75

Circa 1925-1930. "Chromium" blade.

N-9 APPROACHING
PUTTER $50   60   80

Circa 1920s. Lofted line scored face.

ALUMINUM-HEAD
PUTTER $80   100   150

Circa 1920s. "H & B Model H 50".

SCHENECTADY
PUTTER $150   225   350

Circa 1920. Cork grip. "Par-X-L" mark.

GRAND SLAM
SERIES IRONS $35   45   70

Circa 1920s. All irons 2 through 9. "Deck of Cards" mark.

PAR-X-L SERIES
IRONS $40   50   70

Circa 1920s. All irons.

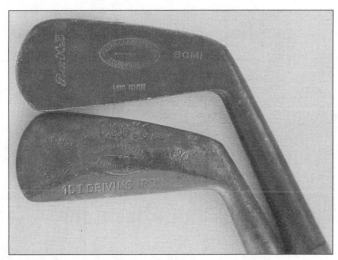

KERNEL SERIES
IRONS $40   50   75

Circa 1920s. Flanged back.

GRAND SLAM WOODS—Carnoustie Model

Steel shafts with black pyratone sheaths, red leather grips with aluminum tips.

No. 11/8—Driver. A Rakish English model with unusually long head. Natural finish with black band at point of contact. Special insert at point of striking with red bulls eye. Steel shafts only. $15.00
No. 12/8—Brassie to match. 15.00
No. 13/8—Spoon to match. 15.00

STANDARD MODEL

No. 11—Driver. The original Grand Slam model. Large head with medium lie. Medium deep and wide face provides large hitting surface. Ebony finish with natural band marking point of impact. Steel shaft, nickel plated. $9.00
Hickory shaft. 7.00
No. 12—Brassie to match. Steel shaft, nickel plated. $9.00
Hickory shaft. 7.00
No. 13—Spoon to match. Steel shaft, nickel plated. $9.00
Hickory shaft. 7.00

SPECIAL PUTTERS

No. 10S—Aluminum head in hammer headed center shafted type. Ebony and nickle finish. Groove across head helps to line up club correctly. Steel shafts with satin nickle finish. No hickory shafts.
Price. $7.50

No. 10P—Aluminum head with patented streamer line design. Runners on sole of club prevent lower edge from catching on grass and stopping stroke. Ebony finish with red arrow marking correct point of impact. Right hand only. Hickory shaft only. $6.00

INVINCIBLE GOLF CLUBS

For right or left hand players.

For those who wish serviceable clubs at a very moderate price, Invincible golf clubs offer a most satisfactory purchase. Standard, large size patterns with wide blades. Second growth hickory shafts, leather grips.

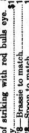

No. 51D—Driver. $2.00

No. 51D1—Driving Iron. $2.00

No. 51M—Mashie. $2.00

No. 51N—Niblick. $2.00

No. 51B—Brassie. $2.00

No. 51M1—Mid-iron. $2.00

No. 51MN—Mashie Niblick. $2.00

No. 51P—Putter. $2.00

GRAND SLAM IRON CLUBS

All standard Grand Slam irons are now chromium plated to resist rust and staining. While these clubs are not guaranteed to be rust proof, the chromium plating is the best protection yet devised for golf club heads.—Chromium plated heads should not be buffed. All that is necessary to keep them clean is to wipe them with a damp cloth. Do not permit them to be used on the wheel, since continued buffing will remove plating.

Hickory shafts in Grand Slam clubs are extra select. Steel shafts are the new true temper type. Grips are of calf skin with aluminum tip. Stainless steel heads can also be furnished as priced under each illustration.

No. 1—FAIRWAY IRON

Full shot value 185 to 195 yards for average good player. Lengths 38 to 39½ inches.

No. 1—Hickory shaft, chromium plated.**$6.00**
No. 1—Steel shaft, chromium plated....**$7.50**
No. 1W—Ladies' right hand only, hickory shaft, chromium plated **$6.00**
No. 1X—Right hand only, stainless steel heads, hickory shafts...............**$7.00**

No. 3—FAIRWAY IRON

Full shot value 155 to 165 yards for average good player.

No. 3—Hickory shaft, chromium plated.**$6.00**
No. 3—Steel shaft, chromium plated....**$7.50**
No. 3W—Ladies' right hand only, hickory shaft, chromium plated............**$6.00**
No. 3X—Right hand only, stainless steel, hickory shaft.......................**$7.00**

No. 2—FAIRWAY IRON

Full shot value 170 to 180 yards for average good player. Lengths 37½ to 39 inches.

No. 2—Hickory shaft, chromium plated.**$6.00**
No. 2—Steel shaft, chromium plated....**$7.50**
No. 2W—Ladies' right hand only, hickory shaft, chromium plated **$6.00**
No. 2X—Right hand only, stainless steel, hickory shaft........................**$7.00**

No. 4—FAIRWAY IRON

Full shot value 140 to 150 yards for average good player.

No. 4—Hickory shaft, chromium plated.**$6.00**
No. 4—Steel shaft, chromium plated....**$7.50**
No. 4W—Ladies' right hand only, hickory shaft, chromium plated **$6.00**
No. 4X—Right hand only, stainless steel, hickory shaft........................**$7.00**

GRAND SLAM IRONS

No. 5—PITCHING IRON

Full shot value 125 to 135 yards.
No. 5—Hickory shaft, chromium plated.**$6.00**
No. 5—Steel shaft, chromium plated....**$7.50**
No. 5W—Ladies' right hand only, hickory shaft, chromium plated **$6.00**
No. 5X—Right hand only, stainless steel, hickory shaft........................**$7.00**

No. 7—PITCHING IRON

Full shot value 95 to 105 yards.
No. 7—Hickory shaft, chromium plated.**$6.00**
No. 7—Steel shaft, chromium plated....**$7.50**
No. 7W—Ladies' right hand only, hickory shaft, chromium plated **$6.00**
No. 7X—Right hand only, stainless steel, hickory shaft........................**$7.00**

No. 6—PITCHING IRON

Full shot value 110 to 120 yards.
No. 6—Hickory shaft, chromium plated.**$6.00**
No. 6—Steel shaft, chromium plated....**$7.50**
No. 6W—Ladies' right hand only, hickory shaft, chromium plated **$6.00**
No. 6X—Right hand only, stainless steel, hickory shaft........................**$7.00**

No. 8—TROUBLE IRON

Especially designed for bunker use. Can be used for fairway pitching shots 50 to 80 yards.
No. 8—Hickory shaft, chromium plated.**$6.00**
No. 8—Steel shaft, chromium plated....**$7.50**
No. 8W—Ladies' right hand only, hickory shaft, chromium plated **$6.00**
No. 8X—Right hand only, stainless steel, hickory shaft........................**$7.00**

No. 9—CHIPPING IRON

For short run up approaches from just off the green.
No. 9—Hickory shaft, chromium plated.**$6.00**
No. 9—Steel shaft, chromium plated....**$7.50**
No. 9W—Ladies' right hand only, hickory shaft, chromium plated............**$6.00**
No. 9X—Right hand only, stainless steel, hickory shaft.......................**$7.00**

No. 10—PUTTER

No. 10—Hickory shaft, chromium plated.**$6.00**
No. 10—Steel shaft, chromium plated....**$7.50**
No. 10W—Ladies' right hand only, hickory shaft, chromium plated............**$6.00**
No.10X—Right hand only, stainless steel, hickory shaft.......................**$7.00**

**INVINCIBLE
SERIES IRONS** $45   60   90

Circa 1915. All irons. Dot "Ball" face.

APPROACHING CLEEK $50   65   90

Circa 1915-1920. "Mussel" back. "Dot-Hyphen" face scoring.

**DIAMOND BACK
IRONS** $50   60   85

Circa 1920. "Stag-dot" face scoring. "Hand Made" and "H & B Monogram" marks.

HAND MADE IRONS $50   60   85

Circa 1920. "Stag-dot" face scoring. "Hand Made" and "H & B Monogram" marks.

**GRAND SLAM
SERIES IRONS** $55   65   85

Circa 1920s. #1 driving iron with the "Deck of Cards" mark.

**INVINCIBLE
SERIES IRONS** $55   70   95

Circa 1915. All irons. Smooth face.

CORK GRIP IRONS $60   75   95

Circa 1915. All irons. Patented 1914. "Hand Made" in circle mark.

DEEP GROOVE IRONS $90   135   190

Circa 1915-1922. All irons with corrugated face. Marked "Baxpin".

**DEEP GROOVE
IRONS** $100   150   225

Circa 1915-1922. All irons with slot grooves.

**DEEP GROOVE
IRONS** $125   175   225

Circa 1920. All Everbrite Monel metal slot groove.

**SLOTTED
HOSEL JIGGER** $145   190   250

Circa 1920s. "S-C2 Jigger". Stag-dot face scoring. "Hand Made" mark.

**LO-SKORE
SERIES IRONS** $50   60   85

Circa 1920. All irons.

**INVINCIBLE
SERIES WOODS** $75   95   125

Circa 1920. Driver, brassie or spoon.

**LO-SKORE
SERIES WOODS** $80   100   135

Circa 1920s. Driver, brassie or spoon.

**PAR-X-L SERIES
WOODS** $85   110   145

Circa 1920s. Driver, brassie or spoon.

JUVENILE CLUBS $30   40   65

Circa 1920. Putter, Mid-iron or mashie.

JUVENILE CLUBS $60   80   120

Circa 1920. Juvenile wood.

HORTON, WAVERLY

CHICAGO, IL

Clubmaker from Chicago whose major claim to fame was the patented "Wonder Club" in 1920 with a metal-cased wooden head.

WONDER CLUB $400 675 950

Circa 1920. Patented aluminum shell, wood face.

HUNT MFG. CO.

WESTBORO, MA

A turn-of-the-century manufacturer of rustless clubs. The clubs were a Nickel alloy and had a greenish coloring. "Hunt" in script was their mark. All Hunt-marked clubs are highly desirable to collectors.

NON-RUSTABLE BLADE PUTTER $150 200 300

Circa 1895-1900. Smooth face blade.

NON-RUSTABLE IRONS $100 150 250

Circa 1895-1900. All irons. Smooth face.

HUNTER, CHARLES

PRESTWICK

Professional and clubmaker at Prestwick from 1868 to 1921. His clubs were marked "C. Hunter".

OFFSET BLADE PUTTER $55 65 90

Circa 1915-1920. Hyphen scored face. Stamped "C. & J. Hunter, Prestwick".

DOT-FACE BLADE PUTTER $65 75 100

Circa 1910-1915. Offset hosel. Stamped "C & J Hunter, Prestwick".

LONG-NOSE PUTTERS $850 1450 2200

Circa 1885-1895. Transitional beech head. Marked "C. Hunter".

LONG-NOSE PUTTERS $1250 2250 3750

Circa 1870-1880. Beech-head shallow-face putter. Stamped "C. Hunter".

IMPERIAL GOLF

SUNDERLAND, ENGLAND

Made aluminum-head putters and fairway clubs similar to Mill's Standard Golf Co. Most of its clubs were cast during the late teens and early 1920s.

U MODEL $125 160 250

Circa 1910-1920. Aluminum mallet.

RM MODEL $150 200 275

Circa 1910-1920. Aluminum mallet.

THE VERDEN $175 225 350

Circa 1910-1920. Rounded dome aluminum mallet.

XXX PUTTER   **$200**   **250**   **350**

Circa 1915-1920. Long Aluminum mallet. "Ivorine" sight line.

**ALUMINUM-HEAD
WOODS**   **$125**   **190**   **325**

Circa 1915-1920. All lofts. Marked "Imperial Golf Co, Sunderland, England".

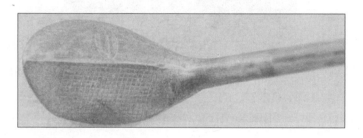

**ALUMINUM-HEAD
NIBLICK**   **$375**   **500**   **800**

Circa 1915-1920. Marked "Imperial Golf Co, Sunderland, England".

JOHNSON, FRANK A

LONDON, ENGLAND

Used a skeleton "Key" as his mark. Made irons from about 1900 through the early teens.

**PREMIER
SPECIAL PUTTER**   **$65**   **85**   **135**

Circa 1910. Line scored blade. "Key" mark.

**SMOOTH-FACE
IRONS**   **$60**   **80**   **130**

Circa 1900-1910. All irons. "Key" mark.

DOT-FACE NIBLICK   **$75**   **100**   **150**

Circa 1910. "Key" mark.

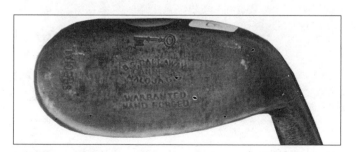

**SMOOTH-FACE
NIBLICK**   **$125**   **175**   **275**

Circa 1900-1910. Medium-size head. "Key" mark.

KROYDON

NEWARK, NJ

Began making clubs after WWI. The ball-face and the brick-face designs are popular collector clubs. The "Banner" series with the degree of loft on the face is also highly collectible although not expensive.

**SHALLOW-FACE
PUTTER**   **$55**   **65**   **85**

Circa 1920. Long blade, offset hosel. "Diamond-Dash" face scoring.

PENDULUM PUTTER   **$350**   **500**   **750**

Circa 1920s. Center shafted. Hatched face scoring.

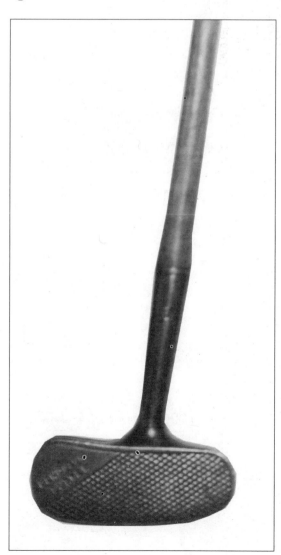

BALL FACE PUTTER $60   70   95

Circa 1920s. "S-7" ball face.

**ALUMINUM
MALLET PUTTERS** $85   110   160

Circa 1920s. "Kroydon S 31 B Putter".

**HEAT-TREATED
IRONS** $30   40   70

Circa 1920s. All irons.

**ROYAL SERIES
IRONS** $35   45   65

Circa 1920s. All irons. Widely spaced line face scoring.

BALL FACE IRONS $45   60   85

Circa 1920s. All irons.

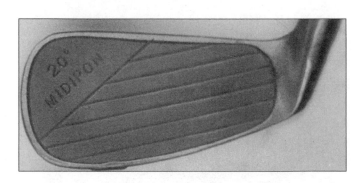

BANNER IRONS $45   60   80

Circa 1920s. All irons. Name and loft of iron at toe of blade.

P SERIES IRONS $55   70   100

Circa 1925-1930. All irons. Alternating "Dashes" and tiny "Diamonds" face scoring.

WAFFLE FACE IRON $85   120   175

Circa 1920s. About 400 tiny waffles on face.

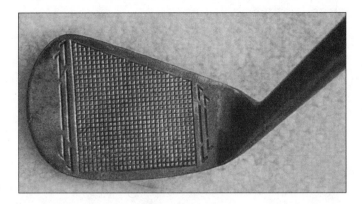

**VERTICALLY SCORED
NIBLICK** $225   275   350

Circa 1920s. "R 2, 50 Degree Niblick" with vertical deep groove face scoring.

BRICK FACE IRONS $350   475   650

Circa 1920. All irons.

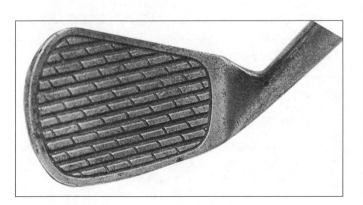

SOCKET WOODS $75   100   150

Circa 1920. All woods. Many have aluminum back weights.

**KROYDONITE
SOCKET WOODS** $75   100   150

Circa 1920. Driver, brassie or spoon.

LEE, HARRY C

NEW YORK, NY

Sporting goods retail business that began about 1900. Famous for marketing the "Schenectady" putter. Most domestic clubs were made by Burke and marked with the "Lee" stampings. It also imported clubs from more than a dozen Scottish and English makers including Jack White, Nicholl, Standard Mills, Spence, and Hendry & Bishop.

DEXTER PUTTER $45   55   75

Circa 1920s. Offset blade. "Acorn" mark.

**DOT-FACE
BLADE PUTTER** $45   55   75

Circa 1915. "Acorn" mark.

**LINE FACE
BLADE PUTTER** $45   55   75

Circa 1920-1925. "Acorn" mark.

**SCHENECTADY
PUTTER** $175   300   500

Circa 1903-1915. Patent date "Mar. 24, 1903" on back.

CONCENTRIC BACK IRONS	$40	50	70

Circa 1915. "Harry C. Lee Co." mark.

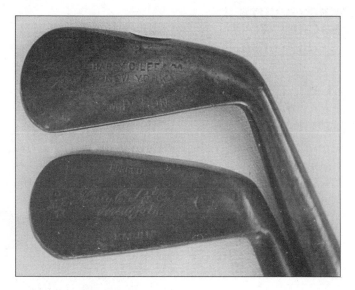

DOT FACE NIBLICK	$50	60	80

Circa 1915-1920. "Acorn" mark.

BALL FACE IRONS	$55	65	95

Circa 1910-1915. All irons. Dot ball face scoring. "Acorn" mark.

HAND MADE SERIES WOODS	$75	95	135

Circa 1920-1925. Driver, brassie or spoon.

LEYLAND & BIRMINGHAM RUBBER CO.

Made many "Rustless" clubs during the late 1920s.

BRASS HEAD PUTTERS	$60	70	95

Circa 1925-30. Stamped "L L M B" inside a "Triangle".

MUSSEL BACK PUTTER	$55	65	95

Circa 1930. "Rustless Putter".

MUSSEL BACK IRONS	$45	60	85

Circa late 1920s. Rustless irons.

STAINLESS STEEL IRONS	$45	55	75

Circa 1925-1930. "Goudie Bear" mark. Dot punched face.

STAINLESS STEEL IRONS	$45	55	75

Circa 1925-1930. "Leyland" mark. Dot punched face.

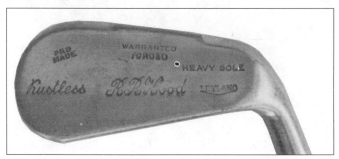

LOCKWOOD & BROWN

LONDON, ENGLAND

Although Lockwood & Brown did not forge its own clubs, they assembled and marked many heads with "Lockwood & Brown, London" in block letters and a monogrammed "LB" mark. They sold clubs from about 1920 through the early 1930s.

SPLICED-NECK PUTTER	$500	650	900

Circa 1910. Persimmon head "Gassiat" style with the back squared off. Stamped "Lockwood & Brown, Lt'd., 2 Jermyn St. S".

GIANT NIBLICK	$1200	1800	2400

Circa 1920s. Rustless giant head. Stamped "Lockwood & Brown, Lt'd., 2 Jermyn St. S".

SPLICED NECK WOODS	$150	225	350

Circa 1910-1920. Driver, brassie or spoon.

BULL DOG WOOD	$90	120	160

Circa 1910. Well lofted wood with "Triangular" black face.

LOGAN, HUGH

Logan was a club designer credited with the famous "Cherokee" aluminum-head putter and the "Genii" model series made by Wm. Gibson.

CHEROKEE PUTTER   **$250**   **350**   **500**

Circa 1915. Round aluminum head marked "H. Logan's, Cherokee", "T" sight line.

MACGREGOR

DAYTON, OH

Crawford, MacGregor and Canby began making golf clubs shortly after 1895. Initially they made wood heads until 1900 when its Willie Dunn was hired to design clubs including irons and putters. Their first iron-head clubs carried a mark similar to a bow tie with the monogram "W. D." Shortly after Dunn's departure, "J. MacGregor, Dayton, O." was the mark used along with a Condie-type flower mark. About 1910 "Par", "Peerless", and an economy line "Edgemont" were introduced. Through the teens, "Superior", "Perfection", "Pilot", and "Bakspin" clubs were offered. During the late 1920s, "Duralite", "Superior" and "Nokorode" irons were the top-of-the-line clubs with "Popular", "Edgemont" and "Go-sum" being the economy brands. Other marks were "Airway-o, "Bap", "Claymore", "Paragon", "Premier", "Pro iron", "Rob Roy", "Tomahawk", "Sink-it", "Down-it", and "Worldwin".

DUNN BOW
TIE MARK PUTTER   **$150**   **200**   **350**

Circa 1900. Smooth face.

DOUBLE CIRCLE
MARK PUTTER   **$100**   **135**   **220**

Circa 1900. Smooth face with "J MacGregor, Dayton, O" around a "Double Circle" mark with a shamrock inside.

J MACGREGOR
SERIES PUTTER   **$55**   **75**   **125**

Circa 1900-1905. Smooth face putting cleek.

EDGEMONT
SERIES PUTTERS   **$50**   **65**   **95**

Circa 1910-1915. Blade putter with a "Diamond" marked face.

"O A" SERIES
PUTTER   **$55**   **70**   **120**

Circa 1915. With a flanged back.

POPULAR
SERIES PUTTER   **$40**   **50**   **85**

Circa 1915. "10X" with a hyphen-scored face.

GO-SUM
SERIES PUTTERS   **$40**   **50**   **75**

Circa 1915-1920. Blade putter.

PILOT SERIES
PUTTERS   **$40**   **50**   **75**

Circa 1915. Blade putter.

ROB-ROY
SERIES PUTTER   **$40**   **50**   **75**

Circa 1920s. Mussel back design.

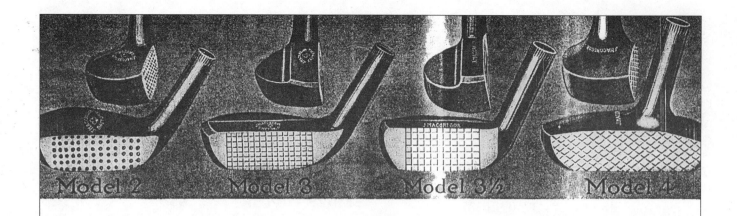

Study your putting

You know—as does every Golfer—that more games are won on the greens than anywhere else.

The man who can putt **always** has his opponent worried. Can **you** putt?

Study your putting—and your putter. Get all there is out of the club—for the club has a lot to do with it. Does your putter fit you? Does it **feel** right? Are you comfortable and natural using it? We call your attention to the

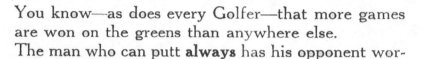

1919

SUPERIOR
SERIES PUTTERS $40   50   80

   Circa 1915-1920. Offset blade putter.

PERFECTION
SERIES PUTTERS $45   55   85

   Circa 1915. Offset blade putter.

RADITE SERIES
PUTTER $50   60   90

   Circa 1920. Offset blade.

DURALITE
SERIES PUTTERS $45   50   75

   Circa 1928-1930. Blade putter with the line and "Pyramid" dot face.

ALUMINUM-HEAD
PUTTERS $80   100   175

   Circa 1920s. "MacGregor, Dayton, 0".

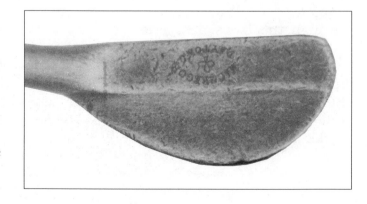

CLIMAX-FIFE
SERIES PUTTERS $55   65   90

Circa 1915-1920. Dot face straight blade.

BRASS-FLANGED
PUTTERS $65   80   125

Circa 1915. Flanged back brass putter marked "60" or "90".

J MACGREGOR
SERIES PUTTERS $175   250   400

Circa 1900. Willie Park style severely bent neck smooth face blade.

SEMI-PUTTER $90   110   160

Circa 1920. Anti-shank type offset hosel.

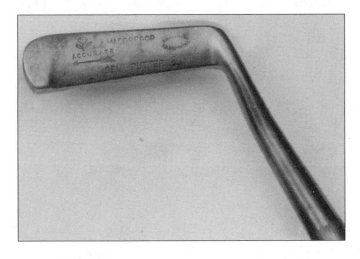

SCHENECTADY
PUTTER $140   190   290

Circa 1915. With "J. MacGregor" markings.

"R A" PUTTER $225   300   475

Circa 1920. "Right Angle" putter. Persimmon head mallet with a black vulcanite "T-" shaped "sight line".

DOWN-IT 486
PUTTER $225   375   575

Circa 1915-1920. Wooden-head mallet putter. Brass face plate with hatched scoring.

WORLD WIN
PUTTER $250   350   500

Circa 1920. Persimmon wood head, center shafted "Schenectady"-style putter. "Ivorine" sight line on head.

IVORA PUTTER $250   350   550

Circa late teens. Brass head with "Ivorine" face insert. Face marked similar to a sun with rays.

DUNN BOW
TIE MARK IRONS $150   200   350

Circa 1900. Smooth face cleek, iron and lofter.

DUNN BOW
TIE MARK IRONS $350   425   800

Circa 1900. Rut niblick.

DOUBLE CIRCLE
MARK IRONS $90   125   200

Circa 1900. Smooth face with "J MacGregor, Dayton, 0" around a "Double Circle" mark with a shamrock inside.

J MACGREGOR
SERIES IRONS $50   65   95

Circa 1900-1905. Cleek with normal shafting.

RUT NIBLICK $300   400   750
Circa 1900-1905. Round concave face.

**J MACGREGOR
SERIES IRONS** $70   95   175
Circa 1900-1905. Cleek with "Carruthers" through-hosel shafting.

**J MACGREGOR
SERIES IRONS** $55   70   125
Circa 1900-1905. Smooth face iron or lofter.

**EDGEMONT
SERIES IRONS** $55   70   125
Circa 1910-1915. "Diamond" face.

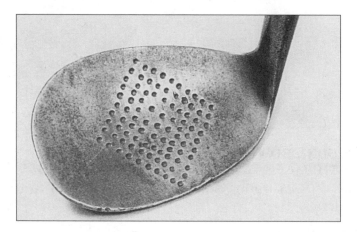

**"O A" SERIES
IRONS** $55   70   120
Circa 1915. Flanged back.

**PEERLESS
SERIES IRONS** $35   45   75
Circa 1925-1930. Stainless steel heads.

**TOMAHAWK
BRAND IRONS** $100   125   190
Circa 1920. "Shield" marked face.

**GO-SUM SERIES
IRONS** $35   45   75
Circa 1915-1925. Hyphen and line scored faces.

PILOT SERIES IRONS $35   45   80
Circa 1912-1920. Various face markings.

**CLIMAX-FIFE
SERIES IRONS** $45   55   85
Circa 1915-1920. "Crown" mark. All irons.

**RADITE SERIES
IRONS** $45   55   80
Circa 1920-1925. A rustless metal head with line-scored face.

**SUPERIOR SERIES
IRONS** $100   125   200
Circa 1918-1920. Slotted hosel patented 1918.

**RADITE SERIES
IRONS** $100   135   200
Circa 1915-1920. Bakspin mashie, mashie-niblick and niblick.

**POPULAR SERIES
IRONS** $40   50   75
Circa 1915. Dot scored face. All irons.

SUPERIOR SERIES
IRONS $35   45   75
Circa 1915-1920. Various face scoring.

POPULAR SERIES
IRONS $40   50   80
Circa 1915. Mussel back irons.

POPULAR SERIES
IRONS $75   100   150
Circa 1915. Concave hyphen scored "B Mashie-niblick".

POPULAR SERIES
IRONS $70   85   125
Circa 1915. "Popular C1/2 Sammy Jigger".

POPULAR SERIES
IRONS $75   100   150
Circa 1915-1920. "Popular G" with a weighted toe bulge similar to the "Smith" patented anti-shank irons.

PERFECTION
SERIES IRONS $60   75   100
Circa 1915-1920. "B-4 Perfection Mashie" with wrap around "Maxwell" holes drilled in the hosel.

DURALITE
SERIES IRONS $35   45   75
Circa 1928-1930. Stainless steel heads with Pyramid dots over line scoring. 1 through 6 and 9 niblick.

DURALITE
SERIES IRONS $50   75   100
Circa 1928-1930. #7 Pitcher.

DURALITE
SERIES IRONS $125   150   250
Circa 1928-1930. #8 Jigger.

AIRWAY-O IRONS $80   100   150
Circa 1925. Concave face, "Goal Post" scoring.

BAKSPIN SERIES
IRONS $175   250   375
Circa 1915-1920. "Ribangle" face. Corrugated deep grooves with lines at an angle over deep grooves.

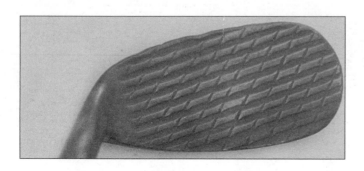

BAKSPIN SERIES
IRONS $95   120   190
Circa 1915-1920. Slot Deep Groove.

BAKSPIN SERIES
IRONS $175   250   375
Circa 1915-1920. Large dot scoring on only half the face.

PRETTY FACE
WOODS $95   125   175
Circa 1920s. Small "Ivorine" inserts set around one large center insert.

SPLICED NECK
WOODS $200   300   500
Circa 1898-1905. Bulger driver with "J. MacGregor, Dayton, O" on the persimmon head.

"BAP" SERIES
WOODS $85   110   160
Circa 1920s. Driver, brassie or spoon. Patented 1923.

YARDSMORE SERIES
WOODS   **$95   125   175**

Circa 1925. Driver, brassie or spoon with a black face having one large round insert and four small inserts.

WORLD WIN
SERIES WOODS   **$85   110   160**

Circa 1920s. Driver, brassie or spoon.

GO-SUM SERIES
WOODS   **$75   100   140**

Circa 1920s. Plain face.

DREADNOUGHT
WOODS   **$90   110   160**

Circa 1920s. Oversized heads. Driver, brassie or spoon.

GO-SUM SERIES
WOODS   **$95   125   160**

Circa 1920s with pretty face design.

BULL DOG WOODS   **$95   120   175**

Circa 1915-1920. Rounded sole. Marked "MacGregor, Dayton, 0" and a black face insert.

EDGEMONT
SERIES WOODS   **$95   115   175**

Circa 1910-1915. Persimmon head driver, brassie or spoon.

ALUMINUM-HEAD
WOODS   **$150   200   350**

Circa 1915-1925. Various lofts.

SAMPSON FIBER
FACE WOODS   **$160   200   275**

Circa 1915-1920. Driver or brassie.

ONE-PIECE WOOD   **$1500   2000   3200**

Circa 1900. Driver or brassie one-piece hickory head and shaft. Has a leather face insert.

JUVENILE CLUBS   **$35   45   80**

Circa 1915. Edgemont putter, mid-iron or mashie.

JUVENILE CLUBS   **$70   100   175**

Circa 1915. Edgemont driver.

McEWAN

MUSSELBURGH, SCOTLAND

The "McEwan" name was associated with club-making from about 1770 through WWII. The earliest marks were simply "McEwan" and a "Thistle". Subsequent family members used either "McEwan" alone or with their first initial. Clubs made by Douglas II from about 1895 were marked "D. McEwan & Sons" and are the most obtainable in today's marketplace.

SPLICED-NECK
WOODS   **$400   650   1250**

Circa 1890-1900. Play club, brassie or spoon. Bulger face. Many have leather face inserts. Transitional head style. "McEwan" mark.

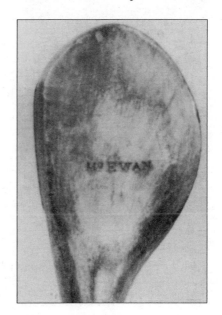

BRASS-HEAD
PUTTERS   **$150   250   350**

Circa 1880-1890. "McEwan" in block letters. "Double Ringed" hosel knurling.

IRON-HEAD PUTTER   **$150   200   375**

Circa 1890-1895. Straight blade. McEwan, Musselburgh mark.

BRASS-HEAD
PUTTER   **$175   225   400**

Circa 1890-1895. Straight blade. McEwan, Musselburgh mark.

LONG-NOSE PUTTERS	$750	1350	2450

Circa 1885-1895. Transitional head style. "McEwan" mark.

LONG-NOSE PUTTERS	$1250	2250	3750

Circa 1870-1880. Long head, large lead back weight. "McEwan" mark.

SOCKET WOODS	$100	125	175

Circa 1905-1915. Persimmon head driver, brassie or spoon.

LONG-NOSE WOODS	$1500	2750	4750

Circa 1870-1880. Play club or brassie. Long head, large lead back weight. "McEwan" mark.

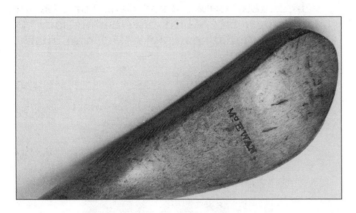

MILLAR, CHARLES

GLASGOW, SCOTLAND

Charles Millar began forging irons about 1895. He used several types of "Thistle Brand" marks to identify his clubs. He also marked his clubs "Glasgow Golf Co." and "Thistle Golf Co."

OFFSET BLADE PUTTER	$50	60	95

Circa 1915. "Thistle Brand" and "The Glasgow Golf Company" marks.

SMOOTH-FACE BLADE	$55	65	90

Circa 1900-1910. "Thistle" mark.

PUTTING CLEEK	$60	75	120

Circa 1900-1910. Smooth face blade. "Thistle" mark.

PREMIER BRAND PUTTERS	$90	110	150

Circa 1920s. Brass blade.

APPROACHING PUTTER	$120	150	200

Circa 1915. Vertical line face scoring. "Thistle" mark.

RUSTLESS IRONS	$50	60	85

Circa 1930-1935. All irons. Dot punched face.

PREMIER BRAND IRONS	$55	65	90

Circa 1915. Dot punched face. "Thistle" mark.

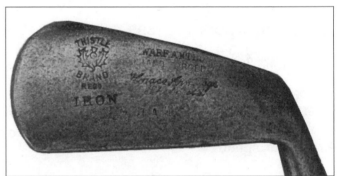

SMOOTH-FACE IRONS	$60	70	110

Circa 1900-1910. All irons. "Thistle-In-Circle" mark.

SMOOTH-FACE IRONS	$75	95	150

Circa 1895-1900. Cleek, iron or lofter. "C L Millar, Glasgow" mark.

D & T SPINNER	$200	275	375

Circa 1915. All irons. Patent #683488. Concave face, dot scoring on bottom.

MORRIS, TOM

ST. ANDREWS, SCOTLAND

Began making clubs in the early 1850s at Prestwick. He opened a shop in St. Andrews in 1864 across the street from the 18th hole and remained there until his death in 1908. The company continued to sell clubs until the Great Depression. His marks were "T. Morris" and "T. Morris, St. Andrews, NB" in oval. After his death "Tom Morris" in script and Old Tom's portrait were used. He purchased many iron heads from Tom Stewart and Robert Condie and added his marks on them. Many of his clubs can be found with shafts marked with "T. Morris, St Andrews, N.B." The "N.B." was for North Britain.

**IRON-HEAD
PUTTER** $175 275 450

Circa 1890-1900. Smooth face usually made by Condie or Stewart.

**SPLICED-NECK
PUTTERS** $350 550 950

Circa 1905-1920. Long narrow head. Persimmon head.

**LONG-NOSE
PUTTERS** $850 1750 2950

Circa 1885-1900. Beech head stamped "T Morris". Transitional head shape.

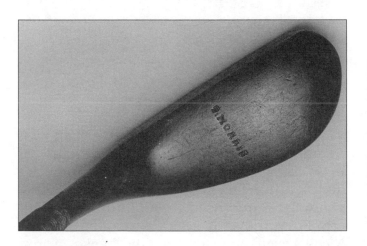

**LONG-NOSE
PUTTERS** $1350 2500 4250

Circa 1860-1880. Beech head stamped "T. Morris". Long head with large lead back weight.

**SMOOTH-FACE
IRONS** $175 325 600

Circa 1890-1905. Cleek, iron or lofter. "T. Morris, St. Andrews" with Condie's "Flower" or Stewart's "Pipe" marks.

PORTRAIT IRONS $85 115 150

Circa 1920s. All irons. Morris' portrait stamped at toe. Most have line-scored face.

RUT NIBLICK $275 500 950

Circa 1890-1905. Smooth face, round head. "T Morris, St Andrews" and Condie's "Flower" or Stewart's "Pipe" marks.

**SMOOTH-FACE
IRONS** $300 475 900

Circa 1880-1890. Cleek or General Purpose iron. "T. Morris, St. Andrews" mark.

RUT IRON $1200 2250 4000

Circa 1880. Small round head. "T. Morris, St. Andrews" mark.

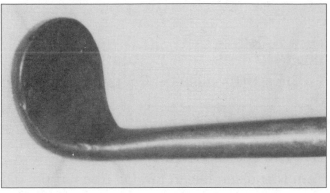

**AUTOGRAPH
SERIES WOODS** $125 175 275

Circa 1915-1925. Driver, brassie or spoon. Two-tone head with "Tom Morris" in script.

**SPLICED-NECK
WOODS** $275 400 675

Circa 1895-1910. Driver, brassie or spoon. Persimmon head stamped "T. Morris".

LONG-NOSE WOODS $1650   3250   7000

Circa 1885-1900. Play club, brassie or spoon. Beech head stamped "T. Morris". Transitional head shape.

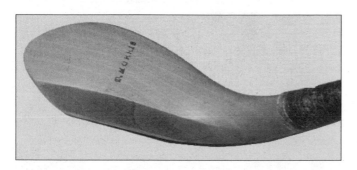

LONG-NOSE WOODS $2500   4000   8000

Circa 1860-1880. Play club, brassie or spoon. Beech or Thorn head stamped "T. Morris". Long head with large lead back weight.

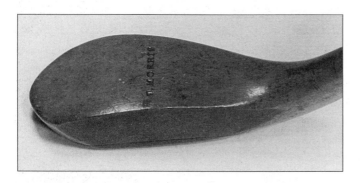

MORRIS MODEL IRONS $100   150   200

Circa 1915. All irons. Dot punched face.

NICHOLSON, T.

PITTENWEEM, SCOTLAND

Tom Nicholson began forging irons in the old cleekmaker's style during the mid 1880s. Prior to winning the Gold Medal at the 1890 Edinburgh Exposition, he marked his clubs "T. Nicholson, Pittenweem" in very tiny lettering. Most of these had the markings "emoried" away and are mistaken for much earlier forgings. After 1890 he used two oval marks on each club; one with "T. Nicholson, Maker, Pittenweem", the other "Gold Medal Exposition, Edinburgh, 1890".

SMOOTH-FACE BLADE PUTTER $125   175   275

Circa 1890-1900. Straight blade. "T. Nicholson, Maker, Pittenweem" football-shaped mark.

GOLD MEDAL IRONS $85   125   225

Circa 1890-1900. All irons.

GOLD MEDAL CLEEK $100   150   250

Circa 1890-1900. Smooth-face cleek.

SMOOTH-FACE IRONS $125   175   300

Circa 1886-1890. All irons. "T. Nicholson, Maker, Pittenweem" in tiny letters.

NICOLL, GEORGE

LEVEN, SCOTLAND
by Roger Hill

Nicoll (pronounced "nickel") of Leven (pronounced lee'-ven) is the most mispronounced maker's name in golf collectibles.

Nicoll's variations of the "hand of friendship" (or hand forging) maker's mark, in most cases, can help date his clubs. There are at least thirteen different hands, beginning about 1898 and used through the steel shaft era. From the early 1880s through 1898, "G. Nicoll Leven" appeared on the backs of iron club heads without the hand mark.

Nicoll's clubs were of high quality and were played by many top amateurs and professionals. Among his lines were the top quality "Zenith" irons as well as clubs such as "Duplicates of Mac Smith's" irons, "Freddie Tait" cleeks and "James Braid" irons". Nicoll is famous for producing the first matched sets of irons called "Indicator". Nicoll also produced socket wood clubs after 1925 marked with either the Nicoll name or the hand mark. Nicoll's long association with champion Henry Cotton came to an end when the company closed in 1983.

APPROACHING
PUTTER $65   90   150

Circa 1890-1898. Without the "Hand" mark. Smooth face straight blade.

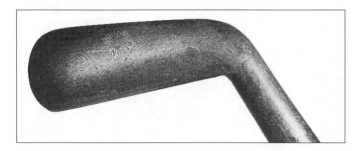

WILLIE PARK PUTTER $250   350   550

Circa 1920. Severely bent neck stamped "Willie Park's Original Bent Neck Putter".

INDICATOR
SERIES PUTTER $45   60   90

Circa 1925-1930. Straight blade, line scored face. "Hand" mark.

WHIPPET PUTTER $45   65   95

Circa teens. Long narrow head, dot-punched face. "Hand" mark.

AGLAIA PUTTER $50   65   95

Circa 1920. Putting cleek. "Hand" mark.

GEM PUTTER $55   90   125

Circa 1930-1935. Rustless rounded back, offset hosel, line scored face. "Hand" mark.

PRECISION PUTTER $60   100   150

Circa 1915. Flanged back and dot punched face. "Hand" mark.

NAP PUTTER $60   70   100

Circa 1920. Offset hosel, line scored face. "Hand" mark.

PREMIER PUTTER $100   135   200

Circa 1915. Wide sole similar to the Auchterlonie holing out putter.

PRE-1898 IRONS $100   125   250

Circa 1895. "G. Nicoll, Leven" in block letters made for "Forth Rubber Company, Dundee".

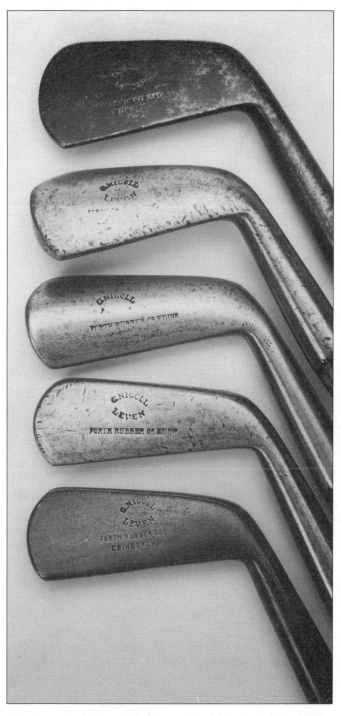

PRE-1898 IRONS $125   175   300

Circa 1890. Cleek with "G. Nicoll, Leven Fife" mark.

| **ABLE IRONS** | **$50** | **75** | **125** |

Circa 1910. Irons with "Geo. Nicoll, Leven Fife" mark and early "Hand" mark.

| **MAC SMITH** | | | |
| **SERIES IRONS** | **$40** | **60** | **90** |

Circa 1920s. "Duplicate of Mac Smith's" with "Hand" mark.

| **INDICATOR** | | | |
| **SERIES IRONS** | **$40** | **50** | **75** |

Circa 1925-1930. 1 through 9 irons. Line-scored or dot face. "Hand" mark.

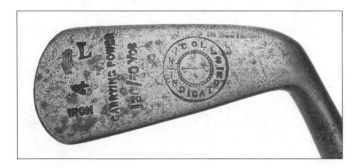

| **ZENITH SERIES** | | | |
| **IRONS** | **$40** | **60** | **90** |

Circa 1925-1930. 1 through 9 irons. "Hand" mark.

| **PIN SPLITTER** | | | |
| **SERIES IRONS** | **$40** | **60** | **90** |

Circa 1925-1930. 1 through 9 irons with flanged backs.

| **NICOLL** | | | |
| **SIGNATURE IRONS** | **$45** | **60** | **100** |

Circa 1915. Dot-punched faces. Driving iron through niblick.

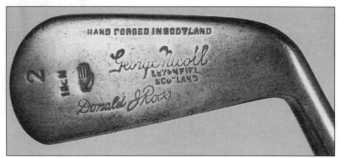

| **BRAID** | | | |
| **SIGNATURE IRONS** | **$60** | **80** | **125** |

Circa 1915. "James Braid" in script. Many had flanged backs.

| **TAIT SIGNATURE** | | | |
| **IRONS** | **$65** | **90** | **140** |

Circa 1915, "Freddie Tait" in script.

| **CRACKER JACK** | | | |
| **SERIES IRONS** | **$70** | **90** | **140** |

Circa 1925-1930. "Carruthers" through-hosel shafting. I through 9 irons.

SMITH

ANTI-SHANK IRONS $100   175   275

Circa 1915-1925. Heel and toe weighted line scored face. "Hand" mark.

**CORRUGATED
DEEP GROOVE IRONS** $125   150   225

Circa 1914-1920. "Zenith Pitcher". "Hand" mark.

**ZENITH
PRECISION JIGGER** $60   85   140

Circa 1920s. Flanged back.

**LEATHER-FACE
IRON** $1500   2000   3500

Patented 1892. Leather face insert. "G. Nicoll, Leven Fife" and Patent numbers.

**GUTTA-PERCHA
FACE IRON** $1750   2250   3500

Patented 1892. Gutta-percha face insert. "G. Nicoll, Leven Fife" and patent numbers. About twice as rare as the leather face.

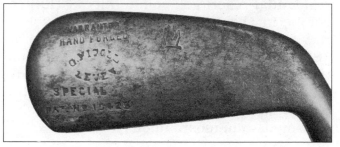

OKE, W G

FULWELL & LONDON, ENGLAND

William Oke began making clubs in the mid-teens and in 1923 registered the "Oak Brand" trademark of an "Oak Tree".

LONG-HOSEL PUTTER $150   200   275

Circa 1920s. Blade putter with seven-inch pencil-thin hosel. "Oak Brand Registered" mark.

DEEP-FACE MASHIE $60   75   125

Circa 1920s. "W. G. Oke, Fulwell, G. C." and the "Oak Brand Registered" mark.

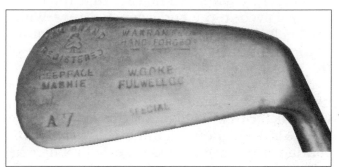

**DOT-PUNCHED
IRONS** $60   70   100

Circa 1910. All irons.

PARK, WILLIE

MUSSELBURGH, SCOTLAND
by Pete Georgiady

Undoubtedly the most versatile of all the great golfers of the 19th century was William Park Jr. Young Willie, as he was known during his lifetime, used his golfing knowledge and skills to be a champion golfer, author, course designer, real estate developer, club and ball designer and, yes, even a clubmaker before he saw his fortieth birthday.

      Born in Musselburgh in 1864, his father, "Auld" Willie, had already won two Open Championships before Junior could even walk. Literally born into the golf business,

Young Willie had little choice but to follow in the footsteps of his father and uncles.

His first assignment, arranged by his Uncle Mungo (himself champion in 1874), was to lay out the course and serve as professional to the golf club at Ryton, Northumberland. While there he started entering professional competitions, winning his first at age 17.

Returning to Musselburgh in 1884, he took control of his father's firm, making his first splash in the business: inventing the bulger driver in 1885 and using it in the 1885 Open. Some years later, he was challenged by Sir Henry Lamb, the prominent amateur, who also claimed to have invented the bulger in the same time frame. Through some lengthy written communications, the pair established they had both devised similar clubs concurrently without knowing that the other was involved in the endeavor. Because Willie was a clubmaker and professional continually in the public eye, he had received most of the popular acclaim for the bulger.

Over the next ten years, Willie was the best known clubmaker in the business. His Open victories in 1887 and 1889 set the stage for the introduction of four new clubs of his invention. He received much acclaim when he brought a new lofter to market. The club was at the forefront of a new development in the game—high approaching shots—and Willie created even more attention when he received a patent for his new implement in 1889.

The Patent Lofter was followed by the Patent Driving Cleek in 1891, the Patent Compressed Driver in 1893, and the most famous club of all, the Park Patent Bent Neck Putter in 1894. His success on the links as well as in the design caused his business to swell and he was acknowledged to be the second largest manufacturer of golf clubs behind the firm of Robert Forgan. In later years, he brought out a patent groove soled brassie called the Pik-up and a patent step faced lofter for imparting backspin.

His patent clubs are easily recognizable because they all are marked as such. He did make many other regular clubs with three types of name stamps. The vast majority of these clubs are smooth faced and it is very difficult to date them accurately since

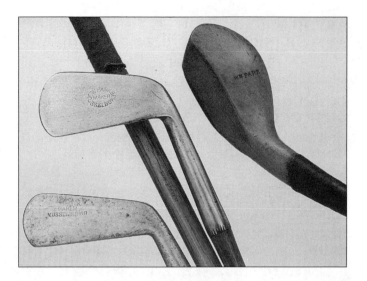

they have minimal markings and were all made in the old style, even after the firm entered the 20th century. Since Park stamped his name on the shafts of all his clubs, many are still identifiable even if the club head markings are illegible.

The range of Park clubs available today is broad and deep. Small-headed niblicks, gunmetal-blade putters, Smith model irons, large-hosel lofters and short-bladed mashie irons are among of the more unusual clubs from his output and some can be found in lady's and children's models as he was one of the first to cater to that growing segment of the market in the 1890s. Park's premium grade clubs are distinguished by his use of greenheart, purpleheart, lemonheart or lacewood for the shafts.

Willie gradually lost interest in clubmaking and the retail business after 1910, concentrating instead in course layout. He spent a considerable amount of time in the United States and Canada, first setting up a retail outlet in New York City, and then course design offices in New York and Toronto.

He was a principal in the first modern residential-resort golf community at Huntercombe in Oxfordshire, although the lack of rail access did not encourage its success. In 1896, Willie Park's *The Game of Golf* became the first published golf instruction book written by a professional. He followed up with *The Art of Putting,* a book that discussed the skill that made him most famous.

It was Willie Park who said, "The man who can putt is a match for any man." Not only was Willie a deft putter but he was the man to beat in club design, retailing and merchandising.

**SMOOTH-FACE
BLADE PUTTER**   **$125   175   300**

Circa 1890-1900. "Wm Park, Musselburgh, Maker" oval mark.

**SPECIAL PATENT
PUTTER**   **$175   225   325**

Circa 1900. Severely bent neck smooth face blade.

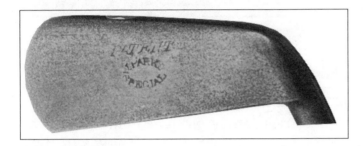

**BRASS-HEAD
PUTTERS**   **$125   190   300**

Circa 1890-1900. Straight blade. "Wm Park, Musselburgh, Maker" oval mark.

**PARK'S
PATTERN PUTTER**   **$175   225   325**

Circa 1900. Severely bent neck smooth face blade. Made for Slazengers.

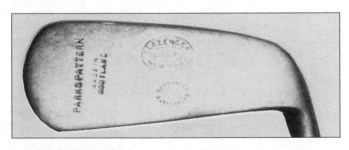

**PATENTED BENT
NECK PUTTER**   **$250   400   650**

Circa 1895-1900. Severely bent neck. "Wm Park, Musselburgh, Maker" oval mark.

LONG-NOSE PUTTER   **$750   1250   2250**

Circa 1895-1900. Transitional beech head. "Wm Park" mark.

**LONG-NOSE
PUTTER**   **$1350   2250   3750**

Circa 1885-1895. Long head, large lead weight. "Wm Park" mark.

DOT-FACE IRONS   **$90   150   200**

Circa 1910-1915. All irons. "Wm Park, Maker, Musselburgh" mark.

**DIAMOND-BACK
IRONS**   **$100   150   250**

Circa 1910. All irons. Smooth face.

**SMOOTH FACE
IRONS**   **$150   200   350**

Circa 1890-1900. All irons. "Wm Park, Maker, Musselburgh" mark.

**PATENTED
DRIVING CLEEK**   **$250   400   600**

Circa 1895-1905. Smooth face compact head. "W. Park's Patent Driving Cleek" mark.

RUT NIBLICK   **$250   400   650**

Circa 1900-1910. Smooth face head. "Wm Park, Maker, Musselburgh" mark.

**PARK
PATENTED LOFTER**   **$300   450   650**

Circa 1890-1895. Concave face.

RUT IRON   **$600   900   1750**

Circa 1885-1895. Small smooth face head. "Wm Park, Maker, Musselburgh" mark.

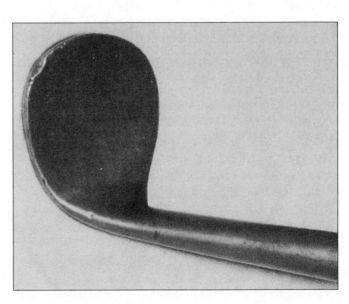

COMPRESSED-HEAD
WOOD $400   600   1250

Circa 1895-1900. Spliced neck. Driver, brassie or spoon. Spoon with "Park's Compressed Patent".

BULL DOG WOOD $150   250   500

Circa 1905-1915. Rounded sole, black triangular face insert.

SOCKET WOODS $150   250   400

Circa 1905-1915. Driver, brassie or spoon. "Wm Park" mark.

PICK-UP PATENT
WOOD $300   450   700

Circa 1910. Metal sole with four runners. Well lofted head.

BULGER-FACE
WOODS $450   700   1450

Circa 1890-1900. Driver, brassie or spoon. "Wm Park" mark.

LONG-NOSE WOODS $900   1900   3750

Circa 1895-1900. Driver, brassie or spoon. Transitional beech head. "Wm Park" mark.

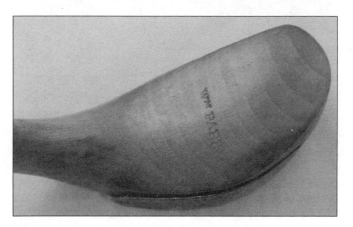

LONG-NOSE WOODS $1500   3750   4900

Circa 1885-1895. Play club, brassie or spoon. Long head, large lead weight. Wm Park" mark.

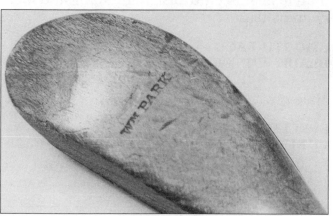

PATRICK, ALEX

LEVEN, FIFE, SCOTLAND

The Patrick family produced clubs from the late 1840s through the 1930s. On their wooden-head clubs the mark "A. Patrick" in block letters was used. They marked their irons and putters with "A. Patrick, Leven, Est. 1847". Shortly after the turn of the century they stamped a "Spur" mark on the backs of their irons, and about 1920 introduced the "Well-Made" horseshoe mark.

TWISTED-HOSEL
PUTTER $75   95   150

Circa 1920. "Well-Made" horseshoe mark.

BRASS-HEAD
PUTTERS $150   250   375

Circa 1890-1895. "A. Patrick, Leven" mark.

LONG NOSE PUTTERS $1000   1850   2950

Circa 1885-1895. Beech head Driving putter. "A. Patrick" in block letters.

HORSESHOE-MARKED
IRONS $50   60   90

Circa 1920s. All irons. "Well-Made" horseshoe mark.

CONCENTRIC-BACK
IRONS $75   100   150

Circa 1900-1910. Smooth face. "A. Patrick, Leven" mark.

SMOOTH-FACE IRONS $80   120   175

Circa 1895-1900. All irons. "A. Patrick, Leven" mark.

SHALLOW-FACE
CLEEK $125   200   350

Circa 1890. Smooth face. "A. Patrick, Leven" mark.

SPLICED-NECK
WOODS $275   575   975

Circa 1900. Bulger face. Driver, brassie or spoon. "A. Patrick" stamping.

ACME WOODS $90   120   160

Circa 1920s. Driver, brassie or spoon.

BULL DOG WOOD $100   135   175

Circa 1910-1915. Rounded sole lofted face. Most have face inserts.

PRETTY FACE WOODS $100   125   175

Circa 1920. Black face insert.

VICTORY SERIES
WOODS $125   175   250

Circa 1920s. Large-head driver, brassie or spoon. "Alex Patrick, Leven, Victory" mark.

SPLICED-NECK
WOODS $175   250   375

Circa 1900. Driver, brassie or spoon. "A. Patrick" stamping.

LONG-NOSE WOODS $650   1100   2250

Circa 1885-1895. Transitional head style. "A. Patrick" mark.

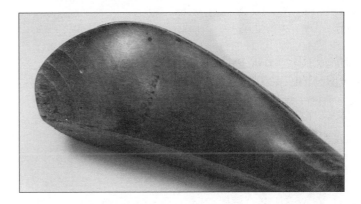

LONG-NOSE WOODS $1250   2250   4750

Circa 1880-1890. Large lead back weight. "A. Patrick" mark.

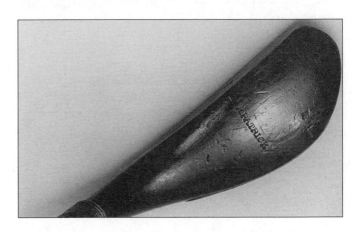

LONG -NOSE WOODS $1250 2250 4750

Circa 1866-1880. Long head with a large lead back weight. "A. Patrick" mark. Neck is more delicate than later woods.

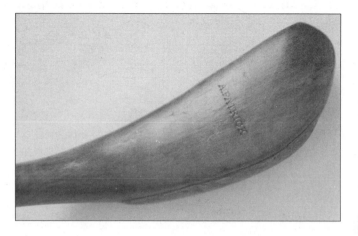

PAXTON, PETER

EASTBOURNE, ENGLAND

Paxton became an apprentice with Tom Hood at Musselburgh. He began designing and forging clubs in the early 1880s. His reputation for quality as a club and ball maker was superb. He marked his clubs "P. Paxton, Eastbourne". He also used a "Crown" mark on transitional style woods.

SMOOTH-FACE
LOFTER $350   500   800

Circa 1890. "P. Paxton, Eastbourne" mark.

SMOOTH-FACE
CLEEK $350   550   900

Circa 1890. Smooth face. "P. Paxton, Eastbourne" mark.

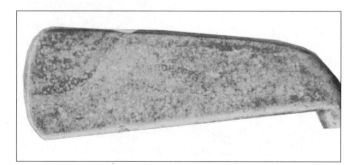

SPLICED-NECK
WOODS $500   750   1350

Circa 1895. Bulger face. Driver, brassie or spoon.

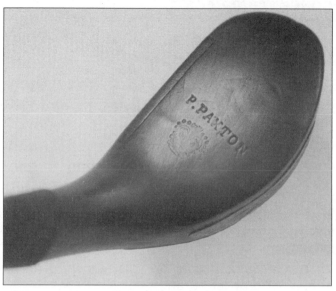

LONG-NOSE WOODS $950   1750 3000

Circa 1885-1895. Play club, brassie or spoon. Transitional head. "P. Paxton" stamp.

LONG-NOSE WOODS $1250 2000 3750

Circa 1880-1890. Play club, brassie or spoon. Long head, large lead weight. "P. Paxton" stamp.

PHILP, HUGH

ST. ANDREWS, SCOTLAND
by Pete Georgiady

As with most other golfing notables who lived prior to 1850, very little is recorded on their lives and pursuits. Hugh Philp is no exception. Much of the information existent today comes in the form of reminiscences from forty or fifty years after his passing.

Philp was born in Cameron, Fife in 1782, the son of a farmer. As a teen he was apprenticed to a carpenter and subsequently pursued a career as a carpenter and joiner. Hugh was never known to have worked with any other clubmaker and his bent towards that avocation apparently stemmed from his expertise as a carpenter and his love of playing golf. In time, these two skills obtained him an affiliation with the St. Andrews Society (later to be the Royal and Ancient Golf Club) for whom he repaired clubs beginning in 1812. The Society had a contract with McEwan's of Edinburgh to supply clubs for its semi-annual meetings, but in 1819 they appointed Philp as their clubmaker, though they did not sever their ties with McEwan until 1827. Also beginning in 1819, Philp served the Scotscraig Golf Club in the town of that name located between St. Andrews and Dundee.

With his new patronage, Philp moved from small quarters outside the town walls to a shop along the links adjacent to the Union Parlor, a popular gathering spot for golfers. Soon afterward he took up a position in a larger shop in the building that is today the Tom Morris shop. This shop would become a social center for golfers, congregating before and after their matches. Overhead in the shop were racks where his favored patrons could store their clubs between outings. The most remembered portion of his career was the last eleven years when he hired James Wilson as an assistant in 1845, and Robert Forgan in 1852. Forgan was his nephew and took over the Philp business when Uncle Hugh died in 1856.

Philp's clubmaking skills have been glorified to superior levels though several contemporary sources say others like Peter McEwan and Alexander Munro were equally proficient. But his mere presence in the town of St. Andrews and his service to the Royal & Ancient may have decidedly aided this repu-

tation by placing him in what little limelight could shine on such a craftsman. The gentleman and golf writer J.G. McPherson left us a romantic bit of insight saying that "the late Hugh Philp had polished an apple tree head for a whole afternoon when modern makers would have considered it quite finished."

Late in his life, he used hickory though he never completely adopted it in making shafts. On chance, he bought a log in the 1850s wondering if he would ever use it all. His heads were made from apple, thorn and beech, long and slender, some straight in the face while others were hooked.

His reputation was again enhanced when the original Mills aluminum putters were patterned after some ancient Philp models whose beauty and utility were still greatly admired fifty years after their heyday.

Historians have also recognized the fact that forgers were prone to producing Philp clubs. As early as the 1860s forged copies of Philp clubs were known to exist, forgeries for unwitting golfers who sought to use good clubs, not for collectors of a later age who would also covet Philp clubs. This legacy is not held by any other maker.

While he was the maker of superior grade clubs, much of the recognition he earned during his own lifetime came from his play and his association with the scions of the golf community. A player he was; like the cracks of his day Philp was a supreme strategist, knowing at precisely which hole he should close out his opponent. He came to play infrequently, usually when he deemed the odds were in his favor. But it is also known that he would occasionally play a three ball with youthful Tom Morris and Allan Robertson.

Hugh Philp was a storyteller with a dry vein of humor. He came on in a crusty way, but in time his inner warmth would shine through. He wore silver spectacles through which he viewed the world with glittering black eyes. In 1859, three years after he passed away, his loss was lamented, "Hugh Philp, how full of bygone pleasant memories of golf land is thy name! Thou didst make clubs for our fathers, and didst mend them for their sons."

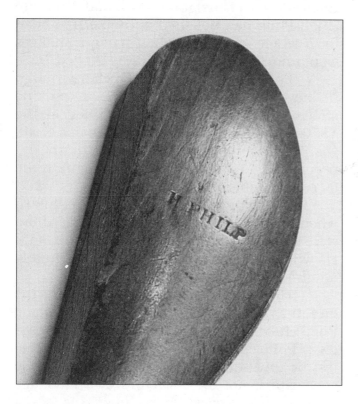

LONG-NOSE
PUTTERS $2000 4500 9500
Circa 1840-1856. "H. Philp" in block letters. Thorn head.

LONG-NOSE
WOODS $4500 10000 20000
Circa 1840-1856. "H. Philp" in block letters. Thorn head.

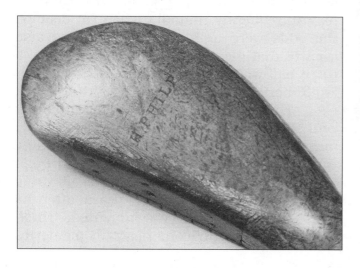

LONG-NOSE
BAFFIE SPOON $5000 12000 25000
Circa 1840-1856. "H. Philp" in block letters. Thorn head.

RODWELL, CHARLES

LONDON, ENGLAND

Charles Rodwell began selling clubs about 1905 and marked his clubs "Charles Rodwell, Lt'd".

IRON-HEAD PUTTER $90   125   190
Circa 1920. Long, shallow blade. Dot-punched face.

ALUMINUM-HEAD
PUTTER $200   325   475
Circa 1920. Raised circular aiming circle. "The Rodwell New Standard Putter# 1981 stamped on the head.

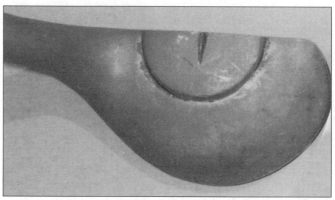

FLANGED-BACK
IRONS $55   65   90
Circa 1915. All irons.

ANTI-SHANK IRONS $150   225   300

Circa 1910-1915. All irons. Fairlie's Patent. Diamond-dot face markings.

ROLLINS & PARKER

REDDICH, ENGLAND

Began selling clubs about 1910 and continued into the early 1930s. Its mark was an "Eye".

EXCELSIOR SERIES IRONS $60   75   120

Circa 1915. All irons. Rounded back. "Eye" mark.

MAXWELL HOSEL IRONS $60   75   120

Circa 1920. Flanged back. "Eye" mark.

DEEP-GROOVE IRONS $100   150   200

Circa 1915-1922. All corrugated groove irons. "Eye" mark.

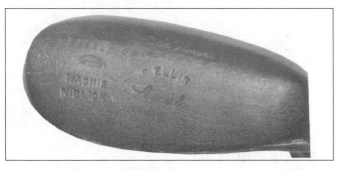

DEEP-GROOVE IRONS $120   160   225

Circa 1915-1922. All slot groove irons. "Eye" mark.

ANTI-SHANK IRONS $150   200   250

Circa 1920s. All irons. Smith's model. "Eye" mark.

SAUNDERS, FRED

LONDON, ENGLAND

Fred Saunders first made clubs in Birmingham about 1896, then later moved to London.

ALUMINUM PUTTER $450   700   1200

Circa 1920. Elongated sight line.

SAYERS, BEN,

NORTH BERWICK, SCOTLAND

The Sayers family began their club business about 1890. They used the markings "B Sayers, N. Berwick" and about 1920 used a "Robin" cleek mark.

BRASS-HEAD PUTTERS $150   200   350

Circa 1890-1900. Smooth face blade. "B Sayers" in block letters.

BENNY PUTTER $150   200   275

Circa 1930. Sole has 17 grooves. "Ben Sayers" in script.

TARGET IRONS $50   60   80

Circa 1920s. All irons. "Target" sweet spot.

MAXWELL HOSEL
IRONS	$60	75	110

Circa 1915. All irons. Flanged back. "Ben Sayers" in script.

SMOOTH-FACE IRONS
	$75	95	150

Circa 1895-1905. All irons. "Ben Sayers North Berwick" marking.

DEEP-GROOVE IRONS
	$100	150	200

Circa 1915-1922. All irons. Corrugated face.

DEEP-GROOVE IRONS
	$120	175	225

Circa 1915-1922. All irons. Slot face.

SELECTED SERIES
WOODS	$90	115	150

Circa 1920s. All woods.

DREADNOUGHT
WOODS	$100	135	175

Circa 1915-1920. Large-head driver, brassie or spoon. "Ben Sayers Dreadnought" stamp.

SPLICED-NECK
WOODS	$150	225	350

Circa 1900-1910. All woods.

GRUVSOL
PATENT WOODS	$150	225	325

Circa 1920s. All woods. "Gruvsol Patent #244925". Grooves on sole plate.

SCOTT, A H

EARLSFERRY, ELIE, SCOTLAND

Andrew Herd Scott began forging clubs about 1894. He was clubmaker to Prince Edward and used the "Plume" mark on his clubs during his reign. About 1910 he adopted the "Lion and Crown" mark.

STRAIGHT LINE
PUTTER	$100	150	200

Circa 1920s. Step down back design. Patent No 349407. "Lion-on-Crown" mark.

ALUMINUM
MALLET PUTTERS	$125	175	250

Circa 1915. "Lion-on-Crown" mark.

LION-ON-CROWN
IRONS	$60	75	120

Circa 1915. Smooth face. "A. H. Scott, Elie, Earlsferry" marking.

SMOOTH FACE
IRONS	$75	100	150

Circa 1895-1905. All irons. "A. H. Scott, Elie, Earlsferry" marking.

LION AND
CROWN WOODS $100   125   160

Circa 1915. All woods.

FORK SPLICED
PATENT WOODS $400   600   750

Circa 1895-1905. All woods. "A H Scott Patent No 21444". "Plume" mark.

SIMPSON, ARCHIE

CARNOUSTIE, SCOTLAND

Began forging clubs during the mid-1880s. During the 1900s his clubmaking business became prominent because of the important clientele patronage. He marked his clubs "A.. Simpson, Carnoustie".

SMOOTH-FACE
PUTTER $60   75   110

Circa 1900. Offset blade. "A. Simpson, Aberdeen" mark.

BRASS-BLADE
PUTTER $85   110   175

Circa 1900. "A. Simpson, Aberdeen" mark.

DOT-FACE IRONS $55   70   95

Circa 1915. All irons.

RUT NIBLICK $225   325   500

Circa 1895-1905. Smooth face. Medium-size rounded head. "A Simpson" mark.

BULGER-FACE
WOODS $200   300   500

Circa 1895-1900. Driver, brassie or spoon. "A. Simpson, Aberdeen" stamp.

SIMPSON, R.

CARNOUSTIE, SCOTLAND

Started forging irons about 1890 with the help of his brothers Jack and Archie. He marked his clubs simply "R. Simpson, Carnoustie". His most famous and highly collectible clubs were the ball-faced irons patented in 1903.

BRASS-HEAD
PUTTERS $100   135   175

Circa 1900-1910. Smooth-face blade. "R. Simpson, Maker, Carnoustie" mark.

PERFECT
BALANCE PUTTER $300   450   650

Circa 1910. "Patent 21307". Simpson's circular mark. Bulge weight in center.

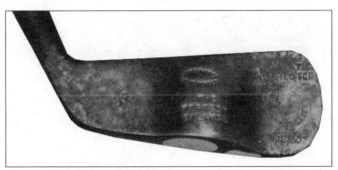

LONG-NOSE
PUTTERS $750   1300   2000

Circa 1890. Beech-head putter stamped "R. Simpson".

LINE-SCORED IRONS $45   55   75

Circa 1920s. All irons. "R. Simpson, Carnoustie" with "S" and the "Anchor" mark.

SMOOTH FACE
IRONS $50   75   100

Circa 1900-1910. All irons. "R. Simpson, Carnoustie" in a double circle.

PERFECT
BALANCE IRONS $350   650   850

Circa 1910. All irons. "Lump" back weighting. "Patent No. 21307" and "R. Simpson, Carnoustie" at toe. "Crescent and Star" mark.

BALL FACE IRONS $750   1500   2500

Circa early 1890s. All irons. Patent Numbers on back.

GUTTA BALL
FACE IRONS $600   800   1350

Circa 1903. All irons. Line cut gutta ball face.

SIMPSON
SPECIAL WOODS $85   110   150

Circa 1910-1915. Driver, brassie or spoon.

PRETTY FACE
WOODS $100   125   160

Circa 1910-1915. Driver, brassie or spoon. "Ivorine" face insert.

MALINKA SERIES
WOODS $100   125   160

Circa 1920s. "Malinka No 367793". Driver, brassie or spoon. "R. Simpson, Carnoustie" mark.

PRETTY FACE WOODS $100   125   160

Circa 1920s. "Diamond"-shaped face insert.

PERFECT
BALANCE WOODS $125   175   225

Circa 1905-1910. Driver, brassie or spoon.

SIMPLEX WOODS $200   300   450

Circa 1900-1910. Spliced neck. "Patent App. For No. 24835". "R. Simpson, Carnoustie" stamp.

LONG-NOSE WOODS $450   650   1000

Circa 1890-1900. Play club, brassie or spoon. Transitional head shape. "R. Simpson" stamp.

LONG-NOSE WOODS $1200 2250   3750

Circa 1883-1890. Play club, brassie or spoon. "R. Simpson" on a beech head. Many have leather face inserts.

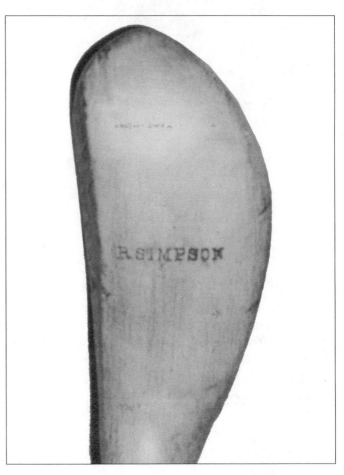

SLAZENGER AND SONS

LONDON, ENGLAND

Slazenger's began marking and selling clubs and balls about 1890. They began by buying clubs from Tom Stewart and Robert Condie and other major makers of the time. During the wood shaft era they had outlets in London and New York and marked their clubs accordingly. The "Six-Pointed Star" was their London mark used during the late 1890s. The other mark was simply "Slazenger". They are presently making golf equipment as a subsidiary of Dunlop.

SLAZENGER NEW YORK PUTTER	$70	90	140

Circa 1900-1910. Smooth face straight blade.

PUTTING CLEEK	$100	160	225

Circa 1895-1900. Smooth face straight blade. "Six-Pointed Star" mark.

SIX POINTED STAR IRONS	$90	140	225

Circa 1895-1900. All irons. Smooth face.

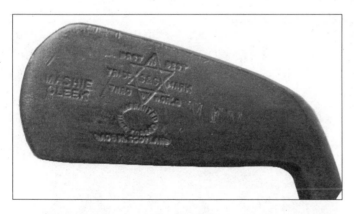

RUT NIBLICK	$350	475	650

Circa 1895. Small smooth face head. "Six-Pointed Star" mark.

SLAZENGER NEW YORK IRONS	$60	80	125

Circa 1900-1910. All irons. Smooth face.

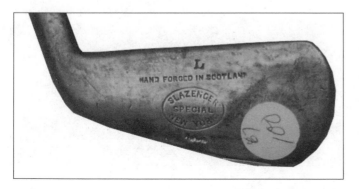

SLAZENGER SPECIAL WOODS	$100	120	160

Circa 1910-1915. Driver, brassie or spoon. "Slazenger Special, New York" stamp.

ALUMINUM-HEAD WOODS	$150	250	350

Circa 1910. All lofts. "Carruthers" through hosel shafting.

SPLICED-NECK WOODS	$175	250	400

Circa 1895-1910. Driver, brassie or spoon.

THREADED SOCKET PATENT	$350	450	650

Circa 1901-1905. "Screw-in shaft" driver or brassie. "Patent No.682,960 Slazenger" on the head.

SPALDING

DYSART, FIFE, SCOTLAND

Spalding began operations in Great Britain about 1900. Clubs from the Dysart, Fife Works carried an "Anvil" mark, "Baseball" mark stamped "Gt. Britain", "Gold Medal" series, "Tong" marked irons and "Argyle" clubs.

Jim Cooper has written the definitive work on Spalding, which is profusely illustrated. Every Spalding collector should have this reference in their library. It is available from the author, or Jim Cooper.

SMOOTH-FACE PUTTING CLEEK	$40	60	90

Circa 1905. "Made in Great Britain" baseball mark.

**MORRISTOWN
PUTTER**   **$75**   **110**   **175**

Circa 1898-1902. "Made in Gr. Britain" baseball mark.

**FLANGED-BACK
PUTTER**   **$50**   **70**   **100**

Circa 1920. "Anvil" mark.

**THISTLE SERIES
PUTTER**   **$40**   **60**   **90**

Circa 1920-1925. Line-face blade.

WRY-NECK PUTTER   **$45**   **60**   **90**

Circa 1920-1925. Line face, "Thistle" mark.

**ARGYLE SERIES
PUTTER**   **$45**   **65**   **90**

Circa 1915-1920. Hyphen scored, offset hosel. "Thistle" marks.

**GOLD MEDAL
SERIES PUTTER**   **$45**   **60**   **90**

Circa 1915-1920. Calamity Jane type with "Wry Neck" and "Anvil" mark.

**TONG BRAND
PUTTING CLEEK**   **$175**   **300**   **400**

Circa 1910. "Tong" mark.

**STANDARD,
LONDON IRONS**   **$60**   **90**   **140**

Circa 1910-1915. "Standard London" on back. Smooth face.

"S R" PUTTER   **$125**   **190**   **300**

Circa 1920s. Long radial blade and 5-1/2 inch hosel. "Anvil" mark.

**SCHENECTADY
PUTTER**   **$150**   **250**   **350**

Pre-1909. "A. G. Spalding, Makers" baseball trademark.

**CALAMITY
JANE PUTTER**   **$200**   **350**   **550**

Circa 1931. "Rustless Calamity Jane" with "Spalding Kro-Flite" mark.

**CENTRA-JECT
MASHIE**   **$40**   **60**   **90**

Circa 1910-15. "Anvil" mark.

JIGGER   **$40**   **60**   **90**

Circa 1910-1915. "Hammer" mark and "Diamond-dot" face scoring.

**HAND-FORGED
IRONS**   **$50**   **70**   **95**

Circa 1915-20. "Anvil" and "Dysart-Fife" marks.

**CRESCENT
SERIES IRONS**   **$50**   **75**   **125**

Circa 1910-1915. Marked "Crescent" with the "Hammer" mark.

THISTLE SERIES
IRONS $40   55   80

Circa 1910-1915. "Spalding" in large block letters.

GOLD MEDAL
SERIES IRONS $50   65   90

Circa 1910-1915. "Dysart-Fife" and "Anvil" mark.

MORRISTOWN
SERIES IRONS $70   100   150

Circa 1898-1902. "Made in Gr. Britain" baseball mark.

TONG BRAND IRONS $125   175   300

Circa 1910-1915. "A G Spalding & Bros., Tong Brand, Scotland" marks.

FOULIS PATENT $125   200   300

Circa 1905-1910. Concave, smooth face. "Hammer" mark.

LEATHER FACE
SOCKET WOODS $100   150   225

Circa 1900-1905. "Baseball" mark.

LARGE-HEAD BRASSIE $75   100   160

Circa 1915-1920 marked " "A. G. Spalding Bros."

SPALDING MEDAL 7 $75   115   165

Circa 1910-1915 Driver, brassie or spoon.

IVORINE FACE
WOODS $100   140   200

Circa 1915-1920. Marked "A. G. Spalding Bros., Scotland".

BULLDOG
TROUBLE WOOD $100   140   190

Circa 1915. Various markings.

SPALDING, A.G. & BROTHERS

USA

Spalding began importing clubs from Scotland about 1893. They were marked with "Spalding" in block letters. During 35 years of manufacturing wooden-shafted clubs, spaulding used a multitude of cleek marks, including the baseball trademark, Morristown, Crescent, Spalding Special, Clan, Harry Vardon, SMCO and A. G. Spalding & Brothers model A, B, and C. From 1906 to 1918 Gold Medal in various configurations was used. In 1919 the "F" Series irons were introduced including the famous Waterfall series. During the 1920s Spalding Medal, Spalding Forged, Dundee, and Kro-Flite, were the dominant markings. In 1930 the wooden shaft Robert T. Jones, Jr. clubs were produced in very limited quantities.

Jim Cooper has written the definitive work on Spalding, which is profusely illustrated. Every Spalding collector should have this reference in their library. It is available from Jim Cooper, or the author. Spalding Retail Catalogue reprints from 1899 to 1932 are also available from the author of this book.

"SMCO" PUTTER $300   450   800

Circa 1895. "Crescent Moon" mark on a straight blade putter.

CLAN SERIES PUTTER $125   225   450

Circa 1895. Blade putter marked "Clan" in large block letters.

SPALDING SPECIAL
SERIES PUTTER $150   200   325

Circa 1894-1896. Steel blade putter.

SPALDING SPECIAL
SERIES PUTTER $225   275   450

Circa 1894-1896. Brass blade putter.

**THE SPALDING
SERIES PUTTER**   **$90**   **125**   **190**

    Circa 1898-1902. "Park" type severe bent neck putter.

**THE SPALDING
SERIES PUTTER**   **$150**   **225**   **350**

    Circa 1898-1902. Deep smooth face steel blade putter.

**THE SPALDING
SERIES PUTTER**   **$90**   **150**   **250**

    Circa 1898-1902. Brass blade putter with a "Diamond" back.

**THE SPALDING
SERIES PUTTER**   **$175**   **275**   **450**

    Circa 1898-1902. Deep smooth face. Brass blade putter .

**MORRISTOWN
SERIES PUTTER**   **$65**   **90**   **145**

    Circa 1898-1900. Steel head blade "Morristown" and "Baseball" marks.

**MORRISTOWN
SERIES PUTTER**   **$70**   **90**   **150**

    Circa 1902-1905. Brass putter with "Baseball" mark.

MORRISTOWN

SERIES PUTTER	$75	100	175

Circa 1898-1902. Brass-head blade. "Morristown" mark only.

MORRISTOWN

SERIES PUTTER	$80	100	140

Circa 1898-1902. Steel-head approaching putter with "Morristown" stamp only.

HARRY VARDON

SERIES PUTTER	$125	175	275

Circa 1900-1903. Gooseneck putter marked "A. G. Spalding & Bros, Makers".

CRESCENT

SERIES PUTTER	$80	100	160

Circa 1902-1905. Brass blade with "Baseball" mark.

GOLD MEDAL

SERIES PUTTER	$50	65	95

Circa 1906-1908 "Spalding Gold Medal 1" with dot ball face.

CRESCENT

SERIES PUTTER	$75	90	150

Circa 1902-1905. Diamond back with "Baseball" mark.

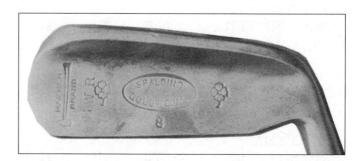

GOLD MEDAL

SERIES PUTTER	$50	65	95

Circa 1906-1908. Brass blade "Spalding Gold Medal".

**GOLD MEDAL
SERIES PUTTER** $70   90   150

    Circa 1912-1919. Flanged back, "Maxwell" drilled hosel.

**GOLD MEDAL
SERIES PUTTER** $50   70   100

    Circa 1912-1919. Ball face.

**GOLD MEDAL
SERIES PUTTER** $75   90   135

    Circa 1912-1919. Brass head.

**GOLD MEDAL
SERIES PUTTER** $70   90   150

    Circa 1912-1919. Flanged back, notched neck.

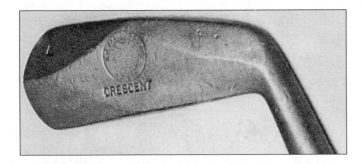

**CALAMITY JANE
PUTTER** $175   290   450

    Circa 1931. Marked "Robt. T. Jones, Jr". Wood shafted.

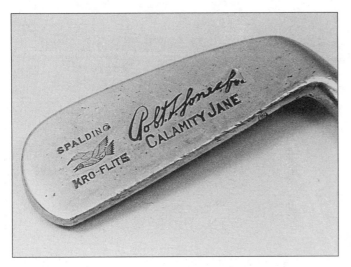

SERIES PUTTER $90   135   175

    Circa 1912-1919. Aluminum-head mallet #4.

GOLD MEDAL SERIES $40   60   95

    Circa 1912-1919. "Gold Medal" in an oval with the "Hammer" mark at toe.

"F" SERIES PUTTER $50   65   90

    Patented 1-3-1922. Blade putter with three deep scoring lines.

"M" SERIES PUTTER $45   60   80

    Circa 1915-1922. "M-11, 12 and 16 all marked "Spalding Forged".

"MEDAL" PUTTER $45   60   85

    Circa 1915-1920. Marked "Spalding Medal" between two "Thistle" marks.

**KRO-FLITE
SERIES PUTTER** $45   60   80

    Circa late 1920s. Blade putter marked "Spalding Kro-Flite" with "H" on the sole.

KRO-FLITE PUTTER $45   60   85

    Sweet Spot "RF" putter with "Pat. Sept 13, 1927" date.

HEATHER PUTTER $40   55   80

    Circa 1915-1920. Marked "Spalding Heather" between two "Rose" marks.

THISTLE PUTTER $40   55   75

    Circa 1920s. Marked "Thistle".

**SEMETRIC
SERIES PUTTER** $40   50   80

    Circa mid to late 1920s. Chromed blade putter.

**MONEL METAL
PUTTER** $80   150   300

    Circa 1912-1913. "Ball-with-Wings" and "Baseball" marks.

"B V" PUTTER $100   150   250

Circa 1910-1915. Crescent head shaped.

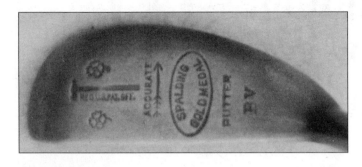

**FLANGED-BACK
PGA PUTTER** $45   60   85

Circa late 1920s. Marked "Pro Golfers Ass'n" with "Crossed Clubs".

**FLANGED-BACK
PUTTER** $45   60   90

Circa 1912-1919. Marked "Spalding Gold Medal 8".

FIRE BRAND PUTTER $60   75   100

One year only, 1923. "Arm & Torch" mark.

CHICOPEE PUTTER $75   100   150

Circa 1920 marked "Spalding Chicopee" on the brass head. There are modern remakes with "Spalding" on the sole.

**MAXWELL
HOSEL PUTTER** $125   175   275

Ten or twelve holes in hosel. Flanged back.

**ALUMINUM
MALLET PUTTER** $70   100   150

Circa 1915-1920. "MR" on the sole. Marked "A. G. Spalding & Bros.".

**HOLLOW BACK
PUTTER** $200   350   550

Circa late 1920s. "HB" putter with hollowed-out back.

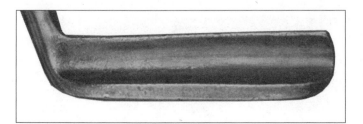

**ALUMINUM
MALLET PUTTER** $90   120   175

Circa 1920. Marked "Reach" with a "Keystone" mark.

ALUMINUM PUTTER $75   100   150

Circa teens. "A. G. Spalding & Bros" and "AHP".

**SCHENECTADY
TYPE PUTTER** $125   175   350

Circa 1910-1920 marked "Spalding Gold Medal H H".

SPRING FACE PUTTER $375   600   1250

Circa 1897-1915. "The Spalding", Crescent" and "Gold Medal" marks.

TRAVIS PUTTER $500   700   1100

Circa 1905-1910. Center-shafted persimmon wood putter with a brass face and sole plate.

OLYMPIC PUTTER $500   700   1200

Circa 1914-1918. Square steel shaft. Pointed toe on the rounded head.

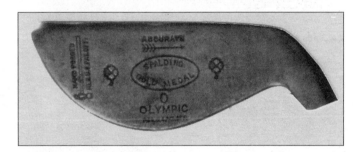

**"SMCO" SERIES
IRONS** $450   700   1200

Circa 1895. Rut niblick with the "Crescent Moon" mark.

Spalding discovered

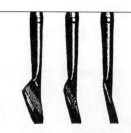

that *mild steel* banishes finger fatigue

So the heads of the world's most accurately matched golf "irons" are made of this superior metal

A STEEL clubhead hits a golf ball with a terrific impact. Where does the shock of the blow go? Spalding has discovered that it depends largely upon the kind of steel used.

Brittle steel resists the blow—transmitting the shock to your fingers. A succession of such blows often causes finger fatigue—that barely perceptible tiring of the finger muscles, which, by the end of a round, can effect the accuracy of your short game.

Mild steel absorbs the shock of the blow. Your fingers are relieved of the strain—a desirable condition in all your golf, a vitally important one in tournament play.

That is why the heads of all Spalding "Irons" are made of mild steel. You notice the difference in the sweeter feel of the impact as the mild-steel clubhead hits the ball.

Mild steel makes the "Sweet Spot" sweeter still

The "Sweet Spot" is the one spot on the club face that gives greatest distance to the ball, and the sweetest feel to the shot. Every golf club has a "Sweet Spot." But it was Spalding who found that by planning the distribution of metal, it could be located in the same position on every club face. And Spalding has marked it there for you to see.

It was Spalding also who originated the idea of having golf clubs match each other. Spalding clubs are so perfectly related in balance and weight that they all *feel* exactly alike. You can time your swing the same for all of them. If you have analyzed the play of champions, you know that such uniformity is the secret of great golf. Spalding has put this uniformity into the clubs themselves.

These clubs have an exact relation of lie to lie. An exact graduation in the pitches of the blades. Even the torsion and resilience of the shafts is matched.

Your wood clubs should match too

You can buy Spalding wood clubs which are as accurately related as the Spalding irons. It is important that this relation exist, too!

At the left is shown an average set of golf clubs. The dotted line connects the centers of balance. There is little relation between them. Your swing and timing for each club would be a trifle different.

At the right are six Spalding clubs. Note that they are so accurately related that a line drawn through the centers of balance parallels the tops of the shafts. The clubs all feel exactly alike. The swing and timing is the same for every one of them.

CLAN LOFTING IRON $150   225   350

Circa 1895. "Clan" in block letters on head and shaft.

**"SMCO" SERIES
IRONS** $150   250   425

Circa 1895 Cleek, iron and lofting iron with the "Crescent Moon" mark.

CLAN SERIES IRONS $125   225   400

Circa 1895. Iron and lofter marked "Clan" in large block letters.

**SPALDING SPECIAL
SERIES IRONS** $90   150   300

Circa 1894-1896. Cleek, Mid-iron, lofting iron.

**SPALDING SPECIAL
SERIES IRONS** $350   550   1000

Circa 1894-1896. Concave-face rut niblick.

**THE SPALDING
SERIES IRONS** $50   85   140

Circa 1898-1902. Cleek, iron and lofting iron.

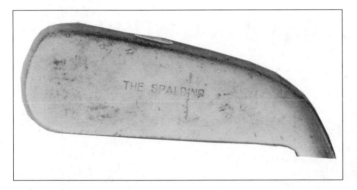

**THE SPALDING
SERIES IRONS** $80   150   275

Circa 1898-1902. Cleek with "Carruthers" through-hosel shafting.

**THE SPALDING
SERIES IRONS** $90   150   300

Circa 1898-1902. Lofter with concave smooth face.

**THE SPALDING
SERIES IRONS** $300   500   950

Circa 1898-1902. Concave-face rut niblick.

**MORRISTOWN
SERIES IRONS** $50   80   145

Circa 1898-1900. Steel head with "Morristown" stamping. Cleek, Mid iron and lofting irons.

**MORRISTOWN
SERIES IRONS** $50   75   135

Circa 1902-1905. Steel head with "Morristown" and "Baseball" marks. Cleek, mid iron and lofting irons.

**MORRISTOWN
SERIES IRONS** $175   300   600

Circa 1898-1900. Smooth-face niblick with "Morristown" stamping.

**BASEBALL
TRADEMARK IRONS** $60   90   140

Circa 1902-1905. "Model B" lofting iron.

**HARRY VARDON
SERIES IRONS** $60   100   175

Circa 1900-1903. Smooth-face cleek, Mid iron and lofter marked "A. G. Spalding & Bros., Makers".

**HARRY VARDON
SERIES IRONS** $200   325   500

Circa 1900-1903. Smooth-face niblick marked "A. G. Spalding & Bros., Makers".

**GOLD MEDAL
SERIES IRONS** $40   60   90

Circa 1909-1912. Various irons with ball face designs.

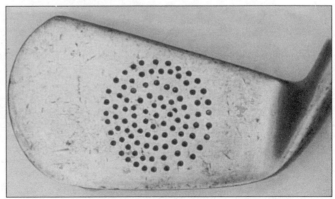

**MODEL SERIES
A, B, C IRONS** $70   100   175

Circa 1899-1902. Cleek, mid-iron and lofting iron with "A. G. Spalding & Bros., Model" in very tiny letters.

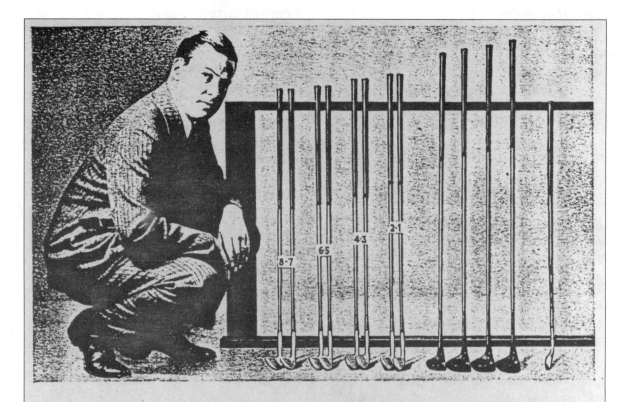

Reading from left to right: BOBBY JONES and the Spalding Clubs he designed

HERE is Bobby Jones examining the first set of golf clubs ever made which offer his idea of what perfect golf clubs should be!

From 8 to 1, is a set of the grandest Irons that the game has ever seen. Jones, now a Spalding Director, and the Spalding experts have, by redistributing weight, succeeded in designing an iron whose head tends to follow through naturally. As Jones himself expressed it, "the blade seems to flow through the ball."

This redistribution of weight—the heavier blade and lighter hosel—gives better control, too. The center of percussion is two inches lower than it is on hickory-shafted irons, and an inch lower than it is on other steel-shafted irons. This makes the clubhead easier to direct, and gives a more perfect instrument for shot control.

Another factor which contributes to control is the flange sole, which seats itself in back of the ball with the accuracy of a putter. This feature relieves the player of the distracting business of fussing with the lie of the blade, and lets him concentrate on the stroke itself.

In these clubs, Jones also cuts the number of stances right in half, by introducing the brand new idea of matching in pairs as to length and lie! This means that you need

master only *one* stance for every *two* clubs. And, every club is matched with every other club in swinging weight—so that one swing and one timing are correct for every club in the set!

"Poems in Wood"

Bobby Jones is recognized as one of the greatest wood players of all time. And his uncanny skill is reflected in the new woods which he designed. One famous expert, when first examining them, said—"They're poems in wood." When perfectly sane golfers get to talking like that about these clubs, they *must* be magnificent!

In addition to the customary woods, Jones contributes a new Senior Set of *Five Graduated Woods*—introducing two completely new woods to take the place of the Numbers 1 and 2 irons. Senior golfers will find, in this Set, a solution of the difficul-

ties they now have with their long iron shots.

Look! It's Calamity Jane!

That interesting looking club on the end is none other than Calamity Jane—an exact duplicate of the famous lady herself. Legend has it that Bobby Jones clings to this great putter because he considers it "lucky." In a way, that's true. Calamity Jane's magnificent balance and deadliness make it a lucky club in any golfer's bag.

Lower prices for all

The new Jones Clubs have the famous Spalding Cushion-neck. The sets are Registered, so that you can always get an exact duplicate of any club. And the prices are the lowest ever asked for Spalding fine clubs.

CUSTOM-BUILT REGISTERED IRONS
Set of 9 $75   Set of 8 $67   Set of 6 $50
(Cushion Shaft Irons, $5 each)
CUSTOM-BUILT DE LUXE
REGISTERED WOODS
Set of 4 $48   Set of 3 $36   Pair $24
CUSTOM-BUILT STANDARD
REGISTERED WOODS
Set of 4 $40   Set of 3 $30   Pair $20
(Autograph Woods, separately, $8 and $10 each)
Custom-Built De Luxe Senior Graduated Registered Woods, $60 for set of 5. Senior Graduated Matched Woods, $40 for set of 5. Calamity Jane Putter, $6.

Spalding
ROBERT T. JONES, JR.
GOLF CLUBS

MODEL SERIES
A, B, C IRONS   **$300**   **600**   **1000**

Circa 1902-1905. Rut niblick with concave face.

CRESCENT
SERIES IRONS   **$50**   **75**   **125**

Circa 1902-1905. Cleek, mid-iron, lofter and specialty clubs. Smooth face with "Baseball" mark.

GOLD MEDAL
SERIES IRONS   **$50**   **60**   **85**

Circa 1912-1919. "Jigger".

GOLD MEDAL
SERIES IRONS   **$50**   **75**   **135**

Circa 1906-1908. "Gold Medal" in block letters. "C" lofter with "Diamond-dot" face scoring.

GOLD MEDAL
SERIES IRONS   **$60**   **85**   **125**

Circa 1906-1908. "Gold Medal" in block letters. Iron, lofter and niblick.

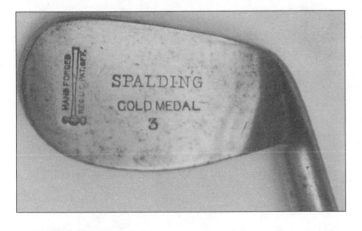

GOLD MEDAL
SERIES IRONS   **$50**   **75**   **135**

Circa 1906-1908. "Gold Medal 6" in block letters with a concave "Stag-dot" face.

GOLD MEDAL
SERIES IRONS   **$125**   **175**   **325**

Circa 1906-08. Foulis concave mashie-niblick with "Gold Medal 3" in block letters.

CORRUGATED DEEP
GROOVE IRONS   **$85**   **125**   **175**

C-54, C-67 and "C-98. Mashie, mashie-niblick and niblick.

CORRUGATED DEEP
GROOVE IRONS   **$85**   **125**   **175**

"F" Series Mid-iron, mashie, mashie-niblick and niblick.

SLOT DEEP
GROOVE IRONS   **$95**   **140**   **195**

"C-91, Dedstop mashie-niblick" on the sole.

A G SPALDING & BROS.
SERIES IRONS   **$30**   **40**   **75**

Circa late teens-early 1920s. Irons 1 through 9.

A G SPALDING & BROS.
SERIES IRONS   **$60**   **80**   **120**

Circa late teens-early 1920s. "Bobbie iron" on a "radial" sole.

"F" SERIES LINE
GROOVES IRONS   **$40**   **55**   **80**

Patented 1-3-1922. 2 through 9 irons. "F" numbers marked on sole at toe.

KRO-FLITE
SERIES IRONS   **$30**   **40**   **70**

Circa 1925-1930. Irons 1 through 7, and 19.

KRO-FLITE
SERIES IRONS   **$50**   **65**   **95**

Circa 1925-1930. Irons 8 Sky iron, 15 through 18, and 29 Sand Dabber.

R T JONES
KRO-FLITE IRONS   **$100**   **200**   **350**

Irons 2 thru 8.

R T JONES
KRO-FLITE IRONS   **$120**   **225**   **400**

#1 Driving iron and #9 niblick.

R T JONES
KRO-FLITE IRONS   **$2000**   **3500**   **7500**

Complete set 1-9 irons and Calamity Jane putter.

CUSTOM SERIES
IRONS   **$50**   **65**   **100**

Exactly the same as the Kro-Flite R. T. Jones, but marked "Custom".

CUSTOM SERIES
IRONS   **$500**   **750**   **1400**

Complete set 1-9 custom irons.

"M" SERIES IRONS $35   45   70

Circa early 1920s. Irons 1 through 9 with deep line scoring.

"F" SERIES IRONS $50   65   90

Patented 1-3-1922. #1 iron. "F" numbers marked on sole at toe.

SEMETRIC SERIES IRONS $30   40   75

Circa late 1920s. Irons 1 through 9.

FIRE BRAND SERIES IRONS $50   60   100

One year only, 1923. "Arm and Torch", various irons.

MONEL METAL IRONS $50   65   95

Circa 1912-1913. "Ball with Wings" and "Baseball" mark.

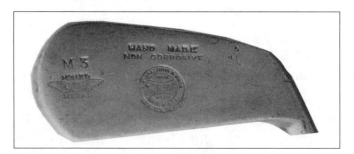

MAXWELL HOSEL IRONS $60   90   135

Ten or twelve holes in hosel. Cleek, mid-iron, mashie, mashie-niblick and niblick all with flanged backs.

WATERFALL IRONS $400   500   800

Circa 1920. Single waterfall "F" Series.

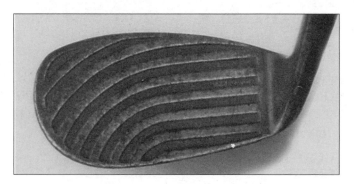

SPRING FACE IRONS $300   550   1000

Circa 1897-1915. "The Spalding", Crescent" and "Gold Medal" marks.

BALL BACK IRONS $400   650   1000

Circa 1905. Smooth-face cleek, iron and lofting iron with large protruding "Ball" back-weighting design.

CRAN IRONS $500   950   1750

Circa 1897-1915. Wood face insert. "The Spalding", "Crescent" and "Gold Medal" marks.

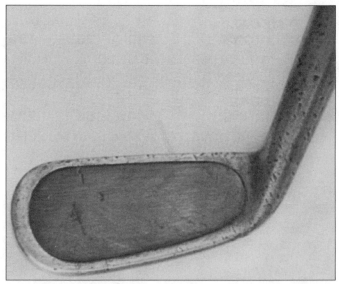

SEELY PATENT IRONS $500   800   1500

Circa 1912-1919. "Forked hosel" with "Gold Medal" marks.

**DOUBLE WATERFALL
IRON**   **$2000   2800   4500**

Circa 1920. "F" series.

**LARD PATENT
IRONS**   **$2750   3500   5500**

Circa 1914-1920. Perforated steel shaft. Corrugated deep groove face scoring, any model.

LARD PATENT IRONS $2200   3000   4500

Circa 1914-1920. Perforated steel shaft. Cleek, mid-iron, mashie, mashie-niblick and niblick.

**THE SPALDING
ONE-PIECE WOOD**   **$1500   2000   3200**

Circa 1898-1902. Driver with leather face insert.

**THE SPALDING
SERIES WOODS**   **$225   350   700**

Circa 1898-1902. Pear-shaped driver, brassie and spoon. Heads were usually made from "Dogwood".

**MORRISTOWN
SERIES WOODS**   **$275   450   700**

Circa 1902-1905. Spliced-neck, bulger-face brassie with "Morristown" and "Baseball" marks.

**CRESCENT
SERIES WOODS**   **$90   135   200**

Circa 1902-1905 Driver, brassie or spoon with "Baseball" mark.

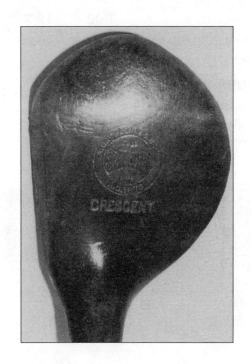

**MORRISTOWN
SERIES WOODS**   **$300**   **475**   **800**

Circa 1902-1905. Spliced-neck semi-long nose play club or brassie with "Morristown" mark.

**HARRY VARDON
SERIES WOODS**   **$200**   **375**   **700**

Circa 1900-1903. Driver, brassie or spoon all with a leather face insert and stamped "Harry Vardon".

**DUNCAN MODEL
WOODS**   **$85**   **110**   **160**

Circa 1920. Patented one-piece sole and back weight.

**FIRE BRAND
SERIES WOODS**   **$100**   **140**   **190**

One year only, 1923. "Arm & Torch" mark.

**SKOOTER
PATENT WOODS**   **$150**   **225**   **375**

Patented August 22, 1911. Marked "A. G. Spalding & Bros." Driver, brassie or spoon.

**ALUMINUM-HEAD
WOODS**   **$150**   **275**   **550**

Circa 1915-1920. Aluminum-head driver and various loft fairway clubs marked "A. G. Spalding Bros., Makers".

**MALTESE CROSS
FACE WOODS**   **$90**   **125**   **160**

Circa 1920s. Red and black Maltese Cross plastic insert.

**JACOBUS PATENT
WOOD**   **$275**   **375**   **650**

Circa 1910. Three Mahogany dowels arranged in the face. "A G Spalding Bros., Gold Medal" markings.

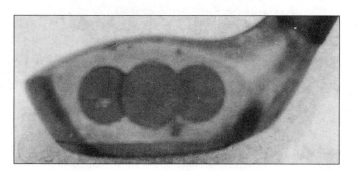

CROW FACE WOODS   **$125**   **175**   **275**

Circa 1920s. Black flying "Crow" in an "Ivorine" insert.

**TRIPLE SPLICE
PATENT WOODS**   **$275**   **350**   **550**

Circa 1920. Driver, brassie and spoon with a "Triple" splice affixing head to shaft.

JUVENILE CLUBS   **$30**   **40**   **65**

"A. G. Spalding Bros., Junior" smooth-face putter, mid-iron and mashie.

JUVENILE CLUBS   **$65**   **90**   **150**

"A. G. Spalding Bros., Junior" driver.

SPENCE & GOURLAY

ST. ANDREWS, SCOTLAND

James Spence and George Gourlay went into partnership in 1895 and by 1908 they had built a great reputation and flourishing business. Their business came to an end in 1914 as a result of WWI. Their mark was a "Clover" with "S & G" inside.

**OFFSET BLADE
PUTTER**   **$50**   **60**   **85**

Circa 1920-1925. "S & G" inside a shamrock mark.

**LONG HOSEL
PUTTER**   **$85**   **110**   **150**

Circa 1920s. "Flag-in-hole". Hosel is 5-1/2 inches.

**DOT-PUNCHED-FACE
IRONS**   **$45**   **55**   **75**

Circa 1915. All irons. "S & G" inside a "Clover" mark.

**DREADNOUGHT
NIBLICK**   **$75**   **95**   **150**

Circa 1915. Dot-punched face.

ANTI-SHANK IRONS   **$120**   **175**   **250**

Circa 1920. All irons. Smith's Patent.

SPENCE, JAMES

ST. ANDREWS, SCOTLAND

After the war, James Spence returned to the business previously operating under Spence & Gourlay. He changed the cleek mark and rebuilt a very successful company. In 1920 he sold out to Robert Forgan & Son. Forgan used the Spence trademark throughout the 1930s, and kept the James Spence (St. Andrews) Limited name for a while. He used the "Flag-In-Hole" and monogrammed "JS" marks.

DRIVING IRON	$50	70	120

Circa 1915-1920. Dot-punched face.

MAXWELL HOSEL IRONS	$55	75	110

Circa 1915-1925. All irons. Flanged back, line or dot faces.

SPECIAL APPROACHING CLEEK	$55	75	110

Circa 1915-1920.

BLACKWELL PUTTER	$60	75	100

Circa 1920s. "Flag-in-Hole" mark on a beveled heel and toe, thick sole offset blade.

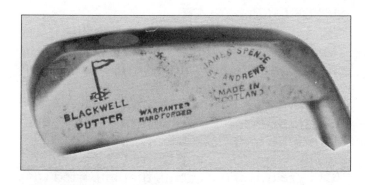

LARGE HEAD NIBLICK	$100	150	250

Circa 1915. Dot punched face. Nearly "Giant" size.

ST. ANDREW GOLF CO.

DUNFIRMLINE & GLASGOW, SCOTLAND

Began making clubs after 1900. They used the "Running Stag" mark and "Stag". It produced many clubs made from "Hawkin's Never Rust", a silvery metal.

SMOOTH-FACE BLADE PUTTER	$55	70	100

Circa 1900-1910. Deep-face, straight, compact blade. "The St. Andrew Golf Co., Ltd, Glasgow" stamping.

BLADE PUTTER	$55	70	100

Circa 1910-20. "Stag" marking.

STANDARD WRY NECK PUTTER	$60	75	110

Circa 1920. Line-scored offset hosel blade.

HAWKINS NEVER RUST PUTTER	$60	90	125

Circa 1920s. Monel metal flanged-back, offset hosel, line-scored blade.

STANDARD JIGGER	$40	55	80

Circa 1915-1920. Hyphen-scored face.

HAWKINS NEVER RUST IRONS	$55	70	95

Circa 1915-1920. All irons flanged back. "Running Stag" mark.

MAXWELL HOSEL IRONS $60 75 110

Circa 1915. Flanged back.

CONVEX FACE IRONS $60 75 100

Circa 1915-1920. "Running Stag" mark. Flanged back.

ANTI-SHANK IRONS $125 175 250

Circa 1920s. All irons. Fairlie's Patent. "Running Stag" mark.

ST ANDREW SPECIAL WOODS $90 120 160

Circa 1915-1920. Driver, brassie or spoon with large heads.

STADIUM GOLF CO.

LONDON, ENGLAND

The Williamson family owned the Stadium Golf Manufacturing Company, Ltd., and Hugh Williamson was in charge of running the business helped by manager Jimmie Ross. They produced particularly modern clubs for that time, and in 1929 the company folded. They used an "Anchor" with a large "S" mark.

KORECTA PUTTER $175 250 375

Circa 1920s. "V" sight groove notched in the "Pagoda" shaped top of the blade. "Anchor and S" mark.

MUSSEL BACK PUTTER $60 75 110

Circa 1925. "Anchor & S" mark. Square punched face scoring.

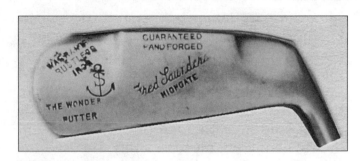

SCUFFLER SEMI PUTTER $175 275 375

Circa 1915-1920. "Rivers-Zambra" Approach putter "Reg'd no. 740870" on head.

DOT-PUNCHED-FACE IRONS $50 60 90

Circa 1915-1920. All irons with a dot punched face. "Anchor & S" mark.

WHITCOMBE JIGGER $50 65 100

Circa 1915-1920. "Anchor" mark at toe.

ANTI-SHANK IRONS $125 175 250

Circa 1920s. All irons. "Anchor-S" mark.

STANDARD GOLF CO.

SUNDERLAND, ENGLAND

William Mills broke tradition in the mid-1890s when he made fairway woods and putters from aluminum. "Standard Golf Company, Sunderland, England" was his mark. The company used markings on the soles to indicate model names and the like. Many aluminum woods and putters were exported to America. The Harry C Lee, Co. and BGI were two of the agents that imported vast numbers of "Mills" aluminum clubs.

Peter Georgiady wrote a three-part series on Mills and Standard Golf in the author's monthly publications #88, 89 and 90. Any collector of Mills clubs should include these articles in their library.

Patrick Kennedy produced a reprint of the 1909 Mills Retail Catalogue and this, too, should be required reading.

NEW RAY MILLS
MODEL   **$50**   **80**   **140**
Circa 1910-1915.

BRAID MILLS MODEL   **$50**   **80**   **140**
   Circa 1905-1915.

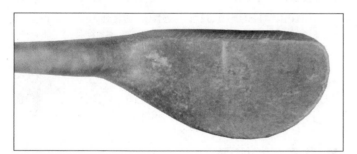

BRAID MILLS 1915
MODEL   **$55**   **85**   **150**
   Circa 1915-1920.

MILLS "SS" MODEL   **$75**   **120**   **175**
   Circa 1915-1920.

NEW MILLS "RNG"
MODEL   **$75**   **125**   **200**
   Circa 1910-1915. "T" Bar sight line.

NEW MILLS "RBB"
MODEL   **$90**   **135**   **200**
   Circa 1910-1915. Thick "sight line" on top.

NEW MILLS "RM"
MODEL   **$75**   **125**   **200**
   Circa 1910-1915.

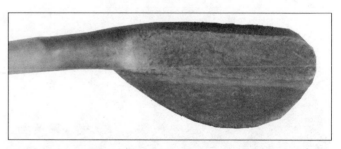

MILLS "L" MODEL   **$150**   **250**   **375**
   Circa 1900-1910. "L" model indicated long nose.

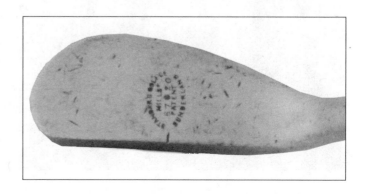

"MNB" MODEL
ALUMINUM HEAD $100   150   250

Circa 1910. Offset hosel. "Blade" type aluminum head with 10 to 12 degrees of loft.

BENT NECK "JM"
MODEL $100   175   250

Circa 1915.

MILLS "YS" MODEL $125   200   325

Circa 1905-1915.

NEW MILLS
"RSB" MODEL $125   175   300

Circa 1910-1915. "Slanted Back" head.

MILLS "Y" MODEL $150   275   450

Circa 1900-1910. Long-nose aluminum putter.

HILTON "X" MODEL $175   275   450

Circa 1910-1915. Long-nose head.

SCHENECTADY-TYPE
PUTTER $175   275   450

Circa 1903-1909. "Sunderland Golf Co" markings.

MILLS "RSR"
MODEL $175   250   400

Circa 1910-1915. Two hollowed out sight bars on either side of a hollowed out sight line.

MILLS "K" MODEL $200   400   650

Circa 1900-1910. Very long head.

MILLS "AK" MODEL $200   400   650

Circa 1910-1915. Rectangular head.

MILLS "RRA" MODEL $200   350   475

"Circa 1910-1915. Raised right angle aiming sight.

MILLS "SB" MODEL $200   300   425

Circa 1910-1915. Head is nearly "D" shaped.

MILLS "Z" MODEL $200   325   475

Circa 1900-1910. Long nose head.

"BSD" ALUMINUM
FAIRWAY WOODS $125   200   375

Circa 1895-1915. Long-head clubs. 1 cleek, 1-1/2 driving iron, 2 iron, and 2-1/2 medium lofter. "BSD" on sole.

"MSD" ALUMINUM
FAIRWAY WOODS $125   200   375

Circa 1895-1915. Short-head Clubs. 1 cleek, 1-1/2 Driving iron, 2 iron, and 2-1/2 medium lofter. "BSD" on sole.

"CB" SERIES
ALUMINUM WOODS $150   250   400

Circa 1915-1920. All clubs.

MSD ALUMINUM
FAIRWAY WOODS $225   350   650

Circa 1895-1915. Short head. 3-1/2. BSD on sole.

ALUMINUM DRIVERS $250   375   575

Circa 1900-1915. "D A" bulger face or "D B" Straight face."

THIS IS THE PUTTER !! YOU ARE ENQUIRING FOR.

The "BRAID-MILLS"
ALUMINIUM PUTTER,

as used by the OPEN CHAMPION, JAS. BRAID, and all the leading Professionals and Amateurs.

Jas. Braid, Open Champion, 1901, 1905, 1906, and 1908, says :—I used the Putter manufactured by you throughout the Championships. I certainly putt more consistently with it than any other.

Harry Vardon, Open Champion, 1896, 1898, 1899, 1903, says :—Since I have taken to your Aluminium Putter, I must say I have been able to putt more accurately with it.

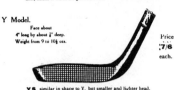

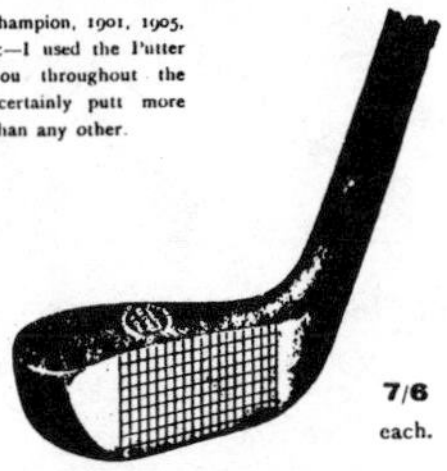

7/6 each.

BEWARE OF SPURIOUS IMITATIONS.

None are genuine unless stamped on top thus ☛ STANDARD GOLF Co MILLS PATENT SUNDERLAND and numbered above the word Patent. :: ::

This Putter (like all our Clubs) is made in any Weight and Lie to suit all players.

When the Leading Players find it an advantage to use our Putters, can you afford to be without one?
THEY INSPIRE CONFIDENCE.
Wonderful Clubs for long or short distances.

Particulars of Putters.

Marks on Sole.
On the Sole is stamped the Model, Lie, and exact Weight of the Head.

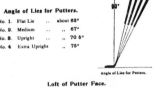

Angle of Lies for Putters.

No. 1. Flat Lie	..	about 63°
No. 2. Medium	.. ,,	67°
No. 3. Upright	.. ,,	70·5°
No. 4. Extra Upright	.. ,,	75°

Loft of Putter Face.
The Loft is made to our Standard (see page 23) but is made more or less to Customers' special requirements, viz. :—The "Braid-Mills" Putter is made equal to Brassie Loft, see page 23.

Weights of Heads.
The Heads are made between the minimum and maximum weights given as stated with each illustration.

As it is impossible to keep on hand the exact weights to suit every requirement, orders will be supplied from the nearest in stock, but exact weights can be made by giving a few days' notice.

Shafts.
The Shafts are made to our Standard, as follows :—
Flat, 36 in. ; Medium, 35 in. ; Upright and Extra Upright, 34 in., unless specially ordered otherwise.

The "MILLS" Patent Aluminium PUTTERS.

In order to suit the physical and other requirements of different players, the "MILLS" Putters are made in various Shapes, Weights, and Lies, details of which are given herewith.

Y Model.
Face about 4" long by about ⅞" deep.
Weight from 9 to 10½ ozs.

Price 7/6 each.

YS similar in shape to Y, but smaller and lighter head. Face about 3½" long by ⅞" deep.
X an exact copy of the Putter used by Mr. H. H. Hilton at the Championship, 1901.

L Model.
Face about 4" long by ⅞" deep.
Weight 9 to 11 ozs.

Price 7/6 each.

Z a Model between **Y** and **L.** This is a beautiful Model. We carry a full line of Left Hand Clubs in each Model. For Lie, Loft, &c., see page 22.

The "MILLS" Patent Aluminium
LONG, MID, BAFFY, AND BULGER SPOONS
as used by all the Leading Players.

ADVANTAGES :

Combine all the advantages of WOOD SPOONS, without their disadvantages. Are impervious to wet and practically indestructible. Will not rust nor alter balance. There are no parts to come loose, such as horn, &c. Perfectly balanced and true. The ball will not skid from face. Inspires confidence in play.

Will play all the Strokes that can be played with Irons. They are much easier to play with than Irons. Invaluable for Approaching.

THE PLAY CLUBS for the TWENTIETH CENTURY.

Prices :—
Finished Clubs, 7s. 6d. each.
Made in a variety of Shapes, Lies, and Weights, to suit all players

---

The "MILLS" Patent Aluminium PUTTERS.

S S Model.
Face about 4" long by about 1" deep.
Weight 9½ to 11 ozs.

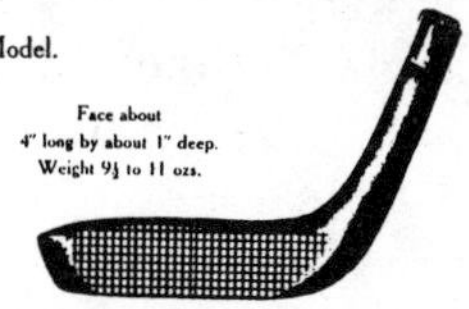

Price 7/6 each.

SB Model, shorter face than **S S**, almost like a Driver Head. This is the shortest and broadest Putter Head we make.

K L Model.
Face about 5" long by ⅞" deep.
Weight 9½ to 11 ozs.

Price 7/6 each.

K Model similar to **K L** but smaller and lighter Head. Face about 4½" long.

LADIES' CLUBS A SPECIALITY.

Booklet, "HINTS ON PUTTING" sent post free on application.

The "MILLS" Patent Aluminium
Long Spoons equivalent to CLEEKS.

M S D 1 Model, with SHORT HEAD and Deep Face.

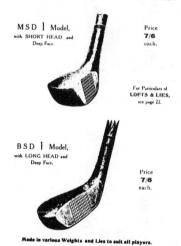

Price 7/6 each.

For Particulars of LOFTS & LIES, see page 22.

B S D 1 Model, with LONG HEAD and Deep Face.

Price 7/6 each.

Made in various Weights and Lies to suit all players.

The "MILLS" Patent Aluminium
MEDIUM LONG SPOONS equivalent to DRIVING IRONS.

M S D 1½ Model, with SHORT HEAD and Deep Face.

Price 7/6 each.

For Particulars of Lofts and Lies, see page 22.

B S D 1½ Model, with LONG HEAD and Deep Face.

Price 7/6 each.

Ladies' Clubs a Speciality, as supplied to H.R.H. The Duchess of Connaught.

The "MILLS" Patent Aluminium
MID-SPOONS equivalent to IRONS.

M S D 2 Model, with SHORT HEAD and Deep Face.

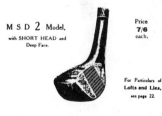

Price 7/6 each.

For Particulars of Lofts and Lies, see page 22.

B S D 2 Model, with LONG HEAD and Deep Face.

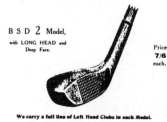

Price 7/6 each.

We carry a full line of Left Hand Clubs in each Model.

The "MILLS" Patent Aluminium
SHORT SPOONS equivalent to MEDIUM LOFTERS.

M S D 2½ Model, with SHORT HEAD and Deep Face.

Price 7/6 each.

For Particulars of Lofts and Lies, see page 22.

B S D 2½ Model, with LONG HEAD and Deep Face.

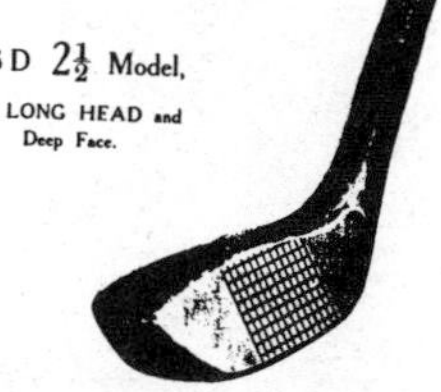

Price 7/6 each.

The Aluminium Spoons have a greater resiliency than Iron.

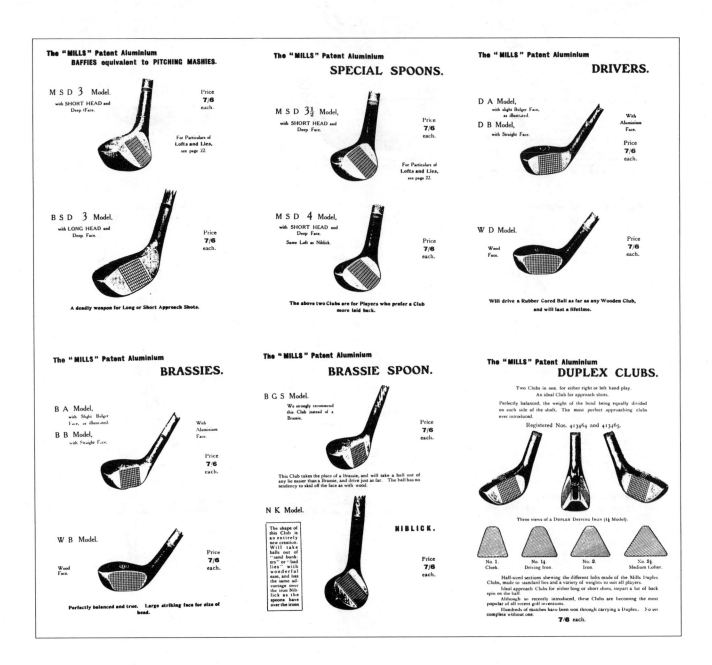

The "MILLS" Patent Aluminium
BAFFIES equivalent to PITCHING MASHIES.

M S D 3 Model.
with SHORT HEAD and Deep Face.

Price **7/6** each.

For Particulars of **Lofts and Lies,** see page 22.

B S D 3 Model.
with LONG HEAD and Deep Face.

Price **7/6** each.

A deadly weapon for Long or Short Approach Shots.

The "MILLS" Patent Aluminium
SPECIAL SPOONS.

M S D 3½ Model,
with SHORT HEAD and Deep Face.

Price **7/6** each.

For Particulars of **Lofts and Lies,** see page 22.

M S D 4 Model,
with SHORT HEAD and Deep Face.
Same Loft as Niblick.

Price **7/6** each.

The above two Clubs are for Players who prefer a Club more laid back.

The "MILLS" Patent Aluminium
DRIVERS.

D A Model,
with slight Bulger Face, as illustrated.

D B Model,
with Straight Face.

With Aluminium Face.

Price **7/6** each.

W D Model.
Wood Face.

Price **7/6** each.

Will drive a Rubber Cored Ball as far as any Wooden Club, and will last a lifetime.

The "MILLS" Patent Aluminium
BRASSIES.

B A Model,
with Slight Bulger Face, as illustrated.

B B Model,
with Straight Face.

With Aluminium Face.

Price **7/6** each.

W B Model.
Wood Face.

Price **7/6** each.

Perfectly balanced and true. Large striking face for size of head.

The "MILLS" Patent Aluminium
BRASSIE SPOON.

B G S Model.
We strongly recommend this Club instead of a Brassie.

Price **7/6** each.

This Club takes the place of a Brassie, and will take a ball out of any lie easier than a Brassie, and drive just as far. The ball has no tendency to skid off the face as with wood.

N K Model.

NIBLICK.

Price **7/6** each.

The shape of this Club is an entirely new creation. Will take balls out of "sand bunkers" or "bad lies" with wonderful ease, and has the same advantage over the iron Niblick as the spoons have over the irons

The "MILLS" Patent Aluminium
DUPLEX CLUBS.

Two Clubs in one, for either right or left hand play. An ideal Club for approach shots.

Perfectly balanced, the weight of the head being equally divided on each side of the shaft. The most perfect approaching clubs ever introduced.

Registered Nos. 413464 and 413465.

Three views of a DUPLEX DRIVING IRON (1½ Model).

| No. 1. Cleek. | No. 1½. Driving Iron. | No. 2. Iron. | No. 2½. Medium Lofter. |

Half-sized sections shewing the different lofts made of the Mills Duplex Clubs, made to standard lies and a variety of weights to suit all players.

Ideal approach Clubs for either long or short shots, impart a lot of back spin on the ball.

Although so recently introduced, these Clubs are becoming the most popular of all recent golf inventions.

Hundreds of matches have been won through carrying a Duplex. No set complete without one. **7/6** each.

"MSD" ALUMINUM
FAIRWAY WOODS   **$275**   **450**   **750**

Circa 1895-1915. Short head. 3 Pitching mashie. "BSD" on sole.

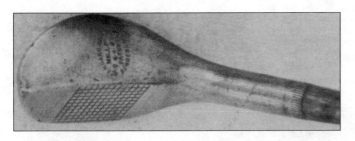

ALUMINUM
BRASSIES   **$250**   **375**   **575**

Circa 1900-1915. "B A" bulger face or "B B" straight face."

BSD ALUMINUM
FAIRWAY WOODS   **$275**   **450**   **750**

Circa 1895-1915. Long head. 3 pitching mashie. "BSD" on sole.

DUPLEX
ALUMINUM WOODS   **$350**   **550**   **1000**

Circa 1900-1915. 1 cleek, 1-1/2 Driving iron, 2 iron, and 2-1/2 medium lofter.

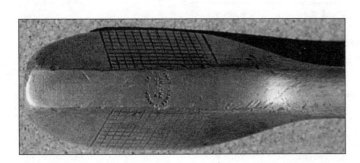

MSD NIBLICK WOOD $400   650   1200

Circa 1895-1915. Short head. 4 or "NK". "BSD" on sole.

STEWART, TOM

ST. ANDREWS, SCOTLAND
by Ralph Livingston

One of the most recognizable maker's marks is the "Clay Pipe"-shaped cleek mark of Thomas Stewart Jr. of St. Andrews, Scotland.

The "Pipe of Peace" cleek mark is stamped into the back of the club head centered along the sole. From 1893 to 1904, Stewart used the pipe and also a "Serpent" (Stewart's mark for a ladies club) cleek mark. In July 1904, his registration mark was approved and from thereafter, the stamping "T.S. St. A. REG. TRADEMARK" was added beneath the "Pipe" mark.

Stewart quickly gained a reputation for making clubs of the highest quality. Many of his clients were the top professionals and amateurs of that time. Today, he is best known for the clubs he made for Bobby Jones, Francis Ouimet, Harry Vardon and countless others.

When Stewart would personally supervise the making of a club, he would stamp a "Dot" into the toe on the back of the club. Approximately one in fifty clubs has Stewart's personal inspection mark. There are other inspection marks and these are attributed to his best associate clubmakers.

One of the most logical aspects of his business was that he sold only club heads. Most of his production was sold to professionals and retailers who would have their staff do the assembly. For a small fee, the club heads were personalized with the professional's name and golf course or the retailer's advertisement. Consequently, many "Pipe" marked irons have names other than "Stewart" stamped on their backs.

ORD PUTTER   **$50**   **65**   **100**

Circa 1920. Line-scored blade. "Pipe" mark.

PUTTING CLEEK   **$55**   **85**   **125**

Circa 1920. Line-scored faced. "Pipe" mark.

SMOOTH FACE
PUTTING CLEEK   **$60**   **85**   **125**

Circa 1910. Marked "Slazenger Special New York". "Pipe" mark.

GEM PUTTER   **$70**   **100**   **150**

Circa 1915-1920. Rounded back. "Pipe" mark.

Excerts From Tom Stewart's 1930 Catalog

LIST OF GOLF IRON HEADS.

PUTTERS OR PUTT. CLEEKS.

1. Putters or Putt. Cleeks, Ordinary.
1. Do.   Round Back.
1. Do.   Diamond Back.
1. Do.   Deep Face.
1. Do.   'Accurate.'
1. Do.   „   Round Back.
1. Do.   „   Diamond Back.
1. Do.   Park Pattern.
1. Do.   Special—Blade bent at neck.
1. Do.   Sherlock Pattern.
1. Do.   F. G. Tait Pattern.
1. Do.   Rowland Jones Pattern.
1. Do.   Gun Metal.
2. Do.   Fairlie Pattern.
3. Do.   Logan Pattern.
3. Do.   Celtic Pattern.
1. Do.   R. T. J. Pattern.

3. Putters—Gem or '100.'
3. Do.   Gem 'Accurate' Bend.
4. Do.   Ballingall.
4. Do.   Smith—Hollow Back.
4. Do.   'Stewart' Patent.
4. Do.   Kinnell.
   Do.   Humphry.
6. Do.   'A.B.' Pattern, as used by Harry Vardon.
3. Do.   Auchterlonie.
6. Do.   'D.S.' Pattern.
   Do.   Aluminium.
4. Do.   Maxwell Pattern.
2. Do.   Citizen.

CLEEKS.

Cleeks—Ordinary, Driving and Approaching.
1. Do.   Ordinary, Long Head.

Sets of Iron Heads made similar to those used by the late Mr. F. G. Tait.

LIST OF GOLF IRON HEADS—Continued.

1. Cleeks—Ordinary, Short Head.
1. Do.   Bevel Heel.
1. Do.   „   and Toe.
1. Do.   Diamond Back.
1. Do.   Round Back.
1. Do.   Mussel Back.
1. Do.   Bulger Back.
1. Do.   Round Sole.
   Do.   Concentrated (Various).
1. Do.   The 'Nipper.'
1. Do.   Sammy.
2. Do.   Fairlie Pattern.
3. Do.   Braid or 'Auchterlonie' Pattern.
3. Do.   Logan Pattern.
3. Do.   Celtic Pattern.
4. Do.   Smith Pattern.
5. Do.   Smith Pattern—Hollow Back.
4. Do.   Carruthers Pattern.
4. Do.   Ballingall Pattern.
4. Do.   Maxwell Pattern.

IRONS.

Irons—assorted.
1. Do.   Mid.
1. Do.   Ordinary.
1. Do.   No. 1.
1. Do.   No. 2.
1. Do.   No. 3.
1. Do.   No. 4.
1. Do.   Bevel Heel.
1. Do.   „   and Toe.
1. Do.   Diamond Back.
1. Do.   Round Back.
1. Do.   Mussel Back.
1. Do.   Bulger Back.
1. Do.   Round Sole.
   Do.   Concentrated (Various).
2. Do.   Fairlie Pattern.
3. Do.   Logan Pattern.
3. Do.   Celtic Pattern.
4. Do.   Smith Pattern.

Sets of Iron Heads made similar to those used by the late Tom Morris.

5. Irons—Smith Pattern—Hollow Back.
4. Do.   Ballingall Pattern.
3. Do.   Auchterlonie Pattern.
4. Do.   Maxwell Pattern.

MASHIES.

Mashies—Assorted.
1. Do.   Deep Face.
1. Do.   Vardon Pattern.
1. Do.   Ordinary Pattern—Narrow Face.
1. Do.   Herd Pattern.
1. Do.   Kirkaldy Pattern.
1. Do.   Jamie Anderson Pattern.
1. Do.   Bevel Heel.
1. Do.   „   and Toe.
1. Do.   Diamond Back.
1. Do.   Round Back.
1. Do.   Mussel Back.
1. Do.   Bulgar Back.
1. Do.   Round Sole.

Mashies—Concentrated (Various).
1. Do.   Extra Deep Face.
1. Do.   Lofting.
2. Do.   Fairlie Pattern.
3. Do.   Logan Pattern.
3. Do.   Celtic Pattern.
4. Do.   Smith Pattern.
5. Do.   Smith Pattern—Hollow Back.
4. Do.   Ballingall Pattern.
3. Do.   Auchterlonie Pattern.
4. Do.   Maxwell Pattern.

JIGGERS.

Jiggers (Assorted).
1. Do.   Ordinary.
1. Do.   Round Back.
1. Do.   Diamond Back.
1. Do.   Hilton Pattern (in four different lofts, Nos. 1, 2, 3 and 4.
Do.   Concentrated (Various).

Driving Irons made similar to that as used by the late Jack Kirkcaldy.

2. Jiggers—Fairlie Pattern.
3. Do.   Auchterlonie Pattern (or ' Braid ').
3. Do.   Logan Pattern.
3. Do.   Celtic Pattern.
4. Do.   Smith Pattern.
4. Do.   Maxwell Pattern.

NIBLICKS.

Niblicks (Assorted).
1. Do.   Ordinary.
1. Do.   Deep Face.
1. Do.   Extra Large Heads.
1. Do.   Diamond Back.
1. Do.   Round Back.
2. Do.   Fairlie Pattern.
3. Do.   Logan Pattern.
3. Do.   Celtic Pattern.
4. Do.   Smith Pattern.
5. Do.   Smith Pattern—Hollow Back.
4. Do.   Maxwell Pattern.

MASHIE NIBLICKS, etc.
1. Mashie Niblick—Deep Face.
1. Do.   ' Benny Pattern.'
3. Do.   ' Young Benny ' Pattern.
1. Do.   Round Top and Straight Sole.
1. Do.   Egg Shape.
2. Do.   Fairlie Pattern—Deep Face.
3. Do.   Logan Pattern.
3. Do.   Celtic Pattern.
4. Do.   Smith Pattern
5. Do.   Smith Pattern—Hollow Back.
4. Do.   Maxwell Pattern.
1. Mashie Cleeks.
1. Do.   Irons—Deep Face.
1. Do.   „   Bevel Heel.
1. Driving Mashie.
1. Do.   Irons.
1. Push-Shot Irons.
1. Lofting Irons, etc., etc.
1. Spade Mashies.

Any pattern of head made to order.
Sets of Iron Heads made as used by Mr. Robert T. Jones.

STEWART'S PATENT PUTTER.

The chief feature of this club is in its broad sole, combined with a heavy top edge, which keeps the ball from 'jumping' when struck.

This pattern of putter is used by many professionals, also many prominent amateurs, including Mr. E. A. Lassen, Ex-Amateur Champion.

"SHERLOCK PUTTER."

This putter is a copy of Jas. Sherlock's own club (Pipe Brand). 'Sherlock' *Autograph* Putters can only be obtained direct from Mr. James Sherlock, Golf Club, Hunstanton.

"A. B." PUTTER.

The 'A. B.' Putter as *used* by Harry Vardon, Open Champion, is after the model of Gem Putter, having a heavy sole and a narrow face.

THE BALLINGALL PUTTER.

This pattern of putter, with a flange sole and invented by Mr. Ballingall, is the favourite style of putter in Ireland, and is used by Mr. Lionel Munn, Irish Amateur Champion, and most of the leading professionals of " Erin."

AUCHTERLONIE APP. CLEEK.

This Approaching Cleek, frequently called the ' Braid App. Cleek,' is the same as made for and played with by James Braid. (The Ex-Open Champion's club is ' *Pipe* ' Brand.) This club, which has a centre-balanced blade, is greatly praised by the Ex-Champion (see ' Braid's Book on Golf '), and has now a great hold on the market, both at home and abroad.

Nos. 1, 2, 3 and 4 Irons.

The professional kit does not seem to be complete now-a-days without this set of Irons, which range in loft from a driving Iron to that of a Lofting Iron.

This set of heads is used and played with (all ' Pipe ' Brand) by Arnaud Massy, Alex. Herd, etc.

"VARDON" MASHIE.

The Vardon pattern of Mashie ('Pipe' Brand) is the most 'sought after' pitching club of the day, and is specially made to the direction of the Open Champion.

"SMITH HEADS."

A pattern of club which has received considerable attention of late is that known as the "Smith" pattern.

R T J PUTTER   **$150**   **250**   **450**
Circa 1930. "Pipe" mark.

NEW ZEALAND CLUBS   **$75**   **125**   **200**
Circa 1910. "Hood & Clements, Christchurch". Bent neck, smooth-face blade putter. "Pipe" mark.

BRASS PUTTER   **$100**   **150**   **275**
Circa 1900. No registration marks under "Pipe" mark.

BRASS PUTTER   **$150**   **225**   **350**
Circa 1895. "Serpent" mark.

R T J PUTTER   **$200**   **375**   **500**
Circa 1930. "R T J" in block letters.

PATENTED "V"
BACK PUTTER   **$300**   **400**   **600**
Circa 1920. "V" groove hollow back design.

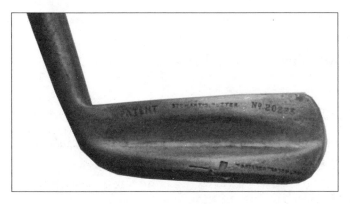

TWEENIE IRON   **$80**
Circa 1920s. Rounded sole line scored club. Similar to a "Bobbie" iron. "Pipe" mark.

LARGE HEAD
NIBLICK   **$150**   **200**   **350**
Circa 1900. Smooth face without registration marks under the "Pipe" mark.

DIAMOND BACK
IRONS   **$45**   **60**   **100**
Circa 1910-1920. Dot-punched face. "Pipe" mark.

JIGGERS   **$50**   **70**   **120**
Circa 1920. With broad flat sole, line scored. "Pipe" mark.

HARRY VARDON
IRONS   **$60**   **95**   **150**
Circa 1920. "Pipe" mark.

BOBBIE IRON   **$70**   **100**   **150**
Circa 1920. Broad, rounded sole. Line-scored face. "Pipe" mark.

SAMMY IRON   **$75**   **100**   **150**
Circa 1915. Dot-punched face. "Pipe" mark.

CONCAVE FACE
LOFTER   **$75**   **125**   **200**
Circa 1900. No registration marks under the "Pipe" mark.

T STEWART
MAKER IRONS   **$75**   **95**   **150**
Circa 1910. Smooth-face cleek. "Pipe" mark.

CLUBS FOR
CAIRO, EGYPT   **$75**   **125**   **200**
Circa 1915. All irons. "Pipe" mark.

TOM MORRIS IRONS   **$80**   **125**   **200**
Circa 1920s. Line scored face. "Pipe" mark.

"R T J" IRONS   **$90**   **125**   **175**
Circa 1930. Line scored face.

TOM MORRIS IRONS $100   175   300
Circa teens. Dot-punched face. "Pipe" mark."

F O, R T J" IRONS $100   175   250
Circa 1930. (Francis Ouimet, Robert T. Jones) initials at toe. "Pipe" mark.

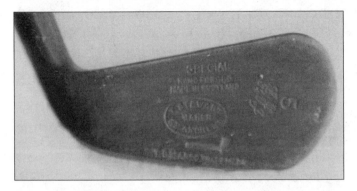

TOM MORRIS IRONS $125   250   400
Circa 1905-1915. Smooth face. "Pipe" mark.

PIPE MARK AT TOE $125   200   350
Circa 1898. Smooth-face general purpose iron.

SERPENT MARK IRONS $125   175   300
Circa 1898-1902. Clubs marked "Slazenger Special New York" smooth face.

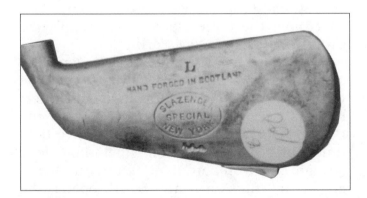

ANTI-SHANK IRONS $125   200   300
Circa 1915-1920. Smith's Model. Dot-punched face. "Pipe" mark.

TOM MORRIS IRONS $175   350   600
Circa Pre-1905. Smooth face. No registration marks below "Pipe" mark.

TOM MORRIS IRONS $175   350   600
Circa pre-1898. Smooth face. "Serpent" mark.

RUT NIBLICK $200   350   600
Circa 1895. Medium-size round head. Smooth face. "Pipe" or "Serpent" mark.

URQUHART, ROBERT

Robert Urquhart first patented an adjustable iron in 1892. His marks were a "U" in a circle and "Urquhart" in large letters on the face of the iron.

ADJUSTABLE IRON
Circa 1900-1905. "Urquhart" across face.

VICKER'S LIMITED

SHEFFIELD, ENGLAND

Vicker's Limited operated from 1924 to 1932. They made stainless steel heads sold under the name "Immaculate". Their market also included North America. They used a double "K" on either side of a "V" as their cleek mark.

RUSTLESS IRONS $45   55   75
Circa late 1920s. All irons. "Double K" mark.

IMMACULATE
RUSTLESS PUTTER $50   60   85

Circa 1925-1930. Double "K" mark.

VULCAN GOLF CO.

PORTSMOUTH, OHIO

Began making clubs during the mid 1920s. Used "Vulcan" in a monogram as its mark. Made the "Burma" 7-inch-long pencil thin hosel putter. "Septum" and "Pirate" were other markings.

LONG HOSEL
PUTTER $100   145   175

Circa 1926-1930. 6-1/2 inch long hosel. "Burma 8 Putter" on back.

PIRATE SERIES
IRONS $35   45   75

Circa 1930. All irons

LONG HOSEL PUTTER $100   135   175

Circa 1926-1930. 6-1/2 inch long hosel. "Septum Putter" on back.

SEPTUM SERIES
IRONS $35   45   75

Circa 1927. All irons.

DRIVING IRON $50   60   90

Circa 1930. Stainless steel.

SEPTUM SERIES
WOODS $75   95   135

Circa 1927. Driver, brassie or spoon.

WALTER HAGEN & L.A. YOUNG CO.

by Pete Georgiady

If the truth were told, Walter Hagen never made a golf club in his life though there are thousands that bear his name. His career as a professional and champion was radically different from any of his peers and Hagen's style of living and playing left an indelible mark on the game of golf.

Born in upstate New York in 1892, he first drew the notice of the golfing world as a dapper young U.S. Open champion at Midlothian in 1914, fast on the heels of Ouimet's sensational victory a year earlier. He was, at that time, the professional to Oak Hill Golf Club in Rochester, New York.

Following his win in 1914, Hagen went on a blitz through the next 13 years where he won every major championship at least once. He was twice the U.S. Open and twice the British Open champion, was a five-time American PGA champion (including four straight), he won both the Eastern and Western opens, the North and South opens, the French Open and a grand number of state championships.

But Hagen did more than win; he won with a style and flamboyance that golf had never witnessed before. He was not the typical pro making clubs and giving lessons. Hagen passed time with royalty and the most celebrated people in society. He wore the fin-

Look at These Clubs!

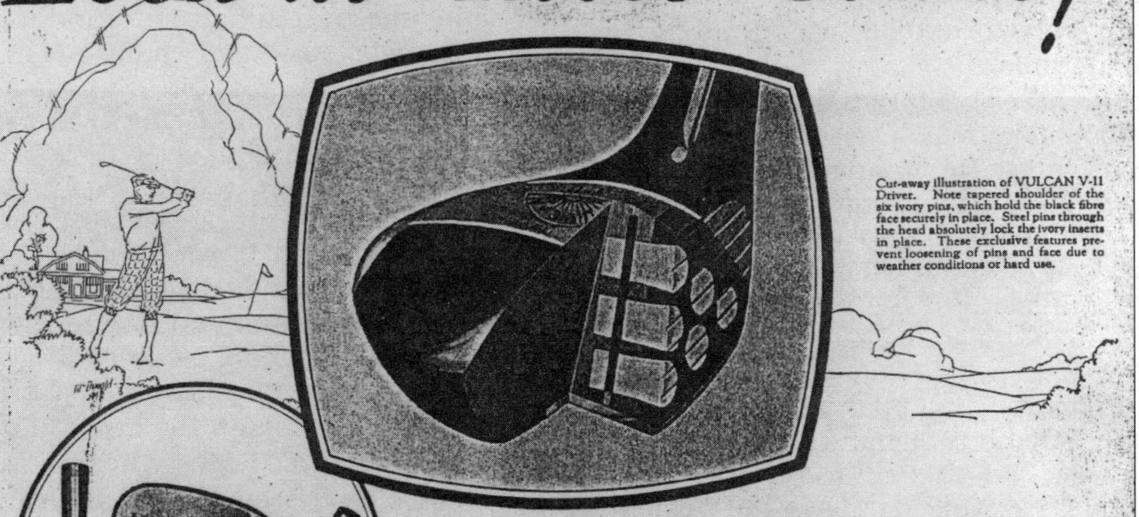

Cut-away illustration of VULCAN V-11 Driver. Note tapered shoulder of the six ivory pins, which hold the black fibre face securely in place. Steel pins through the head absolutely lock the ivory inserts in place. These exclusive features prevent loosening of pins and face due to weather conditions or hard use.

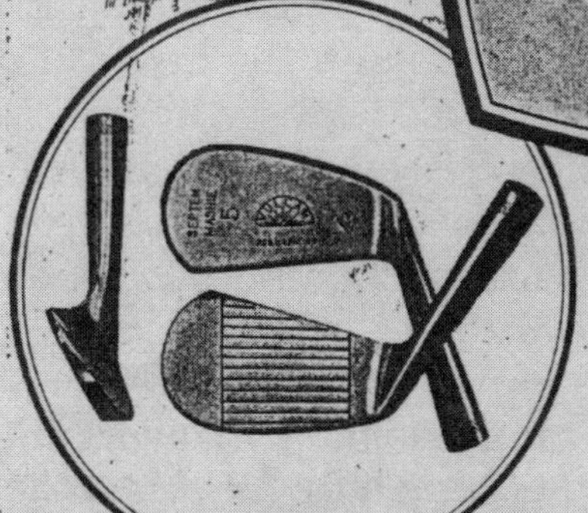

The SEPTEM No. 5 Mashie, shown here, is one of eight perfectly balanced Iron Clubs, including the No. 1 Driving Iron, No. 2 Mid-Iron, No. 3 Mashie Iron, No. 4 Jigger, No. 5 Mashie, No. 6 Mashie Niblick, No. 7 Niblick and No. 8 Putter. VULCAN "Pirate" Irons (popularly priced) are also numbered from 1 to 8.

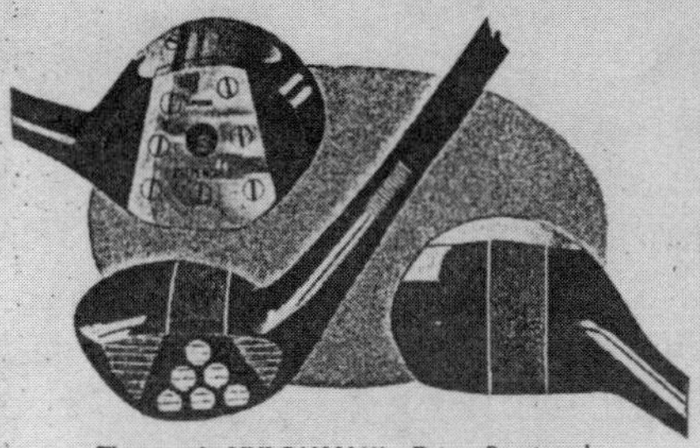

These are the VULCAN V-11's—Driver, Brassie and Spoon (see cross-section above). A wonderful model finished in Ebony, with broad natural stripe. Shafts of finest steel or selected first-grade hickory—15" bell top of best leather.

IT'S time you got your hands on one of these new VULCANS, gave it a heft and a swing—realized the dawn of a new day in golf cooperation. - - - -

Here is *Confidence!* on the end of a shaft of live hickory or steel; confidence that you and these clubs are made for each other—confidence that they are tuned, faced, balanced and shaped to hit a ball how and where you want it to go. - - - - -

Those who made VULCAN Golf Clubs possible, men who have given many years and famous talents to fine club production, call this "Character." The instant you test a VULCAN club you will recognize it, will sense the confidence it instills. - - - - - - - -

And just that closer feeling between hands and club marks the difference between yesterday's finest and VULCAN. - - - - - -

VULCAN Character is the product of a group whose special talents have long been given to fine golf equipment, whose leader has supervised production of five million of America's best known golf clubs. This ripe experience, refreshed with new opportunity, has outdone itself.

VULCAN GOLF COMPANY
PORTSMOUTH, OHIO, U.S.A.

GOLF **VULCAN** GOLF

Clubs of Character for Every Golfer

NOTE: Ask your Club Professional or your favorite dealer to show you a set ot VULCAN Clubs. If he has not yet been supplied ask him to write to us immediately or, better yet, send us his name and address, as well as your own.

© 1927 V. L. Co.

est clothes and drove the most luxurious autos. He lived on his terms and his terms were that he was allowed in the clubhouse where the professional was formerly forbidden. His high style caused consternation in the ranks, but in the end it helped upgrade the lot of the club pro whose existence was generally less than honorable.

The never-bashful Hagen was the original endorsement magnet and lent his image to many products. He was said to have carried 25 clubs in his bag at one time just to cover his endorsements. In the early 1920s, Hagen's primary golf club affiliation was with Burke, which manufactured the monel metal Walter Hagen autograph series. Walter also imported clubs for sale in his shop with Cochrane's of Edinburgh supplying many of the irons bearing Hagen's famous signature.

In the mid-1920s Hagen was enticed to leave New York, while he was at the Westchester-Biltmore, and move to Red Run Country Club in Royal Oak outside Detroit. The auto business was making Detroit a city on the rise and this prosperity created some new opportunities for Walter.

Prior to this time, Hagen's involvement in the golf club business was minimal. He sold clubs through his shop at the various clubs that employed him but actually had little part in the clubmaking end, instead employing good workers who could. He was one of the new breed of pros who sold the clubs of others, spending more time on the course playing competitively.

Hagen's reputation was based on an association with the best of everything. In 1925 he decided to market his own brand of clubs, striking a partnership with his friend, Detroit industrialist Leonard A. Young, owner of a wire and steel company. From 1926 onward, Walter Hagen brand clubs were made exclusively by the L.A. Young Co. Naturally, Hagen played his own brand and to illustrate the change pervading the club business, he played a mixed set. His deluxe model N2 woods were available only with steel shafts while his Walter Hagen De Luxe registered iron sets came with hickory shafts. The complete set of three woods and nine irons, including putter, cost $115. The most expensive bag in his line was $100. Hagen's top-of-the-line goods were not for the economy-minded person.

But there were clubs for those at the lower end. The same iron sets were also sold in forged steel, in a non-registered series. Then came the Autograph brand followed by the Triangle brand and finally WH clubs, with all three brands available in woods and irons. For the beginner were Getaway brand irons at $27.50 for the 11 club set.

In premium woods, the Walter Hagen De Luxe models were also fitted with steel shafts, but the Autograph models came with the choice of wood or steel. By 1930 additional mid-grade models included Arrow, Champion and Star-Line clubs.

The Hagen line contained two unique clubs. Capitalizing on the quality theme, the company produced a very limited number of sterling silver headed blade putters which could be engraved for use as trophies and awards. Made by Lambert Brothers in New York, they are rare today.

The club most associated with the firm is the notorious Hagen concave sand iron, designed and patented by Edwin McClain. It was the first production club with a "flange" on its sole for the use in sand bunkers. It was also concave, which caused it to be banned from use in 1930. However, flat-faced clubs with the same flange followed and have been indispensable ever since. The next model sand iron, the "Iron Man", was also produced with a hickory shaft for a short time before being transitioned to steel.

Another popular club was the aluminum headed putter called "The Haig". Many had the flat ended paddle grip and today a few can be found with hickory shafts, though the vast majority was produced with steel.

GETAWAY SERIES

PUTTER	**$40**	**50**	**70**

Circa late 1920s.

HAGEN

AUTOGRAPH PUTTER	**$45**	**55**	**75**

Circa late 1920s. Chromed blade.

LUCKY LEN PUTTER $250   350   450
Circa 1930-1935. Wooden-head mallet.

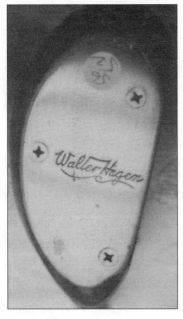

**THE HAIG
ALUMINUM PUTTER** $150   200   250
Circa 1930-1935. Paddle grip.

**STERLING
SILVER PUTTER** $700   900   125
Circa 1930. "Sterling" marked on hosel.

**GETAWAY SERIES
IRONS** $35   45   65
Circa late 1920s. All irons.

**HAGEN
AUTOGRAPH IRONS** $35   45   65
Circa late 1920s. All irons.

**CONCAVE SAND
WEDGE** $300   500   750
Circa 1930. Smooth concave face. Large flange.

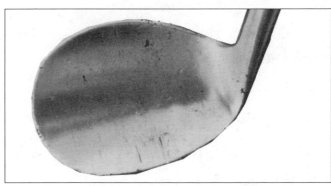

**IRON MAN SAND
WEDGE** $125   200   325
Circa 1930. Large flange. Dot face.

**HAGEN
AUTOGRAPH WOODS** $75   95   150
Circa late 1920s. Driver, brassie or spoon.

**GETAWAY
SERIES WOODS** $75   95   150
Circa late 1920s. Driver, brassie or spoon.

WHITE, JACK

SUNNINGDALE, ENGLAND
Began making clubs in the early 1890s and continued through the late 1920s. Most of his clubs are marked Sunningdale with the "Sun" mark. Famous for making clubs for Bobby Jones.

AUTOGRAPH
RUSTLESS PUTTER $55   65   85

Circa 1925-1930. "Sun" mark.

MUSSEL BACK
IRONS $50   65   95

Circa 1920s. "Sun" mark.

DOT PUNCHED
FACE IRONS $50   60   90

Circa 1915-1920. "Sun" mark.

SUNNINGDALE
WOODS $100   135   190

Circa 1920. Driver, brassie or spoon.

SPLICED-NECK
WOODS $200   325   475

Circa 1900-1910. Driver, brassie or spoon.

WHITE, ROBERT

ST. ANDREWS, SCOTLAND

Began making clubs in the late 1870s. Marked his clubs with "R. White, Maker, St. Andrews" in an oval configuration. Clubs with full Robert White markings are scarce and command a premium.

BRASS-HEAD
PUTTERS $250   375   550

Circa 1880-1890. Straight brass blade. "R. White, St. Andrews, Maker" mark.

SMOOTH-FACE
IRONS $250   400   650

Circa 1880-1890. General purpose iron or lofter. "R. White, Maker, St. Andrews" on back.

SMOOTH-FACE
CLEEK $275   425   675

Circa 1880-1890. Cleek. "R. White, Maker, St. Andrews" on back.

RUT IRON $900   1500   2500

Circa 1880-1890. Small rounded head. "R. White, Maker, St. Andrews" on back.

WILLIAMS, J. H. & CO.

BROOKLYN, NY

Began forging clubs prior to 1900 in Brooklyn, NY. Made iron heads for putters and irons marking them with a tiny "Diamond" and a "W" inside. The mark is found stamped into the hosel. "J H Williams Co, Brooklyn" in block letters was also used. They made fine-quality club heads.

SMOOTH FACE
BLADE $60   90   125

Circa 1895-1900. "Diamond in W" mark on hosel.

PARK STYLE
PUTTER $125   175   250

Circa 1900. Severely bent neck blade. "W" in "Diamond" mark.

WILSON, R. B.

ST. ANDREWS, SCOTLAND

"Buff" began forging clubs during the late 1880's in St. Andrews. He served as an apprentice to Old Tom Morris before opening his own shop. His (OK) brand irons were very popular in America.

OK SPECIAL IRONS $60   90   125

Circa 1900. All irons. Smooth face

SMOOTH-FACE
BLADE PUTTER $60   80   125

Circa 1900. "R. B. Wilson" in block letters.

GOOSE-NECK
PUTTER $75   100   150

Circa 1900. "R. B. Wilson OK Special" mark.

ONE PIECE WOOD $1200 1800 2500

Circa 1900. Smooth face round head.

SMOOTH-FACE
IRONS $70   100   175

Circa 1900. All irons. Smooth face.

RUT NIBLICK $250   400   650

Circa 1900. Smooth face round head.

WILSON, ROBERT,

ST. ANDREWS, SCOTLAND

Began forging clubs about 1870 in St. Andrews and continued until about 1905. His marks were "R. Wilson, St. Andrews" and a bent "horseshoe" nail.

PUTTING CLEEK $300   450   750

Circa 1889-1890. "R. Wilson, Maker, St Andrews" mark.

SMOOTH-FACE
IRONS $250   400   650

Circa 1889-1890. All irons. "R. Wilson, Maker, St Andrews" mark.

ANTI-SHANK IRONS $175   225   300

Circa 1900. All irons. "R. Wilson, Maker, St Andrews" mark.

SMOOTH-FACE
CLEEK IRONS $300   450   750

Circa 1889-1890. "R. Wilson, Maker, St Andrews" mark.

WILSON, THOMAS E.

CHICAGO, IL
by Pete Georgiady

Ever since the first national championship unofficially pitted golfers from Chicago against the Boston/NewYork establishment, the Windy City was a hotbed for early golf in the United States. Its highly developed industrial manufacturing base quickly adapted and the area became the home of several major golf manufacturing companies.

The Wilson Company, like so many of its contemporaries, entered the golf market as an adjunct to its primary products. In 1913 the group that would soon become Wilson was named the Ashland Manufacturing Company. Located on Chicago's Ashland Avenue it was a subsidiary of the meat packing firm of Schwartzchild and Sulzberger. Ashland was an outlet for goods delivered from meat by-products, namely intestines and entrails which they used to produce gut strings for banjoes, violins, tennis rackets and also surgical sutures. Looking to expand its fortunes, the company also began trading in tennis rackets, hunting and camping equipment, bicycles, phonographs and automobile tires.

Within a year, Ashland was in receivership and a New York-based bank assumed control. The bank chose a successful meat packing executive named Thomas E. Wilson to head its new investment because of his demonstrated managerial ability. In 1914, the name was changed to the Thomas E. Wilson Co., and the firm moved from its Ashland Avenue location to Chicago's south side. There was great irony in the hiring of Thomas Wilson because the owners of the company had already decided to name the firm the Wilson Company in an effort to draw upon the successes of the very popular President Woodrow Wilson. Still trading in diverse commodities, the rejuvenated Wilson Co. began manufacturing its own products in 1916.

Thomas Wilson was experienced with company acquisitions and charted a similar course for his new firm. Driven to make the company the best in the sporting goods field, he purchased an Ohio company already making leather balls, baseball gloves and harness gear, and moved it to Chicago. Next, the Indestructo Caddy Bag Manufacturing Co. was purchased and Wilson quickly entered the golf business in a big way.

In 1925, the young company underwent its first name change when it merged with Western Sporting Goods Manufacturing Co., also of Chicago and the newly merged company used the name Wilson-Western Sporting Goods Co. Finally, in 1931, the name changed to the familiar Wilson Sporting Goods.

Earliest Wilson golf clubs are actually marked with the Ashland Manufacturing Company's "A.M. Co." monogram in a circle. Most of these heads were obtained from MacGregor and were additionally stamped with retail or professional's names. The first clubs actually bearing the Wilson name were from the Plus Success series with the model name in very small block letters dating from about 1916 or 1917. Slightly later were irons from the same series where the lettering is contained inside a large W. These irons all date from 1917-1918, although Plus Success clubs were available in several other variations continuing into the 1920s.

In the early 1920s, Wilson introduced its Aim Rite symbol, which would appear on many clubs through the decade. In one of these similar designs, it was commonly placed on the face of the club at the sweet spot. Alternately, a mark of concentric circles was found at the sweet spot. Both of these marks were registered as trademarks and they also served to help golfers align the club face with the ball, useful since the vast ma-

jority of Aim Rite clubs were sold through stores to economy minded customers. But the golf market in the 1920s was booming just as the stock market was and lower-end merchandise was selling very well to the new golfers learning the sport.

The all-time best selling Wilson series was the Wilsonian model of mid-priced clubs. Available throughout the 1920s, it was the mainstay of the company's club selection. All Wilsonian models were available in ladies weights and junior and juvenile sizes. Many of the early Wilsonian irons, as well as other models, were also stamped "Hammer Forged" with the mark of the ball peen hammer, the sign of a better quality product.

Wilson continued low priced domination throughout the post war era with many sets of clubs with names like Carnoustie, Cup Defender, Dixie, Lincoln Park, Linkhurst, Pinehurst, Skokie, Streak and Taplow. Because of their economical nature, most were configured with two woods, four irons (2, 5, 7, 9) and putter. In trying to complete a full set, collectors are often frustrated by searching for the in between numbers which were never produced. In the late 1920s, brightly colored leather grips became fashionable and several lines were sold with bright red, blue or green leather.

One of the more uncommon Wilson clubs produced was the Baxpin model deep-groove mashie which was also stamped for and sold to another Chicago manufacturer, Burrkey. Early deep-groove clubs can also be found with the old Ashland Manufacturing Co., markings, too. Another unique product is the Walker Cup set which featured rainbow pattern grooves on the faces of the irons. Introduced in the mid-1920s, the use of that name on a set of clubs is an indication of how important amateur competitions were during those times.

As the company became solidly established as a maker and seller of golf supplies, it also ventured into the country club market for higher grade equipment. Its Red Ribbon and Blue Ribbon sets were positioned for pro shop sales and were used by many tour golfers. Also in the prestige club category was Wilson's Harry Vardon "72" set with its readily identifiable green grips. Two collectible Wilson putter models from this period are the Amby-dex two-way putter and the Kelly Klub. In the 1940s, Wilson would begin its advisory staff program whose roots were established some fifteen years earlier with endorsements from young Gene Sarazen, Johnny Farrell, and the mature Ted Ray who won the 1920 U.S. Open at age 43. All three golfers lent their signatures to Wilson's first autograph lines of clubs.

WILSONIAN PUTTER $35   45   65
Circa late 1920s.

**CUP DEFENDER
PUTTER** $35   45   65
Circa late 1920s.

RED RIBBON PUTTER $35   45   65
Circa late 1920s.

**JOCK HUTCHISON
MEDALIST PUTTER** $40   50   70
Circa 1925-1930. Offset blade.

**WALKER CUP
PUTTER** $40   50   70
Circa 1925-1930. Offset blade with a five-inch hosel.

PINEHURST PUTTER $40   50   70
Circa 1925-1930. Dot punched face.

**TED RAY SEVENTY-TWO
PUTTER** $40   50   70
Circa late 1920s.

**SUCCESS
PUTTER #2-1/2** $45   55   80
Circa 1920s. Bent neck line scored blade. All original.

**HARRY VARDON
PUTTER** $45   55   75
Circa 1926-1930.

FAIRVIEW PUTTER $50   60   90
Circa 1910-1915. Smooth face blade.

TRIUMPH PUTTER $55   70   100
Circa 1925-1930. Flanged back.

**GENE SARAZEN
PUTTER** $125   175   225
Circa 1925-1930. "Pencil" neck 7-inch long hosel.

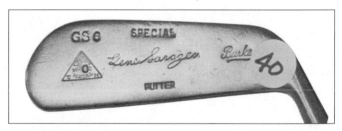

**WILSONIAN
BRASS PUTTER** $70   90   125
Circa 1925-1930. Ball face scoring.

**WALKER CUP
RAINBOW PUTTER** $125   175   250
Circa late 1920s. Rainbow face.

**SCHENECTADY
PUTTER** $150   225   325
Circa 1915-1920.

**JOHNNY
FARRELL IRONS** $35   45   65
Circa 1930. "Matched Models D1002".

| CREST IRONS | $35 | 40 | 60 |

Circa 1930. All irons.

BOB MACDONALD IRONS $35 40 60

Circa late 1920s. All irons.

SUCCESS IRONS $35 40 60

Circa 1920s. All irons.

WALKER CUP IRONS $35 40 60

Circa late 1920s. All irons.

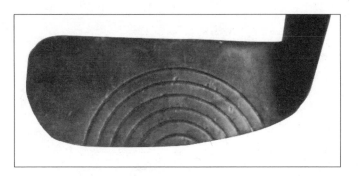

CUP DEFENDER IRONS $35 40 60

Circa 1930. All irons.

JOCK HUTCHISON IRONS $35 45 65

Circa 1930. All irons.

WILSONIAN IRONS $35 40 60

Circa 1920s. All irons.

TED RAY SEVENTY-TWO IRONS $35 45 65

Circa 1930. All irons.

PINEHURST IRONS $40 50 70

Circa 1925-1930. All irons.

HARRY VARDON IRONS $40 50 75

Circa 1930. All irons.

FAIRVIEW IRONS $50 65 95

Circa 1910-1915. All smooth face irons.

DEEP GROOVE IRONS $90 125 175

Circa 1915-1922. All irons. Corrugated deep grooves.

DEEP GROOVE IRONS $100 140 190

Circa 1915-1922. All irons. Slot grooves.

WALKER CUP RAINBOW IRONS $125 175 250

Circa 1930. All irons. Rainbow face design.

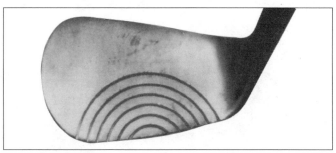

RED RIBBON IRON SET $375 500 750

Circa 1930. Mid-iron, mashie, mashie-niblick, niblick and putter with 2 woods.

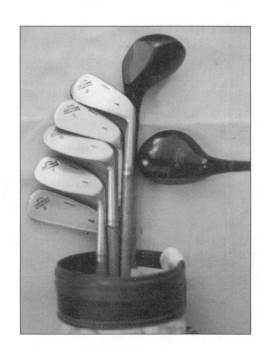

RED RIBBON IRONS $35 40 60

Circa 1930. All irons.

SUCCESS WOODS $75 95 140

Circa 1920s. Driver, brassie or spoon.

WILSONIAN WOODS $75 95 135

Circa 1920s. Driver, brassie or spoon.

RED RIBBON WOODS $75 95 135

Circa late 1920s. Driver, brassie or spoon.

PINEHURST WOODS $80 100 150

Circa 1925. Driver, brassie or spoon.

**SEVENTY-TWO
SERIES WOODS** $85 110 160

Circa late 1920s. Harry Vardon or Ted Ray. Driver, brassie or spoon.

**GENE SARAZEN
WOODS** $85 110 160

Circa 1925-1930. Driver, brassie or spoon.

JUVENILE CLUBS $30 40 55

"Gene Sarazen 11-13" on a circa 1925-1930 line scored mashie. Appears all original.

WILSON, WILLIE

ST. ANDREWS, SCOTLAND

Willie Wilson began forging clubs about 1870 in St. Andrews. He marked his clubs "W. Wilson, St. Andrews" and used the oval "St. Andrews Cross" mark during the 1890s.

**SMOOTH-FACE
IRONS** $250 400 650

Circa 1880-90. General purpose or lofting iron with "W. Wilson, Maker, St. Andrews" stamping.

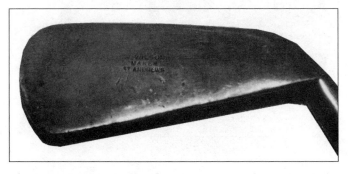

**BRASS-BLADE
PUTTER** $275 400 675

Circa 1880-1890. "W. Wilson St. Andrews, Maker" mark.

**SMOOTH-FACE
CLEEK** $275 425 700

Circa 1880-90. "W. Wilson, Maker, St. Andrews" stamping.

RUT IRON $1000 1750 2750

Circa 1880-90. "W. Wilson, Maker, St. Andrews" stamping.

WINTON, W & CO., LT'D

MONTROSE, SCOTLAND

The Winton family began forging irons about 1890 in Montrose, Scotland. They later added outlets in London and the club heads are marked as such. They used a "Diamond" cleek mark. They also made Bobby Jones' first "Calamity Jane" putters.

TAPLOW PUTTER $45 55 75

Circa 1920s. "Diamond" mark.

**PICCADILLY
BLADE PUTTER** $45 55 75

Circa 1925. "Diamond" mark.

**LINE SCORED
FACE PUTTER** $50 60 80

Circa 1920-1925. Long blade putter. "Diamond" mark.

DODO PUTTER $150 250 350

Circa 1925. Flanged back "Dodo, Little-Johnnie" putter. "Reg'd No. 353972".

**DOT FACE
RUSTLESS PUTTER** $50 60 95

Circa 1925-1930. Offset blade. "Diamond" mark.

THE SPIELIN
PUTTER   **$60**   **75**   **110**

Circa 1925. Step down hosel. "Diamond" mark.

TWO LEVEL

Circa 1915-1920. "Diamond" mark.

BACK PUTTER   **$70**   **100**   **150**

Circa 1915-1920. "Diamond" mark.

FINESSE PUTTER   **$175**   **275**   **375**

Circa 1920. Shallow dot face blade. Oval hosel and shaft.

THE MASCOT
PUTTER   **$200**   **300**   **450**

Circa 1920. Oval hosel and shaft. Large flange and rounded top line coming to a pointed toe.

JIGGER   **$50**   **60**   **85**

Circa 1920. "Diamond" mark on toe.

HARRY VARDON
SERIES IRONS   **$50**   **60**   **85**

Circa 1920s. All irons. Line scored face. "Diamond" mark.

WIN-ON NIBLICK   **$55**   **65**   **80**

Circa 1925-1930. Flanged back.

SMOOTH FACE
IRONS   **$60**   **75**   **120**

Circa 1900. All irons. "Winton, London" mark.

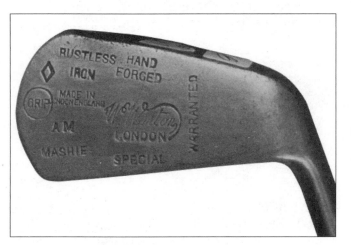

HOYLAKE
SPECIAL IRONS   **$55**   **65**   **95**

Circa 1910-1915. All irons. "Criss-cross" face scoring.

POINTED TOE
CANNON PATENT   **$150**   **225**   **350**

Circa early teens. "Ted Ray's Own". "Diamond" mark.

THE CERT
SERIES IRONS   **$65**   **75**   **100**

Circa 1920s. "Diamond" mark.

DREADNOUGHT
NIBLICK   **$95**   **125**   **175**

Circa 1920. Large head. "Diamond" mark.

BOGIE SERIES
IRONS   **$175**   **250**   **375**

Circa 1920. Cavity back. "Bogie" stamped in the cavity.

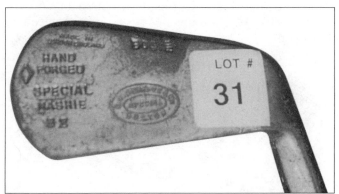

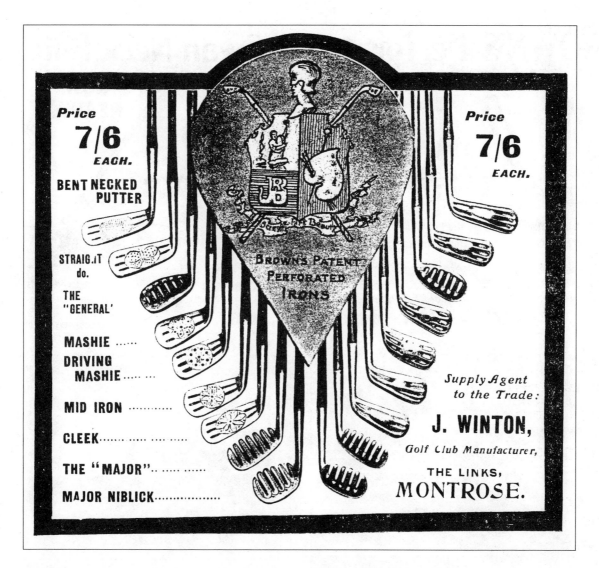

GIANT NIBLICK $1000 1600 2400

Circa 1920. Large head. "Diamond" mark.

ANTI-SHANK IRONS $125 175 250

Circa 1920s. All irons. Smith's Patent. Diamond mark.

ANTI-SHANK IRONS $150 190 275

Circa 1910-1915. All irons. "Diamond" mark. "Fairlie's Patent.

WATER IRONS $3500 5500 8000

Circa 1905. Horizontal slots perforating head at heel and toe. Fancy flower face.

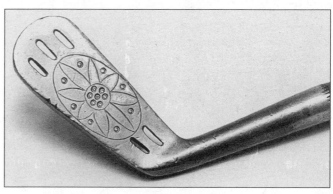

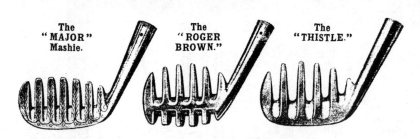

RAKE IRONS   **$4500   6000   8500**

Circa 1905. "The Major". Seven pointed tines.

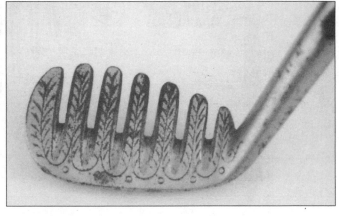

FLANGED BACK IRONS   **$65   75   100**

Circa 1915. Diamond mark at toe.

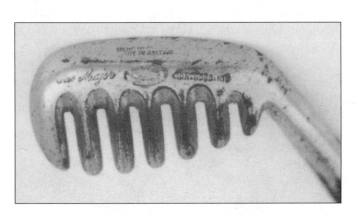

J WINTON WOODS	**$90**	**110**	**160**

Circa 1920. Driver, brassie or spoon.

SPLICED NECK WOODS	**$150**	**225**	**350**

Circa 1910-1920. All woods.

WRIGHT & DITSON

BOSTON, MA

Wright & Ditson began selling golf clubs at their Boston location about 1895. All clubs were purchased from A. G. Spalding & Brothers. Wright & Ditson added their own markings on the blank backs and wood heads for advertising purposes.

Jim Cooper has written the definitive work on Spalding, which is profusely illustrated. Every Spalding collector should have this reference in his or her library. It is available from the author, or Jim Cooper. There are also Wright & Ditson Retail Catalogue reprints from 1913, 1920, 1925 and 1930 available from the author of this book.

SEMI-CIRCLE W & D PUTTERS	**$300**	**550**	**950**

Circa 1895-1897. Brass or Steel smooth-face blade with "Wright & Ditson, Boston" mark in a semi-circle at the toe. Screw-in shaft.

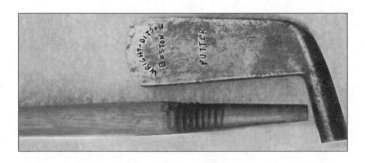

SEMI-CIRCLE W & D PUTTERS	**$200**	**300**	**500**

Circa 1895-1897. Brass or steel smooth-face blade with "Wright & Ditson, Boston" mark in a semi-circle at the toe.

ONE SHOT SERIES PUTTERS	**$45**	**55**	**95**

Circa 1915. Offset blade.

WRIGHT & DITSON SELECTED PUTTERS	**$100**	**140**	**225**

Circa 1898-1903. Severely bent neck in the "Park" style.

ONE SHOT SERIES PUTTERS	**$70**	**90**	**135**

Circa 1915. Smooth-face brass blade.

ONE SHOT SERIES PUTTERS	**$75**	**100**	**160**

Circa 1915. Flanged back with "Maxwell" holes drilled into the hosel.

"F" SERIES PUTTER	**$55**	**70**	**100**

Circa 1922-1925. Deep scoring lines on bottom of face; top is smooth.

A H FINDLAY PUTTERS	**$60**	**75**	**120**

Circa 1900-1905. Smooth face, straight steel blade.

A H FINDLAY PUTTERS	**$70**	**90**	**135**

Circa 1900-1905. Twisted neck gem-type wide-sole putter.

A H FINDLAY PUTTERS	**$75**	**95**	**140**

Circa 1900-1905. Smooth face straight Brass blade.

BEE-LINE SERIES PUTTERS	**$35**	**45**	**75**

Circa 1920s. Offset hosel and a line-scored blade.

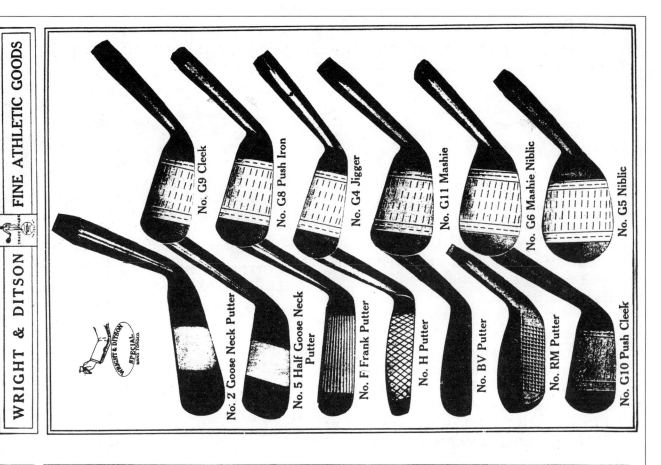

No. G9 Cleek

No. G8 Push Iron

No. G4 Jigger

No. G11 Mashie

No. G6 Mashie Niblic

No. G5 Niblic

No. 2 Goose Neck Putter

No. 5 Half Goose Neck Putter

No. F Frank Putter

No. H Putter

No. BV Putter

No. RM Putter

No. G10 Push Cleek

Wright & Ditson Golf Irons

PUTTERS

Putting is the most important part of Golf. A good putt will make up for many a poor shot, so it is well to have a putter adapted to the player's style.

No. 2 Goose Neck Putter. Has a longer and narrower blade than No. 1. Each, $2.00

No. 5 Half Goose Neck Putter. Same style as No. 1, only half goose neck. " 2.00

No. F. Frank Putter. Goose Neck, twist in neck enabling player to get full view of ball. Long, heavy, shallow blade and keeps ball close to the ground. Each, $2.00

No. H Putter. Goose Neck, with very heavy head and shallow straight face; a splendid club for heavy greens. . . . . Each, $2.50

No. BV Steel Putter. Has an oval bowl and shaft. Shaft is set in bowl in a straight line with the face, which prevents heeling. . . . . . . Each, $2.50

No. RM. Ray Mills Putter. Aluminum. Careful experiments prove a putter most easily placed in position if the head presents to the eye two long straight lines. This feature is found in the Ray Mills style. . . . . Each, $2.50

GOOSE NECK LINE

This line of clubs is made in a slight goose neck shape, same style as used by a former English champion, who claims it is the ideal shape for golf clubs. The back of each one of these irons is beveled at the bottom so that the sole will go well under the ball.

No. G10 Push Cleek. Has a short head, fairly deep face, and is a very long driving cleek. Extremely useful for long, low push shots against the wind. . Each, $2.00

No. G9 Cleek. Rather thin blade, light weight; medium deep face, with a slight loft; a splendid distance club out of bad lies. . . . . Each, $2.00

No. G8 Push Iron. Thin head, medium weight, mid iron loft. . . . " 2.00

No. G4 Jigger. Long thin blade, well lofted; for long, high shots or short approaches. 2.00

No. G11 Mashie. Medium size head, with regular mashie loft. . . . Each, 2.00

No. G6 Mashie Niblic. Lofted a little more than the mashie. Sole projects in advance of the shaft, so that ball may be picked up cleanly without hitting socket. Each, $2.00

No. G5 Niblic. Well laid back, with the sole projecting in front of the shaft; capital club for playing out of bunkers, and short pitch shots from bunkers. . Each, $2.00

QUINT-ANGLE LINE

A set of irons, including No. 3 Cleek, No. 2 Driving Iron, No. 3 Mid Iron, No. 3 Mashie and No. 1 Approach Iron, all having the same lie, but with different lofts. These Irons have a fairly short hosel, and blade with a little extra weight behind the point of impact. Many poor shots are made because of a player using clubs of different lies. The Quint-Angle line eliminates this difficulty and gives the player added confidence. They are great favorites with professionals.

The shafts are steely and beautifully balanced, topped off with choice leather grips. All models made for right and left hand players. Ladies' clubs are the same as for men, but a little lighter in weight. When ordering state whether right or left hand clubs are wanted, and if for Ladies or Men.

RULE 27.

BALL IN CASUAL WATER THROUGH THE GREEN

(2) If a ball lie or be lost in casual water through the green, the player may drop a ball without penalty within two club lengths of the margin, as near as possible to the spot where the ball lay, but not make the hole.

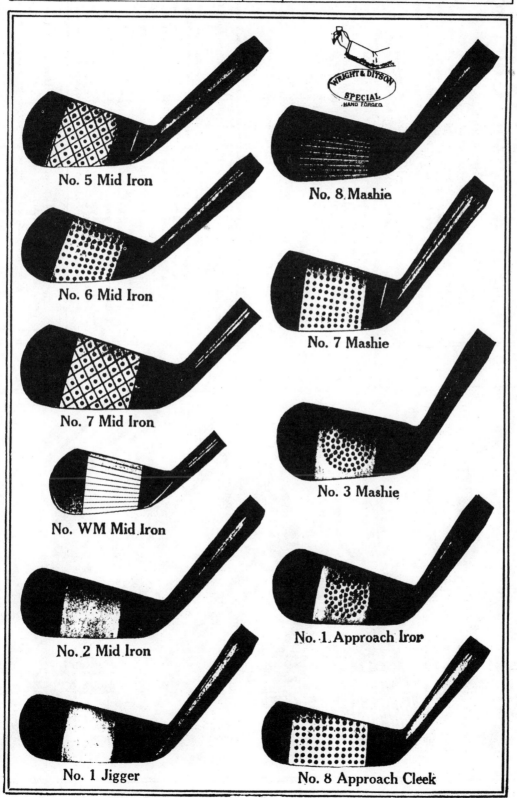

No. 5 Mid Iron

No. 6 Mid Iron

No. 7 Mid Iron

No. WM Mid Iron

No. 2 Mid Iron

No. 1 Jigger

No. 8 Mashie

No. 7 Mashie

No. 3 Mashie

No. 1 Approach Iron

No. 8 Approach Cleek

Wright & Ditson Golf Irons

MASHIE NIBLICS

No. 3 Mashie Niblic. A new club with a flat sole, well laid back, with concave face, and will take a ball out of any bad lie; is also a fine club for pitching over bunkers or on to greens that lie up hill, and puts extreme backward spin on ball.   Each, **$2.00**

No. 6 Mashie Niblic. A wide blade, well lofted, making a splendid approach club and fine for cut shots, causing the ball to drop dead. · · · · · · Each, **$2.00**

NIBLICS

No. M Niblic. Is well laid back, with a long, deep face and a very thin sole, so that a ball may be played out of any hazard. The long blade with the thin sole puts a back spin on the ball that is certain to make it drop "dead" with hardly any roll, which makes this club an ideal one for short pitching. · · · · · Each, **$2.00**

No. 4 Niblic. A very heavy club for digging ball out of sand or other hazards. "   **2.00**

No. 6 Dreadnought Niblic. Has a very broad and flat face. · · · · "   **2.00**

PUTTING CLEEKS

No. 8 Putting Cleek. Has long blade; medium weight; the same length as a putter and is upright in lie. The face is slightly laid back in order to put a "drag" on the ball, and is the nicest club to use on rough putting greens. · · Each, **$2.00**

No. 7 Putting Cleek. Similar to No. 8, but lighter weight and shorter blade. "   **2.00**

PUTTERS

Putting is the most important part of Golf. A good putt will make up for many a poor shot, so it is well to have a putter adapted to the player's style.

New Model Fownes. Made of wood and beautifully balanced. Splendid for either short or approach putts. · · · · · · · · · · · · Each, **$3.00**

No. RL. Wood face and brass back. A very handsome and useful putter. "   **3.00**

No. BM. Aluminum. Very popular with expert players, and is used for long approach putts. Flat, medium and upright lie. · · · · · · · · · Each, **$2.50**

Hammer-Head Aluminum Putters improve your putting. Used and highly endorsed by many prominent players. · · · · · · · · · · · Each, **$2.50**

Straight Face Putter. Regular style, in gun metal and steel; for novice and juvenile.   **2.00**

No. 1 Goose Neck Putter. Bent slightly in the neck, so that one can get a direct sight on the ball. Tapers gradually from a narrow top to a wide sole without any loft. Ball runs close to the ground. Has a long, shallow face. · · · · Each, **$2.00**

The shafts are steely and beautifully balanced, topped off with choice leather grips. All models made for right and left hand players. Ladies' clubs are the same as for men, but a little lighter in weight. When ordering state whether right or left hand clubs are wanted, and if for Ladies or Men.

RULE 27.

(1) Casual water in a Hazard, drop behind the Hazard or in the Hazard under penalty of one stroke.   RULE 6.

A competitor shall not ask for or willingly receive advice except from his caddie.   RULE 30.

When the player's ball lies on the putting green he shall not play until the opponent's ball is at rest.

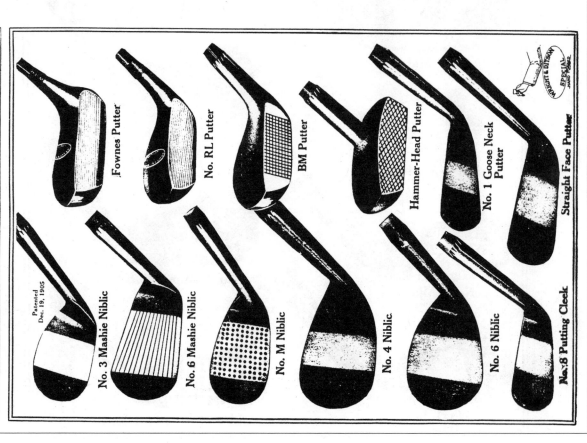

Patented
Dec. 19, 1905

No. 3 Mashie Niblic   Fownes Putter

No. 6 Mashie Niblic   No. RL Putter

No. M Niblic   BM Putter

No. 4 Niblic   Hammer-Head Putter

No. 6 Niblic   No. 1 Goose Neck Putter

No. 8 Putting Cleek   Straight Face Putter

Wright & Ditson Drivers and Brassies

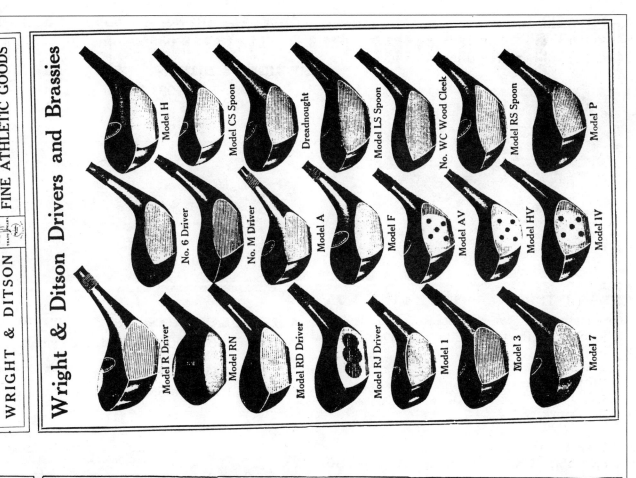

Model R Driver • Model H • No. 6 Driver • Model CS Spoon • No. M Driver • Dreadnought • Model A • Model LS Spoon • Model F • No. WC Wood Cleek • Model AV • Model RS Spoon • Model HV • Model IV • Model P • Model RN • Model RD Driver • Model RJ Driver • Model 1 • Model 3 • Model 7

WRIGHT & DITSON
DRIVERS AND BRASSIES

Special Model R Driver. A club made entirely by hand, of carefully selected material, the shafts being picked from a large stock of hickory, while the head is of best persimmon, of medium size. Has an insertion of brass instead of lead at the back. This brass covers a part of the top and sole of the club, and is immediately behind the point of impact, which, we claim, gives a little more distance. . . . . Each, $3.00

Model R Brassie. Same general style as the Driver, but has an insertion of brass on the sole instead of horn. It is well lofted, picks the ball up cleanly, and drives it a great distance. . . . . Each, $3.00

No. RN Driver. Same as our No. R, but with larger head and more playing face, fairly upright, and a fine club for the average player. . . . . Each, $3.00

No. RD Driver. Is an all-hitting face, which makes socketing an impossibility. They are the straightest and most easily controlled clubs designed; medium size, fairly flat lie. . . . . Each, $3.00

No. RJ Driver. Has three wooden slugs inserted in the face, the striking power coming against the grain instead of with the grain; is resilient as ivory; a very long driving club. . . . . Each, $4.00

Model 1 Driver or Brassie. Medium sized head and medium lie. A very popular model. . . . . Each, $2.50

Model 3 Driver or Brassie. Has a broad head, long face, and flat lie. This is a splendid driving model for a man who likes a good sized head. . . . . . . Each, $2.50

Model 7 Driver or Brassie. Medium sized head, with upright lie. . . . " 2.50

No. 6 Driver. A driving club for distance and accuracy; medium size and lie, with shallow face. . . . . Each, $2.50

No. 6 Brassie. Same as driver. This is a great club for playing close lies or on hard ground. . . . . Each, $2.50

No. M Driver. Medium lie, small head, with small hitting space; for the accurate player, and a great club for cuppy lies. . . . . Each, $2.50

Model A Driver or Brassie. Medium lie, with deep face. A very pretty and popular model. . . . . Each, $2.50

Model F Driver or Brassie. A little smaller model than the other heads ; medium lie. A very popular model. Each, $2.50

Model H Driver or Brassie. Medium sized head, with rather flat lie. . . Each, $2.50

Model P Professional Model Driver or Brassie. This is a very popular model with professionals, who recommend it highly. Medium sized head and lie. Each, $2.50

Ivorine Faced Drivers or Brassies. The Ivorine is very durable and elastic, and it is generally claimed that it drives a little further than the regular wood face. These clubs are made in Models AV, HV, and IV, the "V", meaning Ivorine. Each, $3.50

Dreadnought Drivers or Brassies are made with a very large head, and are popular with a good many players. They drive a ball low, with a long roll. . . . Each, $2.50

Model CS Spoon. Made with a well lofted face, medium length shaft, and medium sized head. . . . . Each, $2.50

Model LS Spoon. Just the same as CS, except that it has a longer face. " 2.50

Model RS Baffy Spoon. Special model and very popular. . . . . " 3.00

No. WC Wood Cleek. This club appeals to all golfers. Constructed for a variety of shots; especially good in cuppy lies or long grass through fairway; fairly long and narrow wood head. . . . . Each, $2.50

The Spoon is a necessity in every golfer's caddy bag. It is surer than the Brassie or Cleek out of bad lies, giving the player great distance on the carry. Used by all the leading players.

ST. ANDREWS
SERIES PUTTERS   **$45**   **55**   **90**
    Circa 1910. Square punches on face.

KRO-FLITE
SERIES PUTTERS   **$35**   **45**   **75**
    Circa 1926-30 Sweet Spot "R F" Putter with long hosel and offset blade. Patented Sept. 13, 1927.

VICTOR SERIES
PUTTER   **$35**   **45**   **75**
    Circa 1920s. Blade putter.

RAINBOW
SERIES PUTTERS   **$40**   **50**   **80**
    Circa 1920s. Dot-punched face. "Rainbow" mark.

ALUMINUM HEAD
PUTTERS   **$100**   **140**   **200**
    Circa 1915-1920. "B M" Wright & Ditson Special".

WRIGHT & DITSON, MAKERS,
ST. ANDREWS   **$70**   **90**   **150**
    Circa 1898-1903. All irons.

WRIGHT & DITSON

SELECTED IRONS   **$55**   **75**   **125**
    Circa 1898-1903. All irons.

WRIGHT & DITSON   **$70**   **90**   **150**
    Circa 1898-1903. All irons.

A H FINDLAY IRONS   **$75**   **90**   **150**
    Circa 1900-1905. Smooth-face cleek.

A H FINDLAY IRONS   **$60**   **75**   **125**
    Circa 1900-1905. Smooth-face iron or lofting iron.

ONE SHOT SERIES
IRONS   **$50**   **65**   **100**
    Circa 1910-15. All smooth-face irons.

ONE SHOT SERIES
IRONS   **$125**   **150**   **225**
    Circa 1920. Corrugated deep groove "Dedstop Jigger".

"F" SERIES IRONS   **$40**   **50**   **85**
    Circa 1922-1925. F-2 through F-7 or F-9 with deep scoring lines on bottom of face, top is smooth.

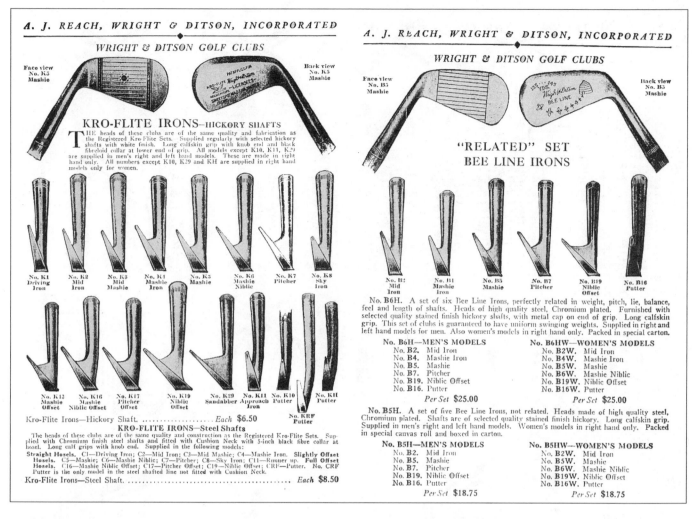

A. J. REACH, WRIGHT & DITSON, INCORPORATED

WRIGHT & DITSON GOLF CLUBS

Face view
No. K5
Mashie

Back view
No. K5
Mashie

KRO-FLITE IRONS—HICKORY SHAFTS

THE heads of these clubs are of the same quality and fabrication as the Registered Kro-Flite Sets. Supplied regularly with selected hickory shafts with white finish. Long calfskin grip with knob end and black fibreloid collar at lower end of grip. All models except K10, K11, K29 are supplied in men's right and left hand models. These are made in right hand only. All numbers except K10, K29 and KH are supplied in right hand models only for women.

No. K1 Driving Iron · No. K2 Mid Iron · No. K3 Mid Mashie · No. K4 Mashie Iron · No. K5 Mashie · No. K6 Mashie Niblic · No. K7 Pitcher · No. K8 Sky Iron

No. K15 Mashie Offset · No. K16 Mashie Niblic Offset · No. K17 Pitcher Offset · No. K19 Niblic Offset · No. K29 Sandabber · No. K11 Approach Iron · No. K10 Putter · No. KRF Putter · No. KH Putter

Kro-Flite Irons—Hickory Shaft .... *Each* $6.50

KRO-FLITE IRONS—Steel Shafts

The heads of these clubs are of the same quality and construction as the Registered Kro-Flite Sets. Supplied with Chromium finish steel shafts and fitted with Cushion Neck with 5-inch black fibre collar at hosel. Long calf grips with knob end. Supplied in the following models:
Straight Hosels. C1—Driving Iron; C2—Mid Iron; C3—Mid Mashie; C4—Mashie Iron. **Slightly Offset Hosels.** C5—Mashie; C6—Mashie Niblic; C7—Pitcher; C8—Sky Iron; C11—Runner up. **Full Offset Hosels.** C16—Mashie Niblic Offset; C17—Pitcher Offset; C19—Niblic Offset; CRF—Putter. No. CRF Putter is the only model in the steel shafted line not fitted with Cushion Neck.
Kro-Flite Irons—Steel Shaft. .... *Each* $8.50

A. J. REACH, WRIGHT & DITSON, INCORPORATED

WRIGHT & DITSON GOLF CLUBS

Face view
No. B5
Mashie

Back view
No. B5
Mashie

"RELATED" SET BEE LINE IRONS

No. B2 Mid Iron · No. B4 Mashie Iron · No. B5 Mashie · No. B7 Pitcher · No. B19 Niblic Offset · No. B16 Putter

No. B6H. A set of six Bee Line Irons, perfectly related in weight, pitch, lie, balance, feel and length of shafts. Heads of high quality steel, Chromium plated. Furnished with selected quality stained finish hickory shafts, with metal cap on end of grip. Long calfskin grip. This set of clubs is guaranteed to have uniform swinging weights. Supplied in right and left hand models for men. Also women's models in right hand only. Packed in special carton.

No. B6H—MEN'S MODELS	No. B6HW—WOMEN'S MODELS
No. B2. Mid Iron	No. B2W. Mid Iron
No. B4. Mashie Iron	No. B4W. Mashie Iron
No. B5. Mashie	No. B5W. Mashie
No. B7. Pitcher	No. B6W. Mashie Niblic
No. B19. Niblic Offset	No. B19W. Niblic Offset
No. B16. Putter	No. B16W. Putter
Per Set $25.00	*Per Set* $25.00

No. B5H. A set of five Bee Line Irons, not related. Heads made of high quality steel, Chromium plated. Shafts are of selected quality stained finish hickory. Long calfskin grip. Supplied in men's right and left hand models. Women's models in right hand only. Packed in special canvas roll and boxed in carton.

No. B5H—MEN'S MODELS	No. B5HW—WOMEN'S MODELS
No. B2. Mid Iron	No. B2W. Mid Iron
No. B5. Mashie	No. B5W. Mashie
No. B7. Pitcher	No. B6W. Mashie Niblic
No. B19. Niblic Offset	No. B19W. Niblic Offset
No. B16. Putter	No. B16W. Putter
Per Set $18.75	*Per Set* $18.75

ONE SHOT SERIES
IRONS $45   60   90
Circa 1915. All marked face irons.

"F" SERIES IRONS $50   65   95
Circa 1922-1925. F-1 with deep scoring lines on bottom of face; top is smooth.

BEE-LINE SERIES
IRONS $30   40   65
Circa 1920s. All irons.

ONE SHOT SERIES
IRONS $50   65   95
Circa 1920. "#8" Sky-iron or Jigger.

ST. ANDREWS
SERIES IRONS $30   40   70
Circa 1915-1925. All irons.

WRIGHT & DITSON "BEE" LINE IRONS

Models B6 and B7 are made with corrugation cut in a compound curve, as this presents a uniform path of travel regardless of the angle at which the ball crosses the face.

Model B1. Driving Iron.

Model B2. Mid Iron.

Model B3. Mid Mashie.

Model B4. Mashie Iron.

Model B5. Mashie.

Model B6. Mashie Kompound Dedstop Corrugated Ribbed Effect (Patent Applied For).

Model B7. Pitcher, Kompound Dedstop Corrugation Ribbed Effect (Patent Applied for).

Model B8. Jigger.

Model B9. Niblic.

Above supplied in left hand models also.

No. B1. Driving Iron

No. B2. Mid Iron

No. B3. Mid Mashie

No. B4. Mashie Iron

No. B5. Mashie

No. B6. Dedstop Mashie Iron

No. B7. Pitcher

No. B8. Jigger

No. B9. Niblic   .   .   Each, $6.00

"Bee" Line Irons. Models as above, with specially prepared calf grip.

Wright & Ditson Premier Quality Steel Putters

No. LW.   Very popular style.   .   .   Each, $6.00

No. CH.   Chicopee model. Oval hosel.   Each, $6.00

No. C94.   New model. Oval hosel, goose neck,   Each, $6.00

No. HB.   Hollow back model. Oval hosel.   Each, $6.00

No. LW Putter

No. CH Putter

No. C94 Putter

Front View

Premier Quality Aluminum Putters

No. MR.   Embraces the good points of various styles we have made during the past few years. Made in two lies—medium and upright.   Each, $6.00

No. NH.   "Hammer Brand" Putter. Aluminum. Raised top. Upright lie and medium lie.   Not legal in England.   .   Each, $6.00

No. MR Putter

No. BB Putter

Front View

Wright & Ditson Wood Putter

No. 10.   Heavily weighted with lead. Scored brass face. Specially prepared calf grip.   .   Each, $6.00

No. 10 Gold Medal Putter

No. NH Putter

Front View

**"F" SERIES
"SKY-IRON"**   **$60**   **80**   **125**

Circa 1922-1925. Deep scoring lines on bottom of face, top is smooth.

**ONE SHOT SERIES
IRONS**   **$100**   **135**   **175**

Circa 1915-1922. Corrugated or slot-type deep groove mashie, mashie-niblick or niblick.

**KRO-FLITE SERIES
IRONS**   **$30**   **40**   **70**

Circa 1926-1930. Sweet spot. 1 through 8 and 19.

VICTOR SERIES IRONS   **$30**   **40**   **70**

Circa 1920s.

**RAINBOW SERIES
IRONS**   **$35**   **45**   **75**

Circa 1920s. Dot-scored face.

WATERFALL IRONS   **$400**   **500**   **800**

Circa 1920. "Bee-Line" markings.

**DOUBLE
WATERFALL IRONS**   **$2000 2800 4500**

Circa 1920. "Bee-Line" markings.

**SPLICED-NECK
WOODS**   **$150**   **250**   **450**

Circa 1898-1903. "Wright & Ditson" in script. Driver, brassie or spoon. Some have leather face inserts.

**SPLICED-NECK
WOODS**   **$250**   **350**   **700**

Circa 1898-1903. Pear-shaped, persimmon head, bulger-face driver or brassie. Some have leather face insert.

A H FINDLAY WOODS   **$95**   **120**   **175**

Circa 1900-1905. Driver, brassie or spoon. Many with leather face inserts.

A H FINDLAY WOODS   **$125**   **150**   **250**

Circa 1900. Bulger driver or brassie with a leather face insert. Very thick, oval shaped socket hosel.

**WRIGHT &
DITSON WOODS**   **$75**   **95**   **140**

Circa 1910-1920 Driver, brassie or spoon.

**BEE-LINE
SERIES WOODS**   **$75**   **95**   **140**

Circa 1920s Driver, brassie or spoon.

**ST. ANDREWS
SERIES WOODS**   **$75**   **95**   **140**

Circa 1920s. Driver, brassie or spoon.

**ST. ANDREWS
SERIES WOODS**   **$95**   **120**   **175**

Circa 1920s. Small head wooden cleek or Bull Dog head.

**VICTOR SERIES
WOODS**   **$75**   **95**   **140**

Circa 1920s Driver, brassie or spoon.

**ALUMINUM HEAD
WOODS**   **$125**   **160**   **275**

Circa 1910-1920. Various lofts.

JUVENILE CLUBS   **$30**   **40**   **60**

Circa 1920. "Y" Youth series. putter or irons.

Chapter 5

Golf Balls

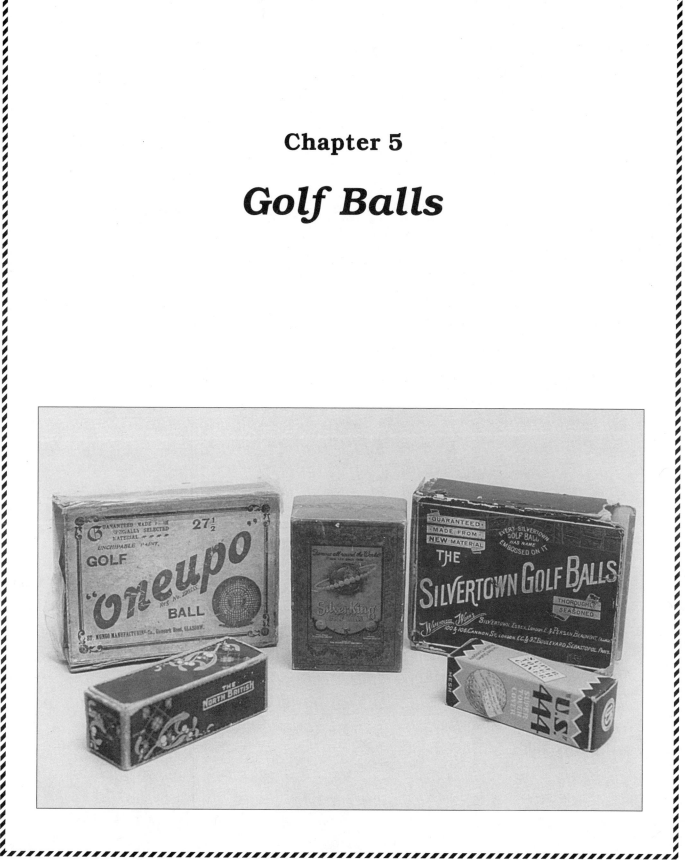

Chapter 5

Golf Balls

Golfers through the ages played with balls made from wood, feathers stuffed into a leather cover, gutta-percha, wound rubber centers with celluloid covers, balls with "honey" centers, solid balls made of "space age" plastics, graphite windings, Cadwell Geer, syrlin, balata and zinthane covers.

The ball most people associate with pre-1850 golf is the "Feather" ball. A skilled worker took three pieces of leather, two round and one rectangular strip, and sewed the three together with heavy waxed thread. Before the last few stitches were completed, it was turned inside out to hide the seams. A quantity of boiled feathers, enough to fill a top hat, were stuffed through the tiny unsewn opening and the closing stitches finished the ball. Many ball makers soaked the leather in "Alum" and when the cover dried, it shrunk. At the same time, the drying feathers inside expanded, making a surprisingly hard, very playable golf ball. The *Encyclopedia of Golf Collectibles* by Olman and *The Curious History of the Golf Ball* by Martin provide lengthy descriptions of how the feather ball was made.

Only three or four good balls could be made in a day by a skilled worker and, as a result, the balls were rather expensive. It is thought that a feather ball in the early 19th century (expressing value in 1990s dollars) cost the golfer $50 or more! Only royalty and the very wealthy could afford these expensive balls.

In the 1840s, experiments making golf balls from gutta-percha transformed the ancient game that had been played nearly unchanged for 400 years. Gutta-percha, dried sap of the Malasian sapodilla tree, was used during that time the same way we use styrofoam peanuts to pack fragile items. The gutta-percha was heated in boiling water and rolled

This gutty ball was made by Allan Robertson, ca. 1853.

into a sphere by hand, then left to "cure" for a few weeks before being painted. In a day's work, a skilled worker could make ten times as many "gutties" as he could featheries. The price of the gutties was about one fifth the price of the feather ball, with remade balls even less, and many who before could not afford to play began to use this new inexpensive ball.

The transition from the feather ball to the gutta-percha ball was not as rapid as most golf writers and auctioneers make it out to be. Robert Forgan recalled: "...(in 1856) gutta-percha balls were just getting established, and as they were much cheaper than the feather ball golf soon began to spread...". Featheries were most likely still played by many traditional Scotsmen well into the 1860s.

Gutta balls that had been scuffed and nicked during play were found to fly straighter and longer than the new smooth balls. Some players gave new balls to their caddies to "knock them around" before play began. Somewhere along the line, an enterprising ball maker used the "claw" of his hammer to nick the ball's surface. Patterns were cut into the ball using a chisel, until another enterprising maker decided a metal mold with raised markings could mold the gutta-percha into a uniform ready made "scored" ball.

A hand-hammered gutta ball, ca. 1855.

Golf was propelled into the modern game we know today by the Haskell Patent of April 11, 1899. Working for B.F. Goodrich of Akron, Ohio, Coburn Haskell and Bertram Works developed a process, in 1898, of winding thin rubber strips around a central core and covered these windings with a cover of gutta-percha. Again, everyone did not change from the guttie to the rubber-core balls overnight. In fact, the only player in the 1902 British Open field playing the new Haskell ball was Sandy Herd, the eventual winner. By 1910 though, only the diehards were playing gutties.

As the game grew during the later part of the 19th and early 20th centuries, golfers demanded a better ball, and hundreds of ball makers began molding balls with a variety of cover patterns. Covers had circles, dots, stars, swirls, crescents, squares in circles, triangles, hexagons, octagons, dimples, brambles and were cut with lines. The "Pneumatic" ball was filled with air and there were balls that emitted smoke or an odor to aid in finding it in the rough. There were also balls made to float on the water. Literally thousands of patterns and combinations of patterns were used by the manufacturers to single out their ball from all others available.

Smooth gutty mold with clamping device, ca. 1850.

THE NEW AMERICAN GOLF BALL.

THE MACGRIPPA : "Here's that Yankee again, blast him! I can't stand the fellow. There's nothing in him except bounce."
THE O'CUBO : "O, I don't know, he's not such a bad sort. He's a bit of a bounder, I admit, and he can't putt for nuts; but he costs 2½ dollars, so let's be charitable."

During the period from 1895 to 1940, most balls came in a wrapper with a paper seal that carried the advertisement and the ball's name. Many companies thought wrapping the ball justified the high prices for golf balls. We must understand that during the Great Depression balls were selling for 50 cents to $1.00. each. Balls were truly *expen-*

sive when considering the price of steak, potatoes and milk. Even in the bountiful "Roaring 1920s", $1.00 was a large sum to pay for a golf ball.

There are several good references on golf balls worth looking into, including *The Curious History of the Golf Ball*, 1968, by Martin; *The Encyclopedia of Golf Collectibles*, 1985, by Olman; and *Antique Golf Ball Reference Guide*, 1993, by Kelly.

My Passion for Old Golf Balls

by Jim Espinola

My first encounter with golf collectibles were the old wooden-shafted clubs. As my collection of clubs began to grow, I wanted examples of golf balls from different eras to display with the clubs. When I began to realize how many different types of balls were available, my collecting interests changed. My passion for ball collecting was fueled by the many different cover patterns I encountered. To me, looking at all these different patterns was like looking at a beautiful painting—a form of art.

Many new collectors I meet ask me why I collect balls, especially the odd cover patterns. I feel the golf ball *is* the history of the game. It is through the ball's advancement that the game and its implements have progressed.

There are literally thousands of different sizes, shapes, center cores and cover patterns, many yet to be discovered. If you join a golfing society, go to auctions and find dealers who publish catalogues, many golf balls will find their way into your collection. There are many fine balls that are not expensive and would make a great display for the collector on a limited budget.

As for advice on collecting balls, your personal taste and budget will be the primary factors. Personally, I began collecting everything regardless of quality and quantity, and condition did not matter. Eventually I realized it was a mistake and began to acquire only the best possible examples. It became evident, as I gained collecting experience, that quality and condition were most important. There are exceptions, though; the rare

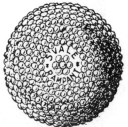

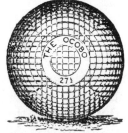

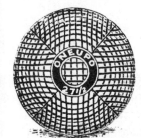

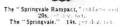

ones or "one of a kind" may not be available in top condition, and because of the scarcity factor, they are desirable. The best advice I can pass along is to collect what you like, in the best condition available that you can afford. It is not quantity, but quality that makes my collection meaningful to me.

Another exciting aspect of collecting is researching the history of golf and golf balls through books, auction catalogues, articles in old magazines, advertisements, talking to old professionals and long time collectors. Developing a resource library and understanding the history of golf has helped me set

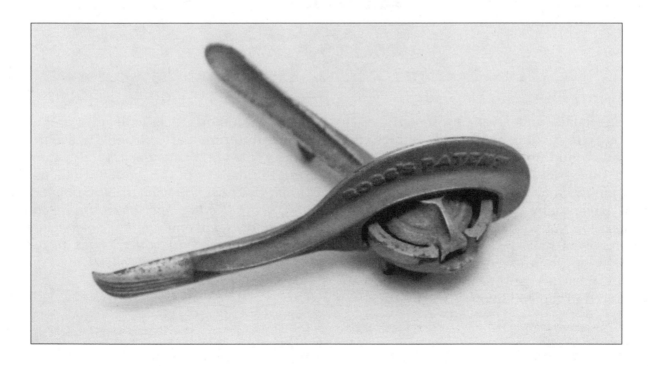

collecting goals and given me insight as to availability and value. Without a library, my collection would not be complete.

With the prices of odd pattern balls, gutties, brambles and wrapped balls escalating at a brisk pace, many collectors cannot afford to purchase top quality examples. For those who want to collect balls in top quality, Signature Balls may be the answer. At present they are plentiful, most are priced under $50 and can be acquired in top condition.

In conclusion, I feel collecting and admiring the different pattern balls is a true form of art. They take me back to the past and bring the history of the game into focus.

Jim Espinola has been a collector of balls for many years. He has specialized in the odd, different and exceptional quality whenever possible. Many of the odd pattern balls pictured in this reference are from his collection.

Golf Balls

	G-5	G-7	G-9

FEATHER BALL

NO MAKER'S NAME $4250 6500 10000

Circa 1800. Large size.

FEATHER BALL

NO MAKER'S NAME $3500 5500 8500

Circa 1840-1860. Average size.

FEATHER BALL

GOURLAY, JOHN, MUSSELBURGH $6500 9000 14000

Circa 1840-1860. "J Gourlay" and size number.

FEATHER BALL

ROBERTSON, ALLAN $6500 10000 18000

Circa 1840-1850. "Allan" and size number.

FEATHER BALL

MORRIS, TOM,
ST. ANDREWS $8000 15000 30000

Circa 1840-1860. "T. Morris" and size number.

SMOOTH GUTTA-PERCHA

NO MAKER'S NAME $1500 3000 6000

Circa 1850-1860. White, brown or black usually with a "test" mark.

HAND HAMMERED GUTTA-PERCHA

NO MAKER'S NAME $1500 2500 5000

Circa 1850-1880. Hand marked with a chisel.

HAND HAMMERED GUTTA-PERCHA

FORGAN, ROBERT,
ST. ANDREWS $1500 3500 7500

Circa 1855-1880. Stamped "R. Forgan" usually with size number.

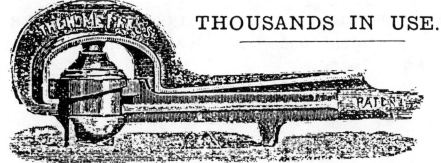

CIRCA 1900 *# 3000 TO $5,000.—*

Musselburgh Golf Ball.

11s. per Doz., Post Paid.

CIRCA 1900

LINE CUT GUTTA-PERCHA

REMADE, NO NAME   **$125**   **300**   **750**
   Circa 1880-1905.

LINE CUT GUTTA-PERCHA

VARIOUS MAKERS   **$250**   **500**   **1500**
   Circa 1880-1905. Maker's name marked on ball.

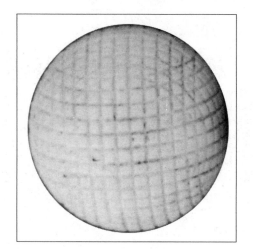

LINE CUT GUTTA-PERCHA

SILVERTOWN   **$250   500   1500**

Circa 1890-1905.

LINE CUT GUTTA-PERCHA

DUNN, WILLIE   **$500   100   2500**

Circa 1895. "Dunn's Record Ball 27".

LINE CUT GUTTA-PERCHA

**HALLEY, J B,
LONDON**   **$400   800   1500**

Circa 1895. "The Ocobo 27 1/2".

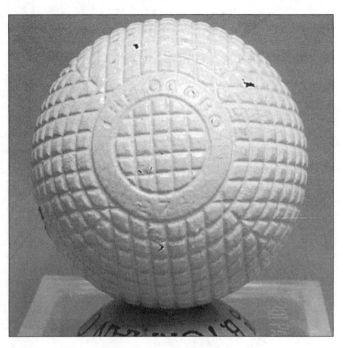

LINE CUT GUTTA-PERCHA

HENLEY'S , LONDON   **$400   800   2000**

Circa 1895. "Henley" in a rectangular panel.

WRIGHT & DITSON GOLF BALLS

Made in different styles to meet the demands of all types of players and conditions of play.

VICTOR 75

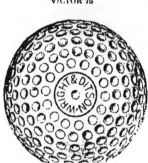

BLACK CIRCLE

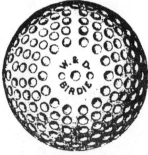

BIRDIE

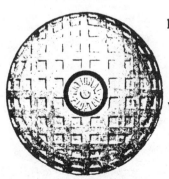

NATIONAL FLOATER

VICTOR 31

VICTOR 29

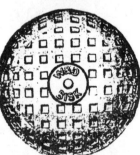

THE BISK

No. 19

VICTOR "75." Small and heavy. Especially for the expert who requires a ball that he can control under all conditions. A wonderful ball for putting.

Each, **$1.00** Dozen, **$12.00**
Compression average 4 1-2. Weight 1.69 ounces.

VICTOR "31." A larger size ball than the "75" and a trifle heavier. Especially adapted to players who desire a large heavy ball for play requiring distance under all conditions.

Each, **$1.00** Dozen, **$12.00**
Compression average 4 1-2. Weight 1.70 ounces.

VICTOR "29." A truly wonderful ball. Same size as the "31," but a little lighter weight. The "29" is the best ball for sixty per cent of the golfers who prefer medium size and weight. Insures better lies, especially when the fair green is heavy. Each, **$1.00** Dozen, **$12.00**
Compression average 6. Weight 1.62 ounces.

BLACK CIRCLE. A size between the Victor "31" and "75" and is now, as it always has been, a ball of championship quality. An ideal ball in every respect.

Each, **90c.** Dozen, **$10.80**
Compression average 6. Weight 1.68 ounces.

THE BISK. Mesh marking, with a lively center; the type ball best suited to players who drive low, depending upon the run for distance. The Bisk is medium size. Very dependable.

Each, **75c.** Dozen, **$9.00**
Compression average 7. Weight 1.67 ounces.

NATIONAL FLOATER. A large light ball, floats in water, mesh marking, and is considered by a great many golfers to be the best floater ever produced.

Each, **75c.** Dozen, **$9.00**
Compression average 8. Weight 1.44 ounces.

BIRDIE, or, Yellow Circle. Medium size and weight, has always been and always will be one of the most popular balls ever introduced, being suitable to all types of play. Each, **75c.** Dozen, **$9.00**
Compression average 7 1-2. Weight 1.52 ounces.

W. & D. No. 19. New this year. Large size, medium weight, recessed marking. and is beyond all doubt the very best for golfers who want a fine playing and durable ball at a low price.

Each, **60c.** Dozen, **$7.20**
Compression average 7. Weight 1.63 ounces.

LINE CUT GUTTA-PERCHA

PARK, WILLIE, MUSSELBURGH $1500   3000   5000

   Circa 1890s. "Park" in rectangular panel. Also collectible as a signature ball.

CIRCA 1930 DIMPLE BALLS

REACH, WRIGHT & DITSON $20   45   100

   Circa 1930. Many names. Balls in boxes or wrappers are worth double. (Above)

LINE CUT GUTTA-PERCHA

UNKNOWN MAKER $800   1200   2000

   Circa 1895. "Allaway" in rectangular panel.

BLUE BIRD DIMPLE

HENRY C LYTTON,
CHICAGO $40   90   250

Circa 1920s. No name, just a flying bird on pole.

DARBY FLYER MESH

ASSOCIATED
GOLFERS $50   100   250

Circa 1920s. "Darby Flyer" at poles. Standard square mesh pattern.

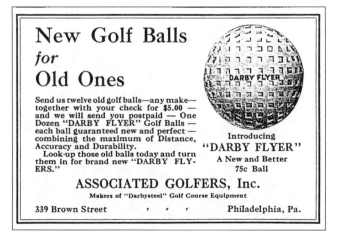

GRAY GOOSE MESH

BAKER & BENNETT,
NEW YORK $50   100   300

Circa 1920s. Standard square mesh pattern. They came in an individual box. A G-7 box will double the value.

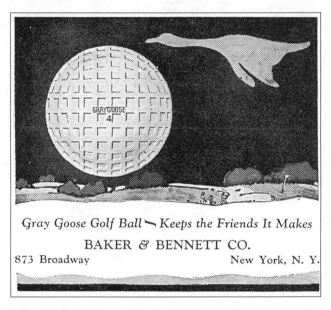

REACH EAGLE DIMPLE

REACH, A J,
PHILADELPHIA $50   100   250

Circa 1920s. "Reach Eagle" at poles. Balls in boxes or wrappers are worth double.

COLONEL MESH

ST MUNGO, NEWARK
& GLASGOW $50   100   275

Circa 1915-1920. Many names including "F S", "29", "31", "27", "Click" and others. Balls in boxes or wrappers are worth double.

CIRCA 1930 MESH BALLS

REACH, WRIGHT
& DITSON $50   100   300

Circa 1930. Many names. (Next page, full ad)

BLACK BUG DIMPLE

CAPPER & CAPPER,
CHICAGO $100   250   750

Circa 1920. No name, just a black bug at the pole.

NOBBY MESH

U.S. RUBBER CO.,
NEW YORK $150   350   750

Circa 1930s. Truck tire pattern.

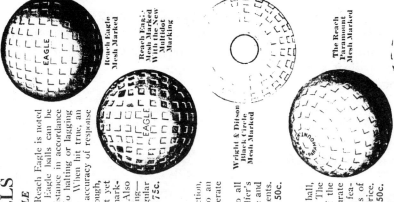

GOLF BALLS

THE REACH EAGLE

The essential qualities for which the Reach Eagle is noted are distance, control and durability. Eagle balls can be depended on for the full measure of distance in accordance with the power put into the stroke. No halting or lagging but straight and sure in flight or roll. When hit true, an Eagle ball flies true. On the green the accuracy of response inspires confidence in putting. The tough, lasting covers, stand terrific punishment yet remain in good playing shape for a remarkable length of time. Mesh marked. Also furnished with the new Multidot marking—twelve colored dots painted on the regular Eagle ball. ...... *Dozen* $9.00 *Each* 75c.

THE WRIGHT & DITSON BLACK CIRCLE

Mesh marked. Exceptionally true in action, remarkable for distance and durable to an extreme degree. Great carry from moderate blow and quick response from all shots.

These balls are particularly suited to all general forms of play—the average golfer's ball. Dependable in every respect. Size and weight conform with standard requirements.
Dozen $6.00 *Each* 50c.

THE REACH PARAMOUNT

Mesh marked. A high grade golf ball, suitable for the discriminating golfer. The quality of this ball has made it one of the most popular on the market. Careful, accurate construction is responsible for playing features which fully meet the expectations of players who prefer to use a ball at this price.
Dozen $6.00 *Each* 50c.

THE WRIGHT & DITSON NATIONAL FLOATER

Mesh marked. Due to its light weight construction, this ball is long in driving quality. Excellent for soft turf conditions. Especially good for ladies' use, for light hitters and beginners. As the name implies, this ball floats in water. The use of this type of ball for water holes reduces mental hazard. Standard floater size and weight. ...*Dozen* $6.00 *Each* 50c.

All the above balls can be supplied in either the 1930 size of 1.62 inches, weight 1.62 ounces or the 1931 size of 1.68 inches, weight 1.55 ounces.

GOLF BALLS

THE WRIGHT & DITSON RECORD

Made for durability and distance. This ball is guaranteed not to cut or nick in actual play. Tests have proven it to be one of the longest distance balls ever made. We have produced in this ball a wonderful degree of durability without sacrificing its distance qualities. *Record* golf balls fully live up to the players' expectations in every kind of shot. Absolute dependability in the continuous uniformity of the Record ball will inspire confidence which improves the player's ability. Mesh marking. Also furnished with the new Multidot marking. Each ball is painted with twelve colored dots. This new marking gives the player greater visibility; easier to identify and easier to hit accurately. ....*Dozen* $9.00 *Each* .75

THE WRIGHT & DITSON BULLET
Dimple Marked

Approved Dimple marking. Made for distance. Special type of marking, and very high-powered. Golfers are surprised at the great distance to be obtained with it. Flies especially well into the wind and holds direction better than any ball we know of. In addition to its wonderful flight, it is very accurate in approaching and putting. Its durability is very satisfactory—more so than is usually found in a high-powered ball. These balls are also furnished with the new Multidot marking. *Dozen* $9.00 *Each* 75c.

THE WRIGHT & DITSON BULLET
Mesh Marked

We furnish the Bullet with a mesh marking. Also with the new Multidot marking. Specify kind, otherwise our regular Dimple Bullet will be furnished on mail orders. ....*Dozen* $9.00 *Each* 75c.

twelve colored dots painted on ball.

All the above golf balls can be supplied in either the 1930 size of 1.62 inches, weight 1.62 ounces or in the 1931 size of 1.68 inches, weight 1.55 ounces. Multidot golf balls are supplied in the following colors: Red, Blue, Green and Maroon.

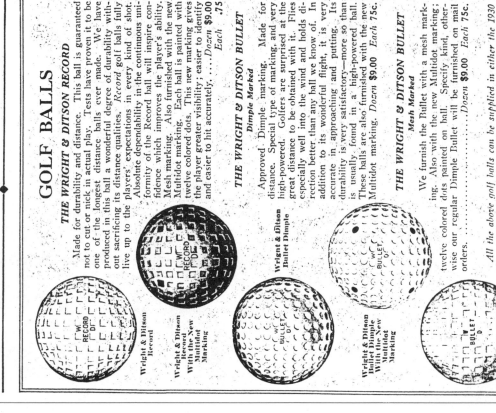

SUPER CHICK DIMPLE

NORTH BRITISH,
EDINBURGH   **$150**   **350**   **750**

Circa 1920. "Super Chick 31" at poles. Large dimples. Very scarce.

WHY NOT BRAMBLE

HENLEY'S, LONDON   **$175**   **350**   **900**

Circa 1915. "Why Not" at both poles.

SPRINGVALE GUTTA

HUTCHISON MAIN,
GLASGOW   **$200**   **450**   **1250**

Circa 1900. Line cut.

LINE CUT GUTTA-PERCHA

VARIOUS MAKERS   **$200**   **450**   **950**

Circa 1895-1905. Maker's name marked on ball.

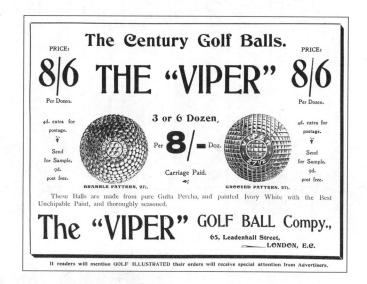

X L CHALLENGER

COCHRANE'S LT'D,
EDINBURGH   **$250**   **700**   **1250**

Circa 1917. "X L Challenger" on equator. New Basket Pattern for 1917.

Wright & Ditson Golf Balls

BABY BLACK CIRCLE

REG. U. S. PAT. OFF.

ALL the great tournaments of 1911 were won by players using the BLACK CIRCLE GOLF BALL. The National Open Championship, the blue ribbon event of American golf, in which all of America's greatest players, both amateur and professional, competed, was won by a player using the Black Circle. In all the great open events of the North and South during 1912, the winners played with the Black Circle. In the National Open Championship of America, the first three prize winners played with the Black Circle. In the Western Open Championship, the first four prize winners played with the Black Circle, and in the Pacific Coast Open Championship the first two prize winners played with the Black Circle. ¶ It is a small heavy ball with Lynx style marking, and sinks in water. It is a long driving ball, flys low and holds its direction against the wind. Its greatest qualities, however, are in its approaching and putting, and a good putt makes up for many poor drives. Per dozen, **$9.00**

ORANGE AND BLACK RINGER

A new ball for 1913; made in the very popular marking that gives distance without great effort. Medium size, light weight, floats in water. . . . Dozen, $9.00

PURPLE RINGER

Also a new ball for 1913; made like the Orange and Black, only heavier, being medium size and weight; sinks in water. Fine ball to use in connection with the Orange and Black when playing against the wind. Dozen, $9.00

ORANGE "BABY" RINGER

Size of the Purple ball; a little lighter in weight; sinks in *water*; a fine all-round playing golf ball. Per dozen, $9.00

RED CIRCLE

Made of the best rubber core center, covered with white gutta; heavy weight, which makes it a desirable ball against the wind. Long driving ball. Dozen, $9.00

GREEN CIRCLE

Floats in water. The players like it because they find it to be the most reliable ball for driving, approaching and putting. The marking is the popular 6-Point style; is known to be the best for accurate flight. Dozen, $8.00

BLUE CIRCLE

Rubber cored; lynx style marking. Very popular. Dozen, $6.00

Purple Ringer

Red Circle

Blue Circle

Orange and Black Ringer

Orange "Baby" Ringer

Green Circle
REG. U. S. PAT. OFF.

REALIZING the necessity that exists for a line of golf balls that shall satisfy not only the taste of every discriminating and critical golfer, but shall cover every variation of weather, season, turf condition, and in fact, any golfing emergency whatever, and firmly believing that these above conditions can be met only by a variety so comprehensive, we submit the following balls for the season of 1913, with recommendations as noted, regarding special merits of different sizes and weights. "Dimple" marking controlled by A. G. Spalding & Bros., under patent dated February 4, 1908. We can also furnish any rubber cored golf balls made under the Haskell patent.

LARGE SIZE BALLS

LIGHT—For moderate hitters, soft turf conditions, water holes.

HEAVY—For distance players, long roll, hard turf, use in wind, steadiness on greens.

No. 1 Spalding Red Dot REG. U.S. PAT. OFF.
Floats in water. Light weight. Dozen, $6.00

No. 2 Spalding Glory Bramble REG. U.S. PAT. OFF.
Red, White and Blue dot. Floats. Light. Dozen, $8.00

No. 3 Spalding Glory Dimple REG. U.S. PAT. OFF.
Red, White and Blue dot. Floats. Light. Dozen, $9.00

No. 4 Spalding Domino Dimple REG. U.S. PAT. OFF.
Four Black dots. Sinks in water. Heavy. Doz. $9.00

MEDIUM SIZE BALLS

HEAVY—For long distance, use in wind, fairly hard turf conditions, and for the players who wish to combine the advantages of both extremes in sizes.

LIGHT—For ladies and light hitters generally, water holes and the accurate "holding" of greens or short holes

No. 5 Spalding Domino Bramble REG. U.S. PAT. OFF.
One Black dot. Sinks in water. Heavy weight. Dozen, $8.00

No. 6 Spalding Domino Dimple REG. U.S. PAT. OFF.
Four Light Blue dots. Sinks in water. Light weight. . Dozen, $9.00

No. 7 Spalding Domino Dimple REG. U.S. PAT. OFF.
Four Red dots. Floats in water. Very light weight. Dozen, $9.00

SMALL SIZE BALLS

MEDIUM—For the average distance man who prefers this size ball, good in wind and on almost any turf.

HEAVY—For extreme distance in carry and roll, for long players particularly, excellent in heavy wind and on smooth, hard courses.

No. 8 Spalding Baby Bramble REG. U.S. PAT. OFF.
One Blue dot. Sinks in water. Medium weight. Dozen, $8.00

No. 9 Spalding Baby Dimple REG. U.S. PAT. OFF.
Two Red and two Blue dots. Sinks in water. Medium weight. Doz. $9.00

No. 10 Spalding Midget Dimple REG. U.S. PAT. OFF.
Green, White and Orange dot. Sinks in water. Heavy weight. Doz., $8.00

No. 11 Spalding Midget Dimple REG. U.S. PAT. OFF.
Two Green and two Orange dots. Sinks in water. Heavy weight, Doz., $9.00

EUREKA LINE CUT GUTTA

**GUTTA-PERCHA CO.,
LONDON** $300   700   1750

Circa late 1890s. Widely spaced lines. "The Eureka 27 1/2" at poles.

LINE CUT GUTTA-PERCHA

**CLARK, J & D,
MUSSELBURGH** $350   750   2000

Circa 1900. "Musselburgh" across the equator.

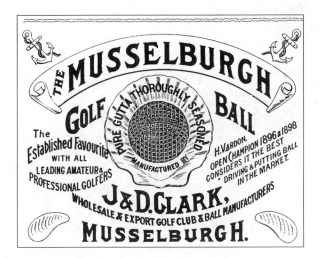

CIRCLE SERIES, RUBBER CORE BRAMBLE

**WRIGHT & DITSON,
BOSTON, MA** $175   350   900

Circa 1906-1915. "Wright & Ditson" and patent dates inside colored circles. Blue, Green, Orange Floater, Black and others.

RUBBER CORED BRAMBLES

SPALDING, USA $175   350   900

Circa 1906-1920. Many including "White", "Wizard", "Dot", "Blue Circle", "Spalding Bramble", "Spalding Bob" and others.

RUBBER CORED BRAMBLES

**KEMPSHALL,
NEW JERSEY** $175   350   900

Circa 1905-1920. Many including "Chick", "Flyer", Arlington", "League" and others.

SPRINGVALE SERIES BRAMBLE

**HUTCHISON MAIN,
GLASGOW** $200   400   1000

Circa 1900. "SVale" Hawk, Falcon, Eagle, Kite and others.

BRAMBLE GUTTA-PERCHA

REMADE, NO NAME $100   200   500

Circa 1895-1905. No name, or maker's name not identifiable.

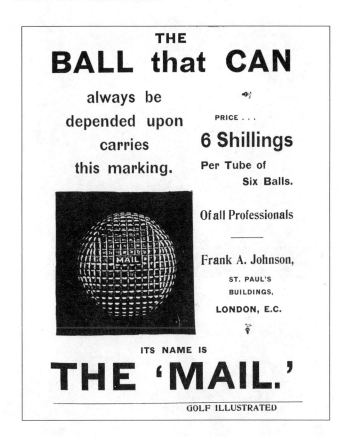

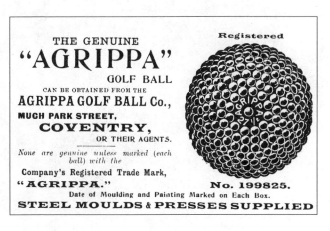

BRAMBLE GUTTA-PERCHA

VARIOUS MAKERS $200 450 950
Circa 1895-1905. Maker's name marked on ball.

BRAMBLE GUTTA-PERCHA

**SPALDING,
VARDON FLYER** $450 950 2000
Circa 1900. "Vardon Flyer" at both poles. Also collectible as a signature ball.

BRAMBLE GUTTA-PERCHA

**AUCHTERLONIE,
ST. ANDREWS** $800 1200 2000
Circa 1895-1905. "Auchterlonie" at pole. (Notice the backwards "N" in the name.) Also collectible as a signature ball.

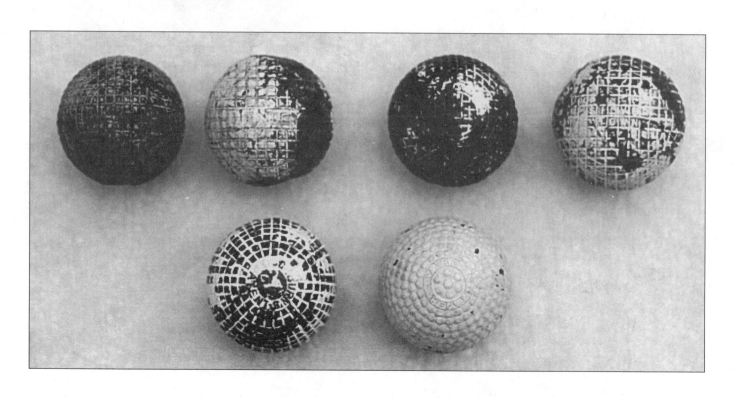

BRAMBLE GUTTA-PERCHA

MORRIS, TOM,
ST. ANDREWS   **$1000   2000   3500**

Circa 1895-1905. "The Tom Morris 27 1/2". Also collectible as a signature ball.

BRAMBLE GUTTA-PERCHA

UNKNOWN MAKER   **$400   900   2000**

Circa 1895-1905. "Maltese Cross", could have been sold by or made by F. H. Ayres, London.

BRAMBLE GUTTA-PERCHA

UNKNOWN MAKER   **$400   800   1750**

Circa 1895-1905. "The Finch".

BRAMBLE, RUBBER CORE

VARIOUS MAKERS   **$125   325   650**

Circa 1900. Gutta-percha cover.

BRAMBLE, RUBBER CORE

VARIOUS MAKERS   **$100   275   550**

Circa 1905-1920. Celluloid or rubber cover.

BRAMBLE, RUBBER CORE

UNKNOWN MAKER   **$1500   3000   7500**

Circa 1900-1905. "The Bruce Cored Center" with a "Spider" and "Web". Gutta-percha cover.

BRAMBLE, RUBBER CORE

GOODRICH, B F,
AKRON, OH   **$750   1250   2250**

Circa 1899-1905. "Haskell" and "Pat. Apr. 1, 1899" at poles. Gutta-percha cover.

LINE CUT RUBBER CORE

GOODRICH, B F,
AKRON, OH   **$1800   3500   5500**

Circa 1902. "Haskell" and "Pat. Apr. 1, 1899" in rectangular panels. Gutta-percha cover.

BRAMBLE, RUBBER CORE

GOODRICH, B F,
AKRON, OH   **$125   325   650**

Circa 1899-1905. "Haskell" and "Pat. Apr. 1, 1899" at poles. Celluloid cover.

BRAMBLE, RUBBER CORE

GOODRICH, B F,
AKRON, OH   **$400   800   1500**

Circa 1910. "Haskell Royal" with a celluloid cover.

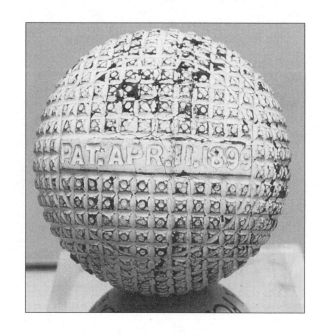

BRAMBLE, RUBBER CORE

IMPROVED GOLF BALLS,
LONDON **$250** **500** **1000**

Circa 1902-1905. "I R" at poles. These were recovered "Haskell or other cored balls". Gutta-percha cover.

BRAMBLE, RUBBER CORE

GOODYEAR
RUBBER CO. **$300** **600** **1500**

Circa 1905. "The Pneumatic" at equator. These were rubber cored with a center of compressed air.

BRAMBLE, RUBBER CORE

GOODYEAR
RUBBER CO. **$700** **1250** **2500**

Circa 1905. "The Pneumatic" at poles. These were rubber cored with a center of compressed air.

BRAMBLE, RUBBER CORE

SILVERTOWN   **$250**   **450**   **1000**

Circa 1905-1915. "Silver King" at poles.

U.S. ROYAL MESH

**U.S. RUBBER CO.,
NEW YORK**   **$30**   **60**   **150**

Circa 1930s. Standard square mesh pattern.

FAIRWAY MESH

U S RUBBER CO.   **$35**   **75**   **225**

Circa 1930s. "Fairway" on poles. Standard square mesh pattern.

CERTIFIED MESH

WALGREEN'S   **$35**   **75**   **225**

Circa 1930s. Standard square mesh pattern.

DUNLOP ENGLAND MESH

DUNLOP   **$40**   **80**   **225**

Circa 1920s. "Dunlop" and "England" at poles. Pattern similar to the "Super Harlequin" pictured here.

BURKE 50-50 MESH

**BURKE MFG CO.,
NEWARK, OH**   **$50**   **100**   **300**

Circa 1920s. "Burke 50-50" at poles. Standard square mesh pattern.

REACH PARAMOUNT MESH

**REACH, A J,
PHILADELPHIA**   **$50**   **100**   **250**

Circa 1920s. "Paramount" at poles. Standard square mesh pattern.

OWL MESH

**DRAPER-MAYNARD,
PORTSMOUTH, NH**   **$50**   **100**   **300**

Circa 1930. "D & M Owl" at poles. Standard square mesh pattern.

NORTH BRITISH MESH

**NORTH BRITISH,
EDINBURGH**   **$50**   **100**   **300**

Circa 1920s-1930s. "North British" at poles. Standard square mesh pattern.

LYNX MESH

SILVERTOWN   **$50**   **100**   **300**

Circa 1930s. "Lynx" at poles. Standard square mesh pattern.

MAXIM MESH

SCOTTISH INDIA RUB., GLASGOW   **$50**   **100**   **300**

    Circa 1920s. "Maxim" at poles. Standard square mesh pattern.

JACK RABBIT MESH

MACGREGOR, DAYTON, OH   **$50**   **100**   **300**

    Circa 1920s. "Jack Rabbit" at poles. Standard square mesh pattern.

FLASH MESH

WANNAMAKER, NEW YORK   **$50**   **100**   **300**

    Circa 1920s. Several varieties marked "Flash". Blue, Yellow, Red, Long and others. Standard square mesh pattern.

DIAMOND SERIES MESH

WORTHINGTON, OHIO   **$50**   **100**   **300**

    Circa 1920s. Diamond King, Jack, Four, Chip and others. Standard square mesh pattern.

DUNLOP GOLD CUP MESH

DUNLOP   **$50**   **100**   **250**

    Circa 1920s. "Dunlop" and "Gold Cup" at poles. Standard square mesh pattern.

CUDAHY'S PURITAN MESH

UNKNOWN MAKER: **$50**   **100**   **300**

    Circa 1920s and 1930s. "Cudahy's Puritan" at poles. Standard square mesh pattern.

AVON DELUXE MESH

AVON   **$50**   **100**   **300**

    Circa 1920s. "Avon DeLuxe" at poles. Standard square mesh pattern.

WHIPPET MESH

GOODRICH, B.F.   **$50**   **100**   **300**

    Circa 1920s. Standard square mesh pattern.

WILSON MESH

WILSON, THOMAS E., CHICAGO,   **$50**   **100**   **250**

    Circa 1920s and 1930s. Many including Crest, "W", Top Notch, Success, Pinehurst and Hol-Hi. Standard square mesh pattern.

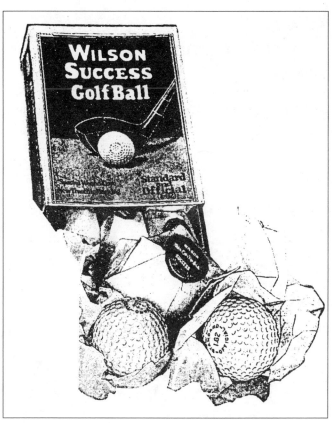

WHIZ MESH

GOODRICH, B F $50   100   300
　　Circa 1920s. Standard square mesh pattern.

BROMFORD MESH

GOLF DEVIL $50   100   250
　　Circa 1930s. Standard square mesh pattern.

TEE-MEE MESH

GOLF DEVIL $50   100   300
　　Circa 1930s. Standard square mesh pattern.

ST. REGIS MESH

UNKNOWN MAKER $50   100   300
　　Circa 1930s. Standard square mesh pattern. There is a steel mold for this ball currently on the market. It sold for $700 in 1995.

REX MESH

**COCHRANE'S LT'D,
EDINBURGH** $50   100   300
　　Circa 1920s and 1930s. Standard square mesh pattern.

REACH PARAMOUNT TRIANGLE

**REACH, A J,
PHILADELPHIA** $75   175   450
　　Circa 1920s. "Reach Paramount" at poles. Triangle pattern.

BRAMBLE, RUBBER CORE

UNKNOWN MAKER $250   450   1000
　　Circa 1905-1915. "The Resilient" at poles.

MESH COVER

SPALDING, USA $50   100   300
　　Circa 1920-1935. "PGA" made in both British and American sizes. Square markings.

MESH COVER

SPALDING, USA   **$50   100   300**

Circa 1920-1935. "Spalding" and "Kro-Flite" at poles. Square markings.

MESH COVER

ST. MUNGO, NEWARK
& GLASGOW   **$50   125   350**

Circa 1920-1935. "Arch Colonel" and "1.55", "1.62" or "1.68" at poles. Square markings.

DIMPLE COVER

SPALDING, USA   **$50   125   375**

Circa 1908-1925. Many markings including Midget Dimple, 40, 50, 60, Dot, Baby Dimple, Domino, Glory Dimple, Honor, and others.

DIMPLE COVER

SPALDING, USA   **$15   30   75**

Circa 1920-1940. "P G A".

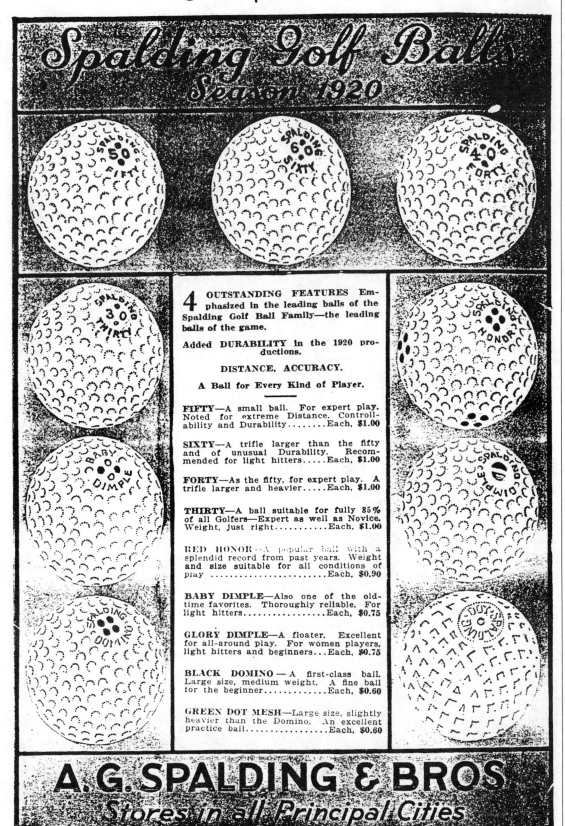

PARK ROYAL HEXAGONAL FACES

PARK, WILLIE,
MUSSELBURGH   **$9000   20000   40000**

Circa 1896. Supposedly designed to minimize speed on downhill putts. RARE!

CHEMICO DE LUXE

COUNTY
CHEMICAL CO.   **$800   1500   3000**

Circa 1900. "Horseshoe" type markings with "Dots". "Chemico De Luxe" at poles. Very scarce.

STARS AND STRIPES GUTTA

DUNN, WILLIE,
NEW YORK   **$7500   15000   40K**

Circa 1897. "Willie Dunn's Stars and Stripes" and "Patented July 27, 1897, No 27441" at the poles. Extremely RARE.

ZOME TWO

MARTINS,
BIRMINGHAM   **$400   800   1750**

Circa 1900-1910. "Zome Two" at poles. Large circles with a raised center.

WHITE FLYER

CRAIG PARK,
GLASGOW $500   1200   2250

Circa 1915. "White Flyer" at poles. Circles with a "Cross" inside. Very scarce!

THE RESILIENT

UNKNOWN MAKER $1000   2000   4000

Circa 1910. "The Resilient" at the poles. Ringed "Diamonds" pattern. Very scarce.

THE DIAMOND GUTTA

WHIT & BARNES $1000   2000   3500

Circa 1895-1900. "Diamond W & B Co" at equator. "Diamond" pattern line cut gutta-percha. Very RARE.

DIAMOND CHICK

NORTH BRITISH,
EDINBURGH $1500   2500   5000

Circa 1910-1915. "Diamond Chick" at poles. A very odd pattern. Very scarce.

THE FALCON

UNKNOWN MAKER $800   1250   2500

Circa 1910. "The Falcon 27" at poles. Similar design to the "Diamond Chick".

CAPON HEATON

UNKNOWN MAKER $600   1200   2500

Circa 1910. "Capon Heaton" at poles. Five pointed stars inside a large dimple. Very scarce.

HEAVY COLONEL

**ST. MUNGO, NEWARK
& GLASGOW $450   850   2000**

Circa 1915. "Heavy Colonel" at poles. Large widely spaced dimples.

STAR CHALLENGER

**COCHRANE'S LT'D,
EDINBURGH $350   750   1500**

Circa 1905-1910. "The Challenger" surrounding a "Star" on the poles. Joined stars circle the ball.

BURBANK

STOW-WOODWARD $600 1000 2000

Circa 1930s. "Burbank" crossed vertically and horizontally at poles. An unusual swirl cover pattern. Very scarce.

HENRY'S RIFLED BALL

HENRY, ALEX $6000 15000 40000

Circa 1903. "Henry's Rifled Ball" at poles. Cover is a swirl pattern similar to a rifle barrel.

FAROID

UNKNOWN MAKER $2000 4500 10000

Circa 1920. "Faroid, This End Up" at poles. Ringed pattern. Very scarce.

GAMAGE'S ARIEL

THE GAMAGE, LONDON $300 650 1400

Circa 1920. "Gamage's Ariel" at poles. Large widely spaced dimples.

WILSON BRAMBLE

WILSON, THOMAS E., CHICAGO $600   1200   2250

Circa 1920. "Wilson" at poles. Pattern is large flat brambles.

WHITE FLAT BRAMBLE

WORTHINGTON, OHIO $600   1250   2250

Circa 1910-1915. "White Worthington" at poles. Large flat brambles. Very scarce.

HENLEY

HENLEY'S, LONDON $3500   6500   12000

Circa 1920s. "Henley" at equator. Triple line pattern that resembles the British "Union Jack" flag. Very scarce.

CLINCHER CROSS

NORTH BRITISH, EDINBURGH $200   450   950

Circa 1915. "Clincher Cross" and size number at poles. Ball is lined into four sections. Triangles and rectangles make up the pattern.

CHEMICO TRIUMPH

**COUNTY
CHEMICAL CO.**   **$75   175   450**

Circa 1920. "Chemico Triumph" surrounding a "Cross" at the poles. Small concentric squares form the pattern.

U. S. TIGER

**U S RUBBER CO.,
NEW YORK**   **$200   450   1000**

Circa 1920. "U. S. Tiger" at poles. Large circles. Was made in white and yellow cover colors.

DIAMOND COVER

SPALDING, USA   **$75   150   400**

Circa 1920-1930. Entire cover with diamonds. "Spalding" at poles.

WARWICK

DUNLOP, BIRMINGHAM, ENGLAND $75   175   450

Circa 1925-1935. Alternating rows of square and dimple markings.

THE METEOR

GOODRICH, B F, OHIO $250   500   1350

Circa 1920. "The Meteor" at poles. Concentric triangles.

GOODYEAR "A"

GOODYEAR RUBBER CO., OHIO $75   150   400

Circa 1920. "Goodyear A" at poles. Odd pattern of squares.

SUPER HARLEQUIN

HARLEQUIN $150   350   850

Circa 1920s. "Super Harlequin" crossed at poles. Unusual arrangement of squares.

HARRINGTON SPECIAL

UNKNOWN MAKER $100   250   550

Circa 1920s. "Harrington Special" at poles. Squares and rectangles in an odd design.

CRESCENT COLONEL

ST. MUNGO, NEWARK
& GLASGOW   **$175   350   800**

Circa 1920s. "Crescent Colonel" surrounds a "Crescent". Pattern is opposing crescents.

WRAPPED BALLS

Golf ball manufacturers began wrapping balls about 1895. Dunlop, Slazenger, Penfold, Spaulding, Wilson and several other companies continued through the 1980's. The first wrappers were made of paper with an advertising seal; later wrappings were of colored cellophane.

CIRCA 1924 DIMPLE BALLS

WANNAMAKER,
NEW YORK   **$15   35   100**

Circa 1925. Dimple patterns. Many names including "Red Flash", "Radio Crown", "Xray", "Taplow" and others.

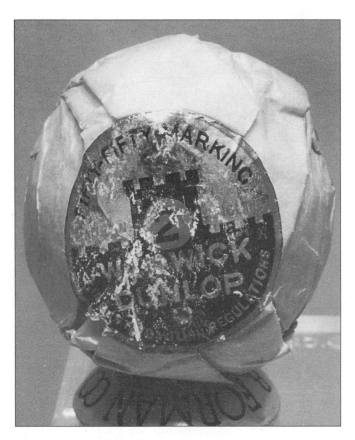

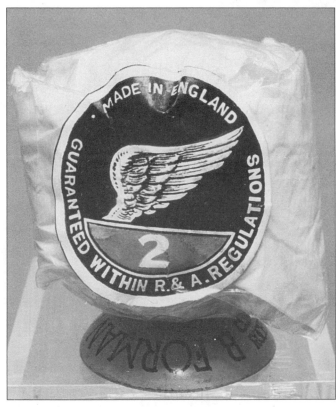

RED FLASH RADIO CROWN *Silver King* REG U S PAT OFF XRAY TAPLOW

All Leaders

IN this group of Wanamaker golf balls, each grade of golfer is represented. There is a ball here to fit your game and your pocketbook — and every one is a leader in its class.

The world-renowned Silver King, "King O' Them All" is the leading golf ball in every country on earth where golf is played. "There's a Silver King for every grade of golfer." Price $1.00 each.

Radio Crowns are the choice of thousands upon thousands of golfers — the recess mould is unusually attractive, and the paint is durable. Radio Crown never disappoints its users. Price 75c each.

Praises of the Xray are now being sung all over America. Xray is earning new plaudits daily. The reason is clear to those who have given this new ball a try. True, firm, from cover to core. Price $1.00 each.

The Red Flash — improved each year — is the best moderate priced ball. It is an exceptionally fine putting ball. Price 65c each.

Taplow golf balls are made in floaters or regular size and weight. The Taplow has unusual durability — undoubtedly the longest lived 50c ball sold.

John Wanamaker, New York

Philadelphia   Chicago   Boston   Los Angeles

Sole, authorized distributors in America of Silver King Golf Balls

BALL BOXES AND CONTAINERS

All prices given are for empty boxes and containers.

ONEUPO DOZEN BOX

ST. MUNGO,
GLASGOW   **$100   225   500**

Circa 1900. Box for gutta-percha balls.

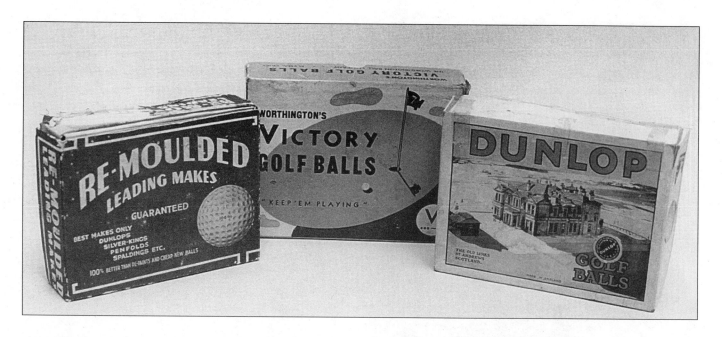

ARCH COLONEL MESH DOZEN BOX

ST. MUNGO,
NEW JERSEY $75   150   350

Circa 1920s. Colorful box picturing "The Colonel".

SILVERKING DIMPLE DOZEN BOX

SILVERTOWN $75   150   300

Circa 1930. Balls encircling the globe dozen box.

SILVERTOWN GUTTA DOZEN BOX

SILVERTOWN $100   225   450

Circa 1900. Slip case type dozen box.

NORTH BRITISH SLEEVE BOX

NORTH BRITISH,
GLASGOW $40   75   150

Circa 1920s. Cardboard sleeve box for three balls, mesh or dimple.

US 444 SLEEVE BOX

U S RUBBER,
NEW YORK $30   60   150

Circa 1930s. Cardboard sleeve box for three balls, mesh or dimple.

RE-MOULDED DOZEN BOX

UNKNOWN MAKER $50   90   175

Circa 1920s. Dozen box dimple or mesh. (Above)

WORTHINGTON DOZEN BOXES

WORTHINGTON,
OHIO $35   60   100

Circa 1930s and 1940s. Dozen boxes for mesh or dimple.

WORTHINGTON DOZEN BOXES

WORTHINGTON,
OHIO $50   90   150

Circa 1920s. Dozen boxes for mesh or dimple.

DUNLOP 65 BALL TUBE

DUNLOP $10   25   60

Circa late 1930s-1950s. Three-ball screw-top tube sleeve.

DUNLOP 65 BALL BOXES

DUNLOP $20   50   100

Circa late 1930s-1950s. Boxes for dimpled Dunlop 65 marked "Recessed".

DUNLOP BALL BOXES

DUNLOP $40   75   125

Circa 1920s-1930s. Boxes for mesh or dimple pattern balls.

DUNLOP METAL DISPLAY BOX

DUNLOP   **$300   500   1000**

Circa 1920s. Metal box for displaying two dozen balls on counter top.

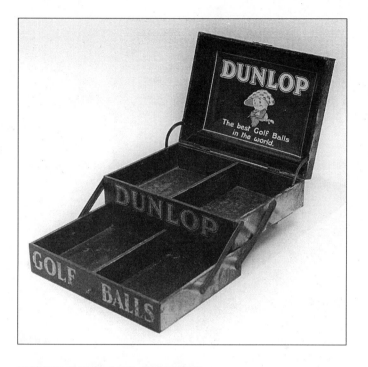

DUNLOP BALL BOXES

DUNLOP   **$75   125   250**

Circa 1905-1920. Boxes for bramble pattern balls.

INDIVIDUAL DIMPLE BALL BOXES

VARIOUS MAKERS   **$5   20   50**

Circa 1940s-1960s. Individual boxes for dimple balls.

INDIVIDUAL DIMPLE BALL BOXES

VARIOUS MAKERS   **$15   35   75**

Circa 1920s-1930s. Individual boxes for dimple pattern balls from the period pre-1935.

INDIVIDUAL MESH BALL BOXES

VARIOUS MAKERS   **$20   45   90**

Circa 1920s-1930s. Individual boxes for mesh pattern balls from the period pre-1935.

Chapter 6

Signature Balls

Chapter 6

Signature Balls

One of the most asked questions by would-be ball collectors is "What is a signature ball?" Signature balls are imprinted, at the time of manufacturing, with a professional's name. Golf balls signed, or autographed by a professional, president or celebrity (usually with a "Sharpie" felt tip pen) are NOT SIGNATURE balls, but autographed balls and classified as autographed items.

The first signature golf balls were feather balls. Willie Park, about 1890, made gutta-percha balls and simply marked them "Park". Harry Vardon was the first professional golfer to receive monetary compensation for the use of his name when, at the turn of the century, A.G. Spalding & Brothers made the "Vardon Flyer" gutta-percha ball.

Over the years literally thousands of different named balls and varieties bearing those names (about 140 different varieties of the MacGregor-made balls marked with Jack Nicklaus' name have been classified) have been collected singly, in sleeves or in original half dozen and dozen boxes.

Paul Biocini has authored the *Signature Golf Ball Collector's Guide*, 1995, and has been gracious enough to write the introduction to this chapter.

Collecting Signature Golf Balls

by Paul Biocini

It all started in Scotland when the names Morris, Gourlay, Allan (Robertson), etc., were imprinted on the feather balls they had made. Forgan, Park, Auchtrerlonie, etc. were the best ball makers during the gutta-percha period, 1860-1900, and they, too, imprinted their names on balls.

But why were the names put on the ball? Quality, recognition, favorite professional, posterity, or just a way to promote sales; whatever the reason, it was here to stay.

Originally, many of the early American golf professionals were golf pros from Scotland and England. This was the case with John Dunn of New York who remodeled used gutties. His mold was imprinted with his namel, thus creating the first signature ball made in the USA!

A.G. Spalding & Bros. introduced the Vardon Flyer with Bramble markings in 1900 which became the first manufactured signature ball. During 1905-1915 there were hundreds of newly formed golf ball manufacturing companies producing a variety of exotic balls, but only the J. H. Taylor Company's "H" Bramble Ball (1915) and later the "H" Mesh Ball (1925) were stamped with a professional's name.

Starting in the late 1920s, Worthington, Wilson and other companies produced both mesh and dimple design balls imprinted with the names of the stars who played them. As a result, collectors today ardently search for balls bearing the names of Walter Hagen,

Gene Sarazen, Jock Hutchison, Johnny Ferrell, Tommy Armour and others. This was the first attempt by ball companies to create the "Professional Staff" concept.

Wilson was also the first company to sign a lady professional in 1933 and "Helen Hicks" became the first woman's name to appear on a manufactured ball. "Babe" Didrickson was the second when the Goldsmith Co. made a ball bearing her name in 1935. Wilson, in 1937, also made a "Didrickson" ball but, to my knowledge, no collector has reported having found one.

Around 1936, the larger golf companies started the "Sold in Pro Shop Only" line of more expensive "Professional" quality balls. This helped promote the sale of the lesser expensive signature balls sold only in retail, sporting goods and department stores.

During the period from the late 1930s through the 1960s, local golf pros like Wiffy Cox, George Buzzini, Andy Silva and others, began having specially made balls with their name imprinted as an advertising ploy (much like the logo balls imprinted with St. Andrews or Pebble Beach) which sold as an inexpensive over-the-counter ball. Approximately 5,000 pros did so, and today more than 2,000 different names have been reported by various collectors.

Signature ball collecting is a relatively new specialty in golf collecting and the new or experienced collector can still find many treasures at local flea markets, garage sales, friends, old golf bags, professional tournaments, collectibles dealers, or trading with other collectors.

Which signature balls to collect should be determined by where your interest lies. There are many who want to "collect them all" and have hundreds or even thousands of balls in their possession. Others may want to collect only winners of the Masters, or only winners of major tournaments. Presidential, ladies or celebrity balls are other collectible venues. One individual collects only signature balls of the pros he has seen play in person.

The field is limited only by your imagination, physical storage or display space, and your pocket book.

When placing a value on a signature ball, keep in mind the overall preservation, how much it has deteriorated from mint new, and the name clarity. If the signature name is scuffed or partially unreadable on a nearly new ball, the ball is technically uncollectible, unless it is very rare or the only example available.

Grading Signature Balls

The G-5, G-7, G-9 pricing values will represent the following conditions:

G-5

An average ball, with a good clear name, may have iron marks (no cuts), some paint loss, or may be slightly out of round.

G-7

An above average condition ball showing only the slightest evidence of play. The name and all markings are bold.

G-9

Mint new as made. No evidence of play.

Pricing
Signature Balls

	G-5	G-7	G-9

VARDON FLYER

SPALDING, USA $500   1000   2250

Circa 1900. Bramble pattern. Gutta-percha. "Vardon Flyer" at pole.

TOMMY ARMOUR—MESH

WORTHINGTON BALL CO. $100   225   450

Circa 1931. "Tommy Armour" in black letters. "Great Lakes" monogram "GL" at poles.

JIMMY HINES

WORTHINGTON BALL CO. $40   75   150

Circa 1938. Dimple ball. "Victory" and "Jimmy Hines".

TOMMY ARMOUR

WORTHINGTON BALL CO. $30   60   100

Circa 1935. Small or large "Tommy Armour" in black letters. Four red and black dots at poles.

ALEX TAYLOR—MESH

ALEX TAYLOR CO., NEW YORK $100   225   450

Circa 1930. Two different mesh pattern balls. A "Taylor Ace" and "Alex Taylor Co" T 30 with a "T" at the poles.

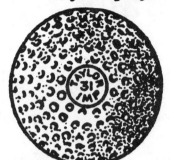

HARRY COOPER—MESH

WORTHINGTON BALL CO.   **$100**   **225**   **450**

Circa 1931. "Harry Cooper" in black letters. "Star" at poles

ALEX TAYLOR—DIMPLE

ALEX TAYLOR CO., NEW YORK   **$75**   **150**   **325**

Circa 1930. "Taylor Imp, 31" at the poles.

TOMMY ARMOUR

WORTHINGTON BALL CO.   **$10**   **15**   **30**

Circa 1958. "Silver Scot".

WIFFY COX—MESH

WORTHINGTON BALL CO.   **$100**   **225**   **450**

Circa 1930. Square mesh pattern.

JOCK HUTCHINSON—MESH

WORTHINGTON BALL CO.   **$100**   **225**   **450**

Circa 1930. Square mesh pattern.

TOMMY ARMOUR—DIMPLE

WORTHINGTON BALL CO.   **$25**   **45**   **75**

Circa 1937. "Tommy Armour" 50 or 60 with name in red block letters.

WALTER HAGEN

HAGEN GOLF CO.   **$125**   **200**   **350**

Circa 1930. Any mesh pattern.

WALTER HAGEN

HAGEN GOLF CO.   **$50**   **75**   **120**

Circa 1935. "Bingo", "Playboy", "Vulcord", "Honey Bee, "It's A Honey", or "288 For Tournament Play".

WALTER HAGEN

HAGEN GOLF CO.   **$20**   **35**   **50**

Circa 1950-1965. "Sir Walter", "Speed-Flo", "Trophy Plus", or "International".

WALTER HAGEN

HAGEN GOLF CO.   **$10**   **15**   **25**

Circa 1955-1965. "The Haig", "The Haig 80-90-100", or "TCW 80-90-100".

CRAIG WOOD

DUNLOP, ENGLAND   **$50**   **90**   **150**

Circa 1939. "Craig Wood" with "2 6 4" below name.

DENNY SHUTE

**WORTHINGTON
BALL CO.**   **$35**   **60**   **100**

Circa 1940. "Medalist".

GENE SARAZEN

**WILSON, THOMAS E.,
CHICAGO**   **$125**   **200**   **350**

Circa 1930. All mesh pattern balls.

GENE SARAZEN

**WILSON, THOMAS
E., CHICAGO**   **$60**   **125**   **200**

Circa 1932-1935. "50", "75", and "Flag". Tough or vulcanized covers.

KY LAFFOON

**WRIGHT & DITSON,
BOSTON, MA**   **$40**   **80**   **150**

Circa 1938. Two orange dots above and below name.

GENE SARAZEN

**WILSON, THOMAS
E., CHICAGO**   **$15**   **25**   **45**

Circa 1940-1952. "Squire".

GENE SARAZEN

**WILSON, THOMAS
E., CHICAGO**   **$15**   **20**   **25**

Circa 1960. "Strokemaster" and "Autograph".

DENNY SCHUTE

**WILSON, THOMAS
E., CHICAGO**   **$40**   **60**   **90**

Circa 1939-1940. "Red 50", "Custom", "Medalist" and "Red 75".

SARAZEN FIFTY

**WILSON, THOMAS
E., CHICAGO**   **$15**   **20**   **25**

Circa 1950. Dimple with "Sarazen" and a "Flag-in Hole" then "Fifty".

RALPH GULDAHL

WILSON, THOMAS E., CHICAGO $75 100 150
   Circa 1935. Radio Active 75.

RALPH GULDAHL

WILSON, THOMAS E., CHICAGO $35 50 75
   Circa 1936-1939. All varieties.

JOHNNY FARRELL

WILSON, THOMAS E., CHICAGO $125 200 350
   Circa 1930. Any mesh cover ball.

JOHNNY FARRELL

WILSON, THOMAS E., CHICAGO $45 70 100
   Circa 1936. "Autograph", "Champion", or "Supreme".

BYRON NELSON

MACGREGOR $35 60 90
   Circa 1935-1938. All varieties.

BYRON NELSON

NORTHWESTERN $25 35 50
   Circa 1962-1968. Steel center.

BYRON NELSON

NORTHWESTERN $15 25 45
   Circa 1962-1968. All varieties.

TOMMY AARON

MADE IN JAPAN $10 15 25
   Circa 1960-1965. Several varieties marked "Japan".

TOMMY AARON

SPALDING, USA $10 15 25
   Circa 1965. "Unicore".

BOBBY CRUICKSHANK

MACGREGOR $50 80 120
   Circa 1936. Two dots, red and black.

BOBBY CRUICKSHANK

WORTHINGTON BALL CO. $45 70 100
   Circa 1938. Worthington cured cover.

JOE KIRKWOOD

WORTHINGTON BALL CO. $30 40 65
   Circa 1940. All varieties.

BILLY BURKE

WORTHINGTON BALL CO. $30 45 75
   Circa late 1930s. Three balls about the same value. "50", "Victory" and "75".

JACK BURKE

WORTHINGTON BALL CO. $10 20 35
   Circa late 1950s. Many varieties all about the same value.

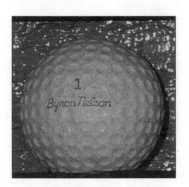

LAURIE AUCHTERLONIE

DUNLOP   **$40**   **60**   **100**

Circa 1957. Block letters on Dunlop 65 ball.

JIMMY DEMARET

MACGREGOR   **$25**   **35**   **50**

Circa 1958. All varieties.

WIFFY COX

WRIGHT & DITSON,
BOSTON, MA   **$60**   **90**   **125**

Circa 1936. "Wright & Ditson" with four green dots.

BABE DIDRIKSON

WILSON, THOMAS
E., CHICAGO   **$250**   **350**   **550**

Circa 1936. Wilson 35 and 50.

BABE DIDRIKSON

WILSON, THOMAS
E., CHICAGO   **$450**   **650**   **1000**

Circa 1936. Wilson 75.

BABE ZAHARIAS

WILSON, THOMAS
E., CHICAGO   **$125**   **175**   **300**

Circa 1939. Wilson 75.

GEORGE BAYER

MACGREGOR   **$25**   **35**   **50**

Circa 1958-1962. All varieties.

LLOYD MANGRUM

WILSON, THOMAS
E., CHICAGO   **$20**   **40**   **75**

Circa 1950. Name in block letters.

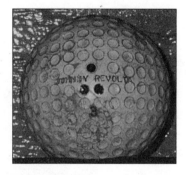

JOHNNY REVOLTA

WILSON, THOMAS
E., CHICAGO   **$25**   **35**   **60**

Circa 1936-1945. All varieties.

TONY LEMA

KROYDON,
NEWARK, NJ   **$30**   **50**   **75**

Circa 1963. With champagne glass.

TONY LEMA

KROYDON, NEWARK, NJ	$15	25	40

Circa 1962-1965. Small or large signature in red or black.

JACK FLECK

SPALDING, USA	$70	100	150

Circa 1956.

JOHNNY REVOLTA

NORTHWESTERN	$15	20	35

Circa 1963-1964.

HELEN HICKS

WILSON, THOMAS E., CHICAGO	$50	75	125

Circa late 1930s. All varieties.

BEN HOGAN

MACGREGOR	$30	45	75

Circa 1950. "Crown".

BEN HOGAN

HOGAN	$20	35	50

Circa 1955-1960. "River Run", "Hogan Construction" or red "Star".

BEN HOGAN

HOGAN	$5	10	15

Circa 1970-1990. Most all varieties.

LOU WORSHAM

MACGREGOR	$20	30	50

Circa 1955-1958.

SAM SNEAD

WILSON, THOMAS E., CHICAGO	$35	50	75

Circa 1938-1939. "White Sulpher" and "Greenbriar".

SAM SNEAD

WILSON, THOMAS E., CHICAGO	$10	15	30

Circa 1950. Blue Ridge.

SAM SNEAD

WILSON, THOMAS E., CHICAGO	$10	15	30

Circa 1960s. "100".

BILLY CASPER

WILSON, THOMAS E., CHICAGO	$25	35	50

Circa 1958. "Wilson Tournament" or "Super Power" with number at bottom.

BILLY CASPER

WILSON, THOMAS E., CHICAGO	$10	15	20

Circa 1960s-1980s. Most all varieties found.

JACK NICKLAUS

MACGREGOR $25   45   75

    Circa 1963. Gold colored Golden Bear.

PATTY BERG

**WILSON, THOMAS
E., CHICAGO** $45   65   100

    Circa 1955-1960. Four balls about the same value: "Autograph", "Trophy", "Classic", or the "Patrician".

JACK NICKLAUS

MACGREGOR $15   25   40

    Circa 1962-1968. "Champion", "Century", "Supreme", "Ambassador", "Embassy", "Diplomat", and "VIP 100".

PEGGY KIRK BELL

SPALDING, USA $25   35   50

    Circa 1965. Spalding Pinehurst.

JACK NICKLAUS

MACGREGOR $10   15   20

    Circa 1970s. Most all varieties.

ARNOLD PALMER

**WILSON, THOMAS
E., CHICAGO** $25   40   75

    Circa 1960. "Personal", "Autograph", "Victory", "S T C", "100", and "Steel Center".

ARNOLD PALMER

SEARS, ROEBUCK $15   20   35

    Circa 1963. Steel center.

ARNOLD PALMER

PRO GROUP $15   20   35

    Circa 1965. Steel center.

ARNOLD PALMER

PRO GROUP $10   15   25

    Circa 1977. Surlyn cover.

DAVE MARR

**WILSON, THOMAS
E., CHICAGO** $10   20   30

    Circa late 1960s. "Stylist" under name. Also "Pinehurst", "Medalist" and "100", all about the same value.

TED MAKALENA

UNKNOWN MAKER $60   100   150

    Circa 1960.

JULIUS BOROS

**WILSON, THOMAS
E., CHICAGO** $20   35   60

    Circa 1958. "100", "Zenith" and others.

SEVE BALLESTEROS

SLAZENGER, UK $15   25   35

    Circa 1980. Name in script.

NANCY LOPEZ

RAM GOLF CO. $15   25   40
   Circa 1970-1972. All varieties.

LAURA BAUGH

**WILSON, THOMAS
E., CHICAGO** $20   30   45
   Circa 1975. Wilson "XK".

CARY MIDDLECOFF

**WILSON, THOMAS
E., CHICAGO** $10   15   25
   Circa 1960. Autograph 100.

JOHNNY MILLER

**WILSON, THOMAS
E., CHICAGO** $10   15   25
   Circa 1969-1980. All varieties.

An assortment of collectible putters, irons and woods.

During the period from 1925 to 1950 many steel-shafted woods had colorful face inserts. These are called "Pretty Faces"; they are highly collectible and make a wonderful display.

(Far right) Some wood-shafted clubs from 1910 to the 1920s were fitted with face inserts. They are highly collectible.

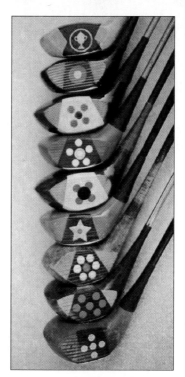

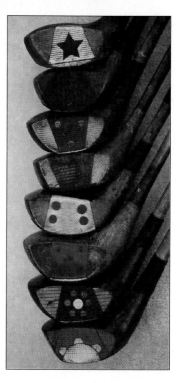

Golf balls from 1900 through the 1950s were usually packaged in colorful boxes, wrappers and sleeves. Many collectors collect boxes as well as balls.

An assortment of collectible putters.

Bronze, plaster and
other types of statuary
are nice office or den
display items.

Collecting golf antiques can mean collecting more than just clubs and balls, as this selection of artifacts attests.

Sets of clubs are a great display, especially if they are in a vintage golf bag.

During the 1920s, several companies used multiple markings on a single club. Kroydon used a line, waffle and circle pattern, while MacGregor punched dots over line scoring.

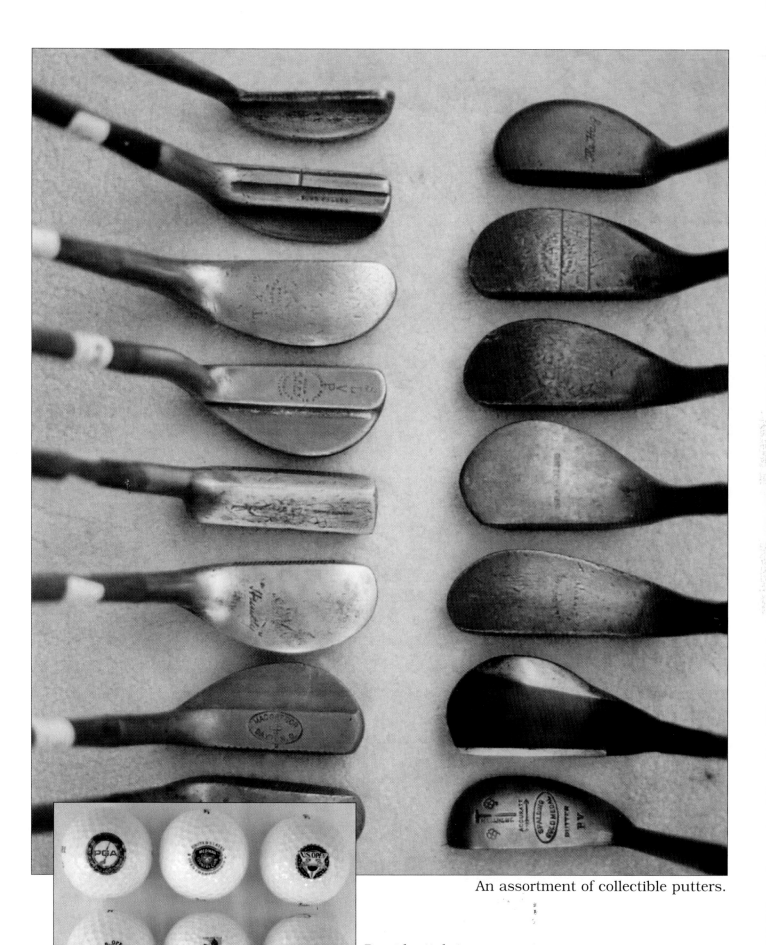

An assortment of collectible putters.

Presidential, tournament and logo balls are among the types that collectors are anxious to acquire.

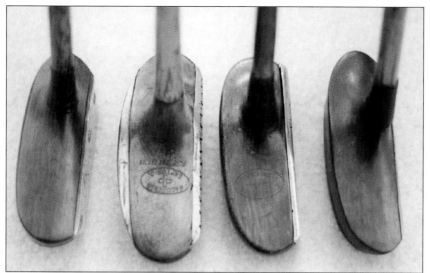

Four different wooden "Schenectady" center-shafted putters.

(Right) Face scoring was not particularly effective in imparting spin on the ball, but looked great in stores and in catalogues, and promoted sales. The Buhrke Company from Chicago made clubs with a "brass plug" for the sweet-spot.

Collectors don't "monkey around" when collecting ceramic pieces, as they are some of the most valuable—and fragile—golf collectibles.

Golf balls are some of the most prized of all golf collectibles.

An example of "The Spalding" driver made from one piece of hickory, a very rare and desirable collectible.

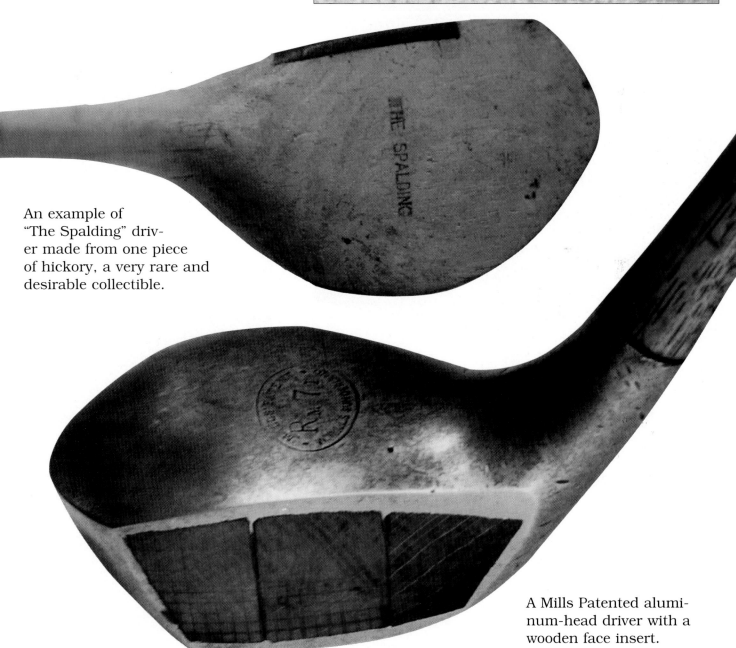

A Mills Patented aluminum-head driver with a wooden face insert.

An unopened foil pack and a selection of cards from the 1992 Pro Set PGA Tour trading card set. The 300-card set included PGA Tour regulars, golfers from the Senior Tour, and even European Tour players.

Authentic autographed photos are great for office or den displays.

Many non-golf magazines have pictured famous golfers on the cover. This *Time* with Bobby Jones on the cover is very scarce and one of the most sought after by collectors.

A long-nose play club with a leather face insert, by McEwan.

Tees are among the most sought after golf collectibles.

Manufacturers of golf goods published catalogs for both retail customers and the "trade." Originals are highly collectible, and reprints like the ones shown here are inexpensive, but valuable reference volumes for collectors.

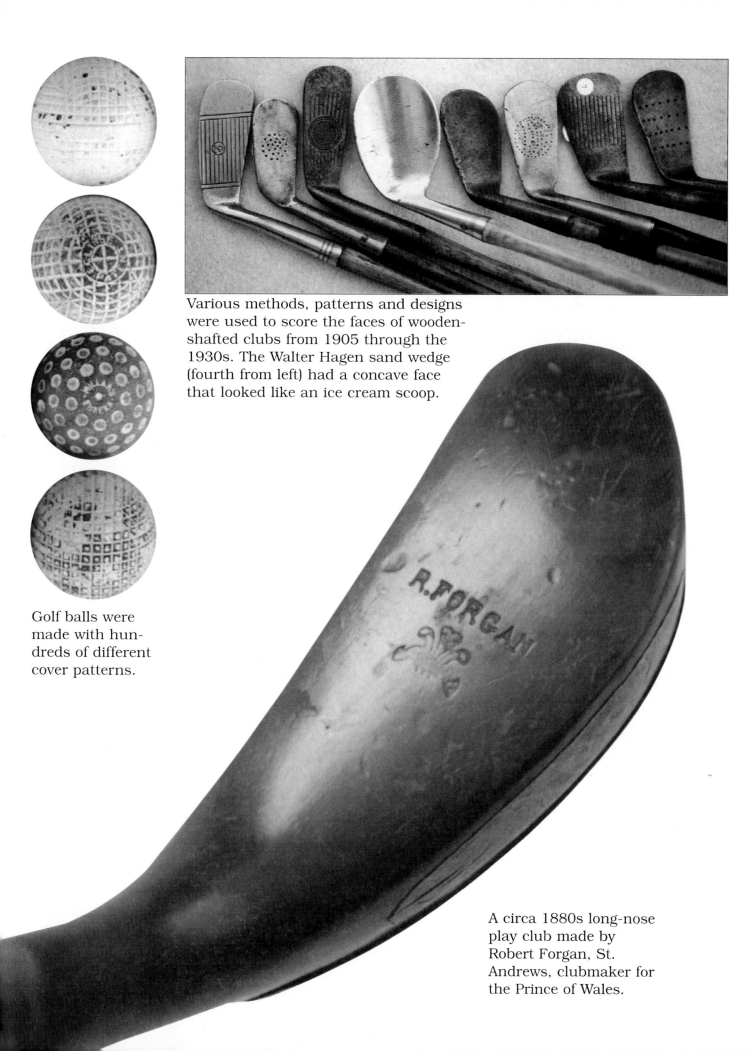

Various methods, patterns and designs were used to score the faces of wooden-shafted clubs from 1905 through the 1930s. The Walter Hagen sand wedge (fourth from left) had a concave face that looked like an ice cream scoop.

Golf balls were made with hundreds of different cover patterns.

A circa 1880s long-nose play club made by Robert Forgan, St. Andrews, clubmaker for the Prince of Wales.

Antique golf paintings are very valuble—both in dollar terms, and in what they teach us about the early days of the game.

Putters made of aluminum were very popular from 1900 through the 1930s.

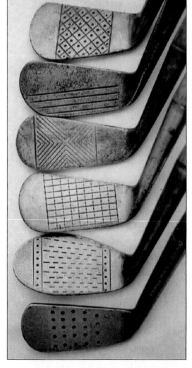

Clubs with unusual face markings make a great display.

An assortment of colorful and various-shaped wooden tees from the 1920s.

Deep-groove irons like these were made illegal for tournament play in 1922.

A "semi-long nose" head design made by Alex Patrick, circa 1890. This design bridged the transition from long-nose clubs to the rounded head we have today.

Money clips with tournament or PGA logos are highly collectible.

Original manufacturer catalogs from Bridgeport Athletic Manufacturing, Wright & Ditson and Spalding.

A selection of line-cut gutta-percha balls and rubber-core bramble-pattern balls, including one painted red for play on snowy days.

A matching set of golf scene-decorated pottery, including a plate, a very valuable and fragile collectible.

Two early, and very collectible, books on golf.

An attractive set of golf pottery, including a large pitcher and a beer stein.

The author, Chuck Furjanic, displays collectibles at a Golf Collectors Society meeting in Palm Springs, California.

A long-nose play club made by Willie Park of Musselburgh, Scotland, circa 1875.

Chapter 7

Collecting Autographs

Chapter 7

Collecting Autographs

Autographed photographs, gum cards, books, golf balls, letters and other items are highly sought after by collectors. The first questions collectors pose is about authenticity and guarantee. There are only two sources from which you can confidently obtain signed items. The first is to get them signed IN PERSON. If you send balls, pictures, cards, etc. by mail to a golf pro, his wife, secretary or an auto pen may do the signing, not the professional. Jack Nicklaus, Lee Trevino and several others use an auto pen to sign pictures. I've seen many "rubber stamp" Ben Hogan items, especially letters and 3 x 5 cards. Several others have their secretaries or family members sign items. Your best bet to get in-person signed items is to go to tournaments on *practice* days. Pros prefer not to sign anything but their official score card on tournament days.

The second, and most convenient, is to purchase your signed items from a *reputable* dealer or experienced collector who will guarantee the signed items for authenticity for LIFE. This means that anytime during the ownership of the signed item, it may be returned if there is a reasonable doubt the signature is not authentic. When a dealer or collector can give you this lifetime assurance, you can be confident it is an authentic signature. Many dealers will issue a "Certificate of Authenticity" that is, in fact, a worthless piece of paper unless backed by a LIFE guarantee. California law mandates all autographed items sold in or to a California resident for $50.00 or more must be accompanied by a certificate of authenticity. Many other states may have—or will have—similar laws. Just remember the certificate is only as good as the guarantee of the issuing dealer.

Most auction houses offer no return of any item when purchasing in person at the sale. Make sure you know the signatures you are purchasing are authentic or hire the services of an expert to inspect signed items for you. Experience is great, but the opinion of an expert is almost essential when purchasing at auctions.

Be careful when purchasing autographed golf balls. (These are not to be confused with "signature" balls that are imprinted with a professional's name at the ball factory as a form of advertising.) The dimple pattern and the small size of a ball makes it difficult to sign and many signatures are hard to authenticate. Forgers are acutely aware of this and will take every advantage. Do yourself a favor, collect only autographed balls you have had signed in person, or again buy only from dealers who offer a life guarantee of authenticity.

Mark Emerson, a recognized expert and a long time collector of quality autographed items, has been kind enough to offer his perspective on collecting autographs.

Golfing Autographs: A Brief History
by *Mark Emerson*

The autograph hobby dates back about 1,000 years, and with the first British Open Championship in 1860, golf began to establish itself as a sport. As a result, autographs of golf's greatest players did not escape interest of collectors.

The first great impresario of the game was Old Tom Morris. Old Tom was the most outstanding player of his day—winner of four British Open titles (1861, 1862, 1864 and 1867)—was a fine clubmaker, golf ball manufacturer and architect. He also was a visionary, understanding the appeal and collectibility of signed material and, even at the turn of the century, he was signing limited edition prints.

The emergence of "The Great Triumvirate," Harry Vardon, James Braid and J.H. Taylor, who between them captured 16 British Open titles, cemented interest in collecting autographs of golf's great stars in the United Kingdom. Signatures were mainly obtained in small leather-covered books designed for collecting autographs. Morris, Vardon, Braid and Taylor were responsible for creating the spark of collecting golf figures overseas.

In the United States, the U.S. Open Golf Championship began in 1895 but initially it attracted small fields. It wasn't until Francis Ouimet stunned the golf world with his 1913 U.S. Open triumph over Ted Ray and Harry Vardon in that memorable playoff that Americans began to take note of golf heroes. Consequently, autographs of early U.S. Open winners are scarce. The boom in American golf was just around the corner when Gene Sarazen, Bobby Jones and the flamboyant Walter Hagen began winning numerous major golfing titles between 1914 and 1930.

In the late 1950s, Arnold Palmer's magnetism electrified galleries and television viewers. Crowds at P.G.A. tour events grew at a larger pace. Today, at nearly any event, players are hounded for signatures on just about anything imaginable.

Why Autographs?

The appeal of autograph collecting generally falls into a few categories. First, collecting signatures in person can be fun and exciting. "In-person" collectors say they enjoy the moment a famous person spends with them, and every once in a while a brief conversation ensues that makes it a life-long memory.

The aspect of collecting older autographed pieces, especially those from deceased individuals, seems to center around the "connection" of an item held by, and then signed by, them.

In addition to the fun of autograph collecting, it can also become an investment that might pay off in time. Quality autographs, just like quality collectibles of all kinds, can appreciate in value.

Autographs can also become an outstanding piece of art that can adorn an office, home, or anywhere. As the collector, you can be the creator of that piece of art which can be fun and satisfying as well.

Whom To Collect

This is a topic every collector should try to come to grips with early on in the process. The best advice in any collecting pursuit is to develop a focus or goal. It is always up to the individual to make this decision, but collecting winners of major championships seems to be the most logical.

Collectible Formats

Once an individual decides whom to collect, it is wise to choose a preferred format for the collection. This is a matter of taste and value. Golf autographs can be on programs, pairing sheets, magazine covers, photos, letters, 3 x 5 cards, golf balls, just to name a few.

Condition

The "quality" of autographs is an important aspect of collecting and involves several factors: the neatness of the actual signature, the boldness of the signature in relation to its background, the instrument with which the autograph is written, and what it's written on.

Prices
Autographed Items

The following list identifies key players and the current values for their autographs. Many autographs are found on pairing sheets, programs, score cards, 3 x 5 cards and autograph book album pages as well as towels, hats and golf gloves. Prices are for ink signatures pre-1975 or "Sharpie" post-1975. Pencil signatures are valued at 30 to 50 percent less.

	G-5	G-7	G-9

TOM MORRIS

**SIGNED CARD
OR PAGE** $1500   2000   3000
Circa 1900.

TOM MORRIS

SIGNED PHOTO $2250   3250   4750
Circa 1900.

HARRY VARDON

**SIGNED CARD
OR PAGE** $300   500   800
Circa 1900-1920.

HARRY VARDON

SIGNED PHOTO $500   950   1500
Circa 1900-1920.

JAMES BRAID

**SIGNED CARD
OR PAGE** $350   600   1000
   Circa 1900-1920.

JAMES BRAID

SIGNED PHOTO $500   800   1500
   Circa 1900-1920.

J.H. TAYLOR

**SIGNED CARD
OR PAGE** $350   550   950
   Circa 1900-1920

J. H. TAYLOR

SIGNED PHOTO $450   750   1250
   Circa 1900-1920

ROBERT T. JONES JR.

SIGNED PHOTO $400   650   1000
   Circa 1955-1970. Shaky ball point pen signature.

ROBERT T. JONES, JR.

**SIGNED CARD
OR PAGE** $400   700   1200
   Circa 1930-1950. Black fountain pen signature.

ROBERT T. JONES, JR.

SIGNED LETTER $750   1250   2000
   Circa 1930-1950. Signed "Bob Jones". Black fountain pen signature.

ROBERT T. JONES, JR.

SIGNED PHOTO $1500   2250   3500
   Circa 1930-1950. Black fountain pen signature.

ROBERT T. JONES, JR.

SIGNED PHOTO $1500   2250   3500
   Circa 1930-1950. Signed "Bob Jones". Black fountain pen signature.

GLENNA COLLETT

**SIGNED CARD
OR PAGE** $125   225   400
   Vintage fountain pen signature

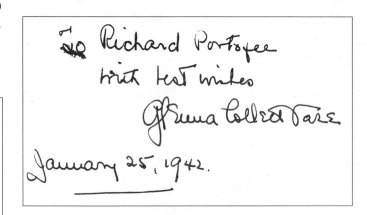

GLENNA COLLETT-VARE

SIGNED PHOTO $150   275   450
   Vintage fountain pen signature.

JOYCE WETHERED

**SIGNED CARD
OR PAGE** $70   120   200
   Vintage fountain pen signature.

JOYCE WETHERED

SIGNED PHOTO $100   200   350
   Vintage fountain pen signature.

JAMES BARNES

**SIGNED CARD
OR PAGE** $200   300   450

Vintage fountain pen signature.

JAMES BARNES

SIGNED BOOK $225   350   500

Most commonly signed book, *Picture Analysis of Golf Strokes*, 1919.

WALTER HAGEN

**SIGNED CARD
OR PAGE** $250   350   550

Vintage fountain pen signature.

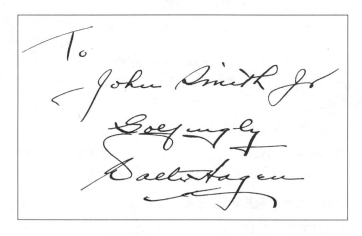

WALTER HAGEN

SIGNED PHOTO $500   850   1500

Vintage fountain pen signature.

TOMMY ARMOUR

**SIGNED CARD
OR PAGE** $75   125   225

Vintage fountain pen signature.

TOMMY ARMOUR

SIGNED BOOK $125   175   275

Most commonly signed book, *How to Play Your Best Golf All the Time*, 1953.

TOMMY ARMOUR

SIGNED PHOTO $175   300   500

Vintage fountain pen signature.

FRANCIS OUIMET

**SIGNED CARD
OR PAGE** $100   175   275

Vintage fountain pen signature.

FRANCIS OUIMET

SIGNED BOOK $175   250   375

Most commonly signed book was *The Rules of Golf*, 1948.

CHICK EVANS

**SIGNED CARD
OR PAGE** $125   225   400

Vintage fountain pen signature.

JOHNNY FARRELL

**SIGNED CARD
OR PAGE** $75   100   150

Vintage fountain pen signature.

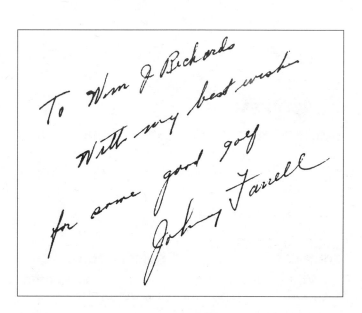

JOHNNY FARRELL

SIGNED BOOK $100   150   225

Most commonly signed book, *If I Were In Your Shoes*, 1951.

DENNY SCHUTE

**SIGNED CARD
OR PAGE** $100   150   225

Vintage fountain pen signature.

DENNY SCHUTE

SIGNED PHOTO $125   200   300

Vintage fountain pen signature.

HORTON SMITH

**SIGNED CARD
OR PAGE** $200   350   500

Vintage fountain pen signature. Most sought after and most difficult Master's winner to obtain.

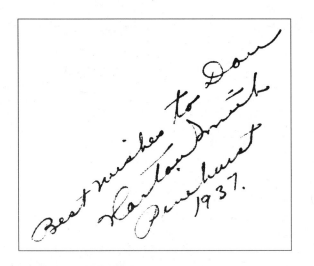

HORTON SMITH

SIGNED PHOTO $350   500   800

Vintage fountain pen signature. Most sought after and most difficult Master's winner to obtain.

JOHNNY GOODMAN

**SIGNED CARD
OR PAGE** $125   200   350

Vintage fountain pen signature. As an amateur won U.S. Open and U.S. Amateur.

LEO DIEGEL

**SIGNED CARD
OR PAGE** $100   150   250

Vintage fountain pen signature.

RALPH GULDAHL

**SIGNED CARD
OR PAGE** $75   125   200

Vintage fountain pen signature.

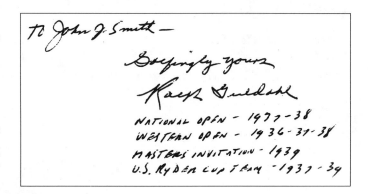

RALPH GULDAHL

SIGNED PHOTO $125   250   400

Vintage fountain pen signature.

JOHNNY REVOLTA

**SIGNED CARD
OR PAGE** $60   90   150

Vintage fountain pen signature.

JOHNNY REVOLTA

SIGNED BOOK $100   150   225

Short Cuts to Better Golf, 1949.

BABE DIDRIKSON ZAHARIAS

**SIGNED CARD
OR PAGE** $200   325   475

Vintage fountain pen signature.

BABE DIDRIKSON ZAHARIAS

SIGNED PHOTO $250   350   550
Vintage fountain pen signature.

LAWSON LITTLE

SIGNED PHOTO $125   200   325
Vintage fountain pen signature.

LAWSON LITTLE

**SIGNED CARD
OR PAGE** $175   225   425
Vintage fountain pen signature.

JIMMY DEMARET

**SIGNED CARD
OR PAGE** $50   75   100
Vintage fountain pen signature.

JIMMY DEMARET

SIGNED PHOTO $100   175   275
Vintage fountain pen signature.

BYRON NELSON

SIGNED CARD $5   10   15
Circa 1960-1990s

BYRON NELSON

SIGNED BOOK $20   25   30
Circa 1980-1990s

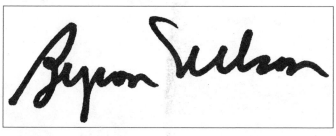

BYRON NELSON

SIGNED PHOTO $30   40   50
Circa 1960-1990s.

BYRON NELSON

SIGNED PHOTO $60   100   150
Circa 1935-1950. Vintage fountain pen signature.

HENRY COTTON

**SIGNED CARD
OR PAGE** $40   65   100
Vintage fountain pen signature.

HENRY COTTON

SIGNED LETTER $75   125   200
Most letters by Cotton were handwritten in fountain pen.

HENRY COTTON

SIGNED PHOTO $75   125   200
Vintage fountain pen signature.

CLAUDE HARMON

**SIGNED CARD
OR PAGE** $50   75   125
Vintage signature.

BOBBY LOCKE

**SIGNED CARD
OR PAGE** $50   75   125
Vintage fountain pen signature.

BOBBY LOCKE

SIGNED PHOTO $75   125   200
Vintage fountain pen signature.

PETER THOMPSON

**SIGNED CARD
OR PAGE** $15   20   25
Vintage fountain pen signature.

PETER THOMPSON

SIGNED PHOTO $20   30   45
Vintage fountain pen signature.

GENE SARAZEN

SIGNED CARD	$5	10	15

Circa 1960-1990s.

GENE SARAZEN

SIGNED PHOTO	$30	40	50

Circa 1960-1990s.

GENE SARAZEN

SIGNED PHOTO	$50	90	125

Circa 1925-1950. Vintage fountain pen signature.

MICKEY WRIGHT

SIGNED CARD OR PAGE	$10	15	20

Vintage ink pen signature.

MICKEY WRIGHT

SIGNED PHOTO	$15	20	30

Vintage ink pen signature.

PATTY BERG

SIGNED CARD OR PAGE	$10	15	20

Circa 1950-1980.

PATTY BERG

SIGNED PHOTO	$20	30	40

Circa 1950-1980.

BEN HOGAN

SIGNED CARD	$75	100	150

Circa 1960-1980. Signature not shaky.

BEN HOGAN

SIGNED BOOK	$175	250	400

Circa 1960-1980. Signature not shaky.

BEN HOGAN

SIGNED PHOTO	$200	300	450

Circa 1960-1980. Signature not shaky.

BEN HOGAN

SIGNED PHOTO	$300	450	750

Circa 1940-1950. Vintage ink pen signature.

SAM SNEAD

SIGNED PHOTO	$20	30	40

Circa 1980s-1990s.

SAM SNEAD

SIGNED CARD	$20	30	40

Circa 1980s-1990s.

SAM SNEAD

SIGNED PHOTO	$75	100	150

Circa 1940-1950. Vintage ink pen signature.

BOB HOPE

GOLF RELATED ITEM	$30	45	75

Pen or sharpie signature.

TONY LEMA

SIGNED CARD OR PAGE	$175	250	400

Ink pen signature.

TONY LEMA

SIGNED BOOK	$300	500	700

Most commonly signed book, *Golfer's Gold*, 1964.

TONY LEMA

SIGNED PHOTO	$350	500	750

Ink pen signature.

JULIUS BOROS

SIGNED CARD OR PAGE	$10	15	20

Ink pen signature.

JULIUS BOROS

SIGNED PHOTO	$20	35	50

Ink pen signature.

ARNOLD PALMER

ALL SIGNED ITEMS	$30	40	50

Circa 1960-1990s.

JACK NICKLAUS

ALL SIGNED ITEMS	$60	75	90

Circa 1960-1990s. Beware of auto pen signatures.

KEN VENTURI

ALL SIGNED ITEMS	$10	15	20

Circa 1964-1990s.

GARY PLAYER

SIGNED CARD OR PAGE	$5	10	15

Circa 1960s-1990s.

LEE TREVINO

ALL SIGNED ITEMS   **$15**   **20**   **25**
    Sharpie signature. Beware of auto pen signatures.

HALE IRWIN

ALL SIGNED ITEMS   **$10**   **15**   **20**
    Sharpie signature.

NICK FALDO

SIGNED PHOTO   **$10**   **15**   **25**
    Circa 1980s-1990s.

GARY PLAYER

SIGNED PHOTO   **$10**   **15**   **25**
    Circa 1960s-1990s.

TOM WATSON

ALL SIGNED ITEMS   **$15**   **20**   **25**
    Sharpie signature.

CORY PAVIN

ALL SIGNED ITEMS   **$10**   **15**   **20**
    Sharpie signature.

SEVE BALLESTEROS

ALL SIGNED ITEMS   **$15**   **20**   **25**
    Sharpie signature.

FRED COUPLES

ALL SIGNED ITEMS   **$15**   **20**   **25**
    Sharpie signature.

ERNIE ELS

ALL SIGNED ITEMS   **$15**   **20**   **25**
    Sharpie signature.

PAYNE STEWART

ALL SIGNED ITEMS   **$15**   **20**   **25**
    Sharpie signature.

TIGER WOODS

ALL SIGNED ITEMS   **$20**   **25**   **30**
    Sharpie signature.

JOHN DALY

ALL SIGNED ITEMS   **$20**   **25**   **30**

Sharpie signature.

GREG NORMAN

ALL SIGNED ITEMS   **$20**   **25**   **30**

Sharpie signature usually with flag-in-hole or word of wisdom.

Chapter 8

Collecting Tees

Chapter 8

Collecting Tees

An Introduction to Golf Tees

by Lee Crist

The "TEE" has played an important role since golf's inception over 500 years ago. Today we take them so matter-of-factly, we usually don't bother to pick them up after a tee shot.

It may surprise you to know tees were not always made of wood and obtainable free by the handfuls at the pro shop. They were made of aluminum, paper, plastic, steel, wire, zinc, rubber—anything that would raise the ball from the turf. Shapes and forms were stars, triangles, domes, tethers, spinners, molds, and just about anything imaginable and even some unimaginable.

They came individually, in boxes, string bags, paper bags, matchbooks, wheels, tins, and any other marketable containers. Pros stocked numerous varieties in their shops, and the greenskeepers lost their tempers when the new wire tees jammed their mowers. The poor tee was berated, bemused and left on the teeing ground until one day Walter Hagen was paid to use a particular tee, and as a gesture to his fans, left them on the teeing ground after a shot. When the last player in his group hit, and strolled down the fairway, a mad scramble ensued—by who else...the collector—to pick up the tee Hagen had just used!

Lee Crist has been a collector of tees for many years and has accumulated a vast collection and assortment. He was kind enough to provide the following for your collecting pleasures.

Everyone knows golf tees are those little white trumpet-looking items approximately 1-7/8 inches long. In reality, golf tees have been around for more than one hundred years and, most likely, the first golf tee was a good swift stomp of a golfer's heel. This raised the ground from a common plain to a higher level giving the player a type of launching pad.

After the heel print came forming a mound of moist dirt (or sand) that would give the ball somewhat of an elevated position, making it easier for contact. Molding each tee by hand constituted a very messy way of accomplishing the feat. Alas, the invention of the sand tee mold came into existence. This approach to forming a consistent tee became popular during the early 1890s. While this form of teeing the ball was not the ultimate, it was definitely a great improvement. Around 1893, more entrepreneurs were at work and individual tees were being developed. Prosper L. Senate of Philadelphia was given credit for inventing and patenting the first portable tee, although I suspect that individuals had made there own ..."one of a kind"... long before this.

As golf became more popular in the United States, so did the quest to find a better way to present the ball for action. The poor golf tee has been the target of abuse ever since and, as of this writing, we have documented 31 variations of sand tee molds.

Collecting golf tees is not a matter of collecting every color in the rainbow or collecting every tee that has a different advertisement. A tee collector, a purist, is a person who has committed his every fiber to finding all the physically different shaped tees that were ever designed, every cloth tee bag ever made, every commercial box manufactured, every advertisement printed and, last but not least, how about patents? Probably none of the collectors started out that way, although it would be very nice to have a few odd looking tees around as a conversation piece.

How to Start a Collection

It is recommended that you communicate with as many of your fellow golfers, friends, golf dealers and antique dealers as you can. Getting the word out and enlisting the help of others will go a long way. Letting people know that you are "looking" does wonders. It's human nature for people to want to help.

Designing your own business/collector card can also be very helpful and lots of fun. Flea markets and garage sales are a great source for finding tees; never pass up an opportunity to go through the pockets of an old golf bag.

Joining one of the antique golf societies, such as the Golf Collectors Society, is another way of finding fellow collectors who will be more than glad to have someone to correspond with. These people love to buy, sell or trade for something they need in their collection; if you have an opportunity to buy more than one unusual tee—buy it. It's always useful to have extras in trading.

How to Display

Once you start accumulating tees, consideration should be given as to how you are going to sort, display, store, and transport your collection. There are numerous ways to display, as there are many categories of tees: Old wooden tees, paper tees, plastic tees, metal tees, pencil tees, surface tees, height tees, novelty tees, tether tees, weighted tees, rubber tees, celluloid tees, swivel tees, and last but not least, sand mold tees.

Some collections are displayed in jewelry-type trays, others are mounted in styrofoam, some are mounted on plywood with very thin wire, and some use file cabinets, housing the collection in various zip lock bags. The latter is a little cumbersome if you plan to transport and show.

How Extensive is Tee Collecting?

When talking to people about collecting, the one thing you always hear is "I had no idea that there were so many different tees." There have been more than 1,275 physically different tees catalogued and numbered; much of the credit for this belongs to Art Eden of Florida and Irv Valenta of North Carolina.

As far as "names" of tees, commercial and otherwise, 394 different have been accounted for.

In the early 1900s, packaging to promote the merchandising of tees became an industry in itself. Tees were packaged in large and small boxes with very ornate designs. Boxes could hold 9, 18, 25, 50, or 100 pieces. There are at least 52 different boxes that have been catalogued.

Another packaging concept was cloth tee bags, similar to a tobacco pouch, which held 50 or 100 tees. Walgreen Drug Co. and Sears Roebuck were two of the early suppliers of the bulk bags; 54 different ones have been catalogued. Paper bags were also used to hold 15 to 25 tees. Most bags were white with the printed advertisement of the golf companies.

Tee packets similar to matchbooks are also collectibles and have been produced since the early 1920s.

Tee advertisements have appeared as early as the 1890s in some sports magazines and are also collectibles.

Pricing

Pricing is a very subjective issue. Many individuals ask what a particular tee is worth. Obviously, the answer is "Whatever someone is willing to pay."

The following entries and photos will make an effort to identify some of the tees that you may find, and estimate their approximate value based on condition.

Prices

Golf Tees

	G-5	G-7	G-9

WALGREEN GOLF TEES
WALGREEN STORES $35   60   100

Circa 1930s. Yellow and black box of yellow-colored wooden tees.

REX ZINC TEES
THE REX CO., CHICAGO $60   100   150

Circa 1930. Red box. Zinc tees.

TEES IN BAGS
VARIOUS MAKERS $30   50   75

Circa 1930s-1940s. Drawstring bags of fifty and one hundred wooden tees. (Below)

PRYDE'S ORANGE TEE
ORANGE MFG. CO. $50   100   150

Circa late 1920s. Carrot shaped wood tees. Blue and orange box.

JUST PERFECT TEES
VARIOUS $35   60   100

Circa early 1930s. Eighteen wooden tees in pale green box.

THE REDDY TEE

NIEBLO MFG CO	$35	70	125

Circa 1930. Wooden tees in green, white and red box.

CRUICKSHANK STEEL TEES

VARIOUS	$60	90	150

Circa 1930. Red wire tees with circular top. Green and red box with Bobby Cruickshank's picture.

BOBBY TEES

VARIOUS   **$40   60   100**

Circa late 1920s. Red wooden goblet-style tees in colorful box.

TOP NOT TEE

VARIOUS   **$40   60   100**

Circa late 1920s. Made of both wood and steel. Orange and white box.

PEG GOLF TEE

VARIOUS   **$40   60   100**

Circa 1930. Yellow box with twelve tees. (Original display boxes are quite valuable.)

GOLD MEDAL GOLF TEE

VARIOUS   **$40**   **60**   **100**

Circa 1930. Twenty wooden tees in box.

THE "YELLO" TEE

VARIOUS   **$40**   **60**   **100**

Circa 1927. Black-and-yellow box of eighteen yellow-colored wooden tees. Endorsed by Walter Hagen and Joe Kirkwood.

NOVEL TEES

VARIOUS   **$50**   **75**   **125**

Circa 1930. Circular Handi-Pack of nine tees.

ALL-MY-TEE

VARIOUS   **$35**   **60**   **100**

Circa 1920. Red rubber with weighted end.

BREAK APART PLASTIC TEES

SPALDING, USA   **$60**   **90**   **150**

Circa 1930s. Twenty red tees that break apart when needed.

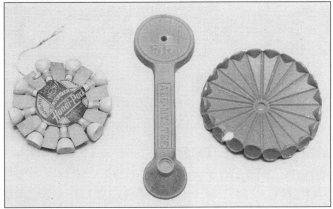

PERFECT GOLF TEE

VARIOUS   **$75**   **100**   **125**

Patented 1927. Molded rubber tee secured in the ground by a nail.

MATCH BOOOK TEES

VARIOUS   **$15**   **25**   **45**

Circa 1930s. Matchbook style with three to six tees. Matchbooks from the 1940s and later are worth considerably less.

NOVEL-TEES

**SPURGIN MFG.,
CHICAGO**   **$45**   **75**   **125**

Circa late 1920s. A book of eighteen paper tees.

THE SCOT-TEE

VARIOUS   **$60**   **100**   **150**

Circa late 1920s. Box of eighteen wooden tees.

RITE PENCIL TEE

**WIMO SPECIALTY
CO., NY**   **$5**   **10**   **20**

Circa 1927. Long tee with pencil lead at tip. Original boxes are scarce. Prices are for single tees.

AVON DOUBLE ARM TEE

VARIOUS   **$75**   **100**   **150**

Circa 1920s. Made in England of rubber with two tee heights. Approximately five inches long.

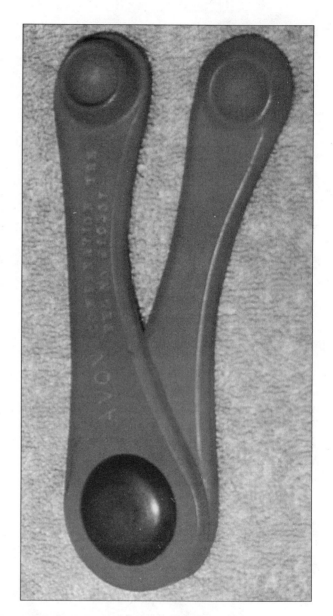

KEYSTONE SAND TEE MOLD

VARIOUS   **$300**   **400**   **500**

Circa 1920-1930. Bakelite plastic with spring plunger.

SAND TEE MOLD

VARIOUS   **$400**   **650**   **850**

Circa 1890-1920. Brass with spring plunger.

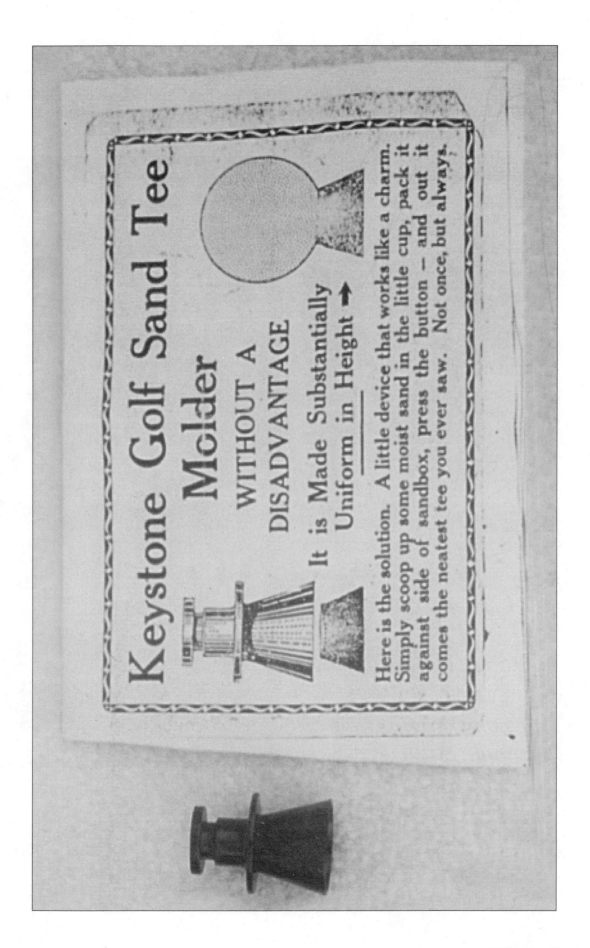

Keystone Golf Sand Tee Molder

WITHOUT A DISADVANTAGE

It is Made Substantially Uniform in Height ➔

Here is the solution. A little device that works like a charm. Simply scoop up some moist sand in the little cup, pack it against side of sandbox, press the button — and out it comes the neatest tee you ever saw. Not once, but always.

K-D SAND TEE MOLD

K-D MFG.,
LANCASTER, PA   **$400   550   750**

Circa 1920s. Polished aluminum with spring plunger.

~and out pops the neatest tee you ever saw!

Scoop up some wet sand, pack the cup against side of sand box, press the button — and there's a tee that's meant to *drive* from!

With the K-D Tee Mold you can make ten million tees of *absolutely uniform height* quicker and neater than by hand. And the tee mold goes in your pocket — not down the fairway.

50c Polished aluminum. Light as a feather. If your "pro" or dealer cannot supply you order direct.

K-D Mfg. Co., Lancaster, Penna.

DOUGLAS SAND TEE GUN

VARIOUS   **$450   600   850**

Circa 1910-1920. Cylindrical plunger made of stainless steel. Made in England.

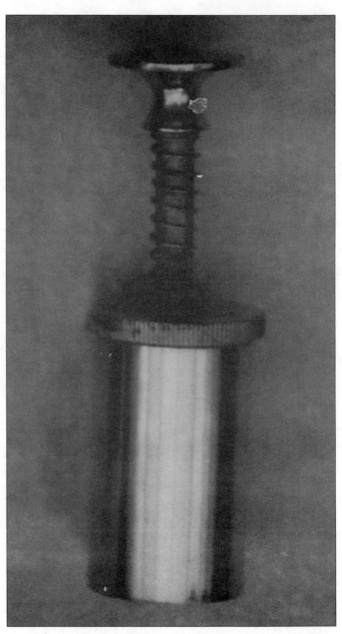

BRASS DOUBLE GOLF TEE STAMP

RANSOME   **$500   750   1000**

Circa 1900. Brass sand tee mold with a deep side for drives and shallow side for irons.

ROUND CUPPED DOME METAL TEES

VARIOUS   **$20**   **35**   **65**

Circa 1920s. Half-dollar sized "Cupped Dome"-type tee. Most had advertisements imprinted on them. Some were made of plastic and are valued less than the metal dome tees. (Above)

ETERNA TEE

VARIOUS   **$35**   **50**   **75**

Circa 1950s. A three height plastic tee. (Right)

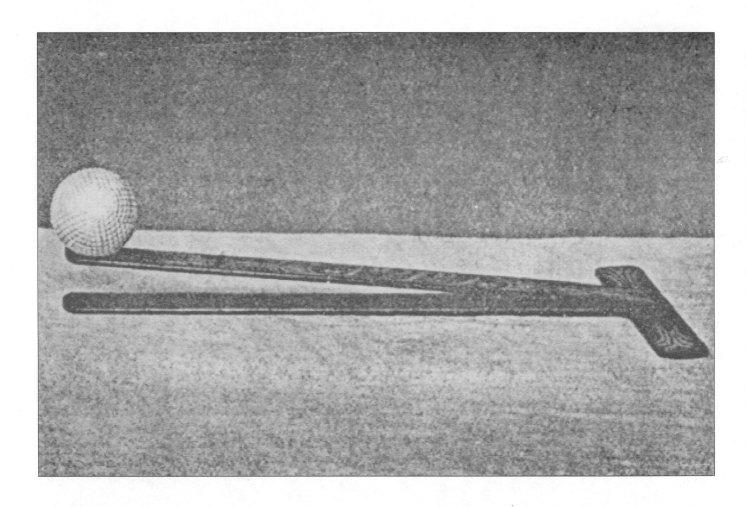

RUBBER MANHATTAN TEE

VARIOUS	$75	100	150

Circa 1920. Five-inch-long rubber tee with round weight at one end, tee at other.

SELF-ADJUSTING GOLF TEE

MILLAR, GLASGOW	$150	250	450

Circa 1900.

INTERNATIONAL GOLF TEE

UNKNOWN MAKER	$75	125	250

Circa 1917. Two rubber tees secured by a rubber tether.

PERFEC TEE

UNKNOWN MAKER   **$50**   **90**   **150**

Circa 1925.

TRIPLE-T GOLF TEE

SIMPLEX MFG.,
CLEVELAND, OH   **$5**   **10**   **20**

Circa 1925. Made for adjusting to three heights. Original boxes are scarce. Prices are for single tees.

NO-LOOZ-TEE

VARIOUS   **$40**   **60**   **80**

Circa 1950s-1960s. Weighted end. Made of rubber.

G & S GOLF TEE

VARIOUS   **$50**   **75**   **125**

Circa 1920s. Brass tee with rubber arm that swivels.

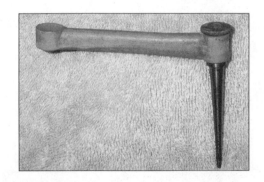

PERMA TEE

VARIOUS   **$75**   **100**   **150**

Circa 1930. Aluminum tee with steel arm that swivels.

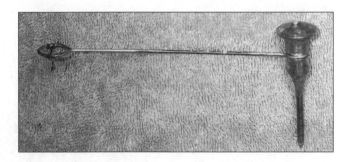

TETHER TEES

VARIOUS   **$50**   **75**   **100**

Circa 1900-1930s. Many varieties with a cord or "Tether" between weight or colorful thistle and the tee.

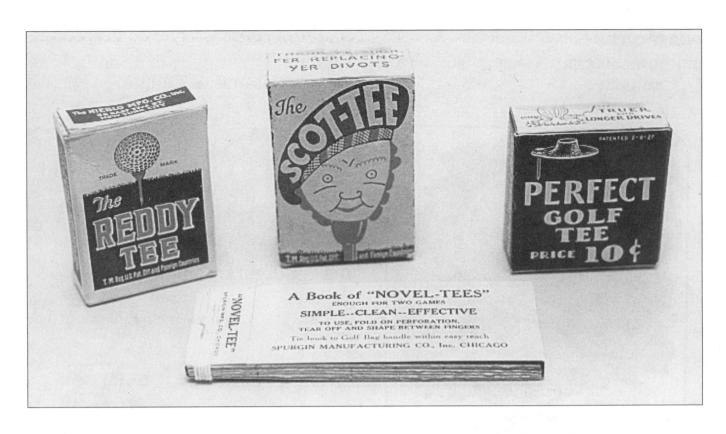

Chapter 9

Collecting Books on Golf

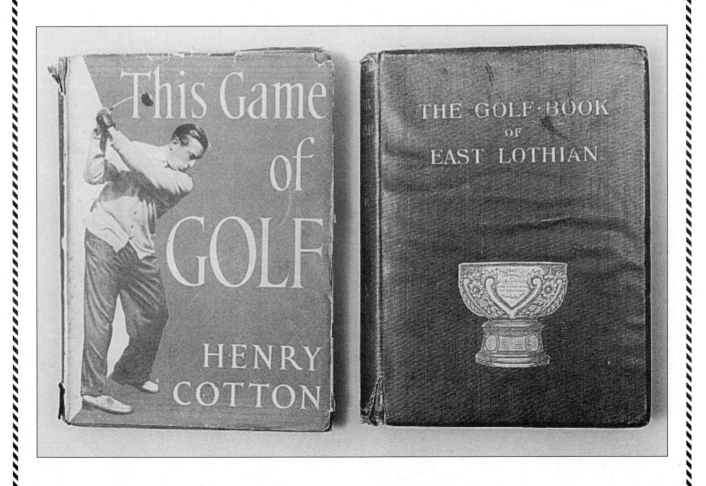

Chapter 9

Collecting Books on Golf

Golf books cover many categories. Instruction, architecture, history, rules and fiction are among the most popular with collectors. Some reference books, generally acquired for information and pricing, are highly collectible as well.

Scotland's King James II, in 1457, issued a decree outlawing golf because his soldiers were golfing more than practicing their archery skills. This decree became the first printed reference to the game of golf. It wasn't until the golf boom of the 1890s that books on golf were published in great quantities.

Richard E. Donovan and Joseph S.F. Murdoch collaborated to publish *The Game of Golf and the Printed Word* (1988) which is a bibliography of golf literature in the English language. This is a highly regarded reference book, and a collectible.

Joseph S.F. Murdoch, well known author, book collector and co-founder of the Golf Collectors Society, has kindly written an introduction to collecting books.

Collecting Golf Books

by Joseph S.F. Murdoch

The collecting of golf artifacts, a hobby that has a history going back several hundred years, has become a major collecting interest in recent years. Among the most popular collectible items are books that relate the history of the game, the stories of great champions and, inevitably, books of instruction calculated to improve our skills. Some cynics may proclaim that no one ever learned to play the game through a book, although there are some notable examples of some who did. Walter J. Travis and Larry Nelson are two who come to mind.

Books of every description have been collected since the first book appeared and it is a hobby which has seized the mind of man throughout the ages. Golf books may not have the lineage of, say, a Gutenburg Bible or the famed poets of England, but for the man who loves the game and likes to read about it, there is a line of books calculated to intrigue any golfer who combines his love of reading with his love of the game.

One of the many allures of book collecting is that one can select a subject or a subject within a subject, and spend a lifetime in pursuit of the books within that chosen field of interest. Books on golf can be divided and subdivided into many different categories, each of which may excite the interest of the collector. Books on golf history, the great champions of the game, the building of golf courses, golf humor, golf fiction, golf poetry, golf instruction, or other facets of the game have been written and published over the years, and the collector has the liberty of selecting that subject which is of his greatest interest.

One can, for example, choose books published in one country or by one writer and form a very nice library of such books. Perhaps a budding young collector may say to himself, "The game has only been played in America for 100 years so I will collect books on the game which have been published only in America." In restricting himself to this one sphere, he will find great treasures and enough books to fill the shelves, floor to ceiling, of a fair-size room.

With the turn of the century, golfers and books proliferated and the books tumbled out of the publishing houses like bogeys from the clubs of a high-handicap hacker. There are books to interest every taste . . . those who strive for the ultimate par in books of instruction; history of the game, records of the great champions, fiction, poetry, the history of venerable clubs and, in more recent years, about the sport of golf collecting.

All of these books, now numbering in the thousands, are testimony to man's addiction to the game and a desire to read about it if fog, sleet and snow conspire to keep him in the house. Should you be of a persuasion to read and to accumulate a few books on the game you love, you will find great treasures in the library of golf.

Determining Condition and Value of Books

by George Lewis

There have been well over 8,000 golf books published in numerous languages, and it would be almost impossible to list prices for them all. Therefore, to help you determine relative values, the following list of about one hundred books includes a few representative titles for each category, such as instruction, history, biography, architecture, essays, reference, etc. Although most of the books listed are still available today with a little legwork, a few of the cornerstone scarce and rare works are also included so that you can get a better feel for the range of pricing.

Prices of books, like so many other collectibles, are determined by condition, edition, scarcity and desirability. More recent books are not listed, because their value has not yet had a chance to fluctuate significantly from the published price. Also not included are rare works which are out of reach of most collectors such as *The Goff* by Thomas Mathison, first published in 1743, last auctioned for over $30,000.

Books that are generally in poor condition (missing pages, broken cover or contents damaged, badly soiled or stained), or library books are not rated. These can be useful for information, but usually are not worth recording as part of your library.

Underlining, margin notes, repair or rebinding all reduce the value of a book. A book which has been beautifully rebound in leather may or may not be worth more than it is with the original binding; most serious collectors would prefer the book in its original state. A leather binding might enhance the value of an inexpensive book, but why spend the money to rebind it? Buy one in very good original condition instead! First printings of first editions command higher prices than later printings.

Lowest price shown is for a first printing in good condition (moderate cover wear, fading, stain, considerable foxing, speckling or browning to pages);

Mid range price is for a very good copy of a first printing (light signs of age, former owner's neatly inked name, date or brief inscription, perhaps a little foxing or speckling to pages) and if a post-1950 book, in a dust jacket (if it was issued with one);

Highest price is for a first printing which is fine (looks like it is virtually new, with no inscriptions, soil, stain or wear, with dust jacket if issued with one). It is usually quite hard to find pre-1950 books in fine condition, so they may command a significant premium, especially with a dust jacket. Very good or fine condition of the dust jacket may also increase the price, in some instances even doubling the value of the book if the dust jacket is very scarce.

If you want to form a golf library of any significance, it is suggested that you discuss your goals with a reputable and knowledgeable dealer who can advise you and assist you to put together a more meaningful collection.

George Lewis, PGA Master Professional, is one of the largest golf book, ephemera and collectibles dealers in the world. Established in 1980, George Lewis/Golfiana can be reached at PO Box 291, Mamaroneck, NY 10543.

Prices

Golf Books

	G-5	G-7	G-9

ALLEN, PETER

| **FAMOUS FAIRWAYS** | $60 | 125 | 150 |

Architecture. 1968.

ARMOUR, TOMMY

| **HOW TO PLAY YOUR BEST GOLF ALL THE TIME** | $8 | 25 | 35 |

Instruction. 1953. Many later printings.

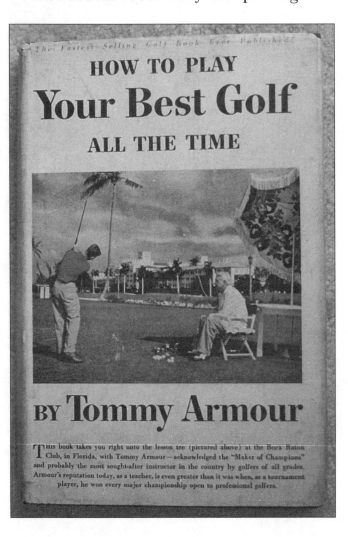

BAMBERGER, MICHAEL

| **THE GREEN ROAD HOME** | $15 | 25 | 40 |

Biography. 1986.

BARNES, JAMES M.

| **PICTURE ANALYSIS OF GOLF STROKES** | $50 | 125 | 200 |

Instruction. 1919.

BOOMER, PERCY

| **ON LEARNING GOLF** | $20 | 40 | 60 |

Instruction. 1942.

BROWN, KENNETH

| **PUTTER PERKINS** | $40 | 80 | 100 |

Fiction. 1923.

BROWNING, R.H.K.

| **A HISTORY OF GOLF** | $100 | 275 | 325 |

History. 1955. An important addition to any library.

CLARK, ROBERT

| **A ROYAL AND ANCIENT GAME** | $800 | 2500 | 3000 |

A library cornerstone. 1875. 1893 and 1899 editions, reissued 1975.

COCHRAN, A. & STOBBS, J.

| **THE SEARCH FOR THE PERFECT SWING** | $40 | 75 | 100 |

Instruction. 1968. Reissued.

COLLETT, GLENNA

**LADIES IN
THE ROUGH**   **$100**   **150**   **250**
   Autobiography. 1928.

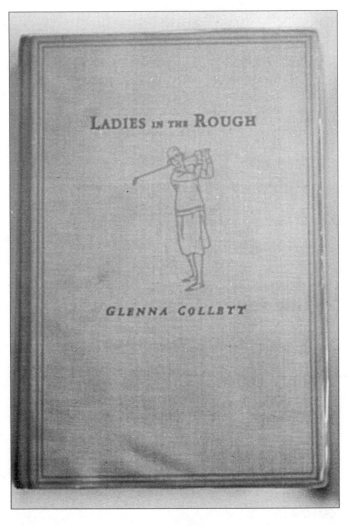

CORNISH, G. & WHITTEN, R.

THE GOLF COURSE   **$30**   **50**   75
   Architecture. 1979.

COTTON, HENRY

THIS GAME OF GOLF   **$25**   **50**   90
   Instruction. 1948.

COUSINS, GEOFFREY

GOLFERS AT LAW   **$40**   **55**   **75**
   Rules. 1958.

DANTE, J. & ELLIOTT, L.

**THE FOUR MAGIC MOVES
TO WINNING GOLF**   **$20**   **35**   **50**
   Instruction. 1962. Reissued.

DARWIN, BERNARD

BRITISH GOLF   **$25**   **50**   **75**
   History. 1946.

DARWIN, BERNARD

**GOLF BETWEEN
TWO WARS**   **$40**   **80**   **100**
   History. 1944. Reissued.

DARWIN, BERNARD

THE GOLF COURSES OF
THE BRITISH ISLES $550   1100   1500
   Architecture. 1910. A library cornerstone.
Reissued.

DARWIN, BERNARD

GREEN MEMORIES $250   450   650
   Autobiography. 1928.

DOBEREINER, PETER

THE GLORIOUS
WORLD OF GOLF $20   40   60
   History. 1973.

DONOVAN & MURDOCH

THE GAME OF GOLF AND
THE PRINTED WORD $40   80   100
   Reference. 1988.

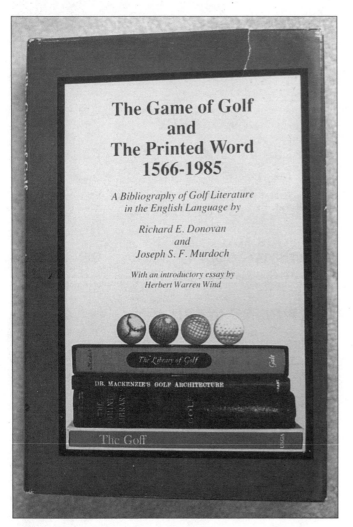

DARWIN, BERNARD, ETAL

A HISTORY OF GOLF IN
GREAT BRITAIN $175   275   400
   History. 1952. Reissued.

DAVIES, PETER

DAVIES' DICTIONARY OF
GOLFING TERMS $20   40   50
   Reference. 1980.

DEMARET, JIMMY

MY PARTNER,
BEN HOGAN $75   140   175
   1954.

DUNCAN, G. & DARWIN, B.

PRESENT DAY GOLF $40   90   165
   Instruction. London, 1921.

EVANS, CHICK

CHICK EVANS'
GOLF BOOK $75   175   225
   Autobiography. 1921.

FLAHERTY, TOM

THE U.S. OPEN
1895-1965 $12   20   35
   History. 1969.

GIBSON, NEVIN

ENCYCLOPEDIA
OF GOLF $15   32   40
   Reference. 1958, 1964.

HAGEN, WALTER

**THE WALTER
HAGEN STORY**   **$35**   **60**   **80**
  Autobiography. 1956.

HAULTAIN, A.

**THE MYSTERY
OF GOLF**   **$90**   **150**   **250**
  Instruction. 1910. Reissued; also 1908 limited edition.

HENDERSON & STIRK

GOLF IN THE MAKING **$50**   **125**   **175**
  Reference. 1979.

HILL, DAVE

TEED OFF   **$10**   **20**   **35**
  1977.

HILTON, HAROLD

**THE ROYAL AND ANCIENT
GAME OF GOLF**   **$1000** **2500** **3000**
  Anthology. 1912.

HOGAN, BEN

POWER GOLF   **$15**   **35**   **50**
  Instruction. 1948.

HOGAN, BEN

**FIVE LESSONS, THE MODERN
FUNDAMENTALS**   **$10**   **30**   **40**
  Instruction. 1957.

HOUGHTON, GEORGE

**CONFESSIONS OF
A GOLF ADDICT**   **$10**   **20**   **35**
  Humor. 1952.

HUNTER, DAVE

GOLF SIMPLIFIED $15   30   50
Instruction. 1921.

HUNTER, ROBERT

THE LINKS $400   650   1200
Architecture. 1926.

HUTCHINSON, HAROLD

FIFTY YEARS OF GOLF $200   400   600
Biography. 1919. Reissued.

HUTCHINSON, HORACE

**GOLF, THE BADMINTON
LIBRARY** $125   275   375
Anthology. 1890 and many later editions; reissued.

JACOBS, JOHN

GOLF $25   40   50
Instruction. 1963.

JENKINS, DAN

**THE DOGGED VICTIMS
OF INEXORABLE FATE** $25   40   60
Essays. 1970.

KERR, JOHN

**GOLF BOOK OF
EAST LOTHIAN** $800   1200   1500
History. 1896. Also large paper editions.

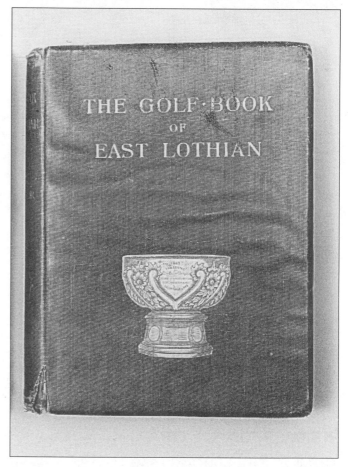

JONES, ERNEST

**SWING THE
CLUBHEAD** $20   30   45
Instruction. 1952. Reissued.

LEMA, TONY

| GOLFERS' GOLD | $20 | 35 | 50 |

Biography. 1964.

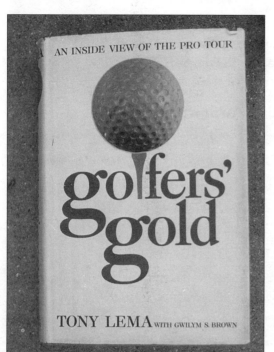

JONES, ROBERT T., JR.

| BOBBY JONES ON GOLF | $35 | 60 | 90 |

Instruction. 1966.

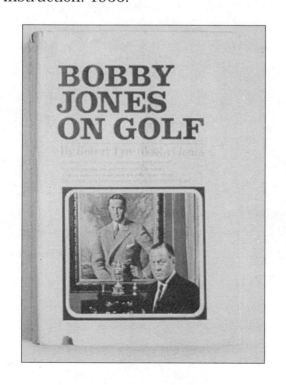

JONES, ROBERT T., JR.

| DOWN THE FAIRWAY | $125 | 300 | 600 |

Autobiography. 1927. Reissued.

JONES, ROBET T., JR.

| GOLF IS MY GAME | $35 | 60 | 90 |

Biography. 1960.

LOCKE, BOBBY

| BOBBY LOCKE ON GOLF | $40 | 60 | 75 |

Instruction. 1953.

LONGHURST, HENRY

| TALKING ABOUT GOLF | $40 | 60 | 80 |

Essay. 1966.

LONGHURST, HENRY

| ONLY ON SUNDAYS | $40 | 60 | 75 |

Essays. 1964.

MacDONALD, C.B.

| SCOTLAND'S GIFT; GOLF | $300 | 600 | 750 |

History. 1928. Reprints $35. Limited Edition.

MACKENZIE, A.

| GOLF ARCHITECTURE | $400 | 750 | 1000 |

Architecture. 1920.

MARTIN, H.B.

| FIFTY YEARS OF AMERICAN GOLF | $250 | 400 | 650 |

History. 1st edition, 1936. Reissued. Limited Edition.

MARTIN, JOHN STEWART

| THE CURIOUS HISTORY OF THE GOLF BALL | $150 | 275 | 325 |

Reference. 1968.

MORRISON, ALEX

A NEW WAY TO
BETTER GOLF $20   30   45
   Instruction. 1932. Many reprints.

MORRISON, ALEX

BETTER GOLF
WITHOUT PRACTICE $25   35   45
   Instruction. 1940.

MURDOCH, JOSEPH S.F.

THE LIBRARY OF
GOLF, 1743-1966. $350   500   650
   Reference. 1968.

PALMER, ARNOLD

MY GAME AND YOURS $10   20   30
   Instruction. 1965.

NELSON, BRYON

WINNING GOLF $20   30   45
   Instruction. 1946.

NICKLAUS, JACK

MY 55 WAYS TO
LOWER YOUR SCORE $10   20   30
   Instruction. 1964.

NICKLAUS, JACK

GOLF MY WAY $10   20   30
   Instruction. 1974.

PRICE, CHARLES

THE WORLD OF GOLF $35   50   75
   Humor. 1962.

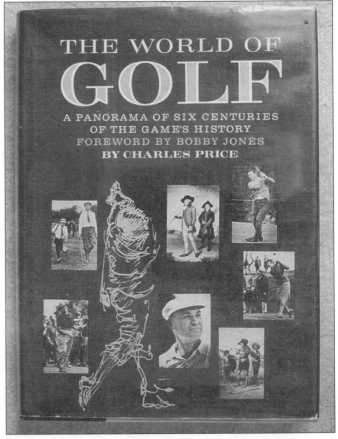

NICKLAUS, JACK

THE GREATEST GAME OF ALL;
MY LIKE IN GOLF $25   40   60
   Biography. 1969.

OLMAN, JOHN & MORTON

THE ENCYCLOPEDIA OF GOLF COLLECTIBLES $5 10 15
Reference. 1985. Also hardcover.

PARK, WILLIE

THE GAME OF GOLF $250 400 500
Instruction. 1896.

RICE, G., EDITOR, & KEELER, O.B.

THE BOBBY JONES STORY $40 65 90
Biography. 1953.

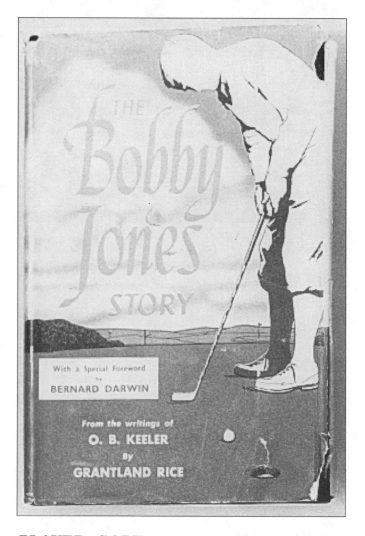

PLAYER, GARY

GARY PLAYER'S GOLF SECRETS $10 20 25
Instruction. 1962.

PLIMPTON, GEORGE

THE BOGEY MAN $10 15 25
Essay. 1968.

PRICE, CHARLES, EDITOR

THE AMERICAN GOLFER $30 50 70
Anthology. 1964. Reissued.

REVOLTA, JOHNNY

SHORTCUTS TO GOOD GOLF $10 20 50
Instruction. 1949 and 1956.

RICE, G. & BRIGGS. C.

THE DUFFER'S HANDBOOK OF GOLF $100 175 275
Humor. 1926. Reissued; also limited edition.

ROBERTS, CLIFFORD

THE STORY OF AUGUSTA NATIONAL GOLF CLUB $45 75 110
History. 1976.

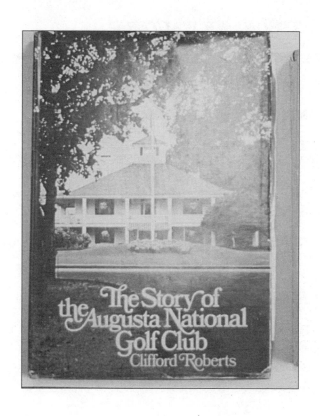

ROTELLA, ROBERT J.

MIND MASTERY FOR WINNING $20   30   40
Instruction. 1981.

SARAZEN, GENE

BETTER GOLF AFTER FIFTY $8   15   25
Instruction. 1967.

SARAZEN, GENE

THIRTY YEARS OF CHAMPIONSHIP GOLF $30   60   90
Biography. 1950. Reissued

SCHAAP, DICK

MASSACRE AT WINGED FOOT $8   15   25
History. 1974.

SHAW, JOSEPH T.

OUT OF THE ROUGH $25   60   80
Fiction. 1934.

SIMPSON, SIR WALTER G.

THE ART OF GOLF $600   750   900
Instruction. 1887, 1892. Reissued.

SMITH, H. & TAYLOR, D.

THE SECRET OF ... HOLDING PUTTS! $12   25   40
Instruction. 1961.

SNEAD, SAM

HOW TO PLAY GOLF $10   20   30
Instruction. 1946, 1952.

SNEAD, SAM

THE EDUCATION OF A GOLFER $20   30   45
Biography. 1962.

SAM SNEAD HOW TO PLAY GOLF

A Complete Course of Instruction by One of the World's Great Golfers
200 ACTION PHOTOGRAPHS
38 PROFESSIONAL TIPS on how to Reduce YOUR SCORE

Plus SPECIAL ILLUSTRATED SECTION—HOW TO CORRECT 19 COMMON ERRORS IN YOUR GOLF SWING

STANLEY, LOUIS T.

THIS IS GOLF $20   30   40
Instruction. 1954.

STEEL, DONALD & RYDE & WIND

THE ENCYCLOPEDIA OF GOLF $60   100   125
Reference. 1975.

STEELE, C.K.

THE GOLF COURSE MYSTERY $60   100   200
Fiction. 1919.

SUGGS, LOUISE

GOLF FOR WOMEN $10   20   30
Instruction. 1960.

TAYLOR, JOHN HENRY

TAYLOR ON GOLF	$200	350	450

Instruction. 1902.

THOMAS, GEORGE C., JR.

GOLF ARCHITECTURE IN AMERICA	$350	650	800

Architecture. 1927. Reissued.

TUFTS, RICHARD S.

THE PRINCIPLES BEHIND THE RULES OF GOLF	$75	120	150

Rules. 1960, 1961. Reissued.

TULLOCH, W.W.

THE LIFE OF TOM MORRIS	$800	1200	1450

Biography. 1908. Reissued.

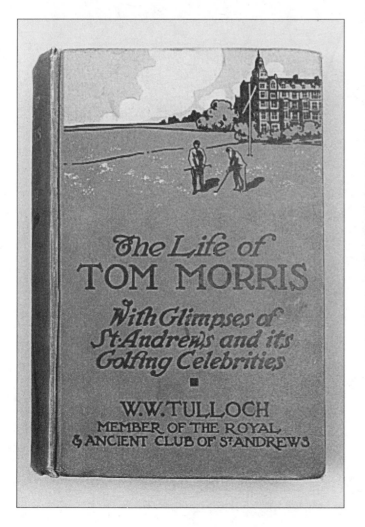

VAILE, P.A.

THE NEW GOLF	$30	50	78

Instruction. 1916.

VARDON, HARRY

THE COMPLETE GOLFER	$50	100	200

Instruction. 1905. Reissued.

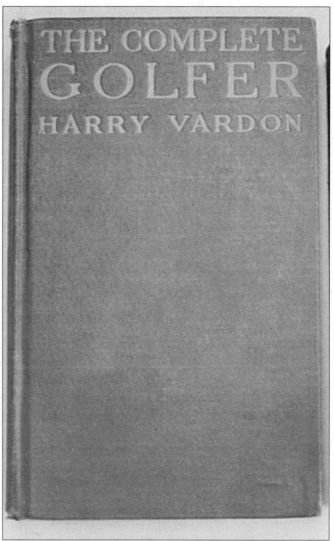

VARDON, HARRY

HOW TO PLAY GOLF	$50	80	140

Instruction. 1912.

WETHERED, JOYCE & ROGER

THE GAME OF GOLF $100   150   200
   Anthology. 1929.

WHIGHAM. H.G.

HOW TO PLAY GOLF $175   225   300
   Instruction. 1897.

WHITLATCH, MARSHALL

**GOLF FOR BE-
GINNERS & OTHERS** $30   60   100
   Instruction. 1910.

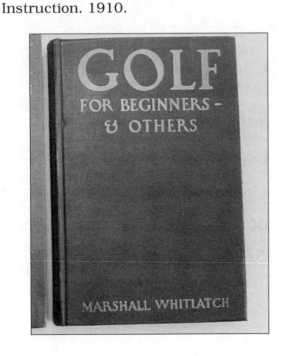

WIND, HERBERT WARREN

COMPLETE GOLFER $25   50   75
   Anthology. 1954.

WIND, HERBERT WARREN

**THE STORE OF
AMERICAN GOLFER** $125   250   350
   History. 1st ed. 1948, 1956, 1975 editions.

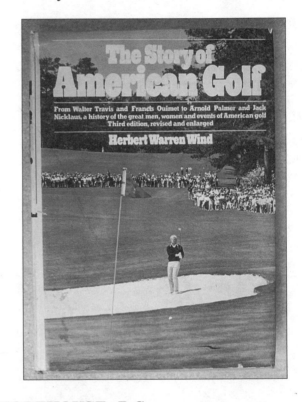

WODEHOUSE, P.G.

GOLF OMNIBUS $40   65   90
   Fiction. 1973.

WODEHOUSE, P.G.

GOLF WITHOUT TEARS $75   150   300
   Fiction. 1924.

WOOD, HARRY B.

**GOLF CURIOS
AND THE LIKE** $900   1400   2000
   Reference. 1910. Reissued.

ZAHARIAS, BABE D.

THIS LIFE I'VE LED $30   50   70
   Biography. 1955.

Chapter 10

Collecting Golf Art

Chapter 10

Collecting Golf Art

We are indebted to David White (GCS, London) for the article that follows, reprinted from THE CONNOISSEUR, July 1902. It appeared in the Golf Collectors Society Bulletin No. 21, January 1975.

The Pictorial History of Golf: A Suggestion for Collectors

by Martin Hardie

At some moment in every student's career the question arises whether he shall know a little about everything or everything about something. So, for the collector there comes the time when he, too, must decide whether he will continue in his pleasant dilettante ways, or devote his research to some special branch of art. Is he to wander at ease in the low-lying meadows, plucking a flower here or there as they please his fancy, or is he to climb the heights in search of edelweiss and the rare blooms? Yet, even when he is drawn to some particular branch of study, be it pictures, or china, or books, or even postage stamps, the possibilities before him are too infinite, and he will feel at once the need of further limitation.

To give an instance from the book world, there is a well-known editor of the present time who devotes his energies to the collection of books of the year 1598.

To suit our present theme, let us suppose that prints are the subject elect for specialization. The study of engravings is endlessly elaborate and complicated, and in making his further limitation the specialist has an unlimited variety of choice. Shall it be a master, a period, or a method? He may give his lifetime to the countless states of Rembrandt, or the two thousand prints of Hollar. He may choose a period, that of Durer and the Little Masters, or the engravers of the eighteenth century. He may be attracted by a method-etching or mezzotint, or the color-prints of Japan. As he faces the subject, there are innumerable pleasing vistas of choice.

Now to the collector who is fond of any manner of sport, we would suggest that in tracing its pictorial history he has a new and interesting subject ready at hand and our present purpose is to show the special attraction offered by the game of golf. And surely every collector ought to be a golfer. Both collecting and golf are games in which the individual depends on himself alone. Both have their glorious possibilities, their successes and disappointments, their moments of fortune, their bunkers of despair. It is a serious question for one who plays both games to decide whether he would prefer a hole in one, or to pick up for five schillings in a country village, a first proof, say of the Salisbury Cathedral by Lucas. Let him search his heart and decide whether he would rather be a better golfer or a better collector.

First it may be pointed out that the collection of golf prints may be of the greatest value in settling disputed points in the history of the Royal Game. For the origin of golf, like that of Mr. Yellowplush, is "wropt in mistry" and it is still a moot point whether Scotland or the Low Countries can claim to be the incunabula of the modern game. For its early literary history the only sources are the Scottish Acts of Parliament and records of Kirk Sessions. "The fut ball and golf be utterly cryit dune" is the stern behest of the Parliament in 1457. So also, a century later in 1593, two golfers were prosecuted by the Town Council of Edinburgh for "playing of the Gowff on the Links of Leith every Sabbath at the time of the sermones."

But, while Scotland can produce this documentary evidence, it is to the Low Countries that we go for the pictorial history of the game. Without any doubt, as our illustrations will show, golf was in vogue in Holland in the sixteenth century, being played on ice as well as on grass. Indeed, early in the seventeenth century, golf balls were imported to Scotland, for in a letter of 1618, the writer says that "no small quantitie of golf and silver is transported yearlie out of his Hienes' Kingdome of Scotland for bying of golf balls." For pictorial records of the earliest period of the game in the Low Countries, one has to search illuminated manuscripts of the fifteenth and sixteenth centuries.

Perhaps the earliest representation of golf, or of a game which must be the primogenitor of golf, is to be found in a manuscript in the Chantilly Collection, and shows figures putting both to a post and to a hole. Mr. W.H. Weale, the well-known authority on Flemish painting, has dated this for me as between 1460 and 1470. Another Flemish "Book of Hours" in the British Museum Library, executed at Bruges between 1500 and 1520, shows distinctly that in this period the golfer putted to a hole. The home green in front of the clubhouse, the red coat of the player, and the steel-faced club, are all curiously modern. Hidden away among collections of manuscripts must be many a treasure which would throw light on the early history of the game.

By the seventeenth century, golf in Holland had become almost entirely a winter game. The Dutch painters of the period seem to have found a peculiar fascination in winter scenes, with their clear, bright atmosphere, and the moving crowds of figures in their various occupations of sledding, skating or golf. As might be expected, many a golfing scene is to be found in the pictures of van de Velde, van der Neer, Avercamp, van Goyen, and others of their school. Several drawings of this period showing single figures or small groups, give perhaps a better idea of golf at the time.

Two such drawings by Avercamp in the Royal Collection at Dresden, of about the year 1610, are obviously character studies from life, and show us players that, except for their costumes, exhibit a startling modernity. How often have we seen a golfer stand in the pose of this stout Dutchman, pipe in hand, his club held loosely resting on the ground, as he surveys a difficult "lie" and swithers for a moment between this club and that. We wonder who the present owner is of the drawing that fetched 18 schillings at the William Esdaile Sale of 1840, catalogued as "Lot 1178, H. Avercamp: Figures playing at Kolf on the ice—capital?"

For the ordinary collector, however, whose aspirations are limited by the length of his purse, the engravings of the period offer the happiest hunting grounds. Juys, Van Schoel, Jan and Adomen van de Velse, Van Sichem and R. de Hooghe are some of the artists whose engraved work contains golfing scenes. A rare etching by Hendrik van Schoel—and the connoisseur will appreciate the fact that neither Bartsch nor Nagler chronicle its existence—shows a reservoir with skaters and golfers, particularly noticeable being a small boy at the top of his swing. Another interesting feature of the picture is the group of curlers in the middle distance on the right. The stones, the kneeling attitude of the player, and the "skip" giving directions with outstretched arm, all show that here we have an early picture of the "roaring game." Several etchings by Jan Van de Velde, from sets representing the twelve months, show figures of golfers playing on ice. Of the late seventeenth century is an engraving by Romeyn de Hooghe, giving us perhaps the best presentment of a golfer with club in hand that can be found among these Dutch prints.

From France, we have an engraving by J. Aliament of about 1750, after a picture in our National Gallery by Adriaen van de Velde. It is interesting to note that the plate is reversed, with the result that the player seems to be left-handed. A thrill runs through the golfer when he notices for the first time in a catalogue of Rembrandt's etchings, the entry "A Kolfer." He is, however, doomed to disappointment, for the Kolf there depicted is the modern Dutch indoor game, only remotely connected with our golf.

In Scotland of the sixteenth and seventeenth century, our "rude fore-fathers" had no Van de Velde or Avercamp to chronicle with brush the annals of the game. Records of Kirk Sessions tell of the chastisement of offenders against the Sabbath laws; club minutes relate the winning of casks of wine; but of pictures we have nothing until the end of the eighteenth century, when there begins a series of excellent portraits of golfers with caddie and clubs. These are interesting to the collector because many have been translated into the beautiful mezzotints for which the period is famous. For the player their value also lies in their historic associations and in the representation they give us of the baffies and spoons and other disused weapons of the game.

One of the best known of these mezzotints is the portrait of William Innes by Val. Green, after L. F. Abbott, dedicated to "the Society of Golfers at Blackheath." Of the original picture no trace can be found, and it may be presumed that it was destroyed in the fire which burned down the Blackheath Clubhouse at the end of the eighteenth century. Another beautiful mezzotint is that by J.

Jones after the portrait by Raeburn, of James Balfour, an early secretary of the Honourable Company of Edinburgh Golfers. This mezzotint carries the inscription: "Published by Wm. Murray, Bookseller, Parliament Close, Edinburgh, October 1796."

An interesting etching is one of Kay's portraits, dated 1803, showing Alexander M'Keller, a well-known character of the Bruntisfield Links, Edinburgh. The engraving by Wagstaffe of the picture by Charles Lees, R.S.A., "A Grand Match at Golf" 1850, is of great historical interest. It depicts a foursome in which Sir David Baird and Sir Ralph Anstruther are matched against Major Playfair and John Campbell, of Saddell. In the group of onlookers are many distinguished Scotchmen of the day, and in the background are seen the towers and spires of St. Andrews. Many similar engravings of championship meetings have been published of late years, but scarcely of sufficient merit to attract the connoisseur.

The collector of wood engravings of "the sixties" will find two interesting golf illustrations by Doyle of "Punch in London Society" for 1863. In more modern times, capital photogravures have been published by the Fine Arts Society after "The Sabbath Breakers," "The Stymie" and other paintings by J. C. Dollman, R.I., and for those clever prints by Mr. Nicholson and Mr. Cecil Aldin, without which the golf collection will be incomplete.

In the case of most collectors, the length of their purse is an important consideration. "Non cuivis contingit adire Corinthum"—not everyone is fortunate enough to dream of acquiring the "Hundred Guider" print, the "Melancholia", the "Abside" or the "Ladies Waldegrave." But these golf prints can, for the most part, be purchased at a reasonable price, and to the connoisseur who is a golfer as well, their acquisition will add a new interest to his game.

Olman's Guide to Golf Antiques, *by John and Mort Olman, 1991, provides the most complete reference on art available to collectors.*

Prices

Golf Art

	G-5	G-7	G-9

THE BLACKHEATH GOLFER

ABBOTT, L.F. $350   500   750

Circa 1900. A colored engraving of the original from 1790.

THE BLACKHEATH GOLFERS

ABBOTT, L.F. $1400   1800   2200

A mezzotint. Original 1790. Many later reprints. (Below)

THE DRIVE

ADAMS, DOUGLAS $200   300   450

Circa 1960. Approximately 16 x 24. Colored engraving from the original oil painting circa 1894.

A DIFFICULT BUNKER

ADAMS, DOUGLAS $200   300   450

Circa 1960. Approximately 16 x 24. Colored engraving from the original oil painting circa 1894.

THE PUTTING GREEN

ADAMS, DOUGLAS $200   300   450

Circa 1960. Approximately 16 x 24. Colored engraving from the original oil painting circa 1894.

Blackheath Golfers

THE DRIVE

BROCK, CHARLES
EDMOND $1200 1800 2500

An engraving, circa 1894.

DEDICATED TO THE FIELD MARSHALL

CHAMBERLAIN, J. $250   350   500

Engraving. Frost & Reed, publishers, 1955. (Below)

THE PUTT

BROCK,
CHARLES EDMOND $1200 1800 2500

An engraving, circa 1894. (Above)

THE RULES OF GOLF

CROMBIE, CHARLES   **$150**   **225**   **300**

A humorous series published in 1905 by Perrier. Many reprints. Prices listed are for reprints. (Above)

GOLF PLAYERS

DE HOOCH, PETER   **$60**   **80**   **100**

Contemporary prints. (Right)

THE SABBATH BREAKERS

DOLLMAN, J.   **$175**   **200**   **300**

Circa 1896 black and white engraving. The original sold for $1,320. in 1992. Prices listed are for circa 1977 lithographs in color.

PUTTING

DOLLMAN,
JOHN CHARLES   **$1200   1800   2500**

An engraving, circa 1900. (Above)

FAIRWAY SHOT

DOLLMAN,
JOHN CHARLES   **$1200   1800   2500**

An engraving, circa 1900. (Right)

ST. ANDREWS CADDIE

EARLE, L.   **$100   200   300**

Original, 1908, second printing 1928 and also 1979.

OLD SCOTCH CADDY

EARLE, L.C.   **$110   150   300**

Circa late 1920s. Approximately 16 x 20. Colored print of the circa 1904 oil painting.

PLAYING OUT OF HEATHER

DOLLMAN,
JOHN CHARLES $1200   1800   2500

An engraving, circa 1900. (Above)

THE TRIUMVIRATE

FLOWER, CLEMENT $300   450   600

1913 painting, prints 1914 and later. (Right)

VARIOUS WATERCOLORS

FROST, A.B. $20   30   50

Circa 1900 including, "By Sheer Strength", "Temper", "Stymied" and others. Prices are for reprints.

JOHN WHYTE MELVILLE

GRANT, SIR FRANCIS $300   450   600

Circa 1970. Color print, London, limited edition of 750.

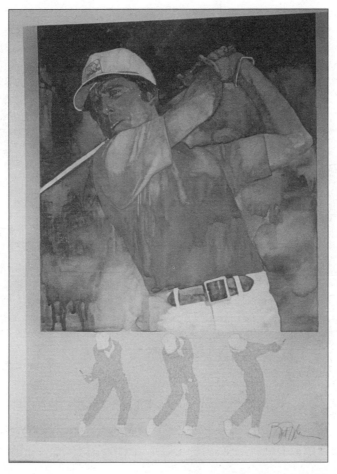

GARY PLAYER

FORBES, BART	$40	60	90

    1980 watercolor reprints.

JOHN WHYTE MELVILLE

GRANT, SIR FRANCIS	$75	100	150

    Circa 1988 color print of the original.

BEN HOGAN

MILOSEVICH, PAUL	$20	30	40

    1980s. Prints in sepia. (Right)

HISTORY OF GOLF IN AMERICA SERIES

GUSTOVSON, LELAND	$400	500	600

    Circa 1960s. Six color prints. "The First Clubhouse in America, Shinnecock", "The Old Apple Tree Gang", "Awarding The First USGA Trophy", "Robert Tyre Jones", "Ouimet Wins The Open" and "Playoff For Masters Championship", Snead and Hogan. Singles are $50-100 ea.

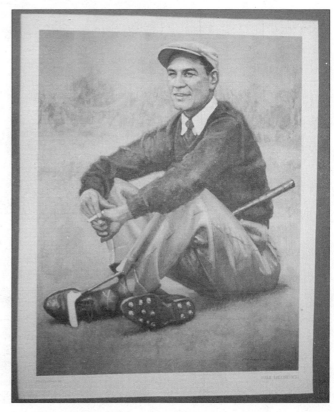

SLAMMIN' SAMMY

MILOSEVICH, PAUL   **$20**   **30**   **40**
     1980s. Prints in sepia.

COPE'S TOBACCO

PIPESHANK, GEORGE   **$20**   **30**   **40**
     Circa 1900 humorous advertisement print for Cope's Tobacco. Reprints 1870s.

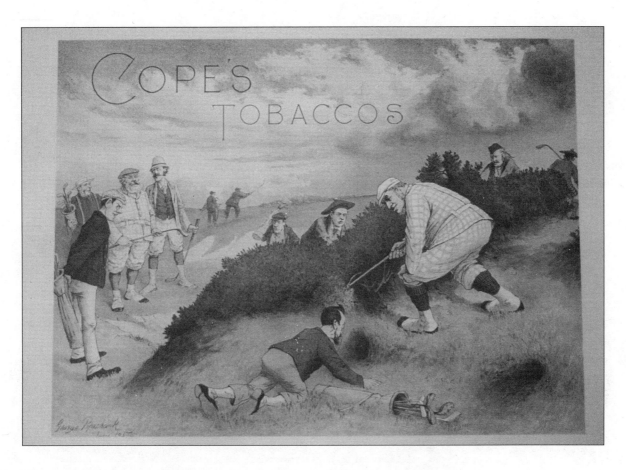

THE GOLFERS

LEES, CHARLES   **$150**   **250**   **350**

Circa 1920. Hand colored. Approximately 21 X 33. Print of the circa 1849 engraving.

CRENSHAW WINS 1984 MASTERS

MILOSEVICH, PAUL   **$150**   **175**   **225**

1985. Limited edition of 600.

TOM MORRIS

REID, SIR GEORGE   **$4000**   **6000**   **8000**

A gravure. 1903.

A LITTLE PRACTICE

SADLER, W.D.   **$300**   **450**   **650**

Original print, black and white, 1915. Many reproductions worth less than $50.

A WINTER EVENING

SADLER, W.D.   **$300**   **450**   **650**

Original print, black and white, 1915. Many reproductions worth less than $50.

ST. ANDREW'S HELL'S BUNKER

SMART, JOHN 250000
   Watercolor, 1889.

CARICATURES OF FAMOUS GOLFERS

**SIR LESLIE
WARD, 'SPY'** $200 300 400
   1890's to 1910. Various amateur and professional golfers. Ward used the pseudonym "Spy".

THE BLACK SHED AT HOYLAKE

SMITH, GARDEN G. 20000
   A watercolor, 1897.

BOBBY JONES

STEVENS, THOMAS E. $250 350 500
   1952. Limited edition prints. Signed prints can bring as much as $3,500.

DUTCH TILES

UNKNOWN MAKER   **$200   300   500**

    Circa 1800.

WALTER HAGEN

VAIL, ARNOLD   **$500**

    1993 original oil. Mr. Vail painted famous golf immortals at the request of Chuck Furjanic. Seventeen were done from 1993 until his death in Feb. 1995. Fourteen of his seventeen works are pictured in the "Linda Craft Auction" catalogue, May 7, 1995, conducted by Chuck Furjanic, Inc.

JIMMY DEMARET

VAIL, ARNOLD   **$500**

    1993 Original oil. Mr. Vail painted famous golf immortals at the request of Chuck Furjanic. Seventeen were done from 1993 until his death in February 1995. Fourteen of his seventeen works are pictured in the "Linda Craft Auction" catalogue, May 7, 1995, conducted by Chuck Furjanic, Inc.

A FROST SCENE

van de VELDE, ADRIAEN $75   125   250

    Prints circa 1920s made from originals circa 1600. (Above)

MAURITS de HERAUGIERES, AGE 2

van der LINDE, ADRIAEN $45000

    1595. Oil-on-panel. (Right)

WINTER LANDSCAPE

van der NEER, AERT   **$75**   **125**   **250**

    Prints circa 1920s made from originals circa 1650. (Above)

ST. ANDREWS

WATSON, J.F.   **$400**   **500**   **650**

    1977. Limited edition print.

OLD TOM MORRIS

WEAVER, ARTHUR   **$200**   **300**   **400**

    Late 1980s. (Right)

YOUNG TOM MORRIS

WEAVER, ARTHUR $200   300   400
  Late 1980s. (Left)

1ST INTERNATIONAL GOLF MATCH

BROWN, MICHAEL J. $500   750   1000

  1903. 1st International Golf Match, England vs. Scotland at Hoylake, 1902. Michael Brown was famous for his "Life Ass'n of Scotland Calendars". (Below)

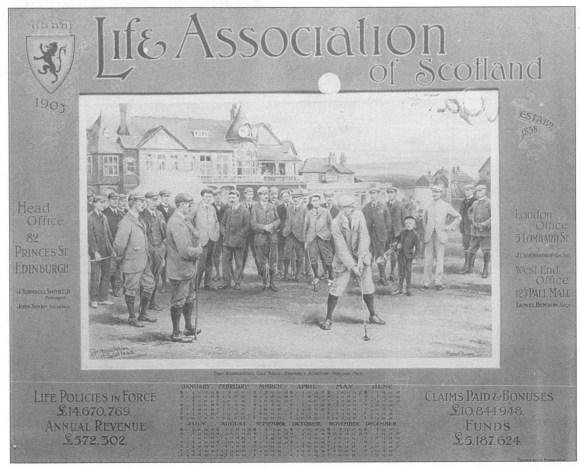

Chapter 11

Collecting Golf Ceramics & Glass

Chapter 11

Collecting Golf Ceramics & Glass

Golf Ceramics

by Wayne Aaron

Wayne Aaron has collected golf ceramics for 25 years and has assembled a very extensive collection. He offers his insight to both the beginner, as well as advanced collector of golf ceramics.

One of the wonders of collecting golf antiquity is the diversity of fields represented. While clubs, balls and books dominate the hobby as collecting themes, there is now a heightened level of interest in golf ceramics.

One reason for this growing popularity may be because many are rapidly discovering that while all fields of golf collecting have intrinsic value, ceramics offers additional aesthetic value. Another reason may be the realization that the true social impact of the game can be better understood by studying (and collecting) the artistic artifacts that evolved with the game—such as ceramics, glass, silver, jewelry, art, toys, statuary, medals and numerous advertising memorabilia items. All of these "aesthetic" categories in their own way help to document, as well as visibly demonstrate, the significant influence golf had on the world around the turn of the century—as it does today.

As one contemplates the joys of collecting golf ceramics, it is wise to recognize at the outset that this endeavor invariably will become a "journey", and as such, never a "destination" that is ultimately reached.

First and foremost, before embarking on this journey it is best to acquire as much knowledge as possible. Only through knowledge can you truly understand what is possible. Also do not be tempted to become a "consumer of quantity" rather than a "collector of quality." A good working definition of quality should not stop at discerning the condition of a potential collectible, it should also encompass historical significance and rarity.

Perhaps the best advice a collector can follow is to always seek out and acquire the very best you can afford. The very scarce items will command a premium price and will appreciate in value at a higher rate than mid to lower end examples. High end items may even become prohibitively expensive in the future and therefore out of the realm of affordability for many collectors.

It is also helpful to establish clear goals before running head long into the world of golf ceramic collecting. In fact, this is sound advice for any field of golf collecting. In summary, acquire knowledge, define your budget, set your goals, collect only quality and buy the best when you see it.

While it is academically interesting to possess an encyclopedic level of knowledge covering the history of pottery and porcelain, including supporting terminology techniques, styles, artists, makers and country of origin, this level of proficiency is not a mandatory prerequisite to become a knowledgeable collector of golf ceramics. While the history of pottery goes back to primitive man, and Chinese porcelain dates to 3000 B.C., ceramics featuring golfers or golfing scenes did not appear until the seventeenth century when they were used as decoration for Delft tiles. For those that do not subscribe to the "Dutch School" origin of golf, you can jump forward to around 1880 onwards when golf clubs gave golf ceramics as prizes and golfing sporting subjects found increasing use as embellishments for vases, pictures, tumblers, bowls, steins, plates and numerous other functional, as well as decorative items. Focusing on a period running from 1880 to 1940 makes the breadth of knowledge you need to acquire a lot more manageable.

Collectors, dealers and even auction houses are often confused by *terminology*. In its simplest form you need to remember the following:

- *Ceramics* is a general term for the study of the art of pottery.

- *Pottery* in its widest sense includes all objects fashioned from clay and then hardened by fire.

- *Porcelain* should only be applied to certain well marked varieties of pottery. It is usually opaque white and is fired at 1,450 degrees centigrade. Also known as Bone China.

- *Stoneware* is vitrified clay fired at temperatures of 1,200 to 1,300 degrees centigrade, which makes it very hard and is tan or gray in color.

- *Earthenware* is not vitrified, retains a porous texture, is fired at no more than 1,200 degrees centigrade and is usually tan in color.

While some may be driven to become an expert on ceramics and submerge themselves into the world of *technique*, which encompasses materials, firing, glazes, colors and metals, it may be best to just understand what is available to collect.

The most definitive discussion to date for golf ceramics can be found in the Olmans' *Guide to Golf Antiques*. Review Chapter 12 pages 153-168. Another excellent reference is *Decorative Golf Collectibles* by Shirley and Jerry Sprung, pages 9-48.

Dates of production by manufacturer including their marks and country of origin with illustrations of objects can be found in both of these recommended references.

An introduction on collecting golf ceramics would not be complete without a brief discussion of what is an acceptable condition (cracks, chips, scratches, repairs, missing parts) before rejecting an object. The following suggestions are offered:

- If the item is truly very rare and you may never see it on the market again, this becomes an issue of price and personal taste. The more the damage, the lower the price. Do not pay a premium for poor quality. Be disciplined enough to walk away, but do not hesitate to purchase if the price is commensurate with condition. A rare item with some damage is a good candidate for a "museum" quality restoration.

- Do not be afraid to acquire an item that has undergone a "museum" level repair. The quality will be so high that only the restorer and the individual that paid for the repair will understand the true condition. If the repair is obvious to suggest the restorer was an amateur, walk away from mid to lower end items at any price. You will never be proud of owning junk and you probably will not be able to trade or sell it either.

Where do you start to find collectible golf ceramics? If you are not already a member, by all means join the Golf Collectors Society.

Write to P.O. Box 20546, Dayton, Ohio 45420 for an application form or call (513) 256-2474. After you meet the requirements for membership you will be provided a directory of all members. Each member indicates their collecting interests. Look for the letter "C", which denotes ceramics. Start both your education (pursuit of knowledge) and search here. Call 10 or 15 people and you will identify through referrals the serious collectors of golf ceramics. They are the ones to contact because they may have duplicates for sale or trade. They will also get you headed in the right direction to other sources.

I have often been asked why I collect ceramics. It is because I have been stricken by an 18th century imagination. During this period it was a popular belief that porcelain was not just another exotic, but a magical and talismanic substance—the substance of longevity, of potency, of invulnerability—now you know why I collect ceramics.

The following listing is presented as an overview of golf ceramic collecting opportunities and is comprehensive for the majority of desired acquisitions, but is by no means all inclusive.

United States

Ceramic Art Company (Pre Lenox)

Lenox

Weller (Dickensware II)

Rookwood

Owens (Utopian)

O'Hara Dial (Waltham Clock Co.)

Robinson Clay Products

Sleepy Eye Indian Mugs

Warwick

American Beleek

Enfield Pottery

Buffalo China

Hanes (Little Arthur)

Viktor Schrechengost (Cowan)

Taylor, Smith & Taylor

England

Doulton Burslem

Doulton Lambeth

Royal Doulton (1902 and after)

- Kingsware
- Series Ware (Charles Crombie) "Pilgrim figures & Proverb sayings"
- Queensware
- Airbrush Brown
- Gibson Series
- Uncle Toby
- H.M. Bateman
- The Nineteenth Hole
- Morrissian
- Bunnykins
- Colonel Bogey
- Old English
- Copeland Spode
- Carleton Ware
- Arcadian
- Bridgewood
- Crown Staffordshire
- Dartmouth

Foley

W.H. Goss

Grimwades

Minton

Taylor Tunnecliffe

Wedgewood

Willow Art

Arthur Wood

Royal Worcester

MacIntyre Burslem

G & S Ltd.

Shelly

Crown Ducal

Radfords

Jasperware

A. Rogers

A.F.C.

Aonian

Burleigh

Cresan

Ambassador

Clifton

Williamson & Sons

Germany

Rosenthal

Royal Bonn

Simon Peter Gerz

Hohr-Grenzhausen

Hauber & Reuther

Royal Bayruth

Schwarzburg

Schaffer and Vater

Frumper Ware

Villeroy & Boch (Metlach)

Goebel

Austria

Amphora (Turn-Tepliz, Bohemia, Riessner)

Italy

Richard Ginori

Japan

Noritake

Nippon

Chikaramachi

France

Limoges

Sevres

Robj

Spain

Lladro (after 1940)

Netherlands

Dutch Delft Tiles (17th century)

Ireland

Irish Beleek

Collectible Glass

by Jerry Sprung

In the waning days of the Victorian period, through the art nouveau and art deco periods, most items of a personal nature carried some complex design, depicting an event or an item in a representational theme; American Indians for instance, were often depicted on pottery, silver, or bronze.

Ever since golf came to the United States in the late 19th century, it became the subject of many media designers who wished to capitalize on the latest fad. Workers in silver and gold took many of their popular sellers, such as cuff links, tie pins, watch fobs and match safes for men, and hat pins and compacts for women, and added a golf motif. This was done either by depicting a figure playing golf, or an implement, golf stick, golf ball or tee.

In addition, silversmiths created trophies with a golfing motif as part of the design. This was done to supply the growing market for tournament prizes. Such makers as Unger Brothers had elaborate catalogs showing a golfer, or a caddy, as the center figure in all of their silver mounted items, from ashtrays to hair brushes to whiskey flasks.

Most bronze golf figures came from Austria. Karl Hagenauer was especially known for his art deco golf figures in the 1920s. Bronze was also used to make decorative humidors and cigarette boxes. Heintz Art Metal Shop and Smith Metal Arts (Silvercrest) of Buffalo, NY were two of the main suppliers of these items.

Most glass golf items were either produced in England or the United States. One of the popular glass designs involved a sterling silver golfer overlay that was attached to the glass bottle, goblet, or pitcher with an adhesive. The same figure is seen in many sizes, adorning glassware made by various manufacturers. Another method was to etch or engrave a golfer or golfing scene directly into the glass. Such companies as Hawkes, Cambridge Glass, and Pairpoint were well-known suppliers of these wares.

Prices
Golf Ceramics

	G-5	G-7	G-9

PORCELAIN HUMIDOR

AONIAN, ENGLAND $1600 1800 2000

Circa 1900s. Comical golf scene.

EARTHENWARE MATCH BOWL

**CARLTONWARE,
ENGLAND** $150   250   375

Circa 1920s.

WOOD & WOOD BISCUIT BARREL

**ARTHUR WOOD &
SON, ENGLAND** $2000 2500 3000

Circa 1900. Hand painted porcelain with silver rim, bail, and ornate lid.

EARTHENWARE HUMIDOR

CARLTONWARE,
ENGLAND   **$450   600   900**
   Circa 1920s.

PORCELAIN ASHTRAY

CHIKARAMACHI   **$400   600   800**
   CIRCA 1930s. Six pieces. Hand painted.

STONEWARE PITCHER

COPELAND SPODE   **$600   800   1200**
   Circa 1900. Golfers in relief, white on blue or green background.

STONEWARE JARDINIERE

COPELAND SPODE   **$700   900   1400**
   Circa 1900. Golfers in relief, white on blue or green background.

STONEWARE EWER

COPELAND SPODE   **$700   850   1200**
   Circa 1900. Golfers in relief, white on blue or green background.

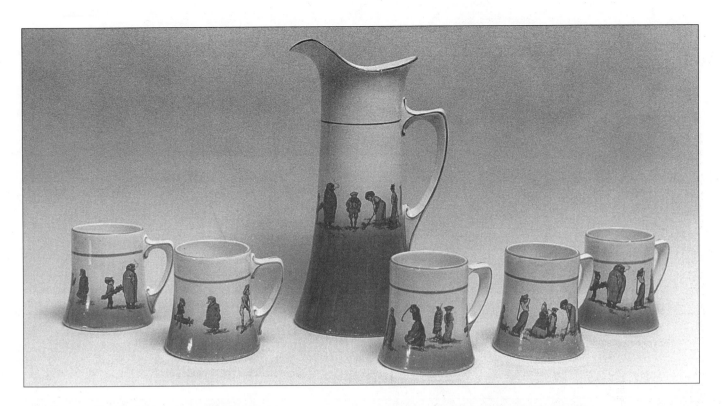

CHINA PITCHER AND CUPS

CRESANT, ENGLAND $1200 1500 1800

Circa 1900s. "Brownie" chocolate pitcher measuring 12-1/2 inches, with matching mugs.

STONEWARE PITCHER

DOULTON, LAMBETH, ENGLAND $1800 2200 2800

Circa early 1900s. Golfers in white relief.

PORCELAIN SPILL VASES

DOULTON, LAMBETH, ENGLAND $700   850   1100

Circa early 1900s.

TRIVET

DOULTON, LAMBETH, ENGLAND $600   800   1000

Circa early 1900s. Uncle Toby Series.

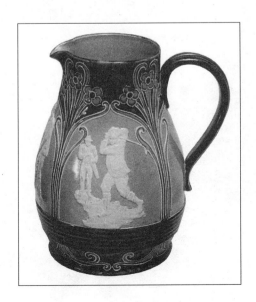

CREAMER

DOULTON,
LAMBETH, ENGLAND $600   800   1000
    Circa early 1900s. Uncle Toby Series. (Left)

HAND PAINTED VASE

DOULTON, LAMBETH,
ENGLAND   **$20000**
    Circa 1885. Burslem.

FLUTE NECK VASE

DOULTON, LAMBETH,
ENGLAND   **$20000**
    Circa 1885. Hand painted, Burslem.

HAND PAINTED HUMIDOR

DOULTON,
LAMBETH, ENGLAND   **$12000**
    Circa 1885. Burslem.

OPEN NECK VASE

**DOULTON,
LAMBETH, ENGLAND**   **$12000**

Circa 1885. Hand painted, Burslem.

ROYAL BONN "DELFT" STEIN

**FRANZ ANTON
MEHLEM**   **$15000**

Circa 1890.

THE BROWNIES PITCHER

**GRIMWADES,
STOKE-ON-TRENT**   **$1000   1200   1400**

Circa 1910. Porcelain.

THE BROWNIES CUP AND SAUCER

**GRIMWADES,
STOKE-ON-TRENT**   **$400   500   600**

Circa 1910. Porcelain.

TOBACCO JARS

HANDLE WARE,
MERIDEN   **$1000   1500   2000**

Circa late 1800.

SILVER LID TANKARD

LENOX,
LAWRENCEVILLE, NJ $1800   2200   2600

Circa 1905. Lady and gentleman golfers on blue background.

SILVER RIM TANKARD

LENOX, LAWRENCEVILLE, NJ $1200   1500   1800

Circa 1905. Lady and gentleman golfers on green background.

HOTEL DINNERWARE

LIMOGE, PARIS, FRANCE $400   500   600

Circa 1900. Hotel dinnerware "Golf Hotel Le Couquet".

PORCELAIN FIGURINE

LLADRO, VALENCIA, SPAIN $300   400   500

Circa 1900s. Figurine.

PORCELAIN CHINA

NORITAKE, JAPAN   **$600**   **700**   **800**
    CIRCA 1930s. Hand painted jar. (Above)

PORCELAIN MUG

NORITAKE, JAPAN   **$400**   **500**   **600**
    Circa 1900s. Hand painted mug marked Nippon.

PORCELAIN HUMIDOR

NORITAKE, JAPAN   **$400**   **500**   **600**
    Circa 1900s. Hand painted humidor marked Nippon.

PORCELAIN VASE AND ASHTRAY

RICHARD GINORI,
ITALY   **$600**   **800**   **1000**
    Circa 1920s. Art deco golfers. (Right, top)

PORCELAIN BOWL

ROYAL BAYRUTH   **$600**   **800**   **1000**
    Circa 1900s. Bowl measuring 10-3/8 inches, signed Brown. (Right, bottom)

PORCELAIN CREAMER

ROYAL DOULTON,
ENGLAND $400   600   800

Circa 1930s. Bunnykins, Royal Doulton.

ROYAL DOULTON, GOLF SERIES WARE

ROYAL DOULTON,
ENGLAND $1500 - 10000

Circa 1900. Decorated with Charles Crombie figures.

ROYAL DOULTON WHISKEY BARREL

**ROYAL DOULTON,
ENGLAND**   **$8000**

Circa 1900. Whiskey barrel with 19th hole scene at one end and The Club House, St. Andrews, on the other; it has silver spout and bucket.

PORCELAIN BOWL

**ROYAL DOULTON,
ENGLAND**   **$400   600   800**

Circa 1930s. Bunnykins, Royal Doulton.

PORCELAIN PLATE

**ROYAL DOULTON,
ENGLAND**   **$200   300   400**

Circa 1930s. Bunnykins, Royal Doulton.

THE NINETEENTH HOLE PLATE

**ROYAL DOULTON,
ENGLAND**   **$400   600   800**

Circa 1900.

HOTEL DINNERWARE

**WARWICK,
WHEELING, W. VA.**   **$300   500   600**

Circa 1900. Hotel dinnerware depicting Bobby Jones.

SUGAR BOWL WITH LID

WEDGEWOOD,
BURSLEM, ENGLAND **$650** **850** **1250**

Circa early 1900s. Golfers in white relief.

CREAMER

WEDGEWOOD,
BURSLEM, ENGLAND **$450** **650** **900**

Circa early 1900s. Golfers in white relief.

HIGH GLAZE VASE

WELLER, ZANESVILLE, OH **$2500**

Early 1900s. Dickinsware pottery. (Left)

TEA SET

WILLIAMSONS &
SONS, ENGLAND **$3000**

Circa 1900-1910. Porcelain tea set depicting golfers of the period—Vardon, Braid, Taylor and various caddies.

Prices

Glass Collectibles

	G-5	G-7	G-9

DECANTER

UNKNOWN MAKER   **$250**   **350**   **550**

Circa 1920s. Sterling silver golfer overlaid on blue glass.

DECANTER

UNKNOWN MAKER   **$300**   **450**   **650**

Circa 1920s. Sterling silver golfer overlaid on blue glass.

CRYSTAL DECANTER

WATERFORD   **$1500** **2000** **2500**

Circa 1920. Sterling silver hallmarked neck. Hand painted golfing scene. (Right)

COCKTAIL SET

UNKNOWN MAKER $1250 1600 2250

Circa 1920s. Shaker, six tumblers and six goblets. Sterling silver golfer overlaid on blue glass.

COCKTAIL SET

UNKNOWN MAKER $550 750 1000

Circa 1920s. Shaker and six glasses. Sterling silver cap and sterling overlaid golfers.

COCKTAIL SET

UNKNOWN MAKER $225 350 475

Circa 1920s. Shaker and four glasses. Sterling silver cap and sterling overlaid golfers on frosted yellow glass.

TANTALUS DECANTER SET

ART DECO CO. $300 500 750

Circa 1920s. Holder and caps are silver plated. Sterling silver golf scenes overlaid on clear glass.

WINE DECANTER

UNKNOWN MAKER   **$250   400   600**

Circa 1920s. Sterling silver golfer overlaid on clear glass.

HAND PAINTED BOTTLE

UNKNOWN MAKER   **$200   275   375**

Circa 1930. 8 inches high.

AFTER SHAVE BOTTLE

A.R. WINARICK CO   **$100   125   175**

Circa 1920. 9-1/2 inches high.

HAND PAINTED GLASS

UNKNOWN MAKER   **$50   75   100**

Circa 1930.

ICE BUCKET

T.G. HAWKES & CO.   **$200   275   400**

Circa 1900. Sterling silver handle. Golf scene engraved on glass.

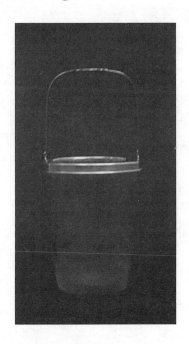

COCKTAIL SHAKER

T.G. HAWKES & CO. $450   600   850

Circa 1900. Sterling silver lid. Golf scene engraved on glass.

WINE BOTTLE

T.G. HAWKES & CO. $225   300   400

Circa 1900. Sterling silver cap. Golf scene engraved on glass.

CLUB SODA BOTTLES

UNKNOWN MAKER $25   35   50

Circa 1920s. Milk glass. Various flavors.

ETCHED GLASSES

HEISSEY $450   650   900

Circa 1920s. Shot glass with etched golfers.

ETCHED GLASSES

HEISSEY $450   650   850

Circa 1920s. Tumbler with etched golfers.

COOKIE JAR

HEISSEY $2000 2750 3750

Circa 1920s. Silver overlay golfers on cut glass.

GLASS SET

CAMBRIDGE $150   200   300

Circa 1920s. Four pink tumblers and carrying tray with handle. Acid etched golfing scenes.

LOCKER BOTTLE, ENGRAVED GLASS

T.J. HAWKES & CO. $275   375   650

Circa 1910. 19th Hole design.

CLAIRET PITCHER

UNKNOWN MAKER   **$800   1200   2000**

Circa 1920. Sterling on glass. 16 inches tall.

CRYSTAL STEIN-STERLING LID

UNKNOWN MAKER   **$1250   1750   2250**

Circa 1900. Golfer in relief on lid.

HAND BLOWN PITCHER

UNKNOWN MAKER   **$500   750   1000**

Circa 1910. Two inch sterling silver neck band.

PERFUME BOTTLE

UNKNOWN MAKER   **$450   600   900**

Circa 1900. Sterling stopper with golfer.

CRYSTAL HUMIDOR-STERLING LID

UNKNOWN MAKER   **$1250   1750   2250**

Circa 1900.

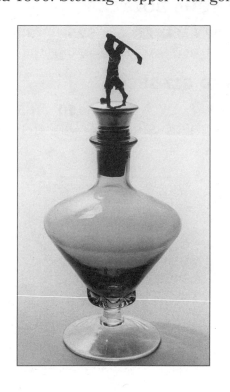

PERFUME BOTTLE

CZECHOSLOVAKIA,
ART DECO   **$450   600   900**

Circa 1930. Cut glass with golfer.

ASHTRAY

H HOFFMAN   **$200   300   400**

Circa 1920s. 5-inch x 3-inch intaglio cut.

TUMBLER

DE PASSE MFG CO   **$60   90   150**

Circa 1915. Sterling overlay.

ASHTRAY

UNKNOWN MAKER   **$40   70   100**

Circa 1940s. 2-1/2-inch x 2-1/2-inch acid etched glass.

ASHTRAY

UNKNOWN MAKER   **$70**   **100**   **175**
    Circa 1940s. 4-inch x 3-inch acid etched glass.

ASHTRAY

UNKNOWN MAKER   **$100**   **150**   **200**
    Circa 1940s. Sterling on glass.

CIGARETTE BOX

UNKNOWN MAKER   **$200**   **300**   **400**
    Circa 1920s. Sterling on glass.

CIGARETTE BOX

UNKNOWN MAKER   **$150**   **225**   **300**
    Circa 1940s. Sterling on glass.

Chapter 12

Golf Medals and Trophies

Chapter 12

Golf Medals and Trophies

Collecting Medals

by Art Di Prospero

One of my favorite collectibles is medals. There's very little written about them and usually the only source is the various world-wide auctions. They come in all shapes and sizes, and are made of bronze, brass, copper, pewter, silver and gold. Most of the silver medals are sterling, whereas the gold medals may vary. The British used mostly 9kt, while Americans used 10kt, 14kt and .900 fine. Some medals are also silver-plated and 12kt gold filled.

I've been drawn to medals for several reasons. The initial visual impact is the artwork. Many are in fine detail, both recessed and in relief. The variety of emblems, golfers, clubs, balls, clubhouses and golfing scenes are sometimes breathtaking.

The pre-1900 British and Scottish medals are not only pieces of art, they tell the history of the game. The names of players, golf course emblems, dates of competition, and other engravings, help identify the better players, where and when they played, and the varied types of competitions of that era.

The early American medals can help "put together" golf in a historical perspective and in chronological order. One of the greatest thrills I can have as a medal collector is to acquire a *documented* piece from Shinnecock, The National, Merion, Baltusrol, Oakmont or any of the other great circa 1890-1910 courses. It gives the collector a humbling feeling as well as awe to know that Willie Anderson, Horace Rawlins, Walter Travis, Walter Hagen, Gene Sarazen and Bobby Jones competed over these hallowed links.

The feeling is purely spellbinding to hold in my hand a medal won by Walter Hagen, or one of my favorites, the medal presented to Olin Dutra upon winning the 1932 PGA Championship. It contains over two ounces of gold and has a 1kt diamond inset. The strike and artwork were absolutely incredible! Just holding it, I can almost feel Mr. Dutra's euphoria from winning the PGA and being presented with his well-earned medal.

The USGA at Far Hills, N.J., has an awesome display of Bobby Jones medals. Other golf clubs such as Chuck Furjanic's home course, The Four Seasons Resort and Club at Las Colinas, where the Byron Nelson Tour event is held, has on display all eighteen medals won by Nelson during 1945, which include those from his incredible eleven straight wins and the PGA Medal.

When collecting, or just looking at medals, you begin to recognize their historical importance, and the part they played in giving the recipients something tangible to remember their "moment of glory." It also gives us a way to identify with the winner's feeling of importance upon being presented with a medal.

Golf Trophies

by Dr. Hank Alperin

A trophy or "prize" for the winner of a competition surely must date the origins of golf. Most notable are the British Open Championship Belt and the British Open Claret Jug, which date from 1860, presented to the winners of the championship. The original Open Championship Belt was retired by the famous young Tom Morris, but the Claret Jug is still being awarded at the end of the championship, with a replica of the original Claret Jug given to the champion. Similar major trophies for the British and United States amateur, and the United States Open Championships are well known. At the Masters a replica of the original trophy (depicting the Augusta National Clubhouse) is presented to the Masters champion.

Many annual golf events in the United States and abroad have individual characteristic trophies, some are glass and others are silver. Medals are still presented in the amateur championships and to the low amateur at the Masters Championship.

A golf trophy may be any item ranging from the classic silver cup, silver bowl or plate, to engraved ribboned medals of gold and silver. Etched and engraved glass trophies are often given at current golf championships particularly in the United States. Many items of metal such as pewter, brass, bronze, plated silver, and ceramics as well, can be found as golf trophies.

The actual item itself presented as the trophy may vary from typical cups, to golf clubs with engraved plaques, mugs, ashtrays, statues, humidors, inkwell sets, sets of decanters, jewelry, mechanical devices including clocks, watches and cigarette lighters. All of these items are both collectible and decorative and while they may cost only a few dollars, they can become a significant investment. There are many collectors within the Golf Collectors Society who specialize in one particular type of trophy; for example items from a certain era, or particular championships. Some individuals may collect only sterling pieces or ceramics, or collect items pertaining to a certain golfer. Others may collect a variety of trophies with no particular theme other than the fact it was presented to a winner of a golf tournament. The prices of these items, like other collectibles, relate to the rarity, condition, and demand.

It is always recommended that collectors buy from reputable dealers who will verify the authenticity, particularly of the more expensive items.

There are many specialized texts available that relate to this field of collecting, particularly artifacts of silver, ceramic, and other metals. Previous major auction house catalogs, and prior catalogs from golf collectible dealers, are also very helpful. The old catalogs with their prices realized are a good guide to the collector as to the prices of the desired trophies.

Where do collectors find trophies? The smaller silver cups and some of the ceramic items can be found in antique shops and flea markets. Occasionally smoking-related items such as ashtrays and engraved lighters, and watches and jewelry, may also be found at these locations. Many golf collectible dealers carry various trophies, and collectors at golf shows display golf trophies for sale. The large golf auction houses both in the United States and Great Britain often carry many trophies, especially important medals and significant trophy cups. Occasionally an entire collection belonging to a famous golfer may be offered, such as in the recent "Bobby Locke" collection, and a large collection of items from the Walter Travis Estate.

The joy of trophy collecting may be obtaining an item from one's favorite golfer, but many enjoy the history behind the trophy relating to a particular golfer, or the golf society that presented it.

At the United States Golf Association Library, one may research some of the inscriptions as to the particular tournament and the correct date. If the inscription does not contain the name of the golfer winning the trophy, it can be obtained here. Often, the trophy was presented with the date and tournament name, but the winner's name had to be engraved by the recipient.

Sterling silver from Great Britain can be dated as to its manufacturer to see if the date of the presentation and the manufacturer correspond. Sterling silver in the United States is marked with the maker of the company and a sterling mark, but no definite date can be attributed.

Medals and Trophies

by Bob Burkett

Medals

From the start of my collecting career in golf, I have always had a special fondness for medals. Unlike clubs, behind each medal there is a story, which can sometimes be found with a little research and imagination. Always, though, they represent man's triumph over an opponent, a golf course, and more importantly, himself.

Medals come in all sizes, shapes, materials and, of course, values. The value rests on a number of factors, the first being composition. A plain brass medal is usually worth less than one made of 18kt gold. However, if the brass was won by, say, Horace Hutchison in a British Amateur Championship, and the gold by a local businessman, the values change.

Beauty, as well as content and history, play a part in the value of medals. Some of the best art in the game of golf is depicted on high quality golf medals and most of these have found their way into collections.

Like most collectibles, medals come in vastly different qualities and price ranges. They may vary in price from $40-50 for a 1950s base metal item, and up to $50,000 or more for an important championship such as the British Open or other majors. Each item is individual, and should be judged as such. Obviously, other factors such as age, wear, engraving and place of origin are to be considered.

The beginning collector should find a focus to his collection. For example, find a specific golf course, a specific time period, famous golfer, or type of medal. Usually your first category choice will be too broad. I started out collecting pre-1930 medals and within a short time it was narrowed to pre-1920 and then, again, to pre-1920 American. It took me 15 years to finally focus on pre-1920 American women's medals.

One last thought: It doesn't matter if you accumulate ten unrelated medals or one hundred related medals, as long as it gives you collecting pleasure. Taking time to research the recipients and places related to your medals may enhance the enjoyment of your collection. On the other hand, you may just want to display them, and that's great too. Remember, the enjoyment of collecting is paramount.

Trophies

Trophies come in a wider range of styles and materials than perhaps any other collectible in golf. The oldest known trophy is a silver golf club from the Edinburgh Burgess Golfing Society. Since then, trophies have appeared in every variation the golfer's twisted mind can conceive. China, crystal, gold, silver, wood, leather, pewter, bronze, and only God knows what else has been fashioned into some sort of symbols of achievement—in the addiction we call golf.

As a broad general statement, trophies are more commonly American than British, while medals are more commonly British than American. Having collected both, I will also make the broad general statement that trophies take up an awful lot more space.

Trophies are very visual and come in a wide variety of sizes and shapes. After 15 years of collecting, I have long since given up trying to find an example of each. Unlike medals, trophies can be striking in appearance and somewhat more modest in cost, owing to the materials being more diverse, and in many cases less costly.

While some of the early high quality trophies will run easily into thousands, many unusual and decorative trophies from the Art Deco 1920s and 1930s can still be found at a relatively modest price. Find a style, period and price that fit your taste and budget.

Please avoid the classic beginner mistake of buying *any* trophy you find at a yard sale, flea market, or antique shop just because it is *golf related*. There are lots of later (1950s and newer) low quality golf items for sale that have little value now and little hope of appreciation in value.

Having said that, I would also advise that you buy what pleases you. Also, buy the best available. It doesn't matter if you have $50 to spend. Buy the best $50 trophy you can find. If you have $5,000 to spend, the rule is the same. Buy the best $5,000 trophy you can find.

The old saying is still true. The bitterness of poor quality remains long after the sweetness of a cheap price has vanished.

Prices

Golf Medals

	G-5	G-7	G-9

BRONZE COIN-SIZE MEDALS

VARIOUS MAKERS $35   50   75

Circa 1900-1930. Nickel to quarter size with club name and date. Medals with ribbons add 50 percent.

BRONZE COIN-SIZE MEDALS

VARIOUS MAKERS $60   100   150

Circa 1900-1930. Half-dollar to dollar size with club name and date. Medals with ribbons add 50 percent.

STERLING COIN-SIZE MEDALS

VARIOUS MAKERS $125   175   250

Circa 1900-1930. Nickel to quarter size with club name and date. Medals with ribbons add 50 percent.

STERLING COIN SIZE MEDALS

VARIOUS MAKERS $200   300   400

Circa 1900-1930. Half-dollar to dollar size with club name and date. Medals with ribbons add 50 percent.

HOLE-IN-ONE MEDALS

VARIOUS MAKERS $20   35   50

Circa 1920s through 1960s. Mostly made of bronze. "Royal" is most common.

BRITISH AMATEUR CHAMPIONSHIP

WALKER AND HALL, SHEFFIELD $6000   8000   10000

Circa 1900. 18kt gold medal in presentation case. Price is for unmarked or unknown winner. Popular winners command a substantial premium.

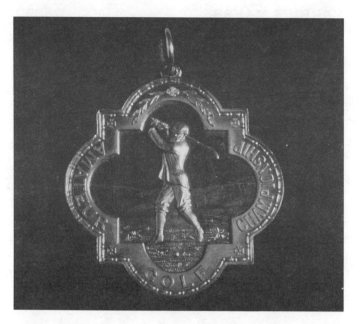

1924 BELGIAN OPEN GOLD MEDAL

UNKNOWN MAKER $7500

14kt gold medal. Won by Walter Hagen. Sold at public auction in 1991 for $1,750. Medals won by less popular players are worth substantially less.

STERLING ST. ANDREWS MEDAL

FRICK JEWELERS, NY $2000

Circa 1900. Presented to members of the golf team at St. Andrews Golf Club, New York.

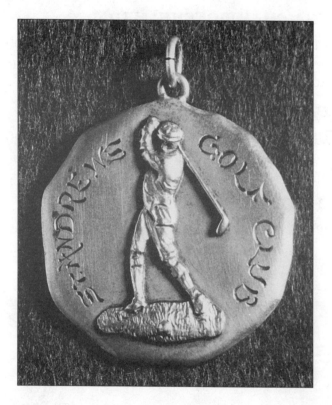

BRITISH OPEN MEDAL

UNKNOWN MAKER $45000

"Open Golf Championship, 1949" gold medal won by Bobby Locke. In red leather presentation case. Sold at public auction in 1993.

BRITISH OPEN MEDAL

UNKNOWN MAKER $40000

"Open Golf Championship, 1950" gold medal won by Bobby Locke. In red leather presentation case. Sold at public auction in 1993.

BRITISH OPEN MEDAL

UNKNOWN MAKER $45000

"Golf Champion Trophy", 1885" gilt medal won by Robert Martin. With blue ribbon and in the original box. Sold at public auction in 1996.

U.S. OPEN GOLF MEDAL

UNKNOWN MAKER $32000

1955 won by Jack Fleck. Sold at public auction in 1993.

PGA CHAMPIONSHIP MEDAL

UNKNOWN MAKER $45000

1921. Won by Walter Hagen. Sold at public auction in 1991 for $8,000.

CANADIAN OPEN GOLD MEDAL

UNKNOWN MAKER $8000

1931. Won by Walter Hagen. Sold at public auction in 1991 for $2,000.

2-INCH STERLING RELIEF MEDAL

WM. DUNNINGHAM, ABERDEEN $2000

1921 from the Caldonia Golf Club, Carnoustie.

WOMEN'S AMATEUR CONTESTANT MEDAL

VARIOUS MAKERS $250

Circa 1920-1935. Quarter size and enameled in different colors through the years.

MEN'S AMATEUR CONTESTANT MEDAL

VARIOUS MAKERS $300

Circa 1920-1935. Quarter size and enameled in different colors through the years.

MEN'S US OPEN CONTESTANT MEDAL

VARIOUS MAKERS $350

Circa 1920-1935. Quarter size and enameled in different colors through the years.

MEN'S WESTERN OPEN CONTESTANT MEDAL

VARIOUS MAKERS $150

Circa 1920-1935. Quarter size and enameled in different colors through the years.

VICTORY GOLF MEDAL

VARIOUS MAKERS $500

A number of medals 2-1/2 inches in diameter were minted to be gifts to participating Golf Clubs in a tournament to raise funds for the United War Work Drive. John D Rockefeller presented the medals.

1897 U.S. OPEN GOLD MEDAL

JOHN FRICK, NEW YORK $50000

Won by Joseph Lloyd. Sold for $21,000 at public auction in 1990.

Prices
Golf Trophies

	G-5	G-7	G-9

STERLING SILVER LOVING CUP

VARIOUS MAKERS $125   175   275

    Circa 1910-1930. Two-handled sterling loving cup without golfing scene. 5 to 6 inches tall. (Below left)

STERLING GOBLET

VARIOUS MAKERS $100   150   250

    Circa 1900-1920. Without golfing scene. 5 to 6 inches tall. (Below center)

STERLING SILVER CUP

GORHAM $200   375   450

    Circa 1900-1920. Two-handled cup without golfing scene. 5 to 6 inches tall. (Below right)

STERLING SILVER CUP

GORHAM $600   800   1000

    Circa 1900-1920. Two-handled cup with golfing scene or crossed clubs and ball. 7 to 8 inches tall.

STERLING SILVER CUP

GORHAM   **$300**   **400**   **500**

    Circa 1900-1920. Two-handled cup without golfing scene. 7 to 8 inches tall.

STERLING CHALICE

UNKNOWN MAKER   **5000**

    Circa 1850. 7 inches tall with golfing scene. Pre-1890 trophies are very rare.

HUMIDOR WITH STERLING LID

VARIOUS MAKERS   **$1000**   **1500**   **2000**

    Circa 1900. Glass or crystal with a sterling lid. 6 to 7 inches tall. (Below left)

STERLING GOLFER ON IVORY BASE

UNKNOWN MAKER   **$2000**   **2500**   **3000**

    Circa 1910. Six inches high including base. (Below right)

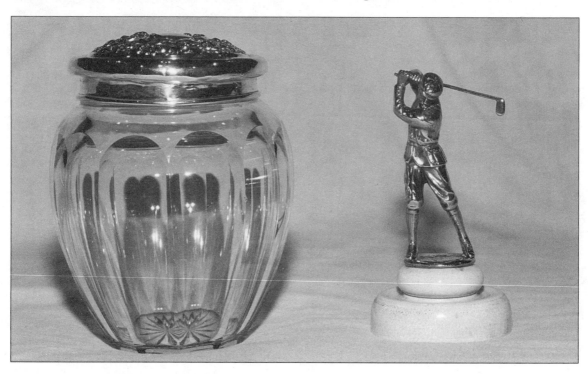

STERLING TEA POT

UNKNOWN MAKER 2500

Circa 1890-1900. 8 inches tall with ornate engravings. Very scarce.

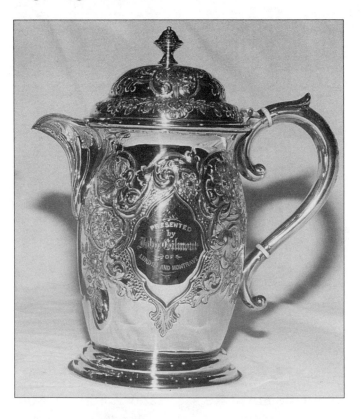

STERLING SILVER LOVING CUP

VARIOUS MAKERS $375 500 750

Circa 1910-1930. Two handled sterling loving cup without golfing scene. 10 to 12 inches tall.

STERLING SILVER LOVING CUP

VARIOUS MAKERS $1000 1500 2000

Circa 1910-1930. Two-handled sterling loving cup with golfing scene or crossed clubs and ball. 10 to 12 inches tall.

STERLING LOVING CUP MADE IN SCOTLAND

J. LAING $600 800 1000

Circa 1920s. 6 inches tall with golfing scene and fine detail.

CERAMIC AND STERLING TROPHY

LENOX $3000 4000 5000

Circa 1900-1910. Opaque green ceramic pitcher with silver overlay. Very scarce.

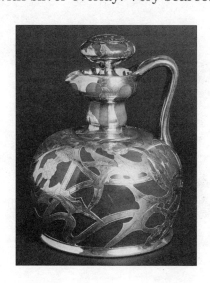

BLUE CERAMIC TROPHY

LENOX   **$750   1000   1250**

     Circa 1900-1920. Three-handled trophy with golfing scene. 7 to 9 inches tall.

STERLING AND BRONZE TROPHY

PAIRPOINT   **$800   1000   1200**

     Circa 1900-1920. Three-handled trophy on legs. Sterling on bronze.

BRONZE GOLFER ON BASE

VARIOUS MAKERS   **$125   200   300**

     Circa 1900-1930. Bronze golfer on wood, bakelite or marble base. 5 to 7 inches tall.

BRONZE GOLFER ON BASE

VARIOUS MAKERS   **$250   400   600**

     Circa 1900-1930. Bronze golfer on wood, bakelite or marble base. 8 to 10 inches tall.

Chapter 13

Golf Trading Cards

Chapter 13

Golf Trading Cards

by Mike Daniels

Although card collecting has been around for more than one hundred years, golf card collecting is still relatively new or unknown to many collectors. Most of us as youngsters collected baseball cards and even though we played golf, we had never seen a golf trading card. We hope that the next few pages will give you additional information and insight into this wonderful and untapped area of golf collectibles.

The History of Golf Cards

Trade and cigarette cards were the first of the collectible cards. Trade cards were handed out by shop owners and manufacturers. These cards depicted the manufacturer's products and were printed with the name and address of the shop or shopkeeper. It was hoped that if they made these cards attractive, the customer would retain them as an informal business card.

The next step was to produce cards in a series with a particular theme. Flowers, fashion, children, pets or country scenes were the first series produced.

If you were to review scrap albums from the middle to the late 1800s, you would find evidence of the success of this new marketing strategy both in the United States and Europe. Hence, the card collecting craze began.

About this same time, 1870-1880, a change was taking place in the tobacco hab-its of people. Cigarettes were taking over from pipes and chewing tobacco. The cigarettes were usually packed in the same fragile packets of their ancestors. This idea of combining a cardboard type of stiffener with the current collecting craze started first in the United States and soon spread to Australia, Britain, and the rest of the world.

In the period from 1880 to about 1940, sets of cigarette cards were issued in profusion. Thousands of sets were made and the foundation was laid for the continuing card collecting hobby.

Since the majority of smokers prior to 1900 were men, subjects were chosen to appeal to men—military, sports, and women were popular choices.

In the United States, Kinney issued a military series in the late 1880s, Allen & Ginter issued its 50-card great generals set, and Duke did a 45-card famous ships series.

A year or two later, Allen & Ginter offered its first sport series called World Champions, which was a 50-card set. About the same time, Goodwin and Co. issued a 50-card Champions set and Kimball & Co. offered its 50-card Champions of Games and Sport set. Yet, in not one of these sets was there a golf card.

Around the turn of the century in England, the first golf cards were produced. Felix Berlyn and Cope Bros. and Co., Ltd. produced 25- and 50-card sets of golf scenes and strokes rather than of players. Original complete sets produced by these companies are extremely rare and sell for thousands of dollars. Do not despair, reprints of these and several other early sets were produced during the 1980s and sell for a fraction of the cost of originals.

The earliest American set to depict a golfer or golf scene was the American Tobacco Series of Champion Athletes and prize fighters of 1910—commonly referred to as the Mecca cigarette set. This set had six (6) famous American golfers of the time: Finley Douglas, Alex Smith, Gil Nicholls, George Low, Jack Hobens and Fred Herreshoff. These are not exactly household names today, but several of these gentlemen had distinguished careers in American golf.

About the same time in England, Odgen's produced its Guinea Gold cigarettes issue of 18 photographic golf cards. This set included Old Tom Morris, Harry Vardon, James Braid, etc. and (6) scenic cards from an early match played between Harry Vardon and James Braid, two of the greatest golfers from this period. By the late 1920s Churchman felt that there was enough interest in the game and a sufficient number of well-known players to issue its famous golfer 50-card series of photographic cards. Over the next several years many other golf sets were produced by Churchman and other tobacco companies.

The success of the cigarette cards became the model for other types of commodities. Cards began to be inserted with newspapers, chocolates, magazines, cereal, tea, and gum packets. Then came a slow and gradual change from a situation where with every stick of gum you were given a few cards, until the time when every pack of cards came with a free stick of gum. Then, finally, why bother putting the gum in the packets at all? We are now in a world of trading cards where series are produced on a commercial basis and sold in packets or as complete sets. Thousands of cards are now produced each year.

Golf cards have gone through a series of cycles over the years with cards and sets being produced for a few years then going into a form of hibernation with only a few cards produced annually. Donruss produced two PGA tour sets of 66 cards each in 1981 and 1982. The PGA tour continued to produce sets from 1983 to 1990. These were very similar to the Donruss sets in style and layout. These sets have become quite scarce in their own right since only a few thousand sheets were produced each year and many of these were destroyed. Only a few collectors knew of their existence and managed to save some sets.

The Pro Set company began producing sets for the PGA tour in 1990 and produced sets for (3) years. The first set consisted of 100 cards, 75 regular PGA tour cards and 25 senior tour cards. These sets were well received by the collecting public and were quite popular by autograph seekers on the American tour.

These sets are no longer being produced and once again the only new sets available seem to be coming out of England. Most of these sets are of one theme or small sets of the 1993 or 1995 Ryder Cup Teams. Hopefully the cycle will continue with the ever increasing popularity of golf among young people throughout the world. Maybe new sets again will be produced in the U.S. to satisfy the collecting interests of golfers. These miniature storybooks tell us much about the history of the game and hopefully some of you will expand your collecting interests into golf cards.

The following new reference books and price guides have been printed in the last few years. These are excellent checklists, and list all known golf cards in the world through 1994.

Recommended Reference Books

A Century of Golf Cards by Bruce Berdock and Michael Baier, 1993.

The Price Guide to Golf Cards, Part I, Tobacco Cards, by Philip Smedley and Bruce Berdock, 1994.

The Price Guide to Golf Cards, Part II, Non-Tobacco Cards, by Philip Smedley & Bruce Berdock, 1995.

Pricing

Golf Cards

	G-5	G-7	G-9

CHAMPION ATHLETES SERIES

AMERICAN TOBACCO CO. $25   50   90

Circa 1910. "Mecca" cigarettes. Six cards: A. Smith, F. Douglas, J. Hobens, F. Herreshoff, George Low and Gil Nicholls.

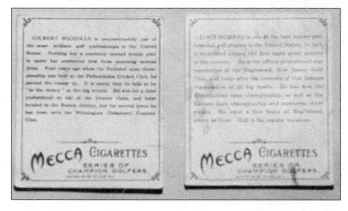

COLLEGE SERIES

AMERICAN TOBACCO CO. $15   30   50

Circa 1914. Seven cards.

COLLEGE SILKS

AMERICAN TOBACCO CO. $25   50   90

Circa 1910. Two sizes of colorful silks. 25 colleges included. Small size 5-1/2 x 3-1/2 inches; large size 7-3/4 x 5 inches.

BURLINE MIXTURE GOLF CARDS, FULL SET

BERLYN, FELIX S, ENGLAND $5500   12000   20000

Circa 1910. 25 small-size cards.

BURLINE MIXTURE GOLF CARDS, ONE CARD

BERLYN, FELIX S, ENGLAND $250   450   800

Circa 1910. 25 small-size cards.

BURLINE MIXTURE GOLF CARDS, ONE CARD

BERLYN, FELIX S, ENGLAND   **$400   1000   1500**

Circa 1910. 25 large-size cards.

BURLINE MIXTURE GOLF CARDS, FULL SET

BERLYN, FELIX S, ENGLAND   **$9500   22000   35000**

Circa 1910. 25 large-size cards.

CAN YOU BEAT BOGEY AT ST. ANDREWS

CHURCHMAN   **$400   750   1250**

Circa 1934. Complete set of 55 cards.

FAMOUS GOLFERS SMALL SIZE

CHURCHMAN   **$700   1450   2250**

Circa 1927. Complete set of 50 cards.

FAMOUS GOLFERS LARGE SIZE

CHURCHMAN   **$800   1350   2250**

Circa 1927. Complete set of 12 cards.

MEN OF THE MOMENT IN SPORTS

CHURCHMAN   **$300   500   850**

Circa 1928. Set of 10 golf cards numbering 24 to 33.

PROMINENT GOLFERS SMALL SIZE

CHURCHMAN   **$550   1100   1750**

Circa 1931. Set of 50 golf cards.

PROMINENT GOLFERS LARGE SIZE

CHURCHMAN   **$550   950   1400**

Circa 1931. Set of 12 golf cards.

SPORTING CELEBRITIES

CHURCHMAN   **$100   150   250**

Circa 1931. Set of 7 golf cards, numbering 30 to 36.

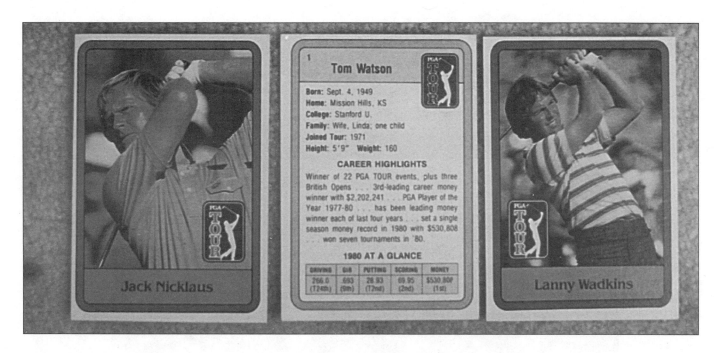

PGA TOUR CARDS

DONRUSS   **$25**   **35**   **50**

1981. Complete set of 66 cards. All are considered "Rookie" cards.

PGA TOUR CARDS

DONRUSS   **$30**   **40**   **65**

1982. Complete set of 66 cards.

GOLF'S GREATEST

MEULLER ENTERPRISES, INC.	**$25**	**30**	**60**

1992. Complete set of 30 cards.

PRO TOUR CARDS

MILLER PRESS	**$90**	**150**	**300**

1983 and 1984. Uncut sheet of 66 cards.

PRO TOUR CARDS

MILLER PRESS	**$65**	**100**	**200**

1985, 1986 and 1987. Uncut sheet of 66 cards.

PRO TOUR CARDS

MILLER PRESS	**$50**	**75**	**120**

1988. Uncut sheet of 66 cards.

PRO TOUR CARDS

MILLER PRESS	**$25**	**45**	**75**

1989 and 1990. Uncut sheet of 66 cards.

THE SEVEN AGES OF GOLF

NATIONAL EXCHANGE BANK	**$850**	**1300**	**2250**

Circa 1902. Seven card set.

OGDEN'S CHAMPIONS OF 1936

OGDEN'S LIMITED,
ENGLAND　　　　　**$10**　　**22**　　　**35**

　Pam Barton, A.H. Padgham and H. Thomson.
(Above)

OGDEN'S GUINEA GOLD

OGDEN'S LIMITED,
ENGLAND　　　　　**$25**　　**50**　　　**100**

　Circa 1901. Unnumbered cards. The Tom
Morris card is worth about double.

POPEYE 2ND SERIES

PRIMROSE
CONFECTIONARY　　**$25**　　**45**　　　**70**

　1961. Card #29

POPEYE 4TH SERIES

PRIMROSE
CONFECTIONARY　　**$8**　　**10**　　　**20**

　1963. Cards #24 and #32. (Right)

NFL FOOTBALL CARDS

PRO SET, INC. $4   7   15

1990. Payne Stewart special card.

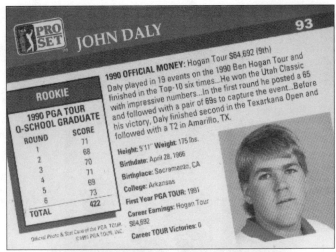

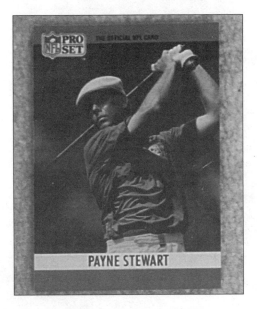

PGA TOUR INAUGURAL SET

PRO SET, INC. $5   6   10

1990. Complete set of 100 cards.

PGA TOUR CARDS

PRO SET, INC. $10   15   25

1991 and 1992. Complete sets of 285 and 300 cards.

THE BOBBY JONES STORY

SHERIDAN
COLLECTIBLES   **$5   7   12**

1993. Complete set of 12 cards.

ARNOLD PALMER HOLOGRAM CARD

PRO SET, INC.   **$50   55   60**

1991.

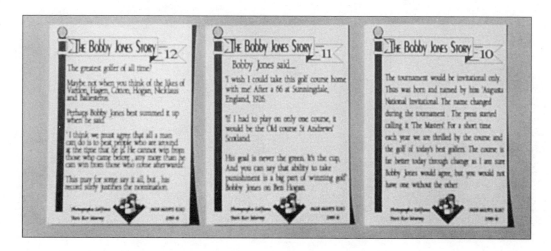

FAMOUS COURSES

WILLS, ENGLAND   **$250**   **400**   **650**
    Circa 1924. 25 card set. (Above)

BEN HOGAN HOLOGRAM CARD

PRO SET, INC.   **$80**   **90**   **100**
    1992.

FAMOUS GOLFERS

WILLS, ENGLAND   **$500**   **800**   **1300**
    Circa 1930. 25 card set.

Chapter 14

Silver and Gold Golf Collectibles

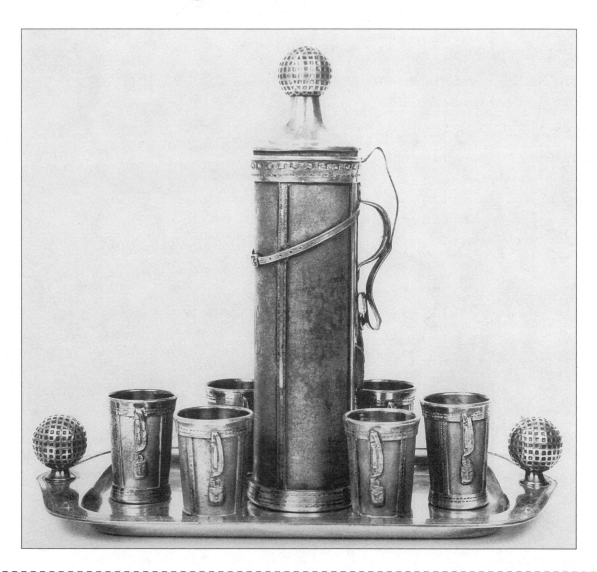

Chapter 14

Silver and Gold Golf Collectibles

Precious metals were used to make many collectible golf items. Here we will discuss and evaluate those made from gold and silver.

Gold came in various qualities ranging from 9kt to 18kt and was mainly used for smaller items such as jewelry in the form of cuff links and tie clasps for men, and brooches, pins and charms for women.

Silver items were very popular around the turn of the century and were made of sterling or were silver plated. Many of these were for ladies and the home. They included toast racks, knife rests, salt and pepper shakers, coffee and tea servers, various utensils, serving trays, hair brushes, coin purses, and pin cushions. Souvenir spoons were also made for both trophies and the tourist trade at famous course locations like St. Andrews, Troon, etc. For the men there were whiskey flasks, cocktail items, match safes, cigarette cases, watch fobs, inkwells, tie clasps, cuff links, and scoring devices. Some of the prominent manufacturers included: Unger Brothers, Tiffany, Gorham, Wm. Kerr, and Whiting.

Following is a listing of collectibles. Several photos were graciously provided by Glentiques, Ltd.

Pricing

Silver and Gold Collectibles

	G-5	G-7	G-9

STERLING CIGARETTE CASE

UNKNOWN MAKER	**$375**	**575**	**900**

Circa 1900-1920. Golfing scene on cover.

STERLING HAT PIN

UNKNOWN MAKER	**$75**	**100**	**150**

Circa 1900-1920s. Wicker basket at top.

STERLING HAT PIN

UNKNOWN MAKER	**$50**	**75**	**100**

Circa 1900-1920s. Iron head at top.

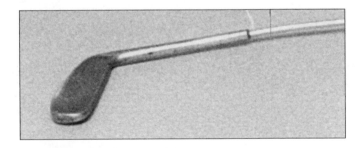

STERLING HAT PIN

UNKNOWN MAKER	**$60**	**90**	**125**

Circa 1900-1920s. Sterling, wood at top.

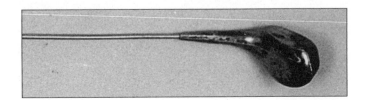

STERLING PIN

UNKNOWN MAKER	**$100**	**150**	**225**

Circa 1910-1920s. 3 inches. Bag and clubs.

STERLING TIE CLASP

UNKNOWN MAKER	**$60**	**90**	**125**

Circa 1910-1920s. 3 inches. Golf club.

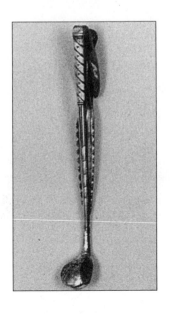

STERLING GOLF BAG PIN

UNKNOWN MAKER $75   125   200

Circa 1910-1920s. 1-1/2 inches. Bag and clubs.

GOLD GOLF BALL CUFF LINKS

DUNLOP, NEW YORK $125   175   250

Circa 1920. Nickel-size 10kt gold mesh golf ball cuff links.

SILVER-PLATED INKWELL

F BRS. LTD. $475   600   900

Circa 1890. 6 x 11 inches in size. Two golf ball inkwells, golfer in center.

COCKTAIL SHAKER, TRAY AND CUPS

DERBY SILVER CO. $1200   1500   2000

Circa 1920. Silver plated. Mesh ball handled tray, six cups and a 13-inch-tall pitcher.

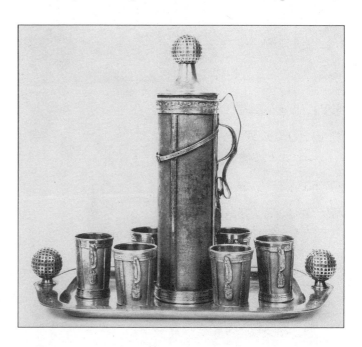

TABLE SCRAPER

UNKNOWN MAKER $225   325   450

Circa 1900-1920. Sterling handle, celluloid blade.

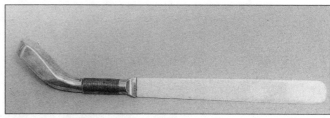

STERLING BOOKMARK

UNKNOWN MAKER $225   325   450

Circa 1900-1920. Caddy with bag.

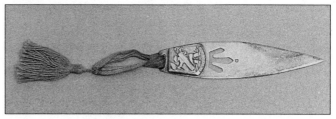

SALT DIP

UNKNOWN MAKER $175   250   375

Circa 1900. Silver plate. Gutta ball design with crossed clubs.

STERLING NUT TRAY

UNKNOWN MAKER $400   500   600

Circa 1900-1910. 5-1/2 inch diameter. Golfer in center.

KNIFE RESTS

UNKNOWN MAKER $250   350   450

Circa 1900-1920. Silver plated.

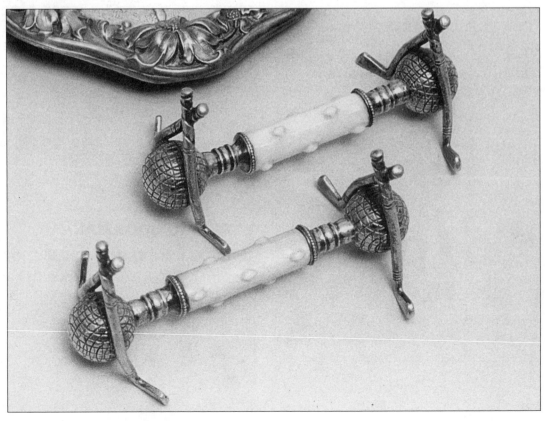

SILVER-PLATED LADY'S COIN PURSE

UNKNOWN MAKER $200   300   450

Circa 1900-1920s. Caddy on front.

STERLING LADY'S COIN PURSE

UNKNOWN MAKER $350   450   650

Circa 1900-1920s. Lady golfer on front.

STERLING PIN CUSHION-WATCH

UNKNOWN MAKER $600   800   1100

Circa 1915-1925. Pin cushion with Swiss watch inside mesh ball cover. (Right)

STERLING PIN CUSHION-HAT PIN HOLDER

UNKNOWN MAKER   **$300**   **450**   **600**
    Circa 1910-1920. Golf bag pin holder.

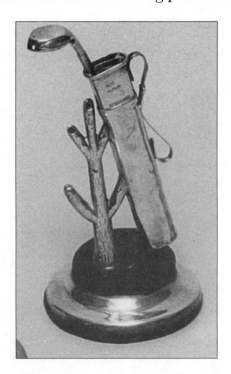

STERLING BELT BUCKLE

UNKNOWN MAKER   **$300**   **400**   **600**
    Circa 1900.

TOAST RACK

DERBY SILVER CO.   **$350**   **500**   **700**
    Circa 1900-1910. Four-slice rack.

STERLING HAT PIN

UNKNOWN MAKER   **$60**   **90**   **125**
    Circa 1900-1920s. Crossed clubs at top.

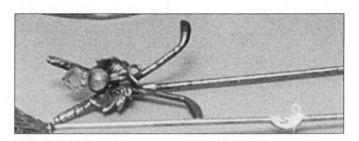

STERLING SILVER SPOONS

VARIOUS MAKERS   **$60**   **80**   **100**
    Circa 1900-1930. Golfers on handle.

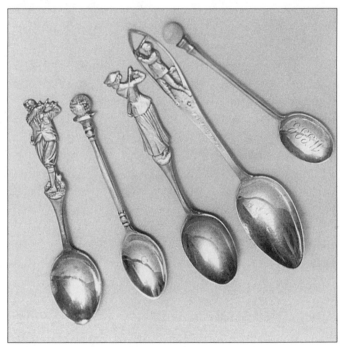

STERLING EGGCUP

UNKNOWN MAKER   **$60**   **100**   **150**
    Circa 1920s. Made in England. 3-1/2 inches tall.

STERLING TEE INFUSER

WATROUS, WALLINGFORD, CT   **$175**   **300**   **450**
    Circa 1910-1915. Shaped like a driver.

STERLING SILVER SPOONS

VARIOUS MAKERS   **$60   80   100**

Circa 1900-1930. Various handle designs. Larger ornate spoons command double the prices listed.

STERLING CIGARETTE CASE

NAPIER CO.   **$200   375   575**

Circa 1930. Golfer on front. Knickers in black enamel.

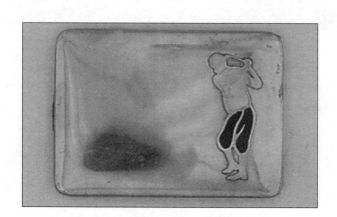

STERLING CIGARETTE CASE

THE THOMAS CO.   **$200   375   575**

Circa 1930. Golfer on front.

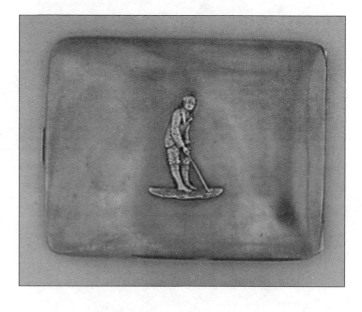

STERLING CIGARETTE CASE

NAPIER CO. $200   375   575

    Circa 1930. Golfer on front. Place for initials at right front.

BLOTTER

UNGER BROS.   500   750   1100

    Circa 1905. Golfer on front.

STERLING MATCH SAFE

UNGER, NEWARK, NJ $400   650   850

    Circa 1900-1910. Caddy with bag.

STERLING MATCH SAFE

ART NOUVEAU $400   650   850

    Circa 1900-1910. Woman golfer in back-swing.

STERLING MATCH SAFE

UNKNOWN MAKER   **$400   750   1000**

Circa 1890. Woman golfer addressing golf ball.

STERLING MATCH SAFE

GORHAM   **$300   450   675**

Circa 1900-1910. Bag of clubs, flagstick and large thistle plant.

STERLING MATCH SAFE

UNKNOWN MAKER   **$300   450   675**

Circa 1900-1910. Ball and crossed clubs.

STERLING MATCH SAFE

La PIERRE MFG. CO.   **$300   450   675**

Circa 1890. Male golfer in backswing.

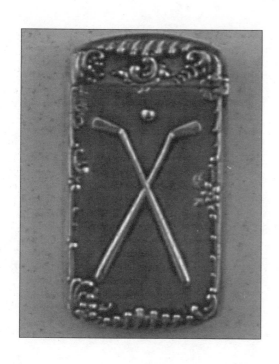

STERLING MATCH SAFE

La PIERRE MFG. CO. $250   375   575

Circa 1900. Small size with crossed clubs and ball.

STERLING MATCH SAFE

UNKNOWN MAKER $300   450   650

Circa 1900. Golf clubs and ball.

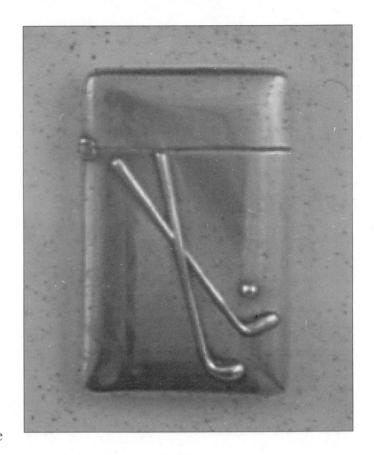

STERLING MATCH SAFE

H.W. LTD, BIRMINGHAM $450   675   950

Circa 1900-1910. Golf ball-shaped with line cut guttie markings.

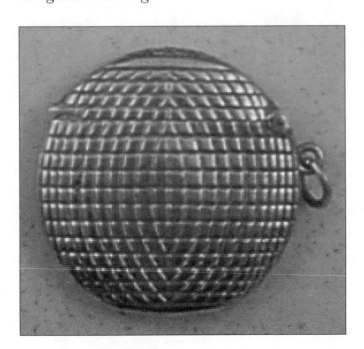

STERLING WHISKEY FLASK

KERR & CO.,
NEWARK, NJ   **$500   800   1100**

Circa 1920s. 4 x 8 inch pint size. Knickered golfers on front.

STERLING WHISKEY FLASK

WATROUS MFG. CO. $350   500   750

Circa 1920s. Half-pint size. Golfing scene on front.

STERLING WHISKEY FLASK

UNGER BROTHERS $650   900   1250

Circa 1905. Small flask. Caddy with bag.

STERLING WHISKEY FLASK

INTERNATIONAL
SILVER CO. $350   500   750

Circa 1920. Small flask in oval shape. Ball and club on front.

NICKEL STERLING FLASK

EVANS CO. $100   200   350

Circa 1920. Golfing scene.

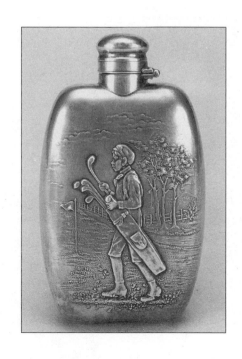

Chapter 15

Miscellaneous Golf Collectibles

Chapter 15

Miscellaneous Golf Collectibles

Many collectors have wide and varied interests that are not limited to clubs, balls and books, and extend their search for golf-related collectibles in antique shops, flea markets and garage sales, as well as fixed price lists, auctions and dealer offerings.

This chapter will include items such as tournament badges from PGA events, U.S. Opens and the Masters. It also includes watches, score keepers, ball washers, drink serving trays, bookends, cigar boxes, games, practice devices, molds, tins, advertising items, golf course equipment, and one-arm bandits.

Pricing
Miscellaneous Golf Collectibles

	G-5	G-7	G-9

TOURNAMENT MEDIA BADGES

VARIOUS MAKERS	$15	20	30

1960s-1980. 2 to 4 inches, in various shapes: round, rectangular, oval, etc. Made of metal and plastic. (Below)

TOURNAMENT CADDIE BADGES

VARIOUS MAKERS	$20	30	45

1960s-1980. 2 to 4 inches, in various shapes: round, rectangular, oval, etc. Made of metal and plastic.

CADDIE BADGES

VARIOUS MAKERS	$75	100	150

1910-1930. Brass or steel. Golf course name and caddie number. Silver-dollar size.

TOURNAMENT ENTRANCE BADGES

VARIOUS MAKERS	$8	12	20

1960s-1980. 2 to 4 inches various shapes: round, rectangular, oval, etc. Made of metal and plastic.

U.S. OPEN BADGES

VARIOUS MAKERS	$15	25	45

1960s-1980. 2 to 4 inches various shapes: round, rectangular, oval, etc. Made of metal and plastic.

U.S. OPEN MEDIA BADGES

VARIOUS MAKERS	$20	30	50

1960s-1970s. Press arm bands. Made of felt with elastic band. Various colors. (Below)

MASTERS BADGES

VARIOUS MAKERS	$40	45	50

1970-1980.

MASTERS BADGES

VARIOUS MAKERS	$60	80	100

1960-1970.

MASTERS BADGES

VARIOUS MAKERS $125   175   275
1950-1960.

MASTERS PRESS BADGES

VARIOUS MAKERS $50   60   75
1960s-1970. Rectangular and round. Made of metal.

POCKET WATCH

U.S. ROYAL $100   150   250
Circa 1920s. Open face with mesh ball background.

POCKET WATCH

DUNLOP $300   400   550
Circa 1920s-1930s. Sterling case in mesh ball pattern.

SCORE KEEPER

VARIOUS MAKERS $150   225   450
Circa 1920s. Pocket-watch size.

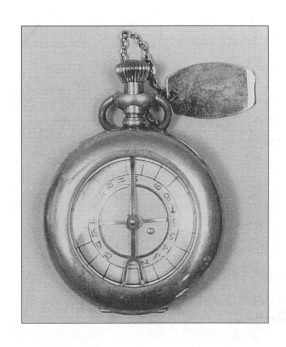

SCORE KEEPER

VARIOUS $150   225   350
Circa 1920s. Wrist-watch style.

HOGAN BELT WATCH

DUNLOP $300 400 550

Circa 1950s.

BALL WASHERS

**HALLEY & CO.,
LONDON** $40 60 90

Circa 1920. Rectangular rubber holder for sponge.

BALL WASHERS

**NORTH BRITISH,
EDINBURGH** $30 45 75

Circa 1920. Square rubber holder for sponge.

BALL WASHERS

UNKNOWN MAKER $150 225 375

Circa 1920. Round silver-plated holder for sponge. Golfing scene on lid.

BALL WASHERS

UNKNOWN MAKER $125 200 300

Circa 1920. Round brass holder for sponge.

GOLF BALL PAINT

VARIOUS   150   225   375

Circa 1900-1920.

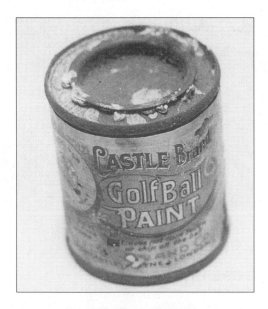

SPOOL OF PITCHED LINEN

VARIOUS   150   225   375

Circa 1900-1930. For repairing golf clubs. Both British and American makers.

GOLF SHOE SPIKES

UNKNOWN   50   75   100

Circa 1920s. "Black Boy" cricket and golf spikes. Colorful red, green and white box.

GOLF SHOE SPIKES

UNKNOWN   50   75   100

Circa 1920s. "Goffix" golfers cleat that attaches to street shoes. Add 50 percent for original box.

LAWN GOLF GAME

UNKNOWN MAKER $250   300   350

Circa 1920s. Four wooden-head clubs, "holes" with discs, one rubber bramble pattern ball, and a wood storage box.

GOLF AROUND THE CLOCK GAME

P.S.P., INC.,
NEW YORK   **$125   200   325**

Circa late 1920s. Cast-iron numerals and hole in an advertising tin.

"PLAY GOLF" GOLF GAME

FERDINAND
STRAUSS, NY   **$125   200   350**

Circa 1910. Metal wind-up game.

ROLA-BOLA GOLF GAME

VARIOUS   **$125   200   350**

Circa 1920s. Putting game.

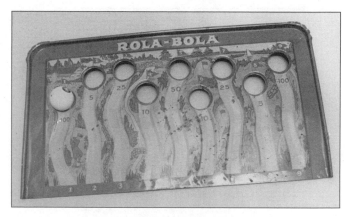

HAND-HELD GOLF GAMES

MINIATURE GAME CO.,
PHILADELPHIA   **$100   150   225**

Circa 1940s. Pocket golf and other hand-held games.

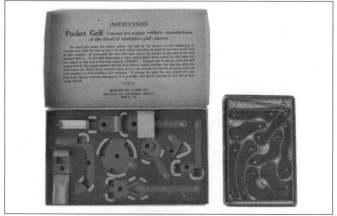

TOMMY GREEN SCHOENHUT GOLFER

SCHOENHUT CO.   **$350   450   600**

Circa 1920s. Five-inch wooden golfer at end of control rod.

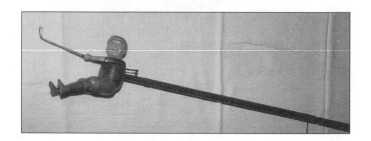

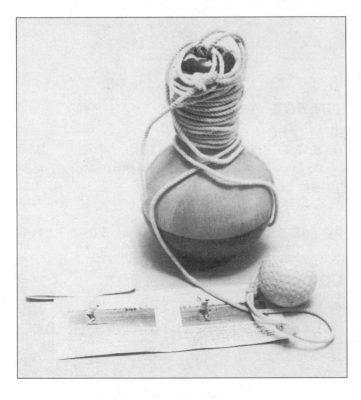

ICE CREAM MOLDS

VARIOUS MAKERS   **$100**   **150**   **200**

   Circa 1910-1920. Made of pewter. Many shapes including a mesh golf ball mold not pictured.

SISSY LOFTER SCHOENHUT GOLFER

SCHOENHUT CO.   **$450**   **600**   **800**

   Circa 1920s. Five-inch wooden golfer at end of control rod.

BOTTLE GOLF PRACTICE DEVICE

UNKNOWN MAKER   **$150**   **225**   **350**

   Circa 1920s. Bottle-shaped device with mesh ball at end of long twine tether. (Left)

SMAKBAK PRACTICE DEVICE

MADE IN ENGLAND   **$75**   **90**   **125**

   Circa 1925. Long metal spike with heavy twine attached to golf ball. In colorful advertising box.

COUNTRY CLUB CIGAR TIN

VARIOUS MAKERS   **$125**   **225**   **350**
    Circa 1920s. Colorful cigar tin.

BISCUIT TIN

ROBERTSON BROS.,
TORONTO   **$200**   **300**   **450**
    Circa 1920s. Hand painted. Approximately 10 inches tall.

SPICE TIN

VARIOUS MAKERS   **$50**   **70**   **100**
    Circa 1920s. Small 1-1/2-inch x 3-1/2-inch tins for spices.

TIN BOX

SPALDING,
DYSART, FIFE   **$150**   **250**   **350**
    Circa 1920s. Large tin box with colorful golfing scenes.

TOMATO CAN

ROYAL BRAND   **$50**   **70**   **100**
    Circa 1920s. Lady golfer on label.

COUNTRY CLUB CIGAR BOX

VARIOUS MAKERS   **$40**   **70**   **100**
    Circa 1920s. Wooden cigar box.

SILVER KING ADVERTISING FIGURE

SILVERTOWN   **$300   450   650**

    Circa 1920s. Papier-mache with mesh ball head. Approximately 10 inches tall.

PENFOLD OR BROMFORD MAN

PENFOLD   **$250   400   600**

    Circa 1920s. Papier-mache golfing figure with large "Hogan"-type hat. Stand marked "He Played a Penfold, or Bromford". Approximately 22 inches tall.

SILVER QUEEN ADVERTISING FIGURE

SILVERTOWN   **$300   450   650**

    Circa 1920s. Papier-mache with mesh ball head. Approximately 8 inches tall.

SCOTTIE DOG ADVERTISING FIGURE

NORTH BRITISH,
EDINBURGH   **$250   375   550**

    Circa 1920s. Made in both metal and pottery. Advertising for the North British Ball.

DUNLOP MAN

DUNLOP   **$250   400   600**

Circa 1920s. Paper-mache colorful golfing figure with golf bag. Stand marked "We Play Dunlop". Approximately 18 inches tall.

PLASTER ADVERTISING PAPER-WEIGHT

UNKNOWN MAKER   **$250   400   600**

Circa 1920s. Whiskey advertisements made of plaster. Usually with golfer and mesh pattern ball.

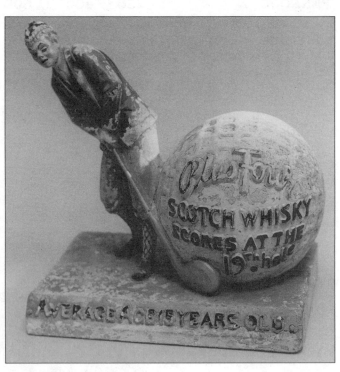

METAL SERVING TRAY

VARIOUS MAKERS   **$50   75   100**

Circa 1930s. Many with beer advertisements.

CAST-IRON DOORSTOPS

VARIOUS MAKERS   **$175**   **250**   **400**

Circa 1920s. Colorfully painted.

WHITE METAL BOOKENDS

VARIOUS MAKERS   **$100**   **125**   **150**

Circa 1920s. Golfer in plus fours.

BOOKENDS

UNKNOWN   **100**   **125**   **150**

Circa 1950s. Heavy granite, 7 inches tall with crossed clubs and ball. (Above)

DESKTOP THERMOMETER

UNKNOWN MAKER   **$250**   **325**   **450**

Circa 1910. 6 inches tall with golfer on top. Made of white metal with dark brown patina. (Left)

HANDKERCHIEF BOXES

UNKNOWN MAKER   **$50**   **75**   **100**

Circa 1920s. Hinged wooden boxes with colorful men and ladies golfers on lid.

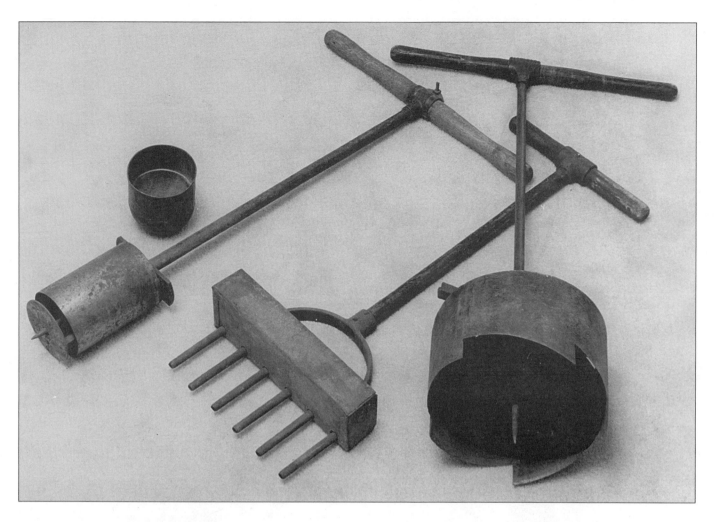

GOLF COURSE EQUIPMENT

VARIOUS MAKERS   **$50**   **75**   **100**

    Circa 1900-1910. Hole or cup liner made of steel.

GOLF COURSE EQUIPMENT

VARIOUS MAKERS   **$150**   **250**   **400**

    Circa 1900-1910. Hole cutter.

GOLF COURSE EQUIPMENT

VARIOUS MAKERS   **$200**   **300**   **450**

    Circa 1900-1910. Green aerifier. The tines were hollow.

GOLF COURSE EQUIPMENT

VARIOUS MAKERS   **$200**   **300**   **450**

    Circa 1900-1910. Sod mover.

GOLF COURSE EQUIPMENT

VARIOUS MAKERS   **$100**   **175**   **275**

    Circa 1920-1930. Fringe mower.

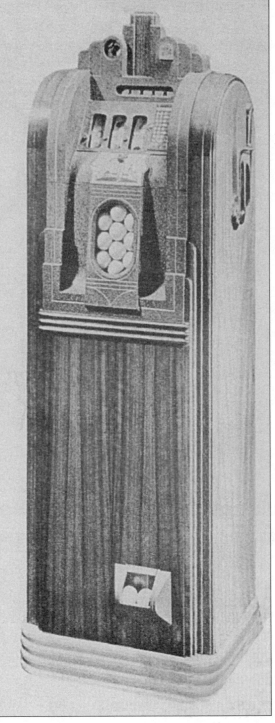

MILLS GOLF BALL VENDER

Built exclusively for Golf Clubs and locations catering to golf players, it's the first machine of its kind to do everything a golf ball vender should do.

It's a full fledged Vender but it pays out, not in mints or checks, but strictly in Golf Balls.

Every coin played in is registered. Every ball paid out is registered.

Capacity 114 Golf Balls. It saves you excessive service, protects you against a needless waste of time and effort.

It is entirely automatic, works just like a Mills Mystery. It comes in a beautiful cabinet, and through a large merchandise display window, shows the Golf Balls, all of them nationally advertised.

If the machine runs out of balls, it may be reloaded without unlocking the rest of mechanism. Each ball thus inserted is then registered.

This brand new Mills machine opens up a brand new market for coin machine amusement. Customers everywhere are reporting cash intakes of $40, $50 and more each day.

GOLF BALL SLOT MACHINE

VARIOUS MAKERS $2500 3750 5500

Circa 1930s-1950s. Jennings and Mills brands. Standing model.

GOLF BALL SLOT MACHINE

VARIOUS MAKERS $2500 3750 5500

Circa 1930s-1950s. Jennings and Mills brands. Countertop model.

GOLF COURSE EQUIPMENT

VARIOUS MAKERS $100 175 275
Circa 1900-1930. Sand tee box. The box pictured was in use at the 11th tee, Baltusrol.

MAGAZINES

GOLFING MAGAZINE 25 40 65
Circa 1930s.

MAGAZINES

AMERICAN GOLFER 60 80 120
Circa 1905-1916. Edited by Walter Travis.

MAGAZINES

GOLF ILLUSTRATED 50 70 110
Circa 1920s. Large size.

MAGAZINES

AMERICAN GOLFER 50 70 100
Circa 1920-1930. Large size.

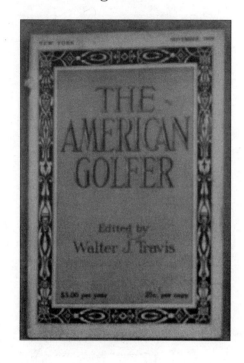

MAGAZINES

GOLFER'S MAGAZINE 60 80 125
Circa Teens.

Bibliography

Berdock, Bruce and Baier, Michael
A Century of Golf Cards, 1993
Published in Canada

Biocini, Paul
Signature Golf Ball Collector's Guide, 1995
Paul Biocini, Modesto, CA

British Golf Collectors Society
Through The Green

Christie's, Glasgow, Scotland
Auction Catalogues

Cooper, J.M.
Early U.S. Golf Clubs by Spalding & Bros., 1994
J. M. Cooper, Kannapolis, NC

Donovan, Richard E. and Murdoch, Joseph S. F.
The Game of Golf and The Printed Word 1566-1985, 1988
Castalio Press, Endicott, NY

Furjanic, Chuck
Auction Catalogues
Golf Collectibles, Irving, TX

Furjanic, Chuck
Monthly Catalogues 1989 to Present
Golf Collectibles, Irving, TX

Georgiady, Peter
Compendium of British Clubmakers, 1994
Airlie Hall Press, Greensboro, NC

Georgiady, Peter
Wood Shafted Value Guide For 1995
Airlie Hall Press, Greensboro, NC

Georgiady, Peter
Wood Shafted Value Guide For 1996
Airlie Hall Press, Greensboro, NC

Georgiady, Peter
Collecting Antique Golf Clubs, 1996
Airlie Hall Press, Greensboro, NC

Georgiady, Peter and Kelly, Leo M., Jr.
Quick Reference Guide to Antique Golf Club Names, 1993
Old Chicago Golf Shop, Matteson, IL

Golf Collectors Society
The Bulletin

Hamilton, Charles
Collecting Autographs and Manuscripts, 1993
Modoc Press, Santa Monica, CA

Jackson, Alan F.
The British Professional Golfers, 1887-1930, A Register, 1994
Grant's Books, Worchestershire, England

Kelly, Leo M., Jr.
Antique Golf Ball Reference & Price Guide, 1993
Old Chicago Golf Shop, Richton Park, IL

Kennedy, Patrick
Golf Club Trade Marks, 1984
Thistle Books, S. Burlington, VT

Oliver's
Auction Catalogues
Kennebunk, ME

Olman, John M. and Morton
The Encyclopedia of Golf Collectibles, 1985
Books Americana, Florence, AL

Olman, John and Morton
Olman's Guide to Golf Antiques, 1992
Market Street Press, Cincinnati, OH

Phillips, Chester England
Auction Catalogues

Smedley, Philip and Berdock, Bruce
The Price Guide to Golf Cards, Part I: Tobacco Cards, 1994
Published in Canada

Smedley, Philip and Berdock, Bruce
The Price Guide to Golf Cards, Part 2: Non-Tobacco Cards, 1995
Published in Canada

Sotheby's, London, England
Auction Catalogues

Sporting Antiquities Auction Catalogues
Melrose, MA

Sprung, Shirley and Jerry
Decorative Golf Collectibles, 1991
Glentiques, LTD., Coral Springs, FL

Listing of Contributors

Chuck Furjanic
P.O. Box 165892
Irving, TX 75016
Phone: (972) 594-7802
Fax: (972) 257-1785
furjanic@onramp.net

Wayne Aaron
9950 Huntcliff Trace
Atlanta, GA 30350
770-993-3611

Dr. Hank Alperin
1450 Winter St.
Augusta, GA 30904
706-738-7317

Archie Baird
Greyfriars
Aberlady, East Lothian
Scotland EH32 0RB

Paul Biocini
4505 Bluff Creek Dr.
Modesto, CA 95355
209-527-1162

Bob Burkett
Old Sport Golf
4297 NE Expressway Access Rd

Doraville, GA 30340
404-493-4344

Jim "Spalding Man" Cooper
1110 Oklahoma St.
Kannapolis, NC 28083
704-782-2493

Lee Crist
103 Windy Peak Ct.
Folsom, CA 95630
916-987-1496

Mike Daniels
Gifts For The Golfer
23 Wilshire Dr.
Albany, NY 12205
518-869-7103

Art DiProspero
Highlands Golf
Box 308
Watertown, CT 06795
860-274-8471

Mark Emerson
4040 Poste Lane Rd.
Columbus, OH 43221
614-771-7272

Jim Espinola
PO Box 54
Dracut, MA 01826
508-459-7165

Pete Georgiady
Airlie Hall Press
6101 O'Briant Ct.
Greensboro, NC 27410
910-665-6457

Johnny Henry
PO Box 776
Ennis, TX 75120
972-875-7360

Roger Hill
2875 Cascade Springs. Dr.
Grand Rapids, MI 49546
616-285-6130

Tom & Karen Kuhl
PO Box 20546
Dayton, OH 45420
937-256-2474

Bob Kuntz
PO Box 300
Dayton, OH 45420
937-228-7767

George Lewis
Golfiana
PO Box 291
Mamaroneck, NY 10543
914-835-5100

Ralph Livingston
831 Freemont NW. Apt #4
Grand Rapids, MI 49504
616-451-6020

Forrest Mc Connell
2740 Fernway Dr.
Montgomery, AL 36111
334-263-6146

Dick Moore
640 E. Liberty St.
Girard, OH 44420
330-545-2832

Norm Moreau
12A Mary Gapper Cres.
Richmond Hill, Ontario
Canada L4C 7L9
905-737-8629

Joseph Murdoch
Cathedral Village
600 E Cathedral Rd #G307
Philadelphia, PA 19128
215-984-8897

Will Roberto
31 Grand St.
Hartford, CT 06116
860-659-0249

Jerry Sprung and Glentiques, Ltd
PO Box 8807
Coral Springs, FL 33075
305-344-9856

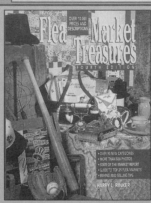

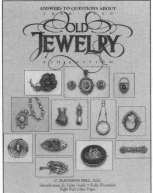